CROCHETING FOR PLEASURE

Crocheting
FOR PLEASURE

MILDRED GRAVES RYAN

ILLUSTRATED BY MARTA CONE

DOUBLEDAY & COMPANY, INC.

GARDEN CITY, NEW YORK

Library of Congress Cataloging in Publication Data

Ryan, Mildred Graves, 1905–
Crocheting for pleasure.

Includes index.
1. Crocheting.   I. Cone, Marta.   II. Title.
TT820.R88   1983   746.43′4   82–45123
ISBN 0–385–18518–9

Rectangular Shawl
(See page 244)

Garden Trellis Afghan
(See page 260)

Hooded Jacket
(See page 253)

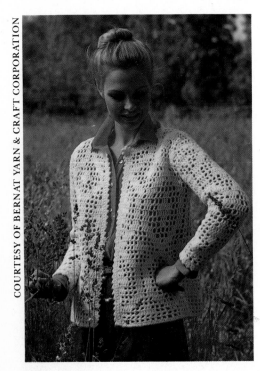

Filet Jacket
(See page 256)

Casual Vest
(See page 246)

Preface

Creating something lovely with one's hands induces a feeling of pleasure. Crocheting can provide this enjoyment and satisfaction. The maneuvering of the thread by the fingers and a hook is fascinating to watch; the results, interesting to behold. It reminds one of a spider spinning an intriguing web. In order that no one can be denied this pleasure, this book has been written.

Little is known about the origin of crocheting. Historians mention a lacy type of crocheting that was available in the sixteenth century. Nuns in Europe were responsible for this creation. Eventually the art spread to Ireland in the early eighteenth century and later to England. There the ladies tried to use their crocheting skill to make copies of lace such as rosepoint and Venetian. In fact, at one time, fine, openwork crocheting was considered a type of American lace in this country.

Today, crocheting is more versatile. It varies from the very delicate and lacy to the coarse and sturdy. This change in feeling gives it an appeal of wider range. Persons of varying abilities, interests, and backgrounds can find creative satisfaction in crocheting.

Although all crocheting is based on one stitch, the interlocking of the loops created by one thread and hook can be done in many ways. This book explains how these variations are attained, starting with the simple-to-do procedures and continuing to the more complicated ones. Throughout the book, step-by-step directions are given, in both words and drawings, to make it easy for the beginning crocheter to use.

The importance of understanding the basics is emphasized. Having a thorough knowledge of the fundamentals and a willingness to practice contributes to the success of future work whether one remains a novice or becomes an expert.

For those who like to create individual designs, suggestions are provided for just that. Dozens of stitch patterns, design details, and sizing tips are mentioned. One chapter is devoted to fashion items, with accompanying directions for making. They are diversified in design function, and ease of construction, so there is something for everyone to crochet and use.

In writing a book, as in other endeavors, one needs the help and encouragement of friends and associates. For such assistance, I am especially grateful to Lonnie Darling, who made the samples used by the artist as a guide for the illustrations, and to Sarah Wellbery, who provided research material for designs and techniques. I am also indebted to the many persons who contributed information concerning supplies and designs, and to those companies who granted permission to reproduce photographs and directions in this book.

M.G.R.

Contents

CROCHETING FOR PLEASURE

1

A Beginning for the Right-handed

Starting to crochet is an experience that may have frustrating moments. You may feel as if all of your fingers are thumbs. Controlling the thread with one hand and the hook with the other seems almost impossible. They just do not want to work together. But do not be dejected. It only requires a little patient practice. Gradually you will find your fingers falling into place. The hook will move over and under the yarn in a productive fashion. A natural feeling will develop.

When this happens, you will find great satisfaction in watching the thread grow into something lovely.

To produce this pleasure requires a careful beginning. Moving step by step, perfecting each technique before trying another, is a good procedure to follow. Plunging ahead too fast can only lead to mistakes and imperfect crocheting. Acquiring a good crocheting skill is most important.

PREPARE THE YARN

The amount of time you have to spend on preparation depends on the type of material you use. If the yarn or thread is purchased in ball form, then you are ready to begin to crochet. If it is not, then it is wise to take time to convert it into this form. Crocheting seems easier if the yarn is wound in a ball. There are various ways to wind it. One is mentioned here. Whichever method you use, be careful not to stretch the yarn.

To rewind the yarn, you will find it easier if someone helps you. It is more difficult to work with the opened skein slipped over the back of a chair than over a friend's hands.

Winding a Ball

This is an easy way to rewind yarn. However, it does allow the ball to roll

away when it is dropped because the end of the yarn is on the outside of the ball. Start by wrapping the yarn loosely around your fingers. Do this about ten times. Then gently remove the loops from your fingers. Put them in your left hand parallel to your fingers. Placing them in this position lets you cross the loops as you continue to wind the yarn

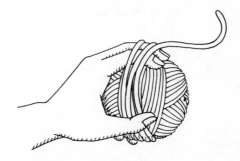

around your fingers. From time to time, turn the ball as it increases in size, slipping your fingers from under the yarn.

Holding your fingers under the yarn keeps the yarn from being stretched. Try to wind a perfectly round ball.

HOLDING THE HOOK

With the yarn or thread ready to be crocheted, you are ready to pick up the hook. There are two ways to grip it. In one, the hook is held like a pencil; in the other it is held more as you would hold a knife.

When using the *first method,* put the crochet hook in the right hand between the thumb and the first finger, as you would a pencil, with the hook facing downward. Place the middle finger near the tip of the hook and the thumb and first finger closer to the center of the hook. The first finger seems to rest on the thumb.

For the *second method,* the hand seems to cover the hook. Pick up the hook with the hook facing downward. Hold the hook with the thumb and the first finger on either side of the shank, and with the middle finger resting against the thumb.

In deciding which method you should use, consider how comfortable the position feels. You do not want to feel awkward as you crochet.

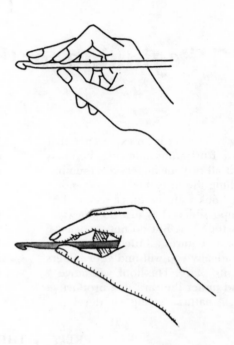

HOLDING THE YARN

When crocheting, grip the yarn with the left hand. Run the ball end of the yarn between the little and ring fingers about 4 inches (10 cm) from the loop on the hook (A). Keeping the palm up, wrap

yarn around the base of the little finger. Weave the yarn between the fingers by bringing it under the back of the ring finger, over the middle, and under the first finger (B).

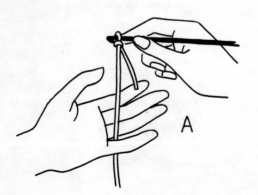

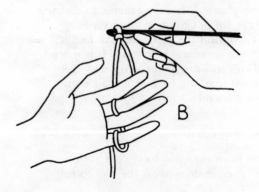

If the length of the yarn needs to be adjusted so you can hold the loop between the thumb and the first finger, gently pull the yarn down. It should lie firmly but not tightly (C). Positioning the yarn this way allows you to regulate the flow of the yarn. The yarn should be taut over the first finger with an even tension so that the hook can be maneuvered around it easily.

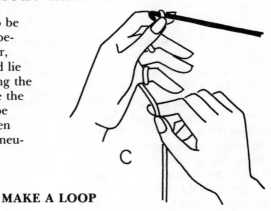

MAKE A LOOP

Crocheting starts with a slip loop or knot. To make it, pick up the yarn or thread about 2 inches (5 cm) from the end. Hold it between your thumb and first finger so you can form a small circle. Do this by bringing the ball end of the yarn over the one in your fingers, letting it fall in back of the circle (A).

Hold the circle in place between the thumb and the first finger. Put the hook through the circle from right to left, holding it in the right hand (B). With the crochet hook, pull the ball end of the yarn through the circle, forming a small loop (C). The loop should be just loose enough to allow the hook to pass through it.

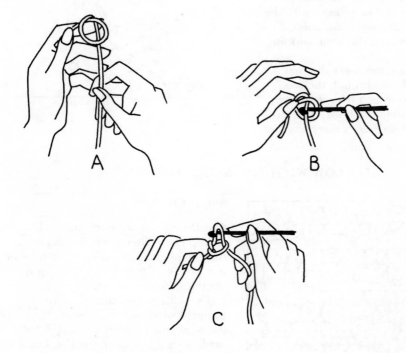

BEGIN WITH A CHAIN STITCH

Crocheting begins with a chain stitch. It forms the foundation row on which other stitches are constructed. Although the chain stitch is easy to make, it does require skill. Keeping the stitches even in size and tension is most important. They should be loose enough to allow the hook to pass through the chain easily. At the same time, they should not be so tight that the edge of the work seems to draw in. If you are a beginner, repeat the procedure over and over again until there is a uniformity of stitches.

Begin by making a slip knot about 6 inches (15 cm) from the end of the yarn. Pass the hook through the loop from right to left. Pull both ends of the yarn until the loop hugs the hook, but not too tightly.

Arrange the yarn in the left hand in the correct way. Hold the slip knot between the thumb and first finger with the first finger lifted slightly; leave about 2 inches (5 cm) between the hook and finger.

Keeping the yarn taut over the first finger, pass the hook through the loop then under the yarn and over it so that it is wrapped around the hook. This procedure is called *yarn over*, a direction you will often find in crocheting. Catch the yarn in the hook, from back to front (A). Draw the yarn through the loop, making the first chain stitch. Repeat this procedure as many times as required (B). As you make the chain, keep the thumb and first finger near the stitch that is being crocheted.

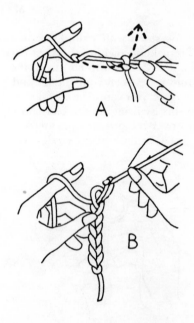

FOLLOW WITH THE BASIC STITCHES

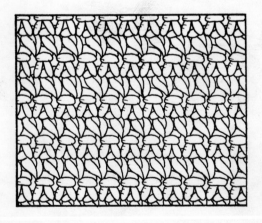

Single Crochet

Crocheting is a series of interlocking loops. They range from the simple to the complicated. No doubt you have noticed the variety of looks that can be made. Although you may be amazed by this versatility, you will be more astounded when you realize that the hundreds of stitch patterns and designs are made with a few basic stitches. Once you have mastered the basic techniques, you will be able to combine the basic stitches in many intriguing ways.

Start with Single Crochet

The basic stitches vary in length. Single
crochet is the shortest. It produces a
flat, firm product that can be made by
proceeding back and forth in a straight
line or can be made in the round, forming a circle.

An item is often finished with single
crochet stitches when other stitch patterns have been used. It can even be
used to join two completed parts.

For a *straight piece,* begin with a foundation chain the required length. Grasp
the chain with the right side toward you.
Put the hook in the second chain from
the slip knot, passing it from the front of
the stitch to the back. As you do this, the
hook slips under the 2 top threads (A).

Slip the hook under and over the
yarn, catching the yarn in preparation to
pulling it through the chain stitch (B).

Draw the yarn through the stitch. Notice that you now have 2 loops on the
hook (C).

Put the yarn over the hook again.
Draw it through the 2 loops on the hook
(D), leaving 1 loop on the hook (E). You
have just made your first single crochet
stitch.

For the second single crochet, insert
the hook in the next stitch of the chain,
remembering that the hook passes under
the 2 top threads. Proceed in this manner until a single crochet is made in
each of the chain stitches.

To end the row, crochet 1 chain stitch
(F). This makes it easier to turn the
work for making the next row.

Turn the crocheting so the reverse
side is toward you (G).

To make the second row of single crochet stitches, insert the hook in the second stitch from the hook, which is the
last stitch of the preceding row. Slip the
hook, from the front, under the 2 top
threads (H). Draw through the yarn to
make a single crochet stitch. Proceed in
this manner until row is completed.

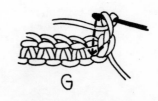

For *single crochet in the round,* make a
short foundation chain in the usual manner. These stitches will form the center
of the circle.

To convert them into a ring or circle,
join the first and last stitch by putting
the hook through the first chain, under
the 2 top threads. Work from the front
(A).

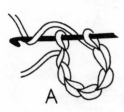

A

Put yarn over the hook. Draw through
chain stitch and loop on hook in a single
motion. This leaves one loop on the
hook (B), and you have made a ring.

To make the first round, crochet 8 single crochet stitches through the center
of the ring (C).

B

Before starting the second round,
mark the end of the first round with a
small safety pin. Put it through the last
stitch (D). Remember to move the pin to
indicate the end of each round when it
is completed. This avoids mistakes.

To crochet the second round, work 2
single crochets into each stitch of the
previous stitch. This allows the circle to
continue to be flat instead of curling up.
At the end of the round, you will have
made 16 stitches.

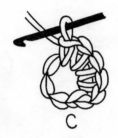

C

To crochet the third round, make a
single crochet in the first stitch and 2
single crochets in the next stitch. Continue in this way so that there is an increase of one stitch in every other stitch
in this round. This leaves 24 stitches on
the round (E). Proceed in this way as
you crochet round and round.

D

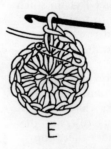

E

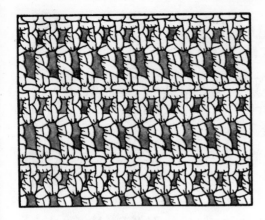

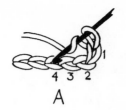

A

B

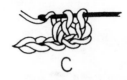

C

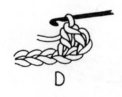

D

E

Follow with Double Crochet

As you might surmise, double crochet is twice as high as single crochet. Because of this, a slightly more open pattern is created. You will find that double crochet is frequently used as the foundation for various pattern stitches.

After making a foundation chain, using an even number of stitches, begin the first row of double crochet by putting the yarn over the hook. Insert the hook in the fourth chain from hook. Be sure to put it under the 2 top strands (A). Put yarn over hook and draw it through the chain, leaving 3 loops on the hook.

Then place yarn over hook (B). Draw it through the first 2 loops.

Put the yarn over the hook again (C), and pull it through the remaining 2 loops. This leaves 1 loop on the hook (D). You have completed your first double crochet stitch.

For the second double crochet, place yarn over hook. From the front, insert the hook in the next chain stitch. Slip it under the 2 top threads. Proceed as you did for the first double crochet.

When the row is completed, make 3 chain stitches (E). To continue, turn the work so that the reverse side is toward you.

To crochet the second row, put yarn over hook. Insert hook in the fifth stitch from the hook (F), passing under the 2 top strands. Continue in the usual manner to complete the stitch.

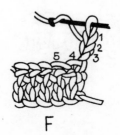

F

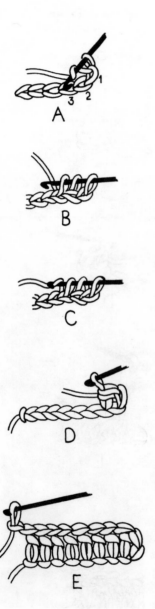

Continue with the Half Double Crochet

This stitch falls between the single and double crochet stitch in size. You will notice that the stitch creates a firm texture with an interesting ridged effect.

Start with a chain the desired length. Put the yarn over the hook before inserting it in the third chain from the hook. Enter from the front of the stitch, passing under the 2 top threads (A).

Draw the yarn through the stitch. Three loops remain on the hook (B), as if you were making a double crochet stitch.

Put yarn over hook. Pull it through all loops on the hook (C), leaving 1 loop on the hook (D). This completes the making of a half double crochet stitch.

For the second half double crochet, place yarn over hook. Insert the hook in the next chain. Enter it from the front under the 2 top threads. Then continue as you did for the first stitch.

At the end of the row, chain 2 stitches (E). Then turn the work ready to begin the second row. Remember the turning chain-2 does not count as a stitch on the following row.

To crochet the second row, place yarn over hook. Put the hook in the first stitch, which is the last stitch of the previous row. Insert the hook from the front under the 2 top loops. Continue to make half double crochet stitches, as you did for the previous row.

Try a Treble or Triple Crochet

For many years, this stitch was known as treble crochet, but now the term triple is

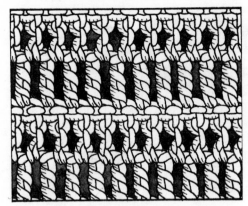

often used. The stitch is longer than double crochet, producing a more open texture. You will find that it is used less frequently than as a double crochet.

Start with a foundation chain the required length.

For the first treble stitch, bring yarn over hook twice (A). Insert hook in the fifth chain from the hook. Enter the chain from the front under the 2 top threads. Place yarn over hook and draw through the chain stitch, leaving 4 loops on the hook (B).

Wrap yarn over hook again. Draw yarn through 2 loops, leaving 3 loops on the hook (C).

Put yarn over hook again. Pull it through 2 loops. Now 2 loops remain on the hook (D).

Place yarn over hook again. Draw it through 2 loops (E), leaving 1 loop on the hook. You have just completed your first treble stitch. (F)

To make the second treble stitch, place the yarn over the hook twice. Insert the hook in the next stitch, passing it under the 2 top threads. Continue to make the second treble stitch the first.

Continue to crochet across the row making a treble stitch in each chain. At the end of the row, chain 4 stitches, which will become the first treble on the second row.

For the second row, place yarn over the hook twice. Insert the hook in the sixth stitch from the hook, entering from the front under the 2 top threads. After making the stitch, you will notice that it is aligned with the second stitch on the previous row. Proceed to crochet as you did for the first row (G).

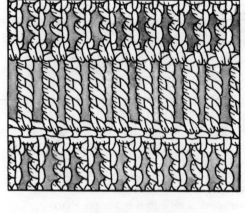

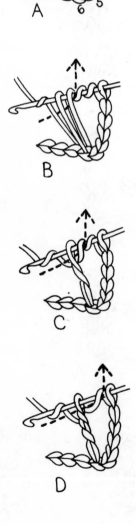

Add a Double Treble Crochet

If you wish, you can extend the length of the stitch, creating a more open effect between the stitches. To do this, start with a foundation chain the necessary length.

Place the yarn over the hook 3 times before inserting it in the sixth stitch from the hook (A).

Wrap the yarn over the hook again. Draw it through the stitch, leaving 5 loops on the hook.

Put the yarn over the hook again (B). Pull it through 2 loops, leaving 4 loops on the hook.

Repeat this procedure (C), leaving 3 loops (D), then 2 loops (E), and finally 1 loop (F) on the hook. At this point, you have made 1 double treble stitch.

After crocheting across the row, make 5 chain stitches. Then turn the work. The chain stitches become the first double treble stitch on the second row. Continue to crochet the stitches as for the first row (G).

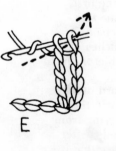

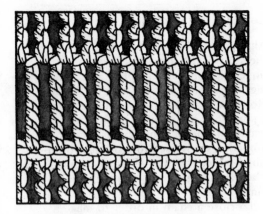

Expand to Triple Treble Crochet

The length of the stitch can be extended by using another yarn-over as you start. Begin with a chain the required length.

Place the thread over the hook 4 times (A) before inserting it in the seventh stitch from the hook.

Put the yarn over the hook. Draw it through 2 loops (B); 5 loops are left on the hook.

Repeat the procedure several times, leaving 4 loops (C), then 3 (D), and 2 (E), and at last only 1 loop (F). In this way 1 triple treble stitch (G) is made. Proceed in this manner to the end of the row.

At the end of the row, make 6 chain stitches. They will be counted as the first stitch in the second row (H). Before starting the row, you should turn the work.

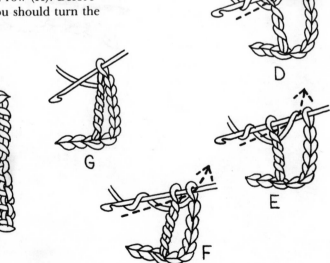

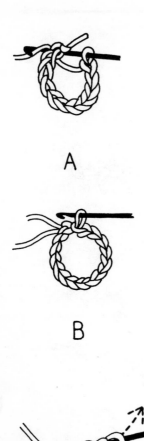

A

B

C

Consider the Slip Stitch

Although the slip stitch is not used like the stitches that have just been mentioned, it does have its place in crocheting. It can be employed in several ways. However, it is most often thought of as a joining or an invisible stitch when making a ring or round medallion. Sometimes it is used to crochet two finished pieces together or as an edging when a piece seems too stretchy and limp.

To close a chain in order to make a ring, insert the hook in the stitch at the end of the chain to be joined (A). Place yarn over hook. Pull it through the stitch and the loop that is on the hook. Doing this in a single motion will make the ring. One loop remains on the hook (B).

Sometimes the directions for making an item indicate that a slip stitch should be made in a row of stitches. In fact, a row of slip stitches can be made across a row. To do this, put the hook into the second stitch from the hook. Place yarn over hook (C). Pull it through the stitch and the loop on the hook. To make another slip stitch, put the hook in the next stitch and repeat the procedure (D).

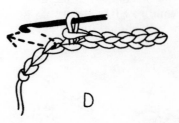

D

2

Tips for the Left-handed

Often one thinks that crocheting with the left hand is completely different from working with the right hand. It really isn't. You crochet in the same way with one exception. The position of the hook and the yarn is reversed. Instead of holding the hook in the right hand, you hold it in the left, and in turn the yarn is positioned in the right hand.

Translating this bit of information into action may be confusing because books are usually illustrated to show working with the right hand. To alleviate this problem, some basic techniques to use if you are left-handed are shown here.

HOLDING THE HOOK

Be sure the yarn or thread is ready for crocheting before you pick up your hook. Suggestions for preparing the yarn are found in Chapter 1.

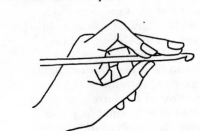

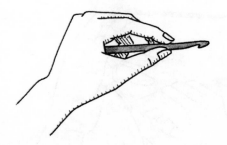

There are two ways to grasp the hook. In one the hook is held as a pencil; in the other it is held more as you would a knife. It is a good idea to try both methods. The one that feels more comfortable in your hand will be the one to use. You won't be able to crochet well if the hook feels awkward.

To use the first method, pick up the crochet hook with the left hand so it is between the thumb and the first finger, as a pencil is held. Keeping the hook facing downward, place the middle finger near the tip of the hook, and the thumb and first finger closer to the center. The first finger seems to rest on the thumb.

In the *second method,* the hand seems to cover the hook. Hold it with the hook facing downward. Grip the hook with the thumb and the first finger on either side of the shank, with the middle finger resting against the thumb.

MAKE A LOOP

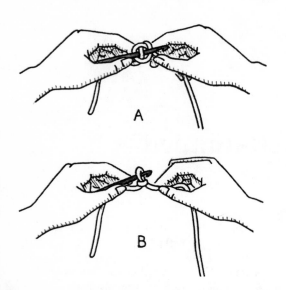

Crocheting begins with a slip loop or knot. To make it, pick up the yarn or thread about 2 inches (5 cm) from the end. Hold it between your thumb and first finger so you can form a small circle. To do this, bring the ball end of the yarn over the one in your fingers, allowing it to fall in back of the circle.

Hold the circle in place between the thumb and the first finger. Put the hook through the circle from left to right, grasping it in the left hand (A). Pull the ball end of the yarn through the circle with the crochet hook, forming a small loop. The loop should be just loose enough to let the hook pass through it freely. If it needs adjusting, pull both ends of the yarn (B).

HOLDING THE YARN

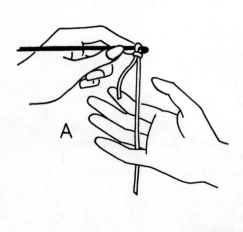

Begin by picking up the yarn in the right hand. Slip the ball end of the yarn between the little and ring fingers about 4 inches (10 cm) from the loop on the hook (A). With the palm up, wrap yarn around the base of the little finger. Run the yarn between the fingers by bringing it under the back of the ring finger, over the middle, and under the first finger (B).

If the length of the yarn does not seem correct for allowing you to hold the loop between the thumb and the first finger, gently pull the yarn downward. It should lie firmly, but not tightly (C). Arranging the yarn this way lets you regulate the flow of the yarn. The yarn should be taut over the first finger so you can move the hook around the yarn easily, keeping an even tension.

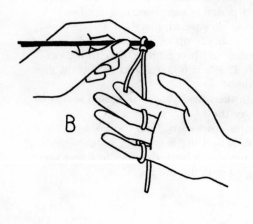

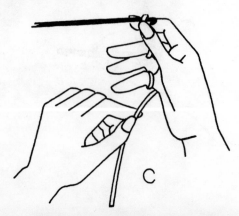

BEGIN WITH A CHAIN STITCH

Each piece of crocheting starts with a chain. It becomes the foundation on which other stitches are made. Although the chain stitch is easy to construct, it does require practice to perfect. Keeping the stitches even in size and tension is not as easy as it seems. A good balance between looseness and tightness must be maintained. The chain should be tight enough for the hook to slip through easily, but not so tight that the edge of the crocheting seems to be drawn up.

Start by placing a slip knot about 6 inches (15 cm) from the end of the thread. Slip the hook through the loop from left to right. Pull both ends of the yarn until the loop hugs the hook, but not too tightly.

Arrange the yarn in the right hand in the proper way. Hold the slip knot between the thumb and the first finger. With the first finger lifted slightly leave about 2 inches (5 cm) between the hook and finger.

Keeping the yarn taut over the first finger, pass the hook under the yarn and over it so that it is wrapped around the hook. This procedure is called *yarn over,* a direction you will often find in crocheting. Catch the yarn in the hook, from back to front (A). Draw the yarn through the loop, making the first chain stitch. Repeat this procedure as many times as required (B). As you make the chain, keep the thumb and middle finger near the stitch that is being crocheted (C). Continue this procedure until the chain is as long as needed.

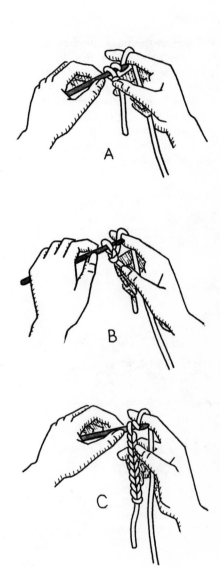

FOLLOW WITH THE BASIC STITCHES

Single Crochet

This is the first of the basic stitches. It is the shortest and produces a firm, flat product. It can be made by proceeding back and forth in a straight line or in the round, forming a circle. Frequently an item is edged with single crochet stitches when other stitch patterns have been employed. It can even be used to join two completed sections.

For a *straight piece,* start with a foundation chain the required length. Hold the chain in the right hand with the right side toward you. Put the hook in the second chain from the slip knot, passing it from the front of the stitch to the back. As you do this, the hook slips under the 2 top threads (A).

Slip the hook under and over the yarn, catching the yarn in preparation for pulling it through the chain stitch (B).

Draw the yarn through the stitch. Notice that you now have 2 loops on the hook (C).

Put the yarn over the hook again (D). Draw it through the 2 loops on the hook, leaving 1 loop on the hook (E). You have just made your first single crochet stitch.

For the second single crochet, insert the hook in the next stitch of the chain, remembering that the hook passes under the 2 top threads. Proceed in this manner until a single crochet is made in each of the chain stitches.

To end the row, crochet one chain stitch. This makes it easier to turn the work for making the next row.

Turn the crocheting so the reverse side is toward you.

To make the second row of single crochet stitches, insert the hook in the second stitch from the hook, which is the last stitch of the preceding row. Slip the hook from the front, under the 2 top threads. Draw through the yarn to make a single crochet stitch. Proceed in this manner until the row is completed.

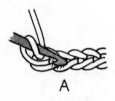

A

B

C

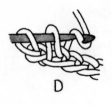

D

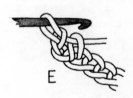

E

For single crochet in the round, make a short foundation chain, perhaps 4 stitches, in the usual manner. These stitches will form the center of the circle.

To convert them into a ring or circle, join the first and fourth stitches by putting the hook through the first chain, under the 2 top threads. Work from the front (A).

Put yarn over the hook. Draw through chain stitch and loop on hook in a single motion. This leaves 1 loop on the hook (B), and you have made a ring.

To make the first round, crochet 8 single crochet stitches through the center of the ring (C).

Before starting the second round, mark the end of the first round with a small safety pin. Put it through the last stitch (D). Remember to move the pin to indicate the end of each round when it is completed. This avoids mistakes.

To crochet the second round, work 2 single crochet stitches into each stitch of the previous row. This allows the circle to continue to lie flat, instead of curling up. At the end of the round, you will have 16 stitches.

To crochet the third round, make a single crochet in the first stitch and 2 single crochets in the next stitch. Continue in this way so that there is an increase of 1 stitch in every other stitch in this round. This leaves 24 stitches on the round (E). Proceed in this way as you crochet round and round. Remember to move the safety pin so you will know where the next round begins.

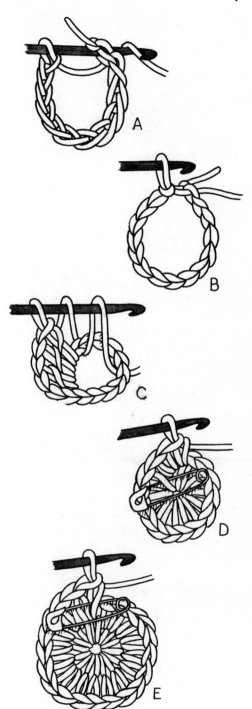

Continue with Double Crochet

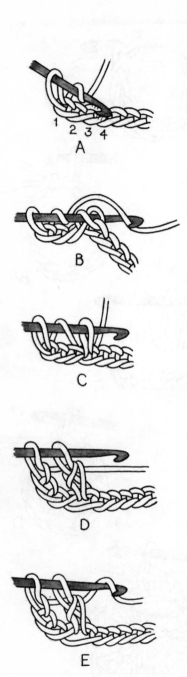

A

B

C

D

E

As you might surmise, double crochet is twice as high as single crochet. This allows the stitch pattern to be slightly more open. Frequently the double crochet stitch is used as a foundation for various stitch patterns.

After making a foundation chain, using an even number of stitches, start the first row of double crochet by putting the yarn over the hook. Insert the hook in the fourth chain from hook. Be sure to put it under the 2 top strands (A). Put yarn over hook (B) and draw it through the chain, leaving 3 loops on the hook (C).

Then place yarn over hook and draw it through the first 2 loops (D).

Put the yarn over the hook again and pull it through the remaining 2 loops (E). This leaves 1 loop on the hook (F). This completes your first double crochet stitch.

For the second double crochet, place yarn over hook. From the front, insert the hook in the next chain stitch. Slip it under the 2 top threads. Proceed as you did for the first double crochet.

When the row is completed, make 3 chain stitches. To continue, turn the work so that the reverse side is toward you.

To crochet the second row, put yarn over hook. Insert hook in the fifth stitch from the hook, passing under the 2 top strands. Continue in the usual manner to complete the stitch.

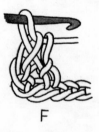

F

Try the Half Double Crochet

This stitch falls between the single and double crochet in size. You will notice that the stitch creates a firm texture with an interesting ridged effect.

Begin with a chain the desired length. Put the yarn over the hook before inserting it in the third chain from the hook. Enter from the front of the stitch, passing under the 2 top threads (A).

Draw the yarn through the stitch. Three loops remain on the hook (B), as if you were making a double crochet stitch.

Put yarn over hook. Pull it through all loops on the hook (C), leaving 1 loop on the hook (D). This completes the making of a half double crochet stitch.

For the second half double crochet, place yarn over hook. Insert the hook in the next chain. Enter it from the front under the 2 top threads. Then continue as you did for the first stitch.

At the end of the row, chain 2 stitches (E). Then turn the work, ready to begin the second row. Remember the turning chain-2 does not count as a stitch on the following row.

To crochet the second row, place yarn over hook. Put the hook in the first stitch, which is the last stitch of the previous row. Insert the hook from the front under the 2 top loops. Continue to make half double crochet stitches, as you did for the previous row.

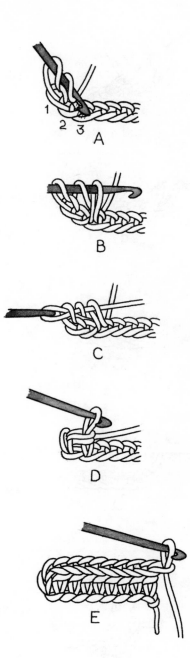

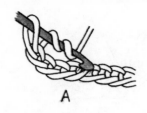

A

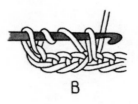

B

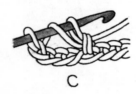

C

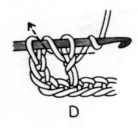

D

E

Add a Treble or Triple Crochet

For many years, this stitch was known as treble crochet, but now the term triple is often used. The stitch is longer than double crochet, producing a more open texture. You will find that it is not used as frequently in crocheting as a double crochet.

Start with a foundation chain the required length.

For the first treble stitch, bring yarn over hook twice (A). Insert hook in the fifth chain from the hook. Enter the chain from the front under the 2 top threads. Place yarn over hook and draw through the chain stitch, leaving 4 loops on the hook (B).

Wrap yarn over hook again. Draw yarn through 2 loops, leaving 3 loops on the hook (C).

Put yarn over hook again. Pull it through 2 loops. Two loops remain on the hook (D).

Place yarn over hook again. Draw it through 2 loops (E), leaving 1 loop on the hook. You have just completed your first treble stitch.

To make the second treble stitch, place the yarn over the hook twice. Insert the hook in the next stitch, passing it under the 2 top threads. Continue to make the second treble stitch as you did the first.

Continue to crochet across the row making a treble stitch in each chain. At the end of the row, chain 4 stitches, which will become the first treble on the second row.

For the second row, place yarn over the hook twice. Insert the hook in the sixth stitch from the hook, entering from the front under the 2 top threads. After making the stitch, you will notice that it is aligned with the second stitch on the previous row. Proceed to crochet as you did for the first row.

Expand to Double Treble Crochet

If you wish, you can extend the length of the stitch, creating a more open effect. To do this, start with a foundation chain the necessary length.

Place the yarn over the hook 3 times before inserting it in the sixth stitch from the hook (A).

Wrap the yarn over the hook again. Draw it through the stitch, leaving 5 loops on the hook.

Put the yarn over the hook again (B). Pull it through 2 loops, leaving 4 loops on the hook.

Repeat this procedure (C), leaving 3 loops (D), then 2 loops (E), and finally 1 loop (F) on the hook. At this point, you have made 1 double treble stitch.

After crocheting across the row, make 5 chain stitches. Then turn the work. The chain stitches become the first double treble stitch on the second row. Continue to crochet the stitches as for the first row.

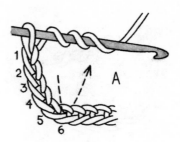

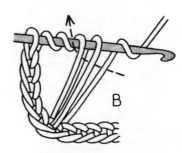

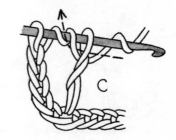

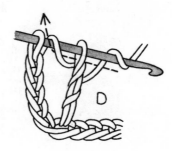

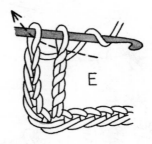

Extend to Triple Treble Crochet

The length of the stitch can be extended further by using another yarn-over as you begin. Start with a chain the required length.

Place the thread over the hook 4 times (A) before inserting it in the seventh stitch from the hook.

Put the yarn over the hook. Draw it through 2 loops (B). Five loops are left on the hook.

Repeat the procedure several times, leaving 4 loops (C). Then 3 (D), and 2 (E), and at last only 1 loop (F). In this way, one triple treble (G) is made. Proceed in this manner to the end of the row.

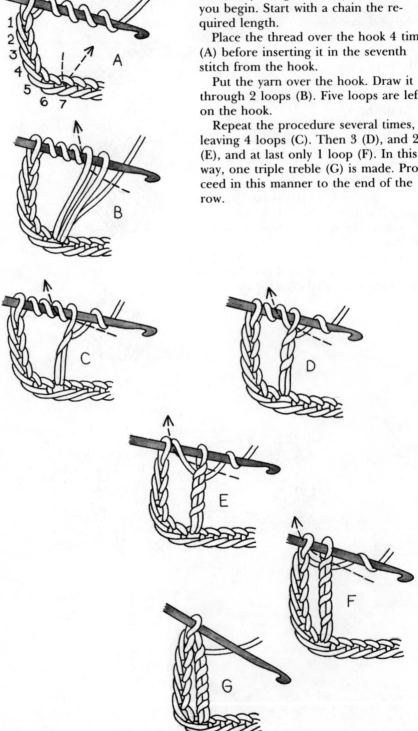

Try the Slip Stitch

The slip stitch has several uses in crocheting, but is seldom employed in the
construction of a stitch pattern. Because
it is the shortest of the stitches, it works
nicely in the linking of 2 stitches to form
a circle or as an invisible stitch in changing from one position to another along a
row of stitches. It can also be used for
the seaming of two finished crocheted
pieces and to strengthen an edge.

For a linking, place the hook in the
stitch at the end of the chain to be
joined (A). Place thread over hook. Pull
through stitch and the loop that is on
the hook in a single motion. One loop
remains on the hook (B).

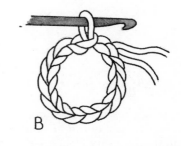

When the directions require a slip
stitch in a row of stitches, use the same
procedure. Insert the hook into the second stitch from hook. Place yarn over
hook (C). Draw a loop through the stitch
and the loop on the hook (D).

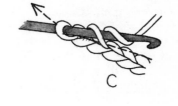

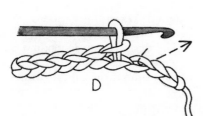

3

Materials to Choose

One of the pleasures of crocheting comes from the wide variety of materials that can be used. Nearly anything that has a stringlike quality can be crocheted. The materials can vary from a very fine tatting thread to twine. This diversity allows you to experiment with the unusual to produce interesting effects. Cord, fabric strips, leather, plastic, raffia, and wire are added to the yarns and threads that are commonly thought of as crochet materials. And in these, there are variations. They can be thin or thick, light in weight or heavy, smooth or textured.

This abundance of variety, however, can produce difficulties. Unless you realize how the distinguishing characteristics respond to crocheting, you may be upset with the final product. Sometimes a material that looks so lovely in the hand appears ugly when worked in an inappropriate design.

Of course it is always best to follow the suggestions for crocheting material that accompany the instructions you are using. There may be times, however, when you cannot find the suggested material or you are in an experimental mood. When this happens, the information that follows should prove helpful. The design is so dependent on the material you use that you cannot think of one without the other. Always remember to select one that is appropriate to the purpose for which it is to be used, and then crochet with a suitable hook.

KNOW THE FIBER CONTENT

Yarns for knitting are usually made of animal and synthetic fibers, used singly or in combination. For crocheting, however, many yarns are made of cotton.

Since it is almost impossible to determine the fiber content by just touching, it is wise to read the label on the yarn. Here you will find the fiber content listed. For instance, it may read "mercerized cotton," "100 percent acrylic," or show a mixture such as 57 percent acrylic, 37 percent wool, 6 percent vinyon. The fibers and the proportions by which they are combined bring features to the yarn that are noteworthy. Understanding what they are helps you to make the correct choice.

Cotton. Cotton fibers are used for both yarns and threads. The thicker strands are usually referred to as yarn; the thinner, threads. The tactile quality also varies widely. It can be soft and spongy or firm and rigid. Some cottons are mercerized to provide extra strength and to add a greater luster. It is also possible to give cotton a special treatment that prevents colors from running and fading.

Wool. The wool from sheep has many outstanding characteristics. Manufacturers have tried to duplicate these natural properties in synthetics, but have never been able to create an exact copy.

Pure wool provides softness and warmth, with some yarns softer than others. And although the yarn is soft, it is strong and elastic. Because of these characteristics a durable, long-wearing yarn is created that can be reused from time to time. It even seems to resist fire better than other fibers. It also seems to absorb moisture without feeling clammy and to maintain a more even temperature. All of these properties make wool yarn an excellent choice.

Other Animal Fibers. Many times yarns in this classification are thought to be wool. Of course they are not. Hairs other than that from sheep are used. Usually they are soft and pretty, produced in various weights from the very thick to the light. The yarns are often more expensive and do not seem to have the elasticity that allows wool to rebound after being stretched. Angora, alpaca, cashmere, and mohair are among the yarns found in this classification.

Synthetic. This group of yarns continues to grow in variety. Each year seems to bring new developments. When you read the labels on the yarn, you will discover a number of names mentioned, sometimes in combination. Acrylic, Dacron, Orlon, polyester, viscose, vinyon, and rayon will be among them. Sometimes they are combined with natural fibers to create different effects. In developing the yarns, easy care and hard wear have been considered, as well as the problems of people with allergies. The nonallergenic feature is a special boon for those who cannot wear wool. Another asset of synthetic yarn is its ability to be washed and dried by machine.

Acrylic seems to be the most popular in this grouping. It seems to have the warmth and versatility of wool. And being able to machine wash and dry their creations is an advantage that many crocheters insist on. Sometimes blocking an article made of an acrylic yarn is difficult because of its spongy nature. You just cannot make it lie flat.

ANALYZE THE CONSTRUCTION

Fiber content is not the only factor contributing to variations in the yarn. The number of strands, the amount of twist, the thickness, and the weight produce different effects.

Check the Ply

This term is often thought of as identifying the weight and thickness of the thread and yarn. It really doesn't. Ply simply pertains to the number of spun threads that are twisted together to make a strand of thread or yarn. In the making of cotton yarns, 2, 3, 4, 6, and 8 strands may be used, and for other yarns 2, 3, or 4. This leads to the designation 2-ply, 3-ply, 4-ply, 6-ply, 8-ply.

Many people are amazed when they learn that a lightweight yarn can be made of 3 or 4 threads, whereas a heavy one is composed of only 2. And you may be more surprised when you find that both a lightweight and heavyweight yarn can be composed of the same number of plies. Although the ply can contribute to the strength of the yarn, it does not influence the thickness or the weight of the yarn.

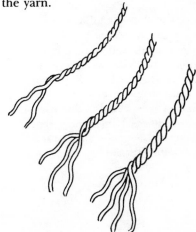

Note the Thickness of Cotton Yarn

Cotton thread is made in a variety of sizes, ranging generally from 3 to 70. This designation indicates the thickness of the yarn. The larger the number, the finer the thread. For instance, thread marked 70 will be very fine, whereas a size 3 thread will be thicker.

Over the years a correlation has been established between the size and the type of thread. Certain names, such as pearl cotton, bring to mind a definite type of thread. This makes it easier to select the correct thread than it is when the yarn is simply called lightweight or heavyweight.

Tatting-crochet cotton is made in a size 70. It is a very firmly twisted 3-ply thread that is available in a large color range. Delicate lace edgings and trims can be made of it.

Three-cord cotton is another very firmly twisted 3-ply thread, made in sizes 10, 20, and 30. Only white and ecru, however, are available in all sizes. Colored threads are only made in size 30. Three-cord cotton works up nicely when used for doilies, tablecloths, edgings, and trims.

Six-cord cotton is also a very firmly twisted thread, but this time it has 6 plies. It comes in sizes 20 and 30, but is available in white and ecru only. Appropriate for placemats, tablecloths, edgings, and trim.

Bedspread cotton is a 4-ply, very firmly twisted thread in about a 5 sizing. Colors are limited to white and ecru. As the name implies it is most appropriate for bedspreads as well as for tablecloths, doilies, placemats, and trimmings.

Pearl cotton is also available in size 5, but it is loosely twisted, having only 2 plies. It comes in a large variety of colors and a distinct luster. Fashion items such as blouses, vests, and accessories as well as baby bonnets, trims, and pot holders can be attractive when worked in this type of cotton thread.

Tatting-crochet cotton

Three-cord cotton

Six-cord cotton

Bedspread cotton

Pearl cotton

Speed-cro-sheen cotton

Glo-tone cotton

Knit-cro-sheen cotton

Metallic Knit-cro-sheen

Speed-Cro-Sheen cotton is a firmly twisted 8-ply thread that is made in about a size 3. The color range is wide, making it suitable for a variety of designs, from bedspreads to accessories.

Glo-tone cotton comes in a 4-ply, firmly twisted thread in about a size 5. It is available in many colors and may be used for various items such as dresses, tops, shawls, as well as decorative fashions for the home.

Knit-Cro-Sheen cotton is another 4-ply, firmly twisted thread made in a wide range of colors in about a size 5. It too creates lovely effects for the home and personal fashions.

Metallic Knit-Cro-Sheen is a 4-ply thread into which a strand of Mylar has been twisted. A color is added to white, making it appropriate for sweaters, tops, and fashion accessories.

Bouclé is distinctive with its nubby surface. It is soft and loosely twisted, having 4 plies. The sizes vary. Bouclé is a fashion item that can create a lovely look in sweaters, skirts, dresses, and accessories.

Recognize the Weights

Weight rather than thickness or size is emphasized in the selection of wool and synthetic yarns. The designation by weight, however, actually relates to the thickness of the yarn, ranging from the very fine to the heavy.

Lightweight yarn comes in various ways. It can have a smooth or fluffy surface and sometimes an unusual texture. The results are equally pleasing whether making a lacy shawl or a closely crocheted fabriclike material. Sweaters, baby garments, and bed jackets are other types of articles frequently made of lightweight yarn.

Medium-weight yarn can be used in a wide range of items. Unless you want a sheer, lacy look or a coarse one, you can work with this weight yarn. Jackets, sweaters, suits, dresses, accessories, and afghans look attractive when made of it.

Heavyweight yarn lends itself nicely to outdoor-wear because of its warmth. Fashions that have a bulky look, such as hats, suits, sweaters, and Aran-style garments, can be constructed with this type of yarn.

Super-weight yarn is a very bulky yarn, although it is often made of only 2 plies. Thick strands of woolen spun yarn are twisted together to form a heavy strand.

Sportsweight yarn is an in-between weight. It comes in 2-, 3-, or 4-ply yarns and is available in a wide range of colors and textures. Try it when the item you want to crochet should be slightly heavier than what you could make using a medium-weight yarn, but a bit lighter than you would construct with a 4-ply worsted yarn.

Experiment with the Unusual

Until recently cotton thread and woolly yarns have been the traditional materials used for crocheting. Recently, however, crocheters have begun to experiment with other types of materials. Generally they are used for decorative pieces and art fabrics. Just as the sculptor uses various products to create her art, so may the crocheter. Materials made of such things as linen, jute, hemp, raffia, real rug yarn, and spun paper are available. Ribbons, plastic straw, leather, and wire are other possibilities. Even fabric strips are worked into attractive fashions. Watch for these different materials in needlecraft shops. And do not be afraid to try them after you have perfected the art of crocheting.

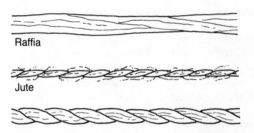

Raffia

Jute

Consider the Textural Interest

Probably one of the most pleasant aspects of working with yarn is the joy of touching and seeing. The airy fineness of some, the luxurious softness of others, and the rainbow of lovely colors can create a most satisfying feeling.

Usually you think of yarn as being smooth and plain. A surface interest, however, can give crocheting a new look. But it should be remembered that yarns with textural interest, such as those that are fluffy and nubby, should not be chosen if you are using a fancy stitch pattern. They are not appropriate for each other. A plain stitch is best to use with yarns of interest. If the yarn, however, is plain, the interest can be created by using a more elaborate stitch pattern.

Textural variations can appear as nubs and loops, producing a three-dimensional effect. Nubs may be spun at equal distances, often in a contrasting color. Sometimes thick dots of cotton are found in the yarn for a stubbed effect. In contrast, there are the frothy yarns that seem so airy and fragile. Then for a change in look, there are the thin yarns that seem so delicate in contrast to the thick, loose strands of yarn. And if you become interested in hard crochet, then the stiff rigidity of the material, such as twine, will provide the textural interest.

SHOP WISELY

Shopping can be a test of how much you know about crochet materials. Deciding which one to use can be frustrating. Unless you have some experience, it is better to follow the suggestion listed for the design you have chosen. The designer and the manufacturer have decided which yarn is best for the effect they wish to create. A change of type and size of yarn often produces a horrible result.

Buy at a Dependable Store

Shopping in a reliable store provides a feeling of security. Generally you will find the yarns of good manufacturers. This makes it easier to judge quality. Also, knowledgeable clerks are found in this type of shop. They can be most helpful.

Another benefit of a reliable store is a policy of accepting returns. There is a tendency to buy more yarn than is needed because of the importance of purchasing sufficient yarn to complete the item at one time. To be able to return the extra yarn is a great service.

When purchasing the yarn, always check the information on the label. You want to be sure that you are buying the same color and that the dye lot number is the same. Colors can vary from one dye lot to another.

Check Quality

Price is often thought of as an indicator of quality—the higher the price, the better the quality. There are, however, other factors to be considered. The fiber, the color, and the ability of the yarn to resist fading, felting, pilling, and rubbing will influence the quality and the price.

Washing causes shrinking, stretching, and fading in some yarns, and can even make them become coarse and rough. Sometimes items made from chemically treated yarn that produces a "shrink-proof" or shrink-resistant product will stretch when laundered, unless they are crocheted with a firm stitch and tension.

The price is also influenced by the color. Soft, subtle hues are more expensive to produce than the brilliant, loud ones.

It is generally assumed that no item is better than the yarn from which it is knitted, but there are different situations that determine the need for top quality. Deciding when less than the best can be used requires painstaking thought in these days of high prices. Estimating the length of time you can use an article and how long it takes you to make it will give some indication as to how much you should spend for the yarn. For instance, a fad item that you can crochet quickly does not require the same top quality as a classic fashion which takes a long time to crochet. For many types of items, the sturdy, cheaper yarns can be used most effectively.

One thing to remember when deciding what to purchase is that good wool can be re-used. Don't throw away an article when you no longer want to use it. Instead rip it apart and rework the yarn into a new fashion.

Think about Suitability

I am not sure that very many people buy crochet material and then wonder what to make of it, as they do with sewing material. It seems as if the project is more often chosen first when crocheting.

But it is possible to select the wrong design for the purpose for which it is to be employed. It is always disappointing when the material does not create the effect or give the service you anticipate.

It is also annoying to crochet something for yourself that looks awful on you although it looks great in your hand. This results when you do not think about the design and the yarn in connection with personal characteristics. This should always be avoided. In sewing the flattering effects of the pattern and fabric are considered. In crocheting so should the yarn, the design, and the stitch pattern complement each other.

Remember, there is a difference in the way yarns can be handled because of their different characteristics. Some create lovely effects when worked in intricate pattern stitches, whereas others should only be used for the simple stitches.

For instance, a fine thread works up beautifully in a Victorian type doily but would be a disaster for a pot holder. A soft yarn makes a lovely lacy shawl, but would be wrong for a man's sweater. Remember that a tightly twisted yarn can create a firm surface finish with durable qualities, whereas a light, airy one produces a soft, frothy finish. Fragile, lacy designs need a fine thread, leaving the heavy yarns for the bold, rough looks.

In case you want to combine yarns, be sure to use the same type. Yarns work up differently when they are blocked. You will be most annoyed if your crocheting is ruined because it stretches in one place and shrinks in another.

Don't Forget Care

Many crocheters consider care all-important. The expense of dry cleaning makes washability an attractive feature. Usually the label on the yarn explains how the article is to be kept clean. Some labels provide more information than others. Before purchasing the yarn, check the label to see whether the yarn can be dry cleaned, hand washed, machine washed, or machine dried. It is always best to follow the listed directions. The finished work will usually look better.

4

Tools to Use

One of the nice things about crocheting is that it requires so little equipment. Actually only a hook is needed. However, hooks are available in such a wide range of sizes and materials that you may be in a quandary when it is time to select a suitable one. Of course, the directions you are following will indicate the size and type you need, but it is wise for you to get a feel for the hook that is just right for the yarn you are using and the look of the item you wish to achieve. Crocheters usually keep a wide range of hooks handy. In this way, they always have the right one.

Although there are other gadgets that may simplify the crocheting process, do not feel that you must have them. Always try them before buying. Then decide which ones will be helpful.

CHOOSE THE CORRECT HOOK

Crochet hooks are made in various types, materials, sizes, and lengths. Understanding the variations will help you in becoming a better crocheter. The material and the hook are so dependent on each other that it is impossible to produce the right effect if they are not compatible.

In purchasing a hook, buy the best you can afford. A good hook will last a lifetime if it is taken care of properly.

Study the Types

There are two types of crochet hooks—the regular and the afghan. Each is made in a variety of materials and sizes.

Regular Hook. Each one is made with a shank or shaft that controls the size of each stitch, and a hook at one end that holds the yarn as the loop is being crocheted. On some metal and plastic hooks

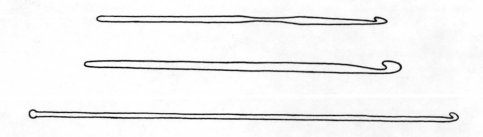

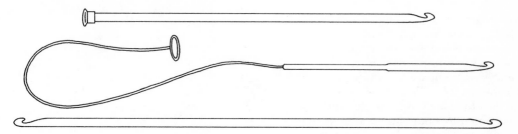

there is a flattened area or indentation on the shank that acts as a platform for the fingers. This makes it easier to hold hooks in the smaller sizes. This feature is seldom found in the larger hooks made of wood or other materials.

Afghan Hook.   This type of hook is sometimes called a tunisian hook. It is different from the regular hook because it is made to hold a complete row of stitches. It resembles a knitting needle with its straight, even shaft and knob at one end, but instead of the other end having a point, it has a hook.

Recently a flexible afghan hook has appeared on the market that allows more stitches to be held on the hook than the regular afghan hook does. It permits most of the weight to be held in the lap, just as circular knitting needles do.

There is also a double-hook tool, a special afghan hook, which can be used for crocheting double-faced fabric in two colors.

In selecting a hook, remember that the hook end is carefully shaped. It should be deeply cut so it can grasp the yarn securely as the stitch is being made. Try to find a hook that is lightweight and comfortable to hold. You want to be able to control it easily.

Examine the Material

Gradually over the years, new materials have been used for making hooks. Years ago a steel hook was the one most frequently used. Today you will find hooks made of aluminum, bone, casein plastic, plastic, and wood.

Steel Hooks.   For a fine, small hook, steel is best. It can remain strong and rigid although drawn very fine. Cotton, linen, and silk in a very fine thread are crocheted with this type of hook. When using a steel hook with a lightweight wool, you must be careful not to let the yarn get pierced.

Aluminum Hooks.   They are usually light in weight and quite rigid. This allows larger-sized hooks to be made in aluminum. They seem to be the most popular type of hook. Standard yarns and heavier threads work up nicely with an aluminum hook.

Bone Hooks.   This type of hook is disappearing. In fact, the bone-type hook of today is often made of plastic. The bone hook has a tapered shaft. Traditionally it was used for fine wool yarn and lightweight crocheting. There is a possibility that bone hooks may break, so handle them carefully.

Plastic Hooks.   This is another hook made of lightweight material. It is used for hooks in larger sizes. Plastic hooks are flexible and so are generally employed for lightweight work in the softer yarns. There is a possibility that the hook may break, so learn to handle it lightly.

Wooden Hooks.   These hooks come in the larger sizes. They are used when you want to make something quickly. Usually they are employed with heavy yarns, such as rug yarn or heavy cord, but there are times when they are used with lightweight threads and yarns to produce a lacy effect. In selecting a wooden hook, be sure that it is smooth and that the hook is carefully made.

Review the Sizing

The sizing of crocheting hooks can be confusing. In choosing a hook, both the diameter, or thickness, and length should be considered. Because of this, I have tried to compare by drawing and chart the sizes available in the various materials. In some instances, the thickness is noted by both letter and number. The number corresponds to the same size in a knitting needle. Except for steel needles, the smaller the number, the smaller the size.

A general rule to remember when selecting a hook is that the thicker the yarn is, the larger the needle should be. Also, the correct size hook is the one that controls the yarn easily. You should be able to hold the yarn with the hook end without splitting the yarn or catching the surface of the crocheting.

Steel hooks are made in a 5 inch (12.5 cm) length and in sizes ranging from 00 to 14. Remember the sizing of the steel hook is different from the sizing of other hooks. The larger the number is, the smaller the size. Usually the diameter is less than ¼ inch (6 mm).

Aluminum hooks are available in sizes B to K and in a 6-inch (15 cm) length. B indicates the smallest size; K, the largest.

HOOK SIZES

Steel	Aluminum	Bone	Plastic	Plastic—Giant or Jiffy	Wood	Wood—Jumbo	Afghan
14							
13							
12							
11							
10							
9							
8							
7							
6							
5							
4							
3							
2	B	1					B
1							
0	C	2					C
00	D	3	D	3			D
		4					
	E	5	E	4			E
	F	6	F	5			F
	G		G	6			G
				7			
	H		H	8			H
	I		I	9	I	10	I
	J		J	10			J
	K		K	10½	L	11	
					M	13	
					N	15	
						16	
				Q			
				S			

(Steel column: "Small" at top, "Large" toward the bottom)

Steel

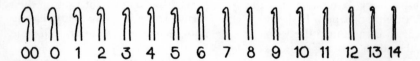

00 0 1 2 3 4 5 6 7 8 9 10 11 12 13 14

Aluminum

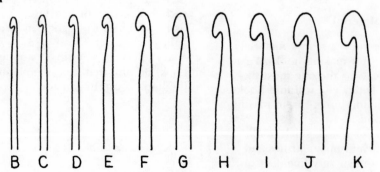

B C D E F G H I J K

If you study the accompanying chart, you will see that there is some overlapping in the available size of steel and aluminum hooks.

Bone hooks have a different sizing formula. They come in sizes 1 to 6. The smallest is number 1 and the largest, number 6. Number 1 corresponds to size B in an aluminum hook and number 6 is equivalent to size F.

Plastic hooks use two systems of size designation—letters and numerals. The letters D to K are employed, with D indicating the smallest size and K, the largest. This system is usually interchangeable with the one for aluminum hooks. If numbers are employed, relate the numbers to the letter system for plastic and aluminum hooks. That is, 3 equals D; 4, E; 5, F; 6, G; 8, H; 9, I; 10, J; 10½, K. Again study the accompanying chart. Plastic hooks are usually 5½ inches (14 cm) long.

There is also a large plastic hook that comes in two sizes, Q and S. The diameter of size Q is ⅝ inch (1.5 cm); size S, ¾ inch (1.8 cm). Hooks made of casein are also available in these two sizes. These hooks are usually about 8 inches (20.5 cm) long.

Wooden hooks are large and long, being 9 or 10 inches (23 or 25.5 cm) long. Crocheting can be done quickly with them.

In order to give you some idea of how thick they are, I have jotted down some diameters for you to study. For instance, 10 indicates a ¼ inch (6 mm) measure-

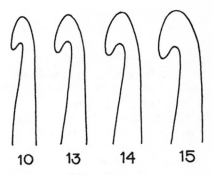

10   13   14   15

ment; 11, ⁵⁄₁₆ inch (7.5 mm); 13, ⅜ inch (9 mm); 15, ⁷⁄₁₆ inch (10.5 mm); 16, ½ inch (12 cm).

Afghan Hooks. Usually this type of hook is made of aluminum. Both letters and numerals are used to indicate sizing. Hooks sized by letter, B through J, are about the same size as aluminum and plastic hooks marked with the same letter. Those hooks using a number to indicate size, 1 through 10, correspond to the size as found in knitting needles. Afghan hooks are the longest of all of the hooks, namely, 9 to 14 inches (23–35.5 cm).

Consider Suitability

The appearance of your crocheting is influenced by the size of the hook you use. Because of this, it is most important that the hook and yarn be appropriate for each other and the article being constructed. The ideal needle size for the yarn is one that will enhance the beauty and texture of the yarn and still keep the work firm enough to hold its shape.

If the hook is too large for the yarn, the crocheting will be loose and may appear sleazy. It will be limp with no body. This allows the crocheting to stretch. It is almost impossible to return the item to its original shape and size even with blocking.

Crocheting with a hook too small produces the opposite results. The item will become rigid. There will be stiffness and too much body.

If you want to make something quickly and easily, work with a hook in a giant size. You may find it isn't quite as easy to control as you expect. A little practice is all you need to perfect the technique.

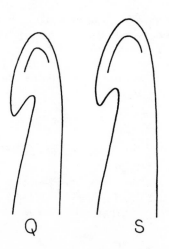

Q   S

ADD SOME AIDS

Although a hook and yarn are the two items necessary for crocheting, there are a few aids that you may find helpful. They include counters, gauges, markers, scissors, tape measure, tapestry needles.

Container. It is always best to keep your tools in a special place. By doing this, you not only work more efficiently, but you can also keep your equipment in better condition. Bags and boxes can be found in a variety of sizes, shapes, and materials. Most people find a bag easier to handle. Trying to find something at the bottom of a box is a problem unless you empty out the contents.

In choosing a bag, look for one that is easy to carry and at the same time big enough to hold the type of crocheting you do. If you only crochet small pieces, then, of course, you will not require as large a bag as if you were crocheting an afghan. Also remember that folding a piece is better than jamming it into the bag.

Keep your small equipment in a small case or envelope. Allowing your tools to move around freely in the bottom of a bag will not only ruin them, but also produce an annoying problem when you are trying to locate a specific article. Some people like to keep their hooks in the original packaging. This makes it easier to identify them.

Counters. These are small devices that help you count stitches and rows when crocheting. They are made in different styles. If you cannot find a flat row counter, you may want to make one. Take a 4-inch (10 cm) cardboard square and cut a 2-inch (5 cm) square in the center. Then mark the various dimensions on the sides.

Gauge. A card for checking hook sizes is useful to have. The better ones are constructed of metal or plastic. The holes in a cardboard gauge are less accurate after they have been used several times. The hook should slip in and out easily. If it does not, you may have a hook in a larger size than you need.

Markers. Colored plastic rings can be used instead of bits of yarn or safety pins for marking separate sections, the beginning and end of a pattern, increases and decreases. The open coil ring is the one to select.

Then there are some sewing aids that you will use. Keeping them with your crochet tools is a good idea.

Needles. They are used in various ways such as for sewing finished pieces together, working in ends of yarn, and splicing yarns. It will be best if the needle has a blunt point and a large eye. A tapestry needle is most frequently used. Available in steel and plastic, the plastic one is known as a yarn needle.

Sometimes a crewel needle is employed for finishing touches. Whichever type of needle you choose, be sure that the eye is big enough for the yarn to slip through it easily.

Needle Threader. Threading a needle with heavy yarn may prove troublesome. To avoid this problem, try a little gadget made especially for this purpose.

Scissors. A small pair for clipping thread and yarn is handy to have. Be sure the points are sharp.

Ruler. Some people find a 6-inch (15 cm) plastic ruler helpful. They find it more convenient to use for taking certain measurements than a tape measure.

Tape Measure. This is an aid you really need. You will work with it constantly in checking the size of the article you are crocheting. Because accurate measurements are so important, choose a good one—one that will not stretch or shrink. Try to keep one with your crocheting tools. By doing this you will be sure to always use the same one when measuring an item.

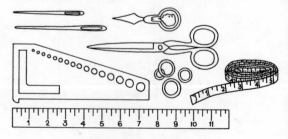

5

How to Interpret the Directions

Directions are often perplexing. Their meaning seems confusing. Because of this, it is wise to understand the significance of each new word and phrase before starting to crochet. Unless you do, creating an item using yarn and a hook can be difficult.

KNOW THE TERMS

Crocheting does seem to have a language of its own. In order to make it easier for you, the basic terms are listed here. They are given in alphabetical order so that it will be easier for you to refer to them. In some instances, the technique is explained in more detail in another section of the book, for example, in the direction for crocheting a specific stitch pattern or article.

Around Bar. This term is found in directions for a special stitch pattern. It indicates a "stitch around bar of stitch in a previous row." To do this, the hook is put around the stitch, instead of into the top of the stitch in the usual manner. If crocheting with the right side toward you, the hook is placed as in A; with the wrong side, as in B.

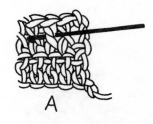

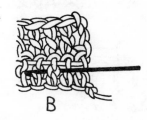

Attaching Thread or Yarn

When joining a new thread to a piece of crocheting, avoid using a knot. A knot creates an unattractive effect. Instead plan the work so the new yarn can be introduced at the end of the row. However, there are times when the new yarn must be joined in the body of the crocheting.

At the end of the row, crochet the last stitch to the final step. Then catch the new thread and draw it through the stitch. Continue crocheting, finishing the last step of the stitch (A). Then cut the original thread to about two inches (5 cm). Turn the work. Lay the ends of the two threads over the previous row. Crochet over them for about four stitches (B).

To join a new thread while crocheting a row, as is often necessary, when introducing a new color: place the thread over the previous row, beginning a few stitches before it is needed (C). Continue to work with the original yarn covering the end of the new one. At the correct place, make a stitch up to the last step. Then pick up the new thread and continue the crocheting, completing the last step of the stitch (D).

By introducing a new thread in this manner, it is not necessary to weave in the ends with a needle when the work is completed.

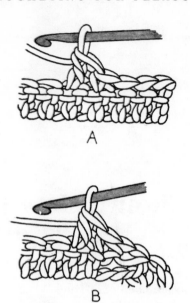

A

B

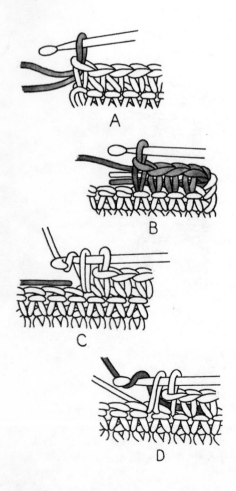

A

B

C

D

Binding Off

Sometimes when crocheting an item it is necessary to shape a certain area, such as an armhole. The instructions will direct you to *bind off*. To do this, several stitches are left unworked at one or both ends of a row. Slip stitch across the top of the required number of stitches at the beginning of the bind off (A). Continue to work a row of stitches as instructed. In order to avoid a sudden change in the height of the stitches, leave the required number of stitches unworked. End the row with a slip stitch. After skipping the slip stitch, work a single crochet stitch in the next stitch (B). Continue to crochet the row.

Blocking

A more professional look can be given a piece of crocheting by blocking. It helps shape the article to specific measurements and may smooth out minor irregularities. There are two basic ways to do the blocking—wet and steam. However, before beginning, check the directions on the yarn label. Often suggestions for blocking are listed, or in some cases, blocking may not be necessary.

Begin by smoothing out the piece to be blocked. Pin it, wrong side up, to a well-padded board, using rustproof pins. Put the pins at the top and bottom of the piece and then the sides. Gently maneuver and shape the article until the article measures the correct size. Place the pins close together to avoid a scalloped edge.

If the crocheting was done with smooth yarns in flat rows, place a damp cloth over it. Press lightly with an iron, allowing the steam to penetrate the article. Be careful not to slide the iron or let it rest on the work. Allow the piece to remain pinned to the board until it is thoroughly dry. This is the wet method.

When you are blocking fluffy yarns and raised pattern stitches, use a steaming technique. Hold the steaming iron close to the article so the steam penetrates it. In case extra steam is needed, you can use a wet pressing cloth. Hold the iron over the crocheting until it is thoroughly dry.

Pieces crocheted with synthetic threads or yarns can be dampened and allowed to dry. Pressing with an iron is not necessary. There is further information on blocking in Chapter 10.

Counting Stitches

Counting seems to be an important part of crocheting. At times, it will be necessary for you to count the number of stitches you have completed. This is not as easy to do as it is when you are knitting. Studying the accompanying drawing will help you determine how this can be done.

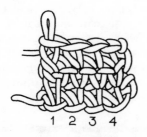

1 2 3 4

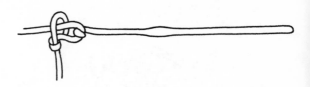

Draw Through

This term is frequently seen in crocheting directions. It describes the pulling through the stitch of the thread or yarn that has been put over the hook. A loop results.

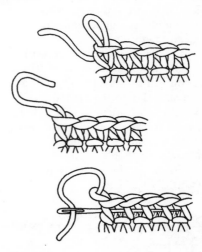

End Off

As you can guess, these words are found at the end of the directions. Cut the thread about three inches (7.5 cm) from the last stitch. Insert hook in the last loop. Place yarn over hook and draw end completely through the loop. Pull the end to tighten the stitch.

You can conceal the end of the yarn by threading a needle with it. Then weave it through the back of the work for about 1 or 2 inches (2.5–5 cm) below the top row of stitches. Cut off the remaining end.

Gauge

One of the most important things to watch when you are crocheting is the gauge. Usually the gauge is stated at the beginning of the crocheting directions.

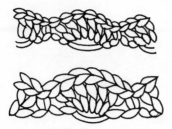

The term refers to the number of stitches and rows required to create a piece of crocheting of a certain size.

The careful attention to the gauge cannot be stressed too much. The size of the article you are making depends on it. Variations in the size of the yarn and the hook as well as the degree of tightness with which you crochet influence the size of the item.

It will be best if you check your work before you begin to make an article. In this way, you will be sure that it will be the correct size. To do this, crochet a swatch 3 inches by 3 inches (7.5 cm by 7.5 cm) using the required pattern stitch, yarn, and hook. After it is completed, block the sample. Then measure it with a ruler, as shown in the accompanying drawing.

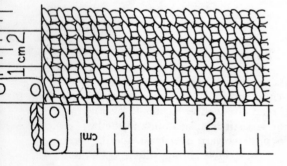

If the stitches and rows are not the same as the stated gauge, you know that you must make some changes. One way to do this is by changing the hook. Use a smaller hook when the number of stitches is less than the number required, a larger hook when more than the necessary number.

Joining Stitches

When the instructions indicate that the stitches must be joined, use a slip stitch.

Working from the front, put the hook under the 2 top threads of a stitch. Place yarn over hook. Draw yarn through stitch and loop on hook in a single motion. One loop is left on the hook, making it possible for you to continue crocheting.

Joining Sections

There are several ways to join crocheted pieces. The one you select depends on the edge and the one you prefer. Whichever method you choose, remember that the seam should be as invisible as possible. You do not want to destroy the beauty of the crocheting. Seams should also be straight and neat. Although they must be strong enough to hold the pieces in position, they should be elastic enough to retain the elasticity of the crocheting.

The edges can be put together as for a plain seam or placed side by side. Even edges can be joined using either method. However, if the edges are uneven but have the same number of stitches, it is best to use the second method.

Seam joining. When a seam is used, the edges may be sewn or crocheted together. Place the two right sides of the pieces together, keeping the edges and stitch pattern even. Then use a backstitch or overhand stitch or a crocheted loop stitch to sew them.

For the backstitch joining. Thread a blunt needle with matching yarn (A). If the yarn is heavy, it may be best to split it. Working as you would in sewing, fasten the end without a knot at the edge. The stitches should be close to the edges being seamed.

A

Bring the needle up two stitches from the edge. Then carry the needle backward, and insert it at the side edge. For the next stitch, move the needle forward four stitches. Carry the needle backward again, and insert it close to the first stitch. Repeat this forward and backward process until the seam is completed. Be careful not to pull the stitches tight.

For an overhand joining. Work this way to make a joining that will open up for a flat finish. As you work, point the needle directly toward you. Slip the needle under the back loop of a corresponding stitch on each edge. Be sure to maintain an even tension that is not too tight (B).

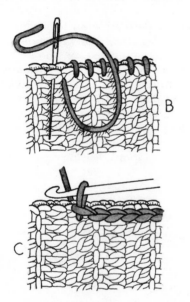

B

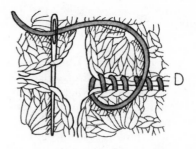

D

tifs. Keep the needle at right angles to the edges. Insert it under the back loop of a corresponding stitch on each edge. Pull the yarn through the stitches gently.

In case you are joining a series of medallions, you do not have to fasten your threads when the corners are reached. Instead continue to join the next two medallions in the same way (D).

For weaving lengthwise edges together. Keep the pieces side by side with the right sides up. Take the stitches over the edges. Begin by bringing needle under the lower half of edge stitch on one piece and then under the upper half of a corresponding edge stitch on the other piece (E). Continue across the edge in this way making an invisible joining.

C

For a slip stitch joining. Crochet along the edge. With the right sides of the pieces together, draw up a loop through 2 corresponding stitches (C), one in each piece. Then put the hook through the next 2 stitches. Pull up a loop through both stitches and the one on the hook. Continue this procedure until joining is completed. A chainlike effect is produced along the seamline.

Edge to edge joining. This type of joining can be done in several ways. Place the two pieces on a flat surface with edges side by side and with corresponding stitches opposite each other.

For an overhand finish. This is most often used to unite granny squares, patchwork squares, medallions, or mo-

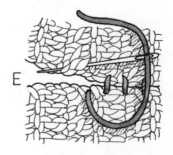

E

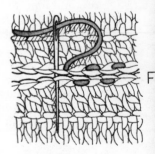

F

For weaving crosswise edges together. When there is an even number of stitches, place the pieces edge to edge. With the right sides up, bring up the needle through a loop. Then insert it through the next loop on the same edge, bringing it up in the corresponding loop on the opposite edge (F). Continue to weave the needle through the two edges, keeping the needle at right angles to the edges. You will notice that you seem to be making a series of running stitches appear along each edge. However, when the joining is completed it will be invisible.

Multiple of

In the making of a pattern stitch, a definite number of stitches is often required. When this happens the directions read "multiple of," indicating that the number of foundation stitches to be made must be divisible by the stated number. For instance, a multiple of 5 would mean that 10, 15, or 20 stitches would be required.

However, if the instructions read "multiple of 5 plus 3," then you know that 3 would be added to the total number, necessitating the use of 13, 18, or 23 stitches.

Shape with Decreases

A variety of shapes or forms can be crocheted by adding and subtracting stitches. It can be done at the ends of the row or within the row. A single increase is made by crocheting twice into the same stitch, whereas a single decrease is made by crocheting through 2 adjacent stitches ending in one final loop. When the increases or decreases are made within a row and repeated in several rows, their position should be noted in order to keep the sequence orderly. Place a marker such as a piece of contrasting yarn or a plastic coil ring.

Decrease for Single Crochet. When it is necessary to eliminate a stitch at the *beginning of row,* you can skip the first stitch or you can work 2 stitches together. The latter gives the neater finish. To do this, make 1 turning chain, which will be counted as the first stitch. Put the hook into each of the next 2 stitches. Draw through a loop so that 3 loops remain on the hook. Place the yarn over the hook. Draw it through the 3 loops, leaving 1 loop.

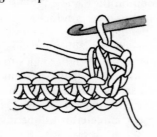

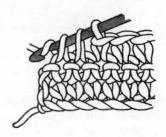

If the decrease must be made at *the end of the row,* you can skip the next to the last stitch or use this method: after crocheting across the row until only 2 single crochet stitches and the turning chain remain, work the 2 stitches together and then make the last stitch into the chain.

When the decrease must be made when *crocheting a row,* the directions will indicate where the decrease is to be taken. Work until 2 loops are left on the hook. With the 2 loops left on the hook, insert it in the next stitch. Place yarn over hook. Pull it through the stitch. Three loops will now be on the hook.

Put yarn over hook again (A). Draw it through the 3 loops, leaving 1 loop on hook (B).

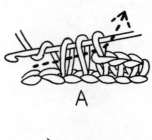

A

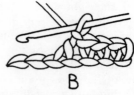

B

In doing this, 2 single crochet stitches have been crocheted together so that there is 1 less stitch in the row. Sometimes it is necessary to remove 2 stitches. To do this, insert hook in stitch. Put yarn over and draw up a loop. Skip the next stitch. Then in the next stitch, insert the hook and pull up a loop. You

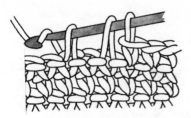

will now have 3 loops on the hook. Put yarn over hook and draw through the 3 loops.

Decrease for Half Double Crochet. Begin by putting yarn over the hook. Insert it in the first stitch. Put yarn over the hook again. Insert the hook into the second stitch. Be sure there are 5 loops on the hook (A). Then put the yarn over the hook. Draw a loop through all loops on the hook (B).

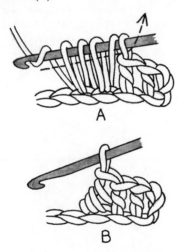

Decrease for Double Crochet. To reduce the number of stitches on the *row by 1,* follow this procedure. Work in double crochet to the point where 2 loops remain on the hook. Place yarn over hook. Draw the hook through the next stitch. Then put yarn over hook. Pull it through the stitch, leaving 4 loops on hook (A).

Place yarn over hook and draw it through 2 loops. Three loops remain on the hook (B).

Bring yarn over hook again. Draw it through the 3 loops, leaving 1 loop on hook (C).

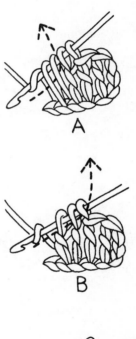

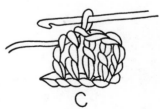

The procedure for removing 1 stitch when crocheting in single crochet can be used for half double stitch. If the decrease is to come at the beginning of the row, crochet 2 turning chains, which will count as the first stitch. Put the yarn around the hook. Insert the hook into the next stitch and draw through a loop. Put the hook into the following stitch. Pull through a loop, leaving 4 loops on the hook. Place the yarn around the hook. Draw it through all 4 loops, making 1 stitch. Proceed across the row until 2 half double crochets and the turning chain of the previous row remain. Work the last 2 stitches together. Then crochet the last stitch into the chain.

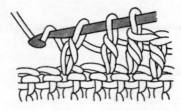

If it is necessary *to remove 2 stitches,* do it this way. Put yarn over hook. Insert it in stitch. Draw through a loop. Bring yarn over hook. Pull hook through 2 loops. Then skip the next stitch. Put yarn over hook. Insert hook in next stitch. Draw through a loop. Put yarn over hook. Draw it through 2 loops, leaving 3 loops on the hook. Put yarn over and draw through three loops.

Decrease for Treble Crochet. In making this decrease, place yarn over hook twice. Put the hook in the stitch at the point where the decrease is to be made. Put yarn over hook. Draw through a loop. Wrap yarn over hook and draw a loop through 2 loops, leaving 3 loops on the hook (A).

Put the yarn over the hook again. Draw it through the 2 loops, leaving 2 loops on the hook (B).

Wrap the yarn over the hook twice. Insert the hook into the second stitch. Draw through a loop. Then put yarn over hook. Draw a loop through 2 loops (C).

Again put the yarn over the hook. Draw it through 2 loops, leaving 3 loops on the hook (D). Put the yarn over the hook. Draw a loop through the 3 loops on the hook (E). After doing this, you have decreased the work by 1 treble crochet (F).

These directions can be followed when the directions indicate a decrease of 2 stitches with this exception. Skip a stitch between the 2 stitches that are worked together as you did for the double crochet decrease.

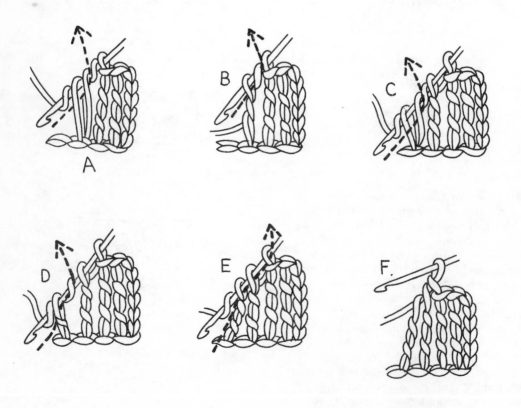

Decrease Several Stitches. Sometimes to obtain a certain shaping in the crocheted piece, it is necessary to eliminate several stitches at the beginning and end of a row. This creates a steplike effect.

At the beginning of a row, make a slip stitch into each of the stitches that must be removed. Eliminate the turning chain.

Start the new row by making a slip stitch into the next stitch. Make the necessary number of turning chains to count as the first stitch. Then continue to work in the stitch pattern you are using to the end of the row.

At the end of a row, follow this procedure. Work to the place where the decrease is to begin. To determine this point, count the turning chain of the previous row as one of the stitches to leave unworked. Turn the work and continue to work the next row.

Shape with Increases

Increases can be made at each end of a row or within a row. The directions you are following will indicate where the increase is to be made. If the increase is made within a row and must be repeated for several rows, it is wise to mark the point where the increasing starts. This allows you to keep the "progression" evenly spaced, moving right to left. When the shaping is to the right, the increase is made before the marker but when it is to the left, it is made after the marker. The marker can be a piece of contrasting yarn or coil ring for easy removal. When crocheting the next row, the order is reversed in order to maintain consistency of the direction.

For a single increase, crochet 2 stitches in 1 stitch instead of the usual one. The technique is used for the various types of stitches (A).

For a double increase, crochet 3 stitches in 1 stitch instead of the usual 1. Again the procedure can be used for the various types of stitches (B).

For an increase of stitches at an end, work a chain of the required number of stitches extending from the edge. Turn the work, crocheting along the chain on the next row (C).

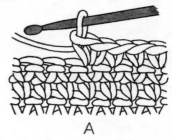

A

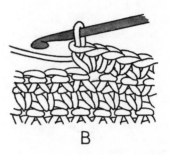

B

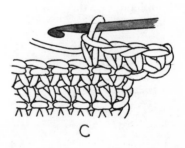

C

Turn Work

You have probably noticed that your crocheting is being turned at regular intervals so the work can progress. In order that the end of the row does not appear puckered, a certain number of chain stitches are made to bring the crocheting up to the level of the stitch. The number depends on the height of the stitch that is to be made. The taller the stitch, the more chains will be needed. The following information lists the number of chains to employ.

1 chain for single crochet (sc)
2 chains for half double crochet (hdc)
3 chains for double crochet (dc)
4 chains for treble crochet (tr)
5 chains for double treble (dtr)
6 chains for triple treble (tr tr)

When the turning chain is made at the end of the row, turn your work from right to left to keep the chain from twisting. Then insert the hook in the indicated stitch. For single and half double crochet, put it in the first stitch. For the other types of stitches, in the second stitch.

Under Two Top Threads

This direction may seem puzzling. When you find it in the instructions you are following, simply slip the hook under the top part of the work. It is so easy to place the hook under or through the wrong stitch.

Work Even

This instruction indicates that you should continue to crochet as before, working with the same number of stitches without increasing or decreasing. Also watch the tension of the work. There is a tendency to draw the work in.

Yarn Over

This direction is continually used in order to create a new loop or stitch. To follow the instruction, pass the hook under and over the yarn or thread so that the end of the hook catches the yarn in preparation for pulling it through the loop or stitch. Sometimes the directions will read "yarn over hook." In case thread is to be used instead of yarn, the instructions may read "thread over."

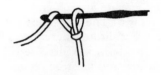

REMEMBER THE ABBREVIATIONS

Deciphering directions can often prove puzzling, especially when they are written in a series of abbreviations. Although you may know the meaning of a term, it may take you a moment to connect its meaning to a letter or symbol. Because the abbreviations vary from author to author, country to country, always study the listing of abbreviations before you begin crocheting. Then read the instructions for the article you are

making. If unfamiliar abbreviations and procedures appear, be sure to check them carefully. This avoids mistakes later. If you think you will need to refer to them, mark the pages on which the abbreviations are listed. A handy reference saves time.

The most widely used abbreviations are listed here. In a few instances, the meaning varies when instructions are prepared for the British market.

ABBREVIATIONS USED IN CROCHET

TERM	AMERICAN	BRITISH
alternate	alt	
beginning	beg	
block (solid mesh)	bl	
chain stitch	ch	
cluster	cl	
decrease	dec	
double crochet	dc	tr
double treble (triple) crochet	dtr, d tr, or dbl tr	tr tr
each	ea	
half double crochet	hdc, h dc, or h.d.c.	h.tr
hook	hk	
inclusive	incl	
increase	inc	
knit	K	
left-hand	LH	
loop	lp	
measure	meas	
number	no.	
open mesh	om	
pattern	pat or patt	
picot	p or P	
popcorn stitch	pc st	
previous row	pr r	
purl	P	
remaining	rem	
repeat	rep * (asterisk) * * (asterisks) ( ) (parentheses)	
right hand	RH	
right side of work	RS	
round	rnd	
row	r	
single crochet	sc	dc
skip	sk	
slip stitch	sl st or ss	sc
space (open mesh)	sp	
stitch	st	
stitches	sts	
together	tog	
treble or triple	tr	long or double treble—dbl tr
treble or triple treble	tr tr	quad tr
turning chain	tch	
wrong side of work	Ws	
yarn over hook or yarn around hook	O, yo, or yoh	

Special Symbols

Asterisks, parentheses, and brackets are often used to simplify the directions. They may indicate certain procedures such as the repetition of a sequence a certain number of times. The number may be stated as a certain number of times or as an order to crochet to the end of the row. For example, when you read directions such as these—*2 dc in next stitch, 1 dc in the following stitch, repeat from * twice—you know that after doing this once you return to the first asterisk and crochet the directions to the second asterisk. In this case, you would repeat the procedure two times. Of course, you understand that you are actually working the stitch sequence three times.

Parentheses ( ) can also be used to indicate repetition. For instance, you might find directions such as these—(1 dc in next st, ch 1) 6 times. At such an instance, you would repeat the sequence 6 times.

You will also find parentheses being used to distinguish a sequence of stitches that are to be made in a stitch or space. The instructions might read, "(sc, ch 1, sc) in next ch." The parentheses make you realize that the enclosed steps must be worked according to the directions following.

Parentheses are also used to indicate variations because of sizing. For instance, the instructions might read, "Directions for size 6–8. Changes for sizes 10, 12, 14, and 16 are in parentheses." Then you will find directions for beginning the crocheting, reading—ch 50 (54 56 60 64).

Brackets [ ] are sometimes used to enclose directions for crocheting a specific stitch or technique.

6

Choosing the Right Project

Choosing a project is always fun. There are so many interesting designs to select. But picking the right one is not always as easy as it seems. There is often a tendency to choose an item beyond one's ability. This can lead to a frustrating experience with unattractive results.

To avoid such a situation, begin by selecting something easy to make. As you become more experienced, you can choose more intricate designs. However, whatever your ability is, select a project that provides a feeling of beauty and pleasure in the making.

TIPS ON RECOGNIZING SIMPLE CHARACTERISTICS

Detecting easy-to-make features is important. Some techniques and yarns are easier to use than others. The size and stitch are influencing forces. Small items are easier to handle and quicker to finish. As you read the directions, note whether the basic stitches of single and double crochet are being used. They are the simplest to crochet.

Although large hooks make an article grow as if by magic, they can be awkward to handle. Medium-sized hooks re-

quire less effort to control. Small hooks create fine work, which is more difficult to make.

Smooth, supple yarn of medium weight seems to make the procedure less difficult. Try to select a color that you like, so that watching the stitches evolve becomes a more pleasurable experience. When there is a color contrast between the hook and the yarn, it is easier to see how each stitch is being made.

THINK ABOUT PERSONAL FEATURES

One aspect of project picking that is often overlooked is the becomingness of the design. The item appears so attractive on the printed page that one forgets about how it will look when worn. This is too bad. Designs and yarns should be selected for their flattering effect. They have the ability to make you look more attractive. Using the correct lines, colors, and textures can make you appear

shorter or taller; smaller or larger; slimmer or more rounded. Design features can even create an illusion that causes one area to seem smaller and at the same time adds fullness to another. It is also possible to draw the eye to a beautiful feature as a less attractive one is camouflaged. The success with which you choose your design and yarn will control the results.

Analyze Your Characteristics

Before you make your project decision, take a searching look at yourself. Don't do it lightly. Too often one looks at oneself through rose-colored glasses. This won't do. Be as critical of yourself as you would be of an acquaintance. Think about your liabilities as well as your assets. Consider size, your shape, and your coloring. Check your posture. Do you stand erect or do you have a tendency to slump? Round shoulders, a hollow chest, a prominent abdomen, and a swayback are probably the results if you do.

As you continue your analysis, decide whether your body seems to appear well-proportioned. Note whether you seem short- or long-waisted for your height. And what about your hips? Do they seem to protrude or appear too rounded? You want to be sure that the design you select does not emphasize such features, especially since there is a tendency for crocheted pieces to cling.

And don't forget to analyze your facial tones. Color plays such an important function in producing a becoming effect. All skins, whether light or dark, have tones of red and yellow. Some skins show a predominance of red; others, yellow. If you recall your paint-box days, you will remember that when you mixed red and yellow together you created orange. Orange can be lightened to create a creamy tone, or darkened to a deep, rich brown. Your skin may be a light tint or a darker shade. If you indulge in sun bathing, you may find that your skin tones fluctuate between light and dark.

Don't Forget Likes and Dislikes

Everyone seems to have certain preferences that influence the clothes they wear. Sometimes these likes and dislikes are not the most flattering. However, before choosing a design, consider your preferences as well as the features that look best on you in an attempt to coordinate these two factors.

Ask yourself whether you prefer tailored designs to dressy ones, classic to high-style, smooth to coarse, soft to stiff, simple to sophisticated, dramatic to understated. Will it be a plain classic pull-

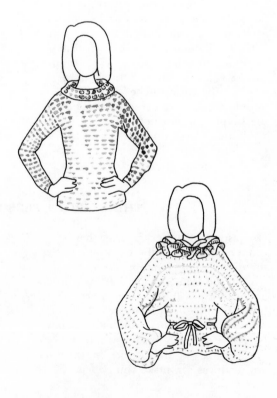

over or a lacy and scalloped one, a simple cardigan or a granny square jacket, a simple crew neckline or a draped cowl. This analysis could continue on and on.

Keep on until you have the answers. Also remember to do this type of analysis when you are making a gift for someone.

PLAN FOR A BECOMING EFFECT

Optical illusion should not be forgotten when selecting a project. It provides a way to create flattering results. When it is used correctly, new effects can be produced as if by magic. It is hard to understand why a person spends so much money and time trying to reduce the size of her figure by dieting and exercise when she could change her apparent size by using the tricks of optical illusion. There are ways to use line, color, and texture to fool the eye.

Tricks with Line

If this is difficult to believe, notice the lines and shapes here. You probably have seen them before. In diagram A, observe how much shorter the lower line seems than the upper, and yet if you measure the lines they are the same length. If this drawing does not convince you, study the heavy lines in diagram B. Isn't it amazing how they seem to bulge. And yet if you place a ruler on them, you will see that they are definitely straight.

In case you still can't believe that your eyes deceive you, study the rectangles (C). They surely do not look the same although they are. The vertical line makes the rectangle seem much narrower and taller than the horizontal line does.

Optical illusion is pure magic when you learn to use it correctly. You can make yourself seem taller or shorter, larger or smaller, thinner or stouter by applying the tricks of optical illusion. And remember that this power can be used for the face as well as the figure.

Before you can apply this magic, you have to understand how the eye reacts to line. Analyze what your eye does. Notice that it follows the direction the line takes. For instance, in drawing D there

are four lines of the same length. But do they look the same length? No. In the first one, notice how your eye moves upward and continues to do just that because there is no other line to stop it. But in the second line, the eye contacts an oppositional line, which encourages it to stop and proceed horizontally instead of vertically. This makes the line seem shorter. However, in the third line, when the eye meets the oppositional line, the eye retreats, and of course the line seems shorter. In the fourth line, when the eye encounters the oppositional lines, it continues upward, making the line appear taller.

If after your analysis of yourself you

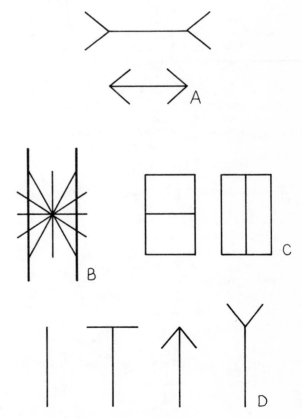

decide you want to appear taller and in turn thinner, then you know that you must keep the eye moving upward. If you want to seem shorter and more rounded, then the eye should move downward. Observe how the design lines of the hats and sweater dresses influence the apparent size of the figure, just as the oppositional lines created illusions in the previous drawings. When you are trying to decide which design to choose, keep this simple trick of optical illusion in mind.

Tricks with Space

The way a space is divided is another way of influencing the reaction of the eye. Remember how the vertical and horizontal lines changed the appearance of the rectangles? Observe how this type of illusion affects the appearance of the

fashion figures (A). It isn't difficult to see that the two-piece effect of sweater and skirt makes the figure appear much shorter than the one-piece dress with its long center front detail.

By dividing large spaces into smaller areas, many creative optical illusions can be achieved. But remember the proportion of the spaces to each other will affect the illusion that is created. Notice the rectangles (B), and how the width of the panel appears to affect the size of the rectangle. When the two parallel lines, which form the panel, are close enough together so the eye has a path in which to move upward, both rectangle and figure appear taller and of course narrower. However, when the lines are placed far apart, the eye has a tendency to move from one side of the panel to the other. This horizontal motion of the eye makes the object seem wider and in

A   B

pears than the one made of vertical lines. The spacing between the lines becomes more important than the direction the lines are taking when the spaces between the lines are arranged so that the eye moves quickly from one line to the next without stopping. Notice how the horizontal lines are the ones that create the vertical illusion. Because of this, always analyze a striped design to determine which way your eyes will move.

Up and Across

Applying these tricks of optical illusion is fascinating. Before you begin, check the analysis you made of your characteristics. Decide whether you should keep the eye moving upward or crosswise. Do you need to camouflage a certain feature? Once you have made these decisions, start to experiment. Some ideas are mentioned here to help you create a flattering illusion when you select a project.

Appear Taller. This isn't always the easiest effect to produce when wearing a crocheted fashion. Very often the crocheted item is a sweater that has a ten-

turn shorter. This trick of optical illusion should be remembered not only when you select a design, but also when you are wearing it. Leaving a jacket or cardigan open just a little bit to form a narrow panel will make you appear thinner, but if you let it fly open so a wide panel results, then you can be sure you will appear much fatter.

One facet of optical illusion that may seem confusing is that which pertains to stripes. Although it is generally thought that vertical lines make an object appear taller and in turn thinner and that horizontal lines have a broadening effect, there are times when this is not true and the illusions are reversed. It is because of this that you should always ask yourself how your eyes see an object. To seem taller, the design must make the eye move upward. As you study diagram C, notice how much narrower and higher the block of horizontal lines ap-

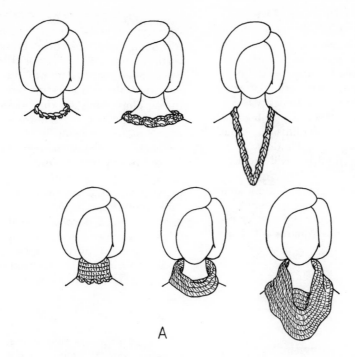

A

dency to make one appear larger and in turn shorter. But remember that straight lines moving in a vertical direction usually produce a lengthening and slimming effect. A collarless neckline with a V-line, a tight-fitting turtle neckline, long, slim sleeves, a straight skirt, and a cardigan worn slightly open are a few design features that can be used to achieve this look. Some stitch patterns that have a ribbed effect may create a vertical illusion.

This type of illusion can also be used to make your face and neck seem more slender. A V-neckline, a narrow collar that forms a V-shape, and a collar worn open at the throat and high at the back of the neck will keep the eye moving upward. If you study the drawings here, you will notice that the shape of the face appears to change as the shape of the neckline does.

Vertical illusions can also be created by accessories. Wearing a long, narrow scarf, a hat with an upturned brim, and a tilted beret will keep the eye moving upward.

Appear Shorter. The eye prefers to move in a horizontal direction. This makes it easier to create an illusion that

makes the figure look shorter and more rounded. A sweater and skirt combination that gives a two-piece effect and a jacket worn open to form a wide panel are two ways to produce this effect. A

B

round neckline, a high round collar, a bulky cowl will seem to add roundness. Short capes and jackets produce the same effect. Wide sleeves and those with cuffs that end at the bustline or hipline seem to draw the eye across the figure adding apparent width to these areas. Patch pockets are another design feature that produces a horizontal illusion. A hat with a turned down brim, a wide scarf draped across the shoulders will seem to shorten the figure.

Stitch patterns with curving lines, such as in shell designs, have the tendency to create this type of illusion. Patchwork effects made with granny squares will also do this.

Concentrate on an Asset

Although the eye usually follows the direction a line takes, it is possible to attract the eye by making one line more important than another. As you look at the accompanying drawing, notice how your eye focuses its attention on the longer or more dominant line in each drawing. Because of this, the eye can be attracted to any part of your costume. By using the trick thoughtfully, you can emphasize an attractive feature and at the same time camouflage a figure problem. A frilly ruffle, a decorative yoke, a pretty edging can draw attention to a pretty face. Out-of-proportion hips may be unnoticed if the eyes are focused on the face.

Select a Becoming Color

This isn't always as easy as it seems. Developing a good feeling for color takes practice. There is often a tendency to use too much or the wrong kind. When color is used correctly, it can be most effective in creating illusions.

Effective Illusions. Color can produce various effects. For example, you can look larger or smaller, or feel warmer or cooler, depending on the color you select. Warm or advancing colors, red and yellow, will make you seem larger, whereas blue, a cool or receding color, will make you appear smaller.

The intensity of a color also influences the look. Bright hues have the ability to make you appear larger, whereas grayed colors seem to make the figure fade into the background, thus appearing smaller. Because of this, a bright blue sweater will make you appear larger than one constructed of a soft, medium blue.

Value is another characteristic of color that influences the apparent size of an object. Light colors will seem to increase size; darker colors decrease it. No doubt you have noticed how much larger your feet appear in white shoes than they do in black ones.

Dividing a design into sections through the use of different colors is another way of creating effective illusions.

Of course if you want to appear taller and thinner, you will have to be careful how you combine the colors. For example, a sweater of one hue and a skirt of another will make the figure appear shorter than the same design in one color. Also, the use of a contrasting color for an accessory, such as a scarf, bag, gloves, or hat tends to make the figure appear shorter, unless the placement of the colors keeps the eye moving upward.

Remember that if you decide to introduce contrasting hues in your costume, the results are usually more pleasing if subdued colors are used for large areas. In fact a good rule to follow is that the larger the area to be covered, the more subdued the color should be. A slender person with a nicely proportioned figure will look attractive in a bright sweater, whereas a fat person will look huge in the same brilliant hue. Therefore, if bright colors are becoming to your face but you do not have a good figure, it is wise to limit their use to a small area, such as a scarf. If, however, you want to use a contrasting color in several acces-

sories, then the value and the intensity of the color should be subdued.

Color has power in another way. A light color can attract the eye and hold its attention in an amazing way. This can be employed to great advantage. You can introduce a light hue to emphasize a good feature so that a figure irregularity may remain unnoticed. For example, if you have hips that are out of proportion, don't emphasize the fact by selecting a design with a white band on the lower edge of a dark sweater. Instead, you will put the light band at the neckline so that the eye is attracted to the face.

Choose a Becoming Texture

Texture plays a definite role in costume design. Often its abilities to make one appear larger or smaller are overlooked. They shouldn't be. The effect of correct lines and colors may be destroyed unless the right texture is used. This is especially so in crocheting because each stitch pattern has a very definite surface interest. The yarn that is used also contributes to the textured effect. Some yarns are stiff and bulky, allowing the garment to stand away from the body, whereas others are soft, clinging to the figure. Shell designs with their scalloped effect seem to add roundness, making the figure seem larger. A double crochet

pattern with its straight lines makes the figure appear smaller. Because of these differences, it is important for you to study a stitch pattern for distinctive characteristics and the effect they have on the figure.

Lightweight or moderate weight yarns seem to be the most becoming for the average figure. The bulky and heavy textures seem to conceal the outline, but at the same time increase the size of the wearer. Yarns of the heavier type should be avoided by the tiny and the plump, but may work extremely well on a tall, well-proportioned, athletic figure.

Yarns that produce a smooth surface when crocheted seem to make the figure appear smaller. In contrast, fluffy and definitely textured yarns seem to add roundness to the figure.

Dull textures, like dull hues, seem to make the silhouette less distinct. It seems to fade into the background. This is an extremely important fact to remember if your figure is not well-proportioned.

In contrast to dull textures, shiny ones, such as the ones found in glittering yarn, seem to increase the apparent size of the figure. They also seem to emphasize the silhouette. Unless you have a perfect figure, it is best to avoid their use.

When choosing a stitch pattern, always consider its effect on the figure. Designs of moderate size and interest and those with an all-over pattern can be flattering. Be sure the lines are indefinite and the colors are nicely blended. If you want to appear taller, then select one in which there is a distinct vertical motion in the design. Usually plain textures make the figure seem smaller than patterned ones.

Note the Fashions

Before you choose a crochet project, check the fashion trends. Thumb through magazines, watch the advertisements, do some window shopping, and be sure to see what ready-to-wear is featuring. If you do this, you will quickly realize that there are extremes in fashion—fads that go out of style quickly. Recently, crocheting has taken its place in high-style fashions. Some are exclusive models, created by name designers. Although the price of these designs is often astronomical, check the group. Usually they provide ideas, telling you what you may expect in the future. Because crocheting is time-consuming, you want to be sure that the project you crochet will still be in fashion when you complete it. Of course you can be sure of the classics. They are perennial favorites.

During your search, you no doubt will find certain styles that will be unbecoming. Don't feel you have to wear them just because they are fashionable. It is better not to dress in style and look attractive than to wear the latest fashions and appear unattractive. Try to adapt fashion to fit your needs. Always choose the lines, colors, and textures that enable you to look the way you want to.

7

Vary the Basic Techniques

Variety is supposed to add spice to life. It certainly does to crocheting. A monotonous texture comes alive by maneuvering the hook in different ways. Each technique creates a special effect, varying from the firm and sturdy to the limp and fragile. The flat textures of the basics can take on new looks. Hundreds of stitch patterns and motifs evolve from a few elementary procedures. In order to become familiar with the new techniques, it is best to make a sample to try each movement. Some helpful hints are suggested here.

COMBINE THE STITCHES

One of the simplest ways to create an interesting stitch pattern is by uniting two basic stitches. Several examples are shown on the following pages. You may be amazed how easy it is to change the look.

By combining a single crochet and a chain stitch, this openwork pattern is created. Inserting a chain stitch between the single crochet stitches, a daintier look is created.

Single Crochet—with Chain-one Spaces

Begin with a foundation chain the required number of stitches. Use a multiple of 2 stitches plus 1, with an additional 2 chains.

For the **first row,** take a single crochet in third chain from hook. Repeat the following procedure to end of row. * Chain 1. Skip 1 chain. Make 1 single crochet in next chain. * Finish with 3 chains. Turn.

For the **second row,** skip first 2 stitches. Repeat the following procedure to end of row. * Take a single crochet in next single crochet. Chain 1. * End with 1 single crochet in second stitch of turning chain. Chain 3 and turn.

Repeat the **second row** until work is completed.

Double Crochet— with Chain-one Spaces

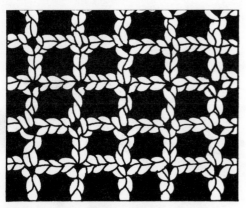

Make a foundation chain the required length. Use multiple of 2 stitches plus 1, with an additional 2 chains.

For the **first row,** make a double crochet in fifth chain from hook. Repeat the following procedure to end of row. * Chain 1. Skip 1 chain. Make a double crochet in next chain. * At end of foundation, chain 4 and turn.

For the **second row,** skip first 2 stitches. Repeat the following procedure to end of row. * Take 1 double crochet in next double crochet. Chain 1. * End row with a double crochet in third stitch of turning chain. Chain 4 and turn.

Repeat the **second row** until work is completed.

Half-Double Crochet— with Chain-one Spaces

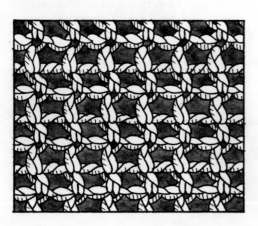

Begin with a foundation chain the required length. Use a multiple of 2 stitches plus 1, with an additional 3 chains.

For the **first row,** make a half double crochet in fourth chain from hook. Repeat the following procedure to end of row. * Chain 1. Skip 1 chain. Make a half double crochet in next chain. * At end of row, chain 3 and turn.

For the **second row,** skip first 2 stitches. Repeat the following procedure to end of row. * Make a half double crochet in next half double crochet. Chain 1. * End with 1 half double crochet in second stitch of turning chain. Chain 3 and turn.

Repeat the **second row** until work is completed.

Treble Crochet—with Chain-one Spaces

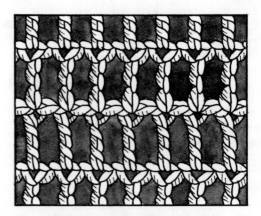

Begin with a foundation chain the required length. Use a multiple of 2 stitches plus 1, with an additional 1 chain.

For the **first row,** make 1 treble crochet in sixth chain from hook. Repeat the following procedure to end of row. * Chain 1. Skip 1 chain. Make 1 treble crochet in next chain. * Finish with 5 chains. Turn.

For the **second row,** skip first 2 stitches. Repeat the following procedure to end of row. * Make 1 treble crochet in next treble crochet. Chain 1. * End with 1 treble crochet in fourth stitch of turning chain. Chain 5 and turn.

Repeat the **second row** until work is completed.

By combining basic and chain stitches, an open, all-over design can be produced. The spaces will vary in size depending on the basic stitch you select and the number of chain stitches between stitches. Some combinations are mentioned here. You can see how they vary in openness.

Double Crochet— with Chain-two Spaces

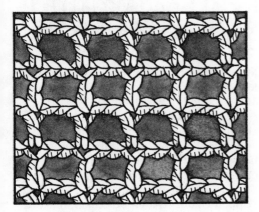

Start with a foundation chain the required length. Use a multiple of 3 stitches plus 1, with an additional 2 chains.

For the **first row,** make 1 double crochet in sixth chain from hook. Repeat the following procedure to end of row. * Chain 2. Skip 2 chains. Take a double crochet in next chain. * At end of row, chain 5 and turn.

For the **second row,** skip first 3 stitches. Repeat the following procedure to end of row. * Take 1 double crochet in next double crochet. Chain 2. * At end of row, take a double crochet in third stitch of turning chain. Chain 5 and turn.

Repeat the **second row** until work is completed.

Treble Crochet—with Chain-two Spaces

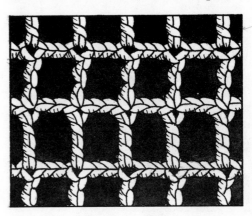

Commence with a foundation chain the required length. Use a multiple of 3 stitches plus 1 with an additional 3 chains.

For the **first row,** take 1 treble crochet in the seventh chain from hook. Repeat the following procedure to end of row. * Chain 2. Skip 2 chains. Take 1 treble crochet in next chain. * Finish with 6 chains. Turn.

For the **second row,** skip first 3 stitches. Repeat the following sequence of stitches to end of row. * Take 1 treble crochet in next treble crochet. Chain 2. * End with 1 double crochet in third stitch of turning chain. Chain 6 and turn.

Repeat the **second row** until work is completed.

Lacy Double Crochet

Start with a foundation chain the required length, using a multiple of 2 stitches plus 1, with an additional 2 chain stitches.

For the **first row,** take 1 double crochet in third chain from hook, leaving 2 loops on hook. Repeat the following procedure to the end of row. * Begin by skipping 1 chain. Take 1 double crochet in next chain to 3 loops on hook. Put yarn over hook and pull through remaining 3 loops. Chain 1. Make 1 double crochet in same stitch to 2 loops on hook. * When the last 2 chains are reached, skip 1 chain. Take 1 double crochet in last chain to 3 loops on hook. Put yarn over hook. Pull through remaining 3 loops. Chain 3 and turn.

For the **second row,** make 1 double crochet in first stitch to 2 loops. Repeat the following procedure to the end of the row. * Begin by skipping 1 chain. Take 1 double crochet in next chain to 3 loops on hook. Put yarn over hook and pull through remaining 3 loops. Chain 1. Make 1 double crochet in same stitch to 2 loops on hook. * At end of row, take last double crochet in top of turning chain. Chain 3 and turn.

Repeat **second row** until work is completed.

Crossed Double Crochet

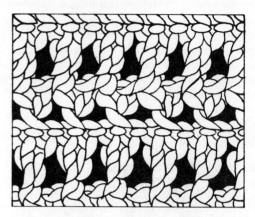

Make a foundation chain the required length. Use a multiple of 2 stitches plus 1 and an additional chain.

For the **first row,** make a double crochet in the fourth chain from the hook, and a double crochet in third chain from hook. Repeat the following procedure to end of row. * Skip 1 chain. Make a double crochet in next chain and also 1 in skipped chain. * At end of chain, make 2 chains and turn.

For the **second row,** skip first 2 stitches. Make 1 double crochet in third stitch and 1 double crochet in second stitch. Repeat the following procedure to end of row. * Skip first stitch. Make a double crochet in next stitch and a double crochet in skipped stitch. * At end of row, chain 2 and turn.

Repeat **second row** until work is completed.

CHANGE A TECHNIQUE

Another way to create variety in stitch patterns is by changing the position of the hook as it enters a loop. Instead of inserting the hook under the 2 top loops as you make the basic stitches, you put it under one loop or between the stitches. If you have never performed these techniques, directions for an article you are making will be easier to follow if you examine the information given here.

Under One Loop

Inserting the hook under 1 loop creates an interesting ribbed effect with more openness in the design.

Back Loop Only. To crochet the back loop only, slip the hook through the loop from front to back with a downward motion. Catch the yarn with the hook and draw it through the loop. Then complete the stitch.

A stitch pattern that uses this technique is shown here.

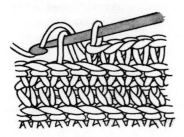

Double Crochet and Half Double Crochet in Alternating Rows

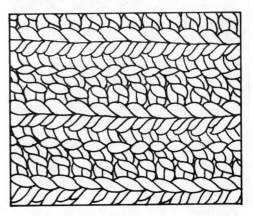

Begin with a foundation chain the required length. Any number of stitches can be used, with the addition of 2 chains.

For the **first row,** make a double crochet in fourth chain from hook. Take 1 double crochet in each chain to end of foundation chain. Then chain 2 and turn.

For the **second row,** skip first stitch. Make 1 half double crochet in each stitch of previous row, ending with 1 half double crochet in top of turning chain. Chain 3 and turn.

For the **third row,** work only into the back loop of each stitch. Skip first stitch. Take 1 double crochet in each stitch of previous row, ending with 1 double crochet in top of turning chain. Chain 2.

Alternate the **second and third rows** until work is completed.

This raised stripe pattern can be made with different combinations of the basic stitches such as those mentioned on the following pages.

Double and Single Crochet in Alternating Rows

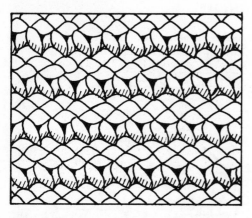

Make a foundation chain the required length, using any number of stitches plus 2 chains.

For the **first row,** make 1 double crochet in fourth chain from hook. Take 1 double crochet in each chain to end of foundation chain. Then chain 1 and turn.

For the **second row,** skip first stitch. Make a single crochet in each double crochet, finishing with a single crochet in turning chain. Chain 3 and turn.

For the **third row,** skip first stitch. Make 1 double crochet in each stitch of previous row. End with 1 double crochet in turning chain. Chain 1 and turn.

Repeat the **second and third rows** until work is completed.

Instead of putting the hook in the back loop, it can be inserted in the front loop. Here is how you will do it.

Front Loop Only.   When working in the front loop, the position of the hook changes. As you insert the hook from front to back, do it with an upward motion of the hook. Catch the yarn, drawing it through the front loop. You are then ready to complete the stitch.

One of the stitch patterns that utilizes this technique is illustrated here.

Albanian Stitch

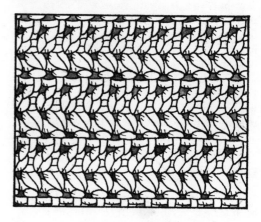

An interesting textural effect results when single crochet stitches are made this way. Begin with a foundation chain the required length. Use an even number of stitches.

For the **first row,** take a single crochet in each chain. Chain 1 and turn.

For the **second row,** make a single crochet in each stitch. Insert hook through front horizontal thread at top of previous row. Chain 1 and turn.

Repeat the **second row** until work is completed.

Between Stitches.   Sometimes directions indicate that a stitch is to be taken between the basic stitches. Be sure to note carefully whether the stitch is to be made through the chain or in the space below, making a stitch over the chain.

For *crocheting through the chain,* insert hook under the 2 top loops and proceed as directed. A stitch pattern that uses this technique is known as Checkerboard. The technique is frequently used for filet crochet.

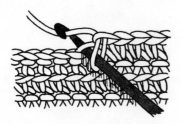

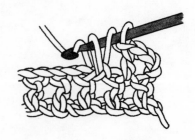

Checkerboard

This stitch pattern is made by combining double crochet with chain-2 blocks. Begin by making a foundation chain the required length, using a multiple of 4 stitches plus 2, with 2 additional chains.

For the **first row,** make 1 double crochet in fourth chain from hook. Repeat the following procedure to end of row. * Chain 2. Skip 2 chains. Take a double crochet in each of the next 2 chains. * At end of row, chain 4 and turn.

For the **second row,** skip first 2 double crochets. Make a double crochet in each chain stitch. Repeat the following procedure. * Chain 2. Skip 2 double crochets. Take 1 double crochet in each chain stitch. At last 2 double crochet, chain 2. Skip 1 double crochet. Take a double crochet in top of turning chain. Chain 3 and turn. *

For the **third row,** skip first stitch. Take 1 double crochet in next chain stitch. Repeat the following procedure. * Chain 2. Skip 2 double crochets. Take 1 double crochet in each chain stitch. * At the last 2 double crochets, chain 2. Skip 2 double crochets. Make 1 double crochet in top of turning chain. Then take 1 double crochet in next stitch of turning chain. Chain 4 and turn.

Repeat the **second and third rows** until work is completed.

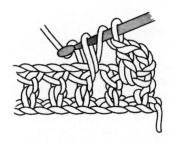

For crocheting in space between stitches, the hook should enter the space instead of the chain. This allows the stitch to be made *over the chain.* Sometimes several stitches are constructed this way. The Lattice Pattern is one that employs this technique.

Lattice Pattern

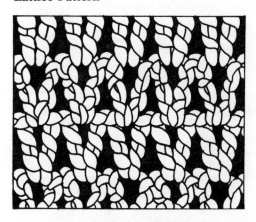

A series of triangular shapes provide a latticelike look to this stitch pattern. Make a foundation chain the required length. Use a multiple of 3 stitches plus 1, with an additional 4 chains.

For the **first row,** make lattice in fifth chain from hook with 1 treble crochet, 1 chain, and 1 treble crochet. Repeat the following procedure to end of row. * Skip 2 chains. Make lattice in next chain. * At the last 3 chains, skip 2 chains and make 1 treble crochet in last chain. Chain 4 and turn.

For the **second row,** make lattice in each chain-1 space to end of row. Make a treble crochet in top of turning chain. Chain 4 and turn.

Repeat the **second row** until work is completed.

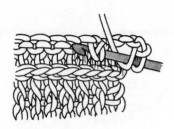

Around the Post. This may seem an odd phrase to use in crocheting. The post refers to the vertical part or shaft of the stitch. It is around this post that the stitch is made, creating an interesting textural surface with a three-dimensional effect. It can be used when crocheting the different basic stitches. To add variety to the look, the stitch can be worked around the front or the back of the post. Sometimes the position changes, alternating from front to back.

When working around the back, place yarn over hook. Then put the hook from the front to back between two adjoining stitches, bringing it up between the stitch you are working on and the next one. Notice that the hook is in a horizontal position in back of the stitch or post. Complete the stitch according to directions.

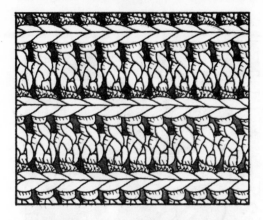

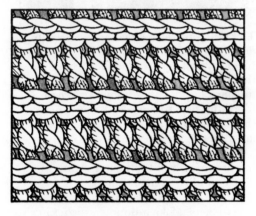

The illustrations shown here indicate how the change in the placement of the hook changes the look of the work. Double crochet stitches were used for both stitch patterns.

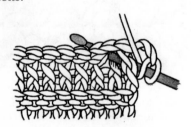

When working around the front of post, the ridged effect becomes more prominent. To create this effect, place yarn over hook. Weave hook under first stitch and over second stitch, letting it slip to the back between the post or stitch being worked and the one next to it. The hook should be positioned horizontally in front of the stitch.

Another way to use this technique to create an effect is in the Waffle Stitch.

Waffle Stitch

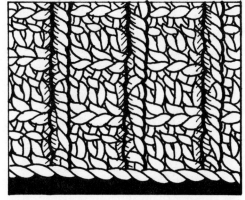

This is one of the popular stitch patterns that creates a raised ridge on the right side, adding textural interest. Begin with a foundation chain the required length. Use a multiple of 4 plus 1.

For the **first row,** make a double crochet in fourth chain from hook. Continue to make a double crochet in each chain to end of row. Chain 1 and turn.

For the **second row,** make a single crochet in first 3 double crochets, picking up only the front loop of each stitch. Repeat the following procedure to end of row. * Chain 1. Skip next stitch. Make a single crochet in next 3 double crochets. * End with chain 1. Skip next stitch. Make a single crochet in last 2 double crochets and in top of turning chain. This makes a horizontal ridge on the right side. Chain 3 and turn.

For the **third row,** work through both loops of each stitch. Skip first single crochet. Make a double crochet in next 2 single crochets. Repeat the following procedure to end of row. * Make a treble crochet around fourth double crochet of first row by inserting hook from right to left under the stitch. Skip the chain-1 space. Make a double crochet in next 3 single crochets. * At end of row, chain 1.

Repeat the **second and third rows** until work is completed.

POSITION THE STITCHES

Although many crocheting techniques have been mentioned, there are ways to arrange these stitches so that they create distinctive designs. Among these designs are the clusters, shells, and popcorns. Although the directions you are following will give you specific instructions, you will find them easier to follow if you understand how the detail is made. Some of the more commonly used designs are mentioned here.

Clusters

To produce this effect, several stitches are worked in one in order to create a cluster. For instance, after crocheting a foundation chain, make 3 double crochet stitches in the fifth chain stitch from hook, leaving the last loop of each double crochet stitch on the hook. Place yarn over the hook and pull through the 4 loops (A). Then make a chain stitch to secure the stitches (B). You have made a cluster. Although double crochet has been used here, it is possible to use treble crochet stitches instead.

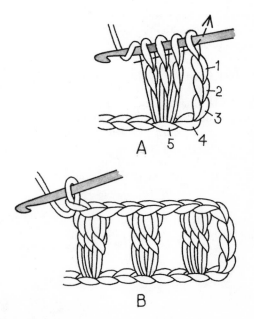

A

B

One stitch pattern that uses a series of clusters is shown here.

Cluster Stitch

When several stitches are grouped together, an openwork block effect results. Begin with a foundation chain the required length. Use a multiple of 2 stitches plus 1 and then add 1 extra chain.

For the **first row,** make 1 single crochet in second chain from hook. Continue with 1 single crochet in each chain to end of chain. Finish with 2 chains. Turn.

For the **second row,** skip the first stitch. Put yarn over hook. Pull up a loop 4 times in next stitch. Now there should be 9 loops on hook. Place yarn over hook and draw through the 9 loops. This forms a cluster. Repeat the following procedure to the last stitch. * Make 1 chain stitch. Skip 1 stitch. Make cluster in next stitch. * When last stitch is reached, take 1 double crochet in last stitch. Chain 2 and turn.

For the **third row,** skip first stitch. Make cluster in top of first cluster. Repeat the following procedure to end of row. * Chain 1. Make cluster in next cluster. * At the end of the row, make a double crochet in top of turning chain. Turn.

Repeat the **third row** until work is completed.

A stitch pattern that has the feeling of the cluster stitch is made with loops instead of stitches. This gives a puffy effect to the clusters. To get this look, follow these directions.

After working a foundation chain and a row of single crochet stitches, you are ready to begin the pattern stitch. This is done in the second single crochet stitch.

Put the yarn over the hook. Insert hook in stitch. Draw up a loop ½ inch (1.3 cm) high. Again place the yarn over the hook, pulling up a loop of the same length. Then for the third time, repeat the process. You should have 7 loops on the hook and all of them worked in the same single crochet stitch. Put the yarn over the hook and draw it through the 7 loops. Make a chain stitch to fasten securely the puff stitch you have made.

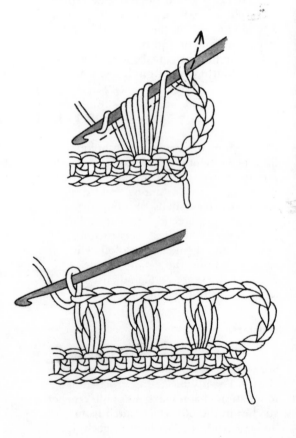

The Puff Stitch that is shown here uses this technique.

Puff Stitch

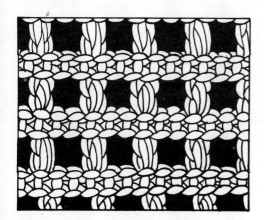

Cluster blocks, alternating with open spaces, produce this puffy design. Begin with a foundation chain of an even number of stitches.

For the **first row,** take a single crochet stitch in each of the foundation chain stitches. Chain 6 and turn.

For the **second row,** put yarn over hook. Skip 1 single crochet. To make the puff stitch, insert hook in next single crochet. Draw through a ½-inch (1.3 cm) loop. Repeat this procedure twice, leaving 7 loops on hook, all made in same stitch. Place yarn over hook and pull through the 7 loops. Chain 1. Then repeat the following sequence of stitches to end of row. * Chain 2. Skip 2 single crochets. Make puff stitch in next stitch. * Chain 1 and turn.

For the **third row,** make a single crochet in each chain stitch and in each puff stitch to end of row. Chain 4 and turn.

Repeat the **second and third rows** until work is completed.

Another type of puffy stitch is the Popcorn Stitch. It is a popular stitch whose history dates back many years.

After making a foundation chain, make 5 double crochet stitches in the sixth chain stitch from the hook. After doing this, pull up a long loop to avoid dropping a stitch. Remove the hook from the loop, placing it in the top of the first double crochet stitch in this grouping. Then slip it through the dropped loop. Draw the long loop through the double crochet stitch. Pull the yarn to tighten the loop. Finish the popcorn with a chain stitch to secure it. Be sure that all double crochet stitches were taken through one stitch.

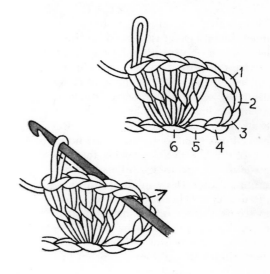

Sometimes the Popcorn Stitch is used for a decorative edging.

Popcorn Stitch

This stitch has been popular for a long time. A puffy effect is created on the surface. It can be worked with or without the bars or posts between each cluster of stitches. Begin with a foundation chain using the required number of stitches.

For the **first row,** make 5 double crochets in the sixth chain from hook. Remove hook from loop. Insert the hook in top of the first double crochet that was made in this grouping and also in the dropped loop. Draw the loop through the double crochet stitch. Make 1 chain to secure the stitch, making the popcorn motif. Repeat the following sequence of stitches to end of row. * Chain 1. Skip next stitch. Make a double crochet in next stitch. Chain 2. Skip next stitch. Make a popcorn in next stitch. * At end of row, chain 3 and turn.

For the **second row,** repeat the following sequence of stitches to end of row. * Make 1 double crochet in popcorn. Take another double crochet in next chain-2 space, also 1 in next double crochet. Follow with a double crochet in chain-2 space. * End with 1 double crochet in popcorn. Make a double crochet in turning chain. Chain 4 and turn.

Repeat the **first and second rows** until work is completed.

Fluffy little knobs highlight this stitch. Edges are frequently given this finish. It can be crocheted on top of any type of stitch. The size of the picot will depend on the number of chain stitches you use and the distance between each picot will depend on the effect you wish.

To make the picot, work a row of single crochet stitches or a foundation chain. Then work 1 single crochet in the second chain from hook. Make 3 chain stitches. Make a slip stitch in top of the single crochet you have just made, creating the picot. Follow with a certain number of single crochet stitches depending on the desired spacing.

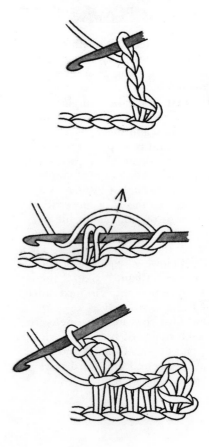

Specific directions for making this decorative edging are given here.

Picot Stitch

This is a popular edge finish. The distance between the picots can be made for any desired spacing. However, in planning the spacing, the placement of the last picot should duplicate the first. Start this edging with the wrong side facing you. Join yarn at side edge.

For the **first row,** work 1 row of single crochet and then turn.

For the **second row,** chain 3. Make 1 single crochet in third chain from hook to form picot. Take a single crochet in each of next 2 stitches.

Repeat until work is completed.

Roll Stitch

This is another stitch that creates a puffy, three-dimensional effect. The vertical bars that give the distinctive character to the stitch pattern can vary in length depending on the number of times the yarn is wrapped around the hook. Although it is easier to draw the hook through the coiled yarn, it is often thought that the longer rolls produce a more interesting look. Also the longer rolls can be pulled into tighter curved rolls. By drawing the thread to the left of the coil tighter, the roll can be curved.

After working the foundation chain, begin by wrapping the yarn over the shank part of the hook a certain number of times, perhaps 16 (A). Do this evenly but loose enough to allow the hook to be pulled through.

Insert hook into the sixth chain stitch. Hold the coiled yarn together with your left hand. Keep the hook pointed downward as you carefully pull the hook through the coil. Chain one stitch to fasten the roll (B). Notice that the completed roll is straight with a strand of yarn the length of the roll to the left (C).

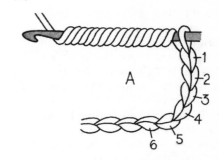

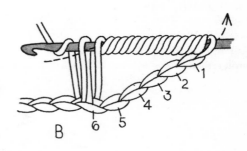

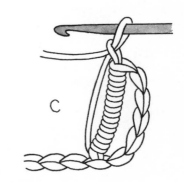

Directions for making this stitch pattern are given here.

Roll Stitch Pattern

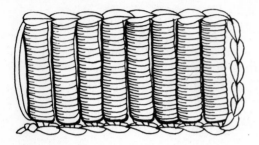

This is an old stitch pattern often found in early-nineteenth-century crochet designs. Yarn is wrapped around the hook to create the raised effect. Begin with a foundation chain the required length. Wrap yarn 16 times around shank part of hook. Do this evenly and loosely. Insert hook in sixth chain from hook. Draw loop through this chain. Put yarn over hook. Hold the wrapped stitches with left hand. Keep the hook pointed downward and carefully draw loop through wrapped stitches. Chain 1 stitch to secure the roll. Work another roll in the next stitch. Continue this way until work is completed.

Shells

Another frequently seen crochet stitch pattern is the shell. It can be made in a wide variety of sizes and combined in many ways.

After making a foundation chain, take 2 double crochet stitches in the fourth chain stitch from the hook to **start the row** (A). Skip the next 2 chain stitches before beginning the first shell. In the next stitch, make 2 double crochet stitches, 2 chain stitches, then 2 more double crochet stitches. Be sure this sequence of stitches is placed in 1 chain stitch (B).

When working the **second row,** start with 2 double crochet stitches or half shell in the first double crochet stitch of the previous row. To make the shell, work in the chain-2 space of the next shell. Remember the shell is made of two double crochet stitches followed by two chain stitches and ending with two double crochet stitches (C).

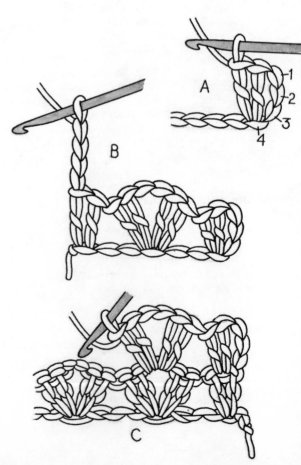

The directions for making a shell pattern using double crochet stitches are given here.

Basic Double Crochet Shell Pattern

Begin with a foundation chain the required length. Use a multiple of 5 stitches plus 1, with an additional 2 chains.

For the **first row,** make 1 double crochet in third chain from hook. Skip 4 chains. Repeat the following procedure to end of row. * For shell, take 5 double crochets in next chain. Skip 4 chains. * At last chain, take 3 double crochets. Chain 3 and turn.

For the **second row,** take 2 double crochets in first stitch. Repeat the making of shell in third double crochet of each shell. End with 2 double crochets in top of turning chain. Chain 3 and turn.

For the **third row,** make 1 double crochet in first stitch. Repeat the making of a shell in third double crochet of each shell. End with 3 double crochets in top of turning chain. Chain 3 and turn.

Repeat the **second and third rows** until work is completed.

The Shell Pattern can also be made using treble crochet. Here are the directions.

Basic Treble Crochet Shell Pattern

Start with a foundation chain the required length. Use a multiple of 5 stitches plus 1, with an additional 3 chains.

For the **first row,** make 1 treble crochet in fourth chain from hook. Skip 4 chains. Repeat the following procedure to end of row. * To make a shell, take 5 treble crochets in next chain. Skip 4 chains. * In last chain, take 3 treble crochets. Chain 4 and turn.

For the **second row,** take 2 treble crochets in first stitch. Make shell, taking 5 treble crochets in third treble crochet of each shell to end of row. Finish with 2 treble crochets in top of turning chain. Chain 4 and turn.

For the **third row,** take 1 treble crochet in first stitch. Make shell, taking 5 treble crochets in third crochet of each shell to end of row. Finish with 3 treble crochets in top of turning chain. Chain 4 and turn.

Repeat the **second and third rows** until work is completed.

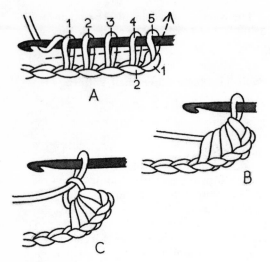

Star Stitch

Another grouping of the loops creates a starlike design. This creates an interesting texture with a striped effect.

After making the foundation chain, start to make the star stitch. Insert the hook in the second chain from hook and pull through a loop. Continue to do this in the next 3 chains. Put yarn over hook (A) and pull through the 5 loops on hook (B). To make the eye on small open circle, chain 1 (C). This completes the first star.

For the next star, insert the hook in the eye and draw through a loop. Pull another loop through the same chain that was last used for previous star stitch and in each of the next 2 chains. Put yarn over hook (D). Pull it through the 5 loops on hook. Chain 1 to make the eye, completing the second stitch (E).

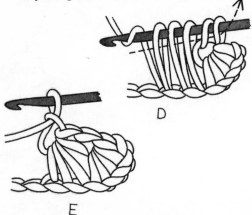

Here are the directions for making the Star Stitch:

Star Stitch Pattern

Begin with a foundation chain the required length.

For the **first row,** insert hook in second chain from hook and pull through loop. Continue to do this in the next 3 chains. Put yarn over hook and pull through the 5 loops on hook. To make eye or small circle, chain 1. This completes the first star stitch. Repeat the following procedure to end of row. * Draw a loop through the eye. Pull another loop through the same chain that was last used for previous star stitch and in each of the next 2 chains. Put yarn over hook and pull through the 5 loops on hook. Chain 1 to make the eye, completing the second star stitch. * At end of row, chain 2 and turn.

For the **second row,** count the chain-2 as 1 half double crochet. Make a half double crochet in first eye. Repeat the following procedure to end of row. Make 2 half double crochets in each eye. End with 1 half double crochet in top of turning chain. Chain 3 and turn.

For the **third row,** draw a loop through the second and third chains from hook. Skip first half double crochet. Draw a loop through each of the next 2 half double crochets. Put yarn over hook and pull it through 5 loops on hook. Chain 1 for eye, completing first star stitch. Repeat the following procedure to end of row. * Draw a loop through the eye just made. Also draw a loop through the same half double crochet last worked and in the next 2 half double crochets. Put yarn over hook and pull yarn through 5 loops on hook. Make 1 chain for eye. * End with last half double crochet of the last star stitch in top of turning chain. Chain 2 and turn.

Repeat the **second and third rows** until work is completed.

Cross Stitch

By arranging the placement of the stitches so one crosses another, an interesting textural effect is created. The contrast between the three-dimensional look of the crossed stitches and the open spaces is distinctive.

After working a **foundation row,** a row of single crochet stitches is made for the **second row.**

For the **third row,** which is the right side of the work, make a double crochet stitch in the second stitch, skipping the first stitch. Then take a double crochet stitch in the skipped stitch, completing 1 cross stitch.

To make the second cross stitch, skip a stitch, then make by a double crochet in the next stitch. Then return to the skipped stitch to make another double crochet.

For the **fourth row,** use a series of single crochet stitches.

Continue to crochet in this way, alternating a row of simple crochet stitches with a row of cross stitches.

One stitch pattern that uses this technique is the Cross Stitch.

Cross Stitch Pattern

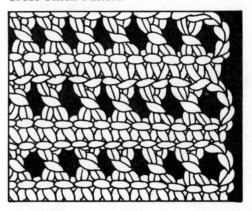

A raised effect is created by rows of crossed stitches. Begin with a foundation stitch the required length, using a multiple of 2 stitches plus 1, with an additional chain stitch.

For the **first row,** make a single crochet in each chain stitch.

For the **second row,** repeat the following procedure. * Skip 1 single crochet. Make 1 double crochet in next single crochet. For the cross stitch, take 1 double crochet in skipped single crochet. * End the row with a double crochet in last stitch. Chain 1 and turn.

For the **third row,** take a single crochet in each stitch across the row. Make a single crochet in top of turning chain. Chain 3 and turn.

Repeat the **second and third rows** until work is completed.

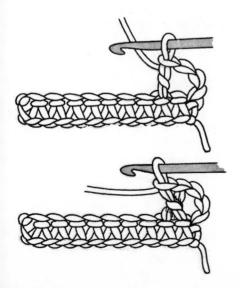

V Stitch

A grouping of stitches in a series of Vs creates an openwork effect. It can be used alone or in combination with other stitches to create interesting stitch patterns. The number of stitches in the V can vary depending on the effect desired. One way in which it can be made is given here.

After working a foundation chain, start the **first row.** Make a double crochet stitch in the fifth chain from the hook. Then chain 1. Follow by placing a double crochet stitch in the fifth chain from the hook. This creates the first V.

To make the next V, skip 2 chains on the foundation chain. Then work 1 double crochet, 1 chain, and 1 double crochet in the next chain stitch.

For the second row, work a V stitch in each of the chain-1 spaces.

A pattern using this technique is shown here.

V Stitch Pattern

This is another of the popular fancy stitches. It produces a lovely openwork effect. Begin with a foundation chain the required length. Use a multiple of 4.

For the **first row,** make a V stitch by placing in the fifth chain from hook 1 double crochet, 3 chains, and 1 double crochet. Repeat the following procedure to end of row. * Skip 3 chains. For the second V, put 1 double crochet, 3 chains, and 1 double crochet in next chain. * At end of row, skip 2 chains. Make double crochet in last chain. Chain 3 and turn.

For the **second row,** repeat the following procedure in V stitch space to end of row. * Make 1 double crochet, 3 chains, and 1 double crochet in the chain-3 space of next V stitch. This places 1 V stitch over V stitch made. * At the end of row, take a double crochet in top of turning chain. Chain 3 and turn.

Repeat the **second row** until work is completed.

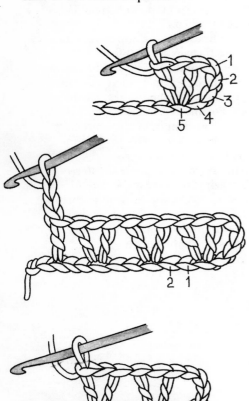

Double Faced

One does not often think of crocheting a thick, sturdy fabric, but it can be done using double crochet stitches.

After making a **foundation chain,** work a double crochet in each of the chain stitches.

To make the **second row,** change the position of the work in order to make it easier to insert the hook. Hold it vertically. Skip the first stitch. Then put yarn over the hook and insert it through the back loops of the next stitch and the foundation chain. Put yarn over hook (A). Pull yarn through the two back loops. Then make a double crochet (B). Continue this way across the row.

For the **third row and continuing rows,** the stitches are made in the same way except the hook passes through the back loop of each double crochet (C).

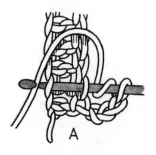

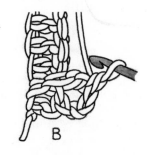

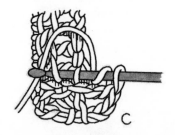

Once you have learned the technique, you can crochet the fabric using the directions that follow.

Double-Faced Fabric

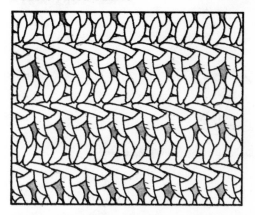

Make a foundation chain the required length. For the **first row,** repeat this procedure to end of row. * Make 1 double crochet in each chain. * Then chain 3 stitches. Turn work.

For the **second row,** crochet with work held sideways. Skip the first stitch. Repeat the following sequence of stitches. * Put yarn over hook. Place hook through the back loop of the next stitch and the back loop of the foundation chain. Put yarn over hook and draw a loop through the 2 loops. Take a double crochet stitch. * At the end of the row, make 3 chain stitches and turn.

For the **third row,** repeat the second row, remembering to slip hook through the back loop of each double crochet of second row. And continue on.

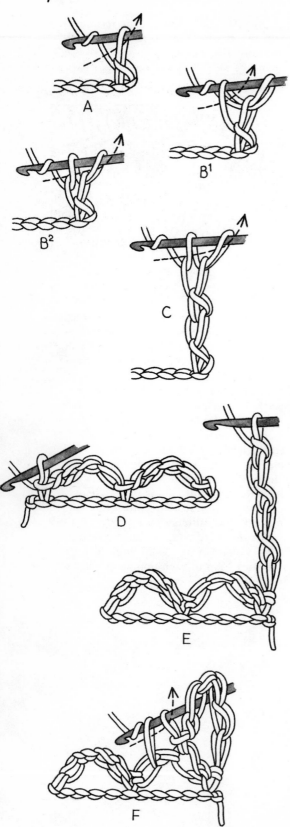

Knotted Effect

By interlocking elongated loops, a lacy, netlike material can be created. Double knots hold the loops together. The length of the loop can vary, depending on the look desired. But the length must be kept consistent throughout the work. Usually a shorter loop is used for a fine yarn than for a thick one.

As you follow the directions mentioned here, note carefully where the hook is placed after the chain is drawn through the long loop. The insertion of the hook is important to creating the correct effect.

After making a foundation chain, start the first row with a single crochet stitch in the second chain from the hook. Then to make the first knot, pull up a ¾ inch (2 cm) loop (A). Put yarn over hook and draw a loop through the longer loop. If you look carefully, you will notice that there is a single strand of yarn to the left of the chain loop that is on the hook (B¹). Take a single crochet in this single strand (B²). This produces a knot stitch. Follow with another knot stitch (C), making the double knot that is necessary for the distinctive character of the stitch pattern made with this stitch.

To continue crocheting, skip 4 chains. Then in the next chain, take a single crochet, and you are ready to make your second double knot (D).

The netlike effect begins to appear when the second row is made. After turning the work, make 3 knot stitches (E). This raises the stitches to the level of the second row. Then in the first long loop of the double knot stitch in the previous row, make a single crochet. Actually the stitch is placed to the right of the knot. Then take another single crochet in the second loop of the same knot stitch to the left of the same knot (F). Make a double knot stitch.

The Knot Stitch uses this technique. Here are the directions.

Knot Stitch

This stitch is also known as the Lover's Knot Stitch. It creates a dainty, gauzy effect. Begin with a foundation chain the required length.

For the **first row,** make a single crochet in the second chain from hook. Repeat the following procedure to end of row. * Begin by drawing up a ¾-inch (2 cm) loop (A). Put yarn over hook and draw a loop through the longer loop. Make a single crochet in single strand of long loop. This procedure produces a knot stitch. Make another knot stitch. Skip 4 chains. Single crochet in next chain. * At the end of the row, turn.

For the **second row,** repeat the following procedure to the end of the row. * Make 3 knot stitches. Then take a single crochet in first long loop of next double knot stitch to the right of knot. Take a single crochet in second loop of the same knot stitch to the left of the same knot. Make a double knot stitch. *

Repeat the **second row** until work is completed.

Looped Effect

A series of loops creates this effect. The loops can vary in length depending on the look desired. An interesting thing to remember is that the loops are made while working on the wrong side of the piece. Crocheting in this way allows the loops to fall to the right side of the work.

After making a foundation chain and a **first row** of single crochet stitches begin the **second row.** One loop stitch is made in each single crochet. To do this, place the yarn over the first finger of your left hand. The distance your finger is from the crocheting depends on how long you wish the loop to be. Then insert the hook in the next single crochet stitch (A). Draw through a loop. With the loop on the hook, put yarn over hook in preparation for making a single crochet stitch (B) that anchors the loop. As you do this remove your finger from the long loop (C).

To continue working in loop stitches alternate a row of single crochet stitches with a row of loop stitches.

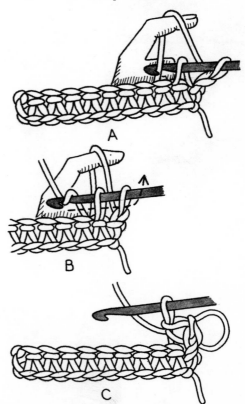

Directions for crocheting in looped stitches are given here.

Loop Stitch

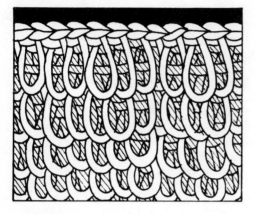

This pattern has a shaggy look. Begin with foundation chain the required length, using any number of stitches plus 1 chain.

For the **first row,** make a single crochet in second chain from hook. Continue to place a single crochet in each chain to end of row. Chain 1 and turn.

For the **second row,** skip first stitch. Repeat the following procedure to end of row. * Insert hook in next stitch. To determine length of loop, place yarn around middle finger of left hand. Draw yarn through stitch. Put yarn over hook and pull through 2 loops. Slip long loop off finger. Continue, keeping loops the same size. * Chain 1 and turn.

For the **third row,** skip first stitch. Make 1 single crochet in each stitch to end of row. Chain 1 and turn.

Repeat the **second and third rows** until work is completed.

8

Experiment with Stitch Patterns

Recently there has been a renewed interest in crocheting. Smart, attractive crocheted fashions are appearing. No longer is the emphasis simply on crocheting for the home. Fashions to wear have taken their place in the realm of crocheting. Stitch patterns that have a long history are being given new looks. Making them in interesting and unusual yarns produces fascinating effects. If you are in the mood to be creative, try some of the stitch patterns shown on the following pages. You will be surprised by what a rewarding experience it is.

Fortunately crocheting lends itself to experimentation. Mistakes can be quickly ripped out and corrected. To get the right look crochet a sample of a new stitch before using it for an article. This makes it possible for you to judge the effect of your handiwork.

As you study the various stitch patterns, you will notice that some seem more difficult than others. Don't let the tough ones frighten you. Just give them a try. Sometimes the ones that seem the hardest are the easiest to crochet.

SINGLE CROCHET VARIATIONS

As you observe the stitch patterns shown in this category, aren't you amazed at the variety of textures you can make with a simple single crochet stitch? Notice the firmness of some and the lacy effect of others. Even if you never perfect another stitch, you can do some interesting crocheting.

Urchin Stitch

Rows of tiny spoked motifs create a raised textural effect. Begin with a foundation chain the required length, using an even number of stitches.

For the **first row,** chain 1. Repeat the following procedure to end of row. * Skip 1 stitch. In next stitch, take 1 single crochet, 2 chains, and one single crochet. *

For the **second row,** follow directions for first row, inserting hook in chain-2 space of previous row for pattern stitches.

Repeat the **second row** until work is completed.

Russian Stitch

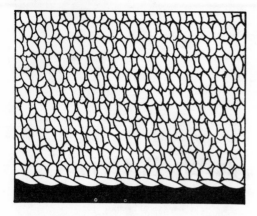

Twisted Russian Stitch

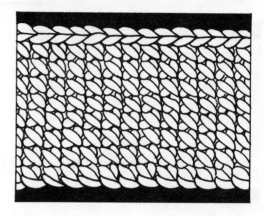

This stitch is worked only on the right side. If it is to be used flat, the yarn is to be joined at beginning of each row and cut at the end.

Start with a foundation chain the required length. Work each row in single crochet, inserting hook under both horizontal loops of each stitch of the previous row. Continue this way until work is completed.

This stitch is worked only on the right side of the piece. If, instead of crocheting round and round, it is made flat, the yarn is joined at beginning of each row and cut at the end. Start with a foundation chain the required length.

For the **first row,** insert hook into second chain from hook. Put hook over yarn and draw through loop. Notice that the hook is passed over the yarn rather than the yarn over the hook. Then put the yarn over hook and pull through 2 loops. Continue to end of row. Fasten thread and clip.

For the **second row,** attach yarn at right-hand end of work. Insert hook under both horizontal loops of each stitch of previous row and pull through a loop as before. Continue as for the first row.

Repeat the **second row** until work is completed.

In addition to making these firm fabrics, single crochet stitches can be used in the making of open, allover designs. To create this effect, the single crochet stitches are combined with the chain stitch as in these Mesh Diamond Stitch patterns. The size of the diamonds varies depending on the number of chain stitches. Directions for different sizes are given here.

Mesh Diamonds—Chain Two

Make a foundation chain the required length. Use a multiple of 3 stitches plus 1, with an additional 3 chains.

For the **first row,** make a single crochet in the fourth chain from hook. Repeat the following procedure to end of row. * Chain 2. Skip 2 chains. Then take a single crochet in the next chain stitch. * At end of row, chain 2 and turn.

For the **second row,** take a single crochet in first chain space. Repeat the following procedure to end of row. * Chain 2. Take 1 single crochet in next chain space. End with a single crochet in last chain space. * Chain 2 and turn.

Repeat the **second row** until work is completed.

Mesh Diamonds—Chain Three

Begin with a foundation chain the required length. Use a multiple of 4 stitches plus 1, with an additional 4 chains.

For the **first row,** make a single crochet in the fifth chain from hook. Repeat the following procedure to end of row. * Chain 3. Skip 3 chains. Make a single crochet in next chain. * At end of row, chain 3 and turn.

For the **second row,** take a single crochet in first chain space. Repeat the following procedure to end of row. * Chain 3. Make a single crochet in next chain space. * End the row with a single cro-

chet in last chain space. Then chain 3 and turn.

Repeat the **second row** until the work is completed.

Mesh Diamonds—Chain Four

Make a foundation chain the required length. Use a multiple of 5 stitches plus 1, with an additional 5 chains.

For the **first row,** take 1 single crochet in the sixth chain from hook. Repeat the following procedure to end of row. * Chain 4. Skip 4 chains. Take a single crochet in next chain. * At the end, chain 4 and turn.

For the **second row,** make a single crochet in first chain space. Repeat the following procedure to end of row. * Chain 4. Make a single crochet in next chain space. * End the row with a single crochet in last chain space. Then chain 4 and turn.

Repeat the **second row** until work is completed.

Mesh Diamonds—Chain Five

Commence with a foundation chain the required length. Use a multiple of 6 stitches plus 1, with an additional 6 chains.

For the **first row,** make a single crochet in seventh chain from hook. Repeat the following procedure to end of row. * Chain 5. Skip 5 chains. Take a single crochet in next chain. * At the end, chain 5 and turn.

For the **second row,** take a single crochet in first chain space. Repeat the following procedure to the end of the row. * Chain 5. Make a single crochet in next chain space. * End with a single crochet in last chain space. Then chain 5 and turn.

Repeat the **second row** until work is completed.

DOUBLE CROCHET DESIGNS

Double Crochet is probably the most
frequently used stitch. Some of the stitch
patterns that depend on it are shown
here.

Arch Stitch

This easy-to-make stitch pattern creates
a very open effect, with curving lines.
Begin with a foundation chain the required length. Use an odd number of
stitches.

For the **first row,** take a single crochet
in each chain.

For the **second row,** chain 5. Take a
double crochet in third stitch of first
row. Repeat the following procedure to
end of row. * Chain 5. Skip 3 stitches.
Take a double crochet in next stitch. *
At end of row, chain 5 and turn.

For the **third row,** make a double crochet by inserting hook in center chain of
chain-5 of previous row. Repeat the following procedure to end of row. * Chain
5. Take 1 double crochet in next chain-5
space. * Finish row with a double crochet in third stitch of turning chain.
Chain 5 and turn.

Repeat the **third row** until work is
completed.

Arch Mesh Stitch

By combining a series of chain stitches
with single and double crochet, an openwork design with a textural quality is
produced. Begin with a row of chain
stitches to form a foundation the required length. Use a multiple of 4
stitches plus 3.

For the **first row,** chain 6 stitches.
Then repeat the following sequence of
stitches to the end. * Make 1 single crochet. Chain 2. Skip 1 stitch. Make 1 double crochet. Chain 2. Skip 1 stitch. *
End the row with 1 double crochet.
Turn work.

For the **second row,** repeat the following sequence of stitches. * Make 1 single
crochet in double crochet of previous
row. Then chain 2. Take 1 double crochet in the single crochet of previous
row. Chain 2. * The row should end
with a single crochet. Turn work.

Repeat the **first and second rows** until
work is completed.

Zigzag Mesh

An interesting arrangement of chain stitches produces a dainty openwork design. Begin with a foundation chain the

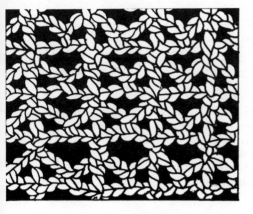

required length. Use a multiple of 4 stitches plus 3.

For the **first row,** chain 6. Repeat the following procedure to end of row.
* Take 1 single crochet. Chain 2. Skip 1 stitch. Make 1 double crochet. Chain 2. Skip 1 stitch. * End with 1 double crochet. Turn.

For the **second row,** repeat the following procedure to end of row. * Make 1 single crochet in double crochet. Chain 3. * End with single crochet in third chain of starting chain-6. Turn.

For the **third row,** chain 5. Repeat the following procedure to end of row.
* Make a single crochet in second chain. Chain 2. Take 1 double crochet in single crochet. Chain 2. * End with 1 double crochet.

Repeat the **second and third rows** until work is completed.

TREBLE CROCHET PATTERNS

An interesting openwork design can be made with the treble crochet stitch. Notice the elongated motion of the stitches as they are crossed.

Crossed Treble Pattern

Begin with a foundation chain the required length, using a multiple of 2 stitches plus 1, with an additional 2 chains.

For the **first row,** take 1 treble stitch in fifth chain from hook, and another in fourth chain from hook. Repeat the following procedure to the end of the row.
* Skip 1 chain. Take 1 treble crochet in next chain and another in skipped chain. * At end of chain, make 3 chains and turn.

For the **second row,** skip first 2 stitches in preceding row. Then make a treble crochet in third stitch and another in second stitch. Repeat the following procedure to end of row. * Skip 1 stitch. Make a treble crochet in next stitch and another in skipped stitch. * At end of row, chain 3 and turn.

Repeat **second row** until work is completed.

By combining the treble crochet stitch with the half double crochet stitch, you can produce an interesting textural effect that is shown on the following pages. It has a subtle striped surface interest.

Raised Stripe Pattern

Begin with a foundation chain the required length. Use any multiple of stitches plus 3 chains.

For the **first row,** take 1 treble crochet in fifth chain from hook. Then take 1 treble crochet in each chain to end of foundation chain. Chain 2 and turn.

For the **second row,** skip first stitch. Make 1 half double crochet in each stitch in the previous row. End with 1 half double crochet in top of turning chain. Chain 4 and turn.

For the **third row,** skip first stitch. Take 1 treble crochet in each stitch in previous use. End with 1 treble crochet in top of turning chain. Chain 2 and turn.

Alternate the **second and third rows** until work is completed.

TEXTURAL INTEREST

You have probably noticed that the textural qualities of crocheting vary widely. Some of the most interesting are mentioned here.

Crescent Pattern

By changing the placement of the hook in making alternating single crochet stitches, an interesting textured effect results. Begin with a foundation chain the required length, using an even number of stitches.

For the **first row,** chain 1. Make single crochet stitches to end of row. Turn.

For the **second row,** chain 1. Make a single crochet in first stitch. Follow with a single crochet, inserting hook into the base of next single crochet of previous row. Alternate these 2 stitches to end of row.

Repeat the **second row** until work is completed.

Cable Pattern

A look similar to that of cable knitting is produced by following this sequence of crochet stitches. Begin with a foundation chain the required length. Use a multiple of 10 stitches plus 1.

For the **first row,** insert afghan crochet hook into second chain from hook. Put yarn over hook and draw through a loop. Then pull through a loop in each chain to end of row. Leave all loops on hook.

For the **second row,** work loops off hook by putting yarn over hook and drawing it through first loop. Repeat the following procedure to end of row. * Put yarn over hook. Pull it through next 2 loops. * End with 1 loop remaining on hook. This loop becomes first stitch of next row.

For the **third row,** pull up a loop under vertical bar of next stitch, holding yarn with thumb in front and below hook. This makes a purl stitch. Repeat the preceding procedure twice. Still keeping all loops on hook, and by holding yarn in back, insert hook from front to back through center of next loop between vertical bar and strand behind it. Put yarn over hook and pull up a loop, making a knit stitch. Repeat this procedure in next 3 stitches. In the last 3 stitches, make 3 purl stitches.

For the **fourth or cable row,** put yarn over hook. Draw yarn through first loop. Put yarn over hook again and draw

through next 2 loops. Do this twice. Slip next 2 stitches onto a double-pointed needle and hold in front of work. Put yarn over hook and pull through loop, working off the next 2 loops twice. Slip loops from double-pointed needle back to hook and work off, making a cable. Work off the 3 purl stitches also.

For the **fifth row,** repeat the third row.

For the **sixth row,** repeat the second row.

For the **seventh row,** repeat the third row.

For the **eighth row,** repeat the fourth row.

Repeat the **first through eighth rows** until work is completed.

Moss Stitch

This stitch produces a solid effect with an interesting textural quality. Begin with a foundation chain the required length. Use a multiple of 2 stitches plus 1, with an additional chain stitch.

For the **first row,** start by taking 1 single crochet and 1 double crochet in the second chain from hook. Repeat the following procedure to end of row. * Skip 1 chain. Then, in the next stitch, make 1 single crochet and 1 double crochet. * At the end, chain 1 and turn.

For the **second row,** skip first 2 stitches. Then take 1 single crochet and 1 double crochet in each double crochet across row. At the end, chain 1 and turn.

Repeat the **second row** until the work is completed.

Arrow Pattern

A raised effect, resembling an arrow, dominates this stitch. To determine length of work, use a multiple of 4 stitches plus 1 chain. Make a foundation chain the required length.

For the **first row,** take a single crochet in the second chain from hook. Make 1 single crochet in each chain to end of row. Then chain 1 and turn.

For the **second row,** skip first stitch. Make 1 single crochet in each stitch to end of row. Chain 3 and turn.

For the **third row,** skip first stitch. Make a double crochet in next single crochet. Repeat the following sequence of stitches. * Skip 3 single crochets. Make 1 half double crochet in next single crochet. Working behind the half double crochet, take 1 double crochet in each of the 3 skipped single crochets. * End the row with 1 double crochet in each of the last 2 single crochets. Then chain 3 and turn.

For the **fourth row,** skip first double crochet. Make 1 double crochet in the next double crochet. Repeat the following sequence of stitches. * Skip 3 double crochets. Make 1 half double crochet in the half double crochet. Working in front of the half double crochet, take 1 double crochet in each of the 3 skipped double crochets. * End the row with a double crochet in each of the last 2 stitches. Chain 1 and turn.

For the **fifth row,** skip first double crochet. Make 1 single crochet in each remaining double crochet. Chain 1 and turn.

Repeat the **second through fifth rows** until work is completed.

Bobble Stitch

Rows of puffy mounds add interest to this openwork stitch pattern. Start with a row of chain stitches to form a foundation the required length. Use a multiple of 2 stitches plus 1 and 1 extra chain stitch.

For the **first row,** make a single crochet in the second chain from the hook. Take a single crochet in each chain to end of row. Then chain 2 and turn.

For the **second row,** skip first stitch. Make a double crochet in next stitch up to where there are 2 loops on the hook. (This is sometimes called a *post.*) Place the yarn over the hook and pull up a loop around the post 3 times. Put the yarn over the hook again and draw through all 8 loops to form a bobble. Repeat the following procedure. * Chain 1. Skip 1 stitch. Make bobble in next stitch. * At end of row, make 1 double crochet in last stitch. Then chain 1 and turn.

For the **third row,** skip first stitch. Make 1 single crochet in each bobble and in each chain 1. End with a single crochet in top of turning chain. Then chain 2 and turn.

For the **fourth row,** skip first stitch. Make bobble in next stitch. Repeat the following sequence of stitches to end of row. * Chain 1. Skip 1 stitch. Make bobble in next stitch. * Then make a double crochet in last stitch. Chain 1 and turn.

Repeat the **third and fourth rows** until work is completed.

Raised Diagonal Pattern

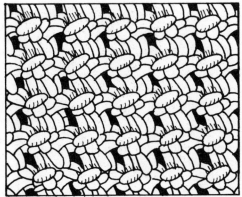

This stitch pattern creates a textural quality by combining slip and half double crochet stitches. Start with a foundation chain using an even number of stitches.

For the **first row,** chain 1. Make a slip stitch in the next stitch and a half double crochet in the next. Then repeat the following sequence of stitches to the end of the row. * Chain 1. Slip stitch in next stitch. Half double crochet in next stitch. * At the end of row, turn.

For the **second row,** repeat the following procedure across the row. * Chain 1. Slip stitch in half double crochet. Then take half double crochet in slip stitch. *

Repeat the **second row** until work is completed.

Point Stitch

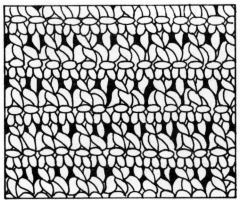

A sequence of loops and single crochets forms this unusual design pattern with a repeating 1-line detail. Begin with a foundation chain the required length. Use a multiple of 2 stitches plus 1 chain.

For the **first row,** skip 2 chains. Repeat the following sequence to end of row. * Bring a loop through each of the next 2 chains, leaving 3 loops on hook. Put yarn over hook and draw through first 2 loops. Put yarn over hook again and draw through last 2 loops. Chain 1. * Turn.

For the **second row,** skip first stitch. Take 1 single crochet in each stitch to end of row. Make 1 single crochet in turning chain. Chain 2 and turn.

For the **third row,** skip first stitch. Repeat the following sequence of stitches to end of row. * Bring a loop through each of the next 2 stitches. Put yarn over hook and draw through first 2 loops. Put yarn over hook again and draw through last 2 loops. Chain 1. * Turn.

Repeat the **second and third rows** until work is completed.

THE POPULAR SHELL

Shell patterns show great versatility. They can vary in size and placement as well as in the openness of the design. Some of the stitch patterns are shown here.

Double Crochet with Single Crochet Row Shell Pattern

Commence with a foundation chain the required length. Use a multiple of 5 stitches plus 1, with additional 1 chain.

For the **first row,** take 1 single crochet in second chain from hook. Make 1 single crochet in each chain to end of foundation chain. Chain 3 and turn.

For the **second row,** take 1 double crochet in first stitch. Skip 4 stitches. Repeat the following procedure to end of row. * To make shell, take 5 double crochets in next stitch. Skip 4 stitches. * In last stitch, take 3 double crochets. Chain 1 and turn.

For the **third row,** skip first stitch. Make 1 single crochet in each stitch of previous row. End with 2 single crochets in top of turning chain. Chain 3 and turn.

Repeat the **second and third rows** until work is completed.

Treble Crochet with Single Crochet Row Shell Pattern

Begin with a foundation chain the required length. Use a multiple of 5 stitches plus 1, with an additional 1 chain.

For the **first row,** make a single crochet in second chain from hook. Take 1 single crochet in each chain to end of chain. Chain 4 and turn.

For the **second row,** take 1 treble crochet in first stitch. Skip 4 stitches. Repeat the following procedure to end of row. * To make the shell, take 5 treble crochets in next stitch. Skip 4 stitches. * End with 3 treble crochets in turning chain. Chain 1 and turn.

For the **third row,** skip first stitch. Make 1 single crochet in each stitch of previous row. End with 2 single crochets in top of turning chain. Chain 4 and turn.

Repeat the **second and third rows** until work is completed.

Treble Crochet with Half Double Crochet Row Shell Pattern

Start with a foundation chain the required length. Use a multiple of 6 stitches plus 1, with an additional 2 chains.

For the **first row,** take 1 half double crochet in third chain from hook. Then make 1 half double crochet in each chain until row is completed. Chain 5 and turn.

For the **second row,** make 1 treble crochet in first stitch. Skip 5 stitches. * Make shell in next stitch by repeating 4 times: 1 treble crochet and 1 chain. Then add 1 treble crochet. Skip 4 stitches. * End with 1 treble crochet and 1 chain made twice. Take 1 treble crochet in turning chain. Chain 2 and turn.

For the **third row,** skip first stitch. Take 1 half double crochet in each stitch of previous row. End with 1 half double crochet in each of 2 top stitches of turning chain. Chain 5 and turn.

For the **fourth row,** take 1 treble crochet in first stitch. Skip 6 stitches. Repeat the following procedure. * Make shell in next stitch. Skip 8 stitches. * End with 1 treble crochet and 1 chain made twice. Take 1 treble crochet in turning chain. Chain 2 and turn.

Repeat the **third and fourth rows** until work is completed.

Treble Crochet with Open Half Double Crochet Row Shell Pattern

Begin with a foundation chain the required length. Use a multiple of 8 stitches plus 1, with an additional 3 chains.

For the **first row,** take 1 half double crochet in fourth chain from hook. Repeat the following procedure to end of row. * Chain 1. Skip 1 chain. Make 1 half double crochet in next chain. * At the end of chain, chain 4 and turn.

For the **second row,** take 3 treble crochets in first chain-1 space. Chain 1. Skip 3 chain-1 spaces. Repeat the following procedure to end of row. * To make shell, place 7 treble crochets in next chain-1 space. Chain 1. Skip 3 chain-1 spaces. * End with 4 treble crochets in last space. Chain 3 and turn.

For the **third row,** skip first stitch. Repeat the following procedure to end of row. * Take 1 half double crochet in next stitch. Chain 1. Skip 1 stitch. * End with a half double crochet in top of turning chain. Chain 4 and turn.

Repeat the **second and third rows** until work is completed.

Lacy Double Crochet Shell Pattern

Begin with a foundation chain the required length. Use a multiple of 5 stitches plus 1, with an additional 3 chains.

For the **first row,** make 1 double crochet in fourth chain from hook. Repeat the following procedure to end of row. * Skip 4 chains. Make a shell in the chain by repeating 3 times: 1 double crochet and 1 chain. Then add 1 double crochet. * End with 1 double crochet, 1

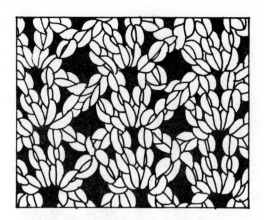

chain, and 1 double crochet in last chain. Chain 4 and turn.

For the **second row,** take 1 double crochet in first chain-1 space. Make a shell in second chain-1 space of each shell. End with 1 double crochet, 1 chain, and 1 double crochet in the last chain-1 space. Chain 4 and turn.

Repeat the **second row** until work is completed.

Lacy Treble Crochet Shell Pattern

Start with a foundation chain the required length. Use a multiple of 6 stitches plus 1, with an additional 4 chains.

For the **first row,** take 1 treble crochet in fifth chain from hook. Repeat the following procedure to end of row. * Skip 5 chains. Make shell in next chain by repeating 3 times: 1 treble crochet and 1 chain. Then add 1 treble crochet. * End with 1 treble crochet, 1 chain, and 1 treble crochet in last chain. Chain 5 and turn.

For the **second row,** take 1 treble crochet in first chain-1 space. Make shell in second chain-1 space of each shell. End with 1 treble crochet, 1 chain, and 1 treble crochet in last chain-1 space. Chain 5 and turn.

Repeat the **second row** until work is completed.

Split Double Crochet Shell Pattern

Start with a foundation chain the required length. Use a multiple of 5 stitches plus 1, with an additional 2 chains.

For the **first row,** take 1 double crochet in third chain from hook. Skip 4 chains. Repeat the following procedure to end of row. * To make shell in next chain, take 2 double crochets, 1 chain, and 2 double crochets. Skip 4 chains. * In last chain, take 2 double crochets. Chain 3 and turn.

For the **second row,** take 1 double crochet in first stitch. Make shell in chain-1 space of each shell. End with 2 double crochets in top of turning chain. Chain 3 and turn.

Repeat the **second row** until work is completed.

Split Treble Crochet Shell Pattern

Commence with foundation chain the required length. Use a multiple of 5 stitches plus 1, with an additional 3 chains.

For the **first row,** take 2 treble crochet in fourth chain from hook. Skip 4 chains. Repeat the following procedure to end of row. * To make shell in next chain, take 3 treble crochets, 1 chain, and 3 treble crochets. Skip 4 chains. * In last chain, take 3 treble crochets. Chain 4 and turn.

For the **second row,** make 2 treble crochets in first stitch. Make shell—3 treble crochets, 1 chain, and 3 treble crochets—in chain-1 space of each shell. End with 3 treble crochets in top of turning chain. Chain 4 and turn.

Repeat the **second row** until work is completed.

Alternating Double Crochet Shell Pattern

This is a popular pattern and is often spoken of as a fancy stitch. The shells can be made in various sizes, depending on the basic crochet stitch used, and placed in different ways for a wide variety of effects. Start with a foundation chain the required length. Use a multiple of 6 stitches plus 1, with an additional 3 chains.

For the **first row,** take 2 double crochets in fourth chain from hook. Repeat the following procedure. * Skip 2 chains. Take 1 single crochet in next chain. Skip 2 chains. For shell, make 5 double crochets in next chain. * At last 6 chains, skip 2 chains. Take 1 single crochet in next chain. Skip 2 chains. Make 3 double crochets in last chain. Chain 3 and turn.

For the **second row,** skip 3 double crochets. Repeat the following sequence of stitches. * Make 1 single crochet in next single crochet. Chain 2. Take 1 single crochet in third double crochet of shell. Chain 2. * At last 6 stitches, take 1 single crochet in next single crochet. Chain 2. Skip 2 double crochets. Take 1 single crochet in top of turning chain and turn.

For the **third row,** take a single crochet in first stitch. Repeat the following procedure to end of row. * Make shell in next stitch. Take 1 single crochet in next single crochet. * End with 1 single crochet in bottom of turning chain. Chain 3 and turn.

For the **fourth row,** take 1 single crochet in third double crochet of first shell. Repeat the following procedure to end of row. * Chain 2. Take a single crochet in next single crochet. Chain 2. Make a single crochet in third double crochet of next shell. * End with a single crochet in last stitch. Chain 3 and turn.

For the **fifth row,** make 2 double crochets in first single crochet. Repeat the following sequence of stitches to end of row. * Take 1 single crochet in next single crochet. Make shell in next single crochet. * End with 3 double crochets in bottom of turning chain. Chain 3 and turn.

Repeat the **second through fifth rows** until work is completed.

Alternating Treble Crochet Shell Pattern

Begin with a foundation chain the required length. Use a multiple of 6 stitches plus 1, with an additional 4 chains.

For the **first row,** take 2 treble crochets in fifth chain from hook. Repeat the following procedure. * Skip 2 chains. Take 1 single crochet in next chain. Skip 2 chains. To make shell, take 5 treble crochets in next chain. * At the last 6 chains, skip 2 chains. Make 1 single crochet in next chain. Skip 2 chains and then take 3 treble crochets in last chain. Chain 4 and turn.

For the **second row,** skip 3 treble crochets. Repeat the following procedure. * Take 1 double crochet in next single crochet. Chain 2. Follow with 1 single crochet in third treble crochet of shell. Chain 2. * At the last 6 stitches, take 1 double crochet in next single crochet. Chain 2. Skip 2 treble crochets. Make 1 single crochet in top of turning chain and turn.

For the **third row,** take 1 single crochet in first stitch. Repeat the following procedure to end of row. * Make shell of 5 treble crochets in next double crochet. Take 1 single crochet in next single crochet. * End with 1 single crochet in bottom of turning chain. Chain 4 and turn.

For the **fourth row,** make 1 single crochet in third treble of first shell. Repeat the following procedure to end of row. * Chain two. Make 1 double crochet in next single crochet. Chain two. Take 1 single crochet in third treble crochet of next shell. * End with 2 chains. Take 1 single crochet in last stitch. Chain 4 and turn.

For the **fifth row,** make 2 treble crochets in first single crochet. Repeat the following procedure to end of row. * Take 1 single crochet in next single crochet. Make shell of 5 treble crochets in next double crochet. * End with 3 treble crochets in bottom of turning chain. Chain 4 and turn.

Repeat the **second through fifth rows** until work is completed.

Graduated Shell Pattern

Begin with a foundation chain the required length. Use a multiple of 5 stitches plus 1, with an additional 2 chains.

For the **first row,** take 1 double crochet in fourth chain from hook. Skip 4 chains. Repeat the following procedure to end of row. * Make shell in next chain by taking 2 double crochets, 1 chain, and 2 double crochets. Skip 4 chains. * Take 2 double crochets in last chain. Then chain 3 and turn.

For the **second row,** make 2 double crochets in first stitch. Then, in each chain-1 space, take 3 double crochets, 1 chain, and 3 double crochets. End with 3 double crochets in top of turning chain. Chain 5 and turn.

For the **third row,** make 2 treble crochets in first stitch. Then, in each chain-1 space, take 3 treble crochets, 1 chain, and 3 treble crochets. End with 3 treble crochets in top of turning chain. Then chain 5 and turn.

For the **fourth row,** make 3 treble crochets in first stitch. Then, in each chain-1 space, take 4 treble crochets, 2 chains, and 4 treble crochets. End with 4 treble crochets in top of turning chain. Then chain 5 and turn.

For the **fifth row,** start with 4 treble crochets in first stitch. Then, in each chain-2 space, take 5 treble crochets, 2 chains, and 5 treble crochets. End with 5 treble crochets in top of turning chain. Chain 6 and turn.

For the **sixth row,** crochet in first stitch 3 times: 1 treble crochet and 1 chain. Also take another treble crochet in same stitch. In each chain-2 space, repeat the following procedure 5 times: 1 treble crochet and 1 chain. Follow with 1 treble crochet and 1 chain repeated 4 times and add 1 treble crochet. End with the following stitches in top of turning chain: repeat 4 times 1 treble crochet and 1 chain. In same stitch, take 1 treble crochet. Chain 6 and turn.

For the **seventh row,** repeat this procedure 4 times in the first stitch: 1 treble crochet and 1 chain. Also in the first stitch, take 1 treble crochet. In each of chain-2 spaces, repeat this sequence of stitches 6 times: 1 treble crochet and 1 chain. Chain 1. Then do this 5 times: 1 treble crochet and 1 chain; add 1 treble crochet. End with 1 treble crochet and 1 chain taken 5 times in top of turning chain. Also add 1 treble crochet in the same turning chain.

This procedure for increasing the size of the shells can be continued until work is completed.

Lacy Alternating Shell Pattern

Begin with a foundation chain the required length. Use a multiple of 8 stitches plus 2, with an additional chain stitch.

For the **first row,** make a single crochet in second chain from hook. Then take another 1 single crochet in the next chain. Repeat the following procedure to end of row. * Chain 2. Skip 2 chains. Then in next chain make a double crochet, 3 chains, and 1 double crochet. Chain 2. Skip 2 chains. Make a single crochet in each of the next 3 chains. * End with single crochet in each of the last 2 chains. Chain 1 and turn.

For the **second row,** take 1 single crochet in first single crochet. Repeat the following procedure to end of row. * Chain 2. Make 7 double crochets in chain-3 space. Chain 2. Make 1 single crochet in second single crochet of 3-single-crochet group. * End with chain 2. Then make a single crochet in last single crochet. Chain 1 and turn.

For the **third row,** make a single crochet in first single crochet. Chain 2. Repeat the following procedure to end of row. * Take 1 single crochet in each of next 7 double crochets. Chain 5. * End with chain 2. Then take a single crochet in last single crochet. Chain 5 and turn.

For the **fourth row,** take 1 double crochet in first single crochet. Repeat the following procedure to end of row. * Start with chain 2. Take a single crochet in each of third, fourth, and fifth single crochets of 7-single-crochet group. Chain 2. In third chain of chain-5 space, make 1 double crochet, 3 chains, and 1 double crochet. * End with 1 double crochet, 3 chains, and 1 double crochet in last single crochet. Chain 3 and turn.

For the **fifth row,** make 3 double crochets in first chain-3 space. Repeat the following procedure to end of row. * Chain 2. Make 1 single crochet in second single crochet of 3-single-crochet group. Chain 2. Take 7 double crochets in chain-3 space. * End with 4 double crochets in turning chain loop. Chain 1 and turn.

For the **sixth row,** take a single crochet in each of first 4 double crochets. Repeat the following procedure to end of row. * Chain 5. Make a single crochet in each of next 7 double crochets. * End with chain 5. Take a single crochet in each of last 3 single crochets. Make a single crochet in top of turning chain. Chain 1 and turn.

For the **seventh row,** take a single crochet in each of first 2 single crochets. Repeat the following procedure to end of row. * Chain 2. In third chain of chain-5 loop, make 1 double crochet, 3 chains, and 1 double crochet. Chain 2. Take a single crochet in each of the third, fourth, and fifth single crochets of the 7-single-crochet group. * End with chain 2. Make 1 single crochet in each of last 2 single crochets. Chain 1 and turn.

Repeat the **second through seventh rows** until work is completed.

Fish Scale Shell Pattern

This is a variation of the shell stitch. Begin with a foundation chain the required number of stitches.

For the **first row,** place in fourth chain 1 double crochet, 3 chains, and 1 double crochet. Repeat the following procedure to end of row. * Chain 3. Skip 3 stitches. Make 1 single crochet in each of next 3 stitches. Chain 3. Skip 3 stitches. In next stitch, take 1 double crochet, 3 chains, and 1 double crochet. * At end of row, turn.

For the **second row,** chain 3. Repeat the following procedure to end of row. * Make 7 double crochets in the chain-3 space between double crochets of previous row. Make 3 chains. Take 1 single crochet in second single crochet. Chain 3. * End with 7 double crochets in last chain-3 space. Turn.

For the **third row,** repeat the following sequence of stitches to end of row. * Take 1 single crochet in each of double crochets of shell. Chain 5. * At end of row, turn.

For the **fourth row,** chain 5. Repeat the following sequence of stitches to end of row. * Make 3 single crochets in 3 middle single stitches of shell. Chain 3. In third stitch of chain-5 space, make 1 double crochet, 3 chains, and 1 double crochet. Chain 3. * End with 3 single crochets in middle of shell. Turn.

For the **fifth row,** chain 5. Repeat the following procedure. * Take 1 single crochet in second single crochet. Chain

3. Make 7 double crochets in chain-3 space between double crochets in previous row. Chain 3. * End with one single crochet, 3 chains, and one single crochet in chain-5 loop. Turn.

For the **sixth row,** chain 5. Repeat the following procedure to end of row. * Take 7 single crochets in double crochet stitches. Chain 5. * End with 1 single crochet in middle stitch of turning chain. Turn.

For the **seventh row,** chain 3. Repeat the following procedure to end of row. * In third stitch of chain-5 space, make 1 double crochet, 3 chains, and 1 double crochet. Chain 3. Take 3 single crochets in middle stitches of shell. Chain 3. * In last stitch, make 1 double crochet, 3 chains, and 1 double crochet.

Repeat the **second through seventh rows** until work is completed.

Shell and Bar Pattern—Double Crochet

Begin with a foundation chain the required length. Use a multiple of 6 stitches plus 1, with an additional 2 chains.

For the **first row,** take 1 double crochet in third chain from hook. Repeat the following procedure to the last 6 stitches. * Skip 2 chains. Take 1 double crochet in next chain. Skip 2 chains. Make 5 double crochets for shell in next chain. * At the last 6 chains, skip 2 chains. Take 1 double crochet in next chain. Skip 2 chains. Then make 3 double crochets in last chain. Chain 3 and turn.

For the **second row,** make 2 double crochets in first stitch. Skip 2 double crochets. Repeat the following procedure to end of row. * Make 1 double crochet in next double crochet. Make a shell of 5 double crochets in the center double crochet of next shell. * End with 2 double crochets in top of turning chain. Chain 3 and turn.

For the **third row,** take 1 double crochet in first stitch. Skip 1 double crochet. Repeat the following procedure to end of row. * Take 1 double crochet in next double crochet. Make a shell of 5 double crochets in center stitch of next shell. * End with 1 double crochet in last double crochet. Then take 3 double crochets in top of turning chain. Chain 3 and turn.

Repeat the **second and third rows** until work is completed.

Shell and Bar Pattern—Treble Crochet

Start with a foundation chain the required length. Use a multiple of 6 stitches plus 1, with an additional 3 chains.

For the **first row,** make 1 treble crochet in fifth chain from hook. Repeat the following procedure. * Skip 2 chains. Take 1 treble crochet in next chain. Skip 2 chains. To make shell in next chain, take 5 treble crochets. * At the last 6 chains, skip 2 chains. Make 1 treble crochet in next chain. Skip 2 chains. Make 3 treble crochets in last chain. Chain 4 and turn.

For the **second row,** make 2 treble crochets in first stitch. Skip 2 treble crochets. Repeat the following procedure. * Take 1 treble crochet in next treble crochet. Make a shell of 5 treble crochets in center stitch of next shell. * End with 1 treble crochet in last treble crochet. Take 2 treble crochets in top of turning chain. Chain 4 and turn.

For the **third row,** make 1 treble crochet in first stitch. Skip 1 treble crochet. Repeat the following procedure to end of row. * Take 1 treble crochet in next treble crochet. Make shell of 5 treble crochets in center stitch of next shell. * End with 1 treble crochet in last treble crochet. Take 3 treble crochets in top of turning chain. Chain 4 and turn.

Repeat the **second and third rows** until work is completed.

CLUSTERS OF STITCHES

By grouping stitches together in small bunches, or clusters, a pretty, puffy effect is created. The clusters vary in size and position depending on the stitches used with them. Some add an interesting touch to a lacy bit of crocheting; others give a softness to a firmer surface. You will notice these variations in the stitch patterns that are shown here.

Meadow Stitch

An interesting arrangement of chain and double crochet produces an allover effect of cluster blocks and triangular spaces. Begin with a foundation chain the required number of stitches.

For the **first row,** chain 5. Take 1 double crochet in sixth chain from hook. Chain 2. Double crochet in same stitch. Repeat the following procedure to end of row. * Skip 2 stitches. Take a double crochet in next stitch. Chain 2. Make a double crochet in the same stitch in which the previous double crochet was taken. * Turn.

For the **second row,** chain 3. Make 3 double crochets in chain-2 space. Repeat the following procedure to end of row. * Make 4 double crochets in each chain-2 space across row. * End with a double crochet in top of starting chain of previous row. Turn.

For the **third row,** chain 4. Repeat the following procedure to end of row. * Between the groups of 4 double cro-

chets, work 1 double crochet, 2 chains, and 1 double crochet. * End with 1 double crochet in the chain-3 space at the beginning of the previous row. Turn.

For the **fourth row,** chain 3. Work 4 double crochets into each chain-2 space. End with 1 double crochet in last stitch. Turn.

Repeat the **third and fourth rows** until work is completed.

Pineapple Stitch

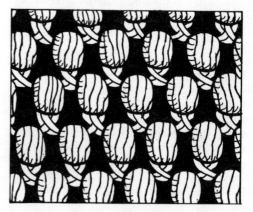

An arrangement of cluster blocks in rows produces a puffy textural effect. Make a foundation chain the required length, using an even number of stitches.

For the **first row,** chain 2. Repeat the following sequence of stitches to end of row. * Begin by repeating this procedure 4 times: put yarn over hook, insert hook in fourth chain, place yarn over hook again, and draw through loop. When there are 9 loops on hook, put yarn over hook and draw through 8 loops. Then put yarn over hook again and draw through last 2 loops on hook. Chain 1. Skip 1 chain. *

For the **second row,** repeat pattern in each chain-1 space of previous row.

Repeat the **second row** until work is completed.

Shawl Cluster Pattern

Open Cluster Ribs

Dainty clusters amid a network of chains give a lacy look to this stitch pattern. Begin with a foundation chain the required length. Use a multiple of 6 stitches plus 1.

For the **first row,** chain 3. Make a cluster in next stitch. To make the cluster, repeat the following procedure 4 times. * Put yarn over hook, draw through a loop. Put yarn over hook again and draw through first 2 loops on hook. Then put yarn over hook and draw through the 4 loops on hook. To secure, chain 1. * Then repeat the following sequence. * Skip 2 stitches. In next stitch, take 1 double crochet, chain 2, and take 1 double crochet. Skip 2 stitches, make one cluster in next stitch. Chain 1. * End with skip 2 stitches. In next stitch, make 1 double crochet, 2 chain stitches, and 1 double crochet. In the last stitch, 1 double crochet. Chain 3 and turn.

For the **second row,** repeat the following sequence of stitches to end of row. * Make cluster in chain-2 spaces between 2 double crochets. Then make 1 double crochet, 2 chains, and 1 double crochet under the 2 threads, securing the cluster of the previous row. * Finish with 1 double crochet in chain-3 space of previous row.

Repeat the **first and second rows** until work is completed.

Clusters of stitches are grouped in vertical rows, giving a ribbed effect to this lacy pattern. Begin with a foundation chain the required length. Use a multiple of 8 stitches plus 1 and an additional chain.

For the **first row,** make a single crochet in second chain from hook. Repeat the following procedure to end of row. * Chain 2. Skip 3 chains. In the next chain, make 1 double crochet, 3 chains, and 1 double crochet. Chain 2, skip 3 chains. Make 1 single crochet in next chain. * At end of row, chain 6 and turn.

For the **second row,** make a single crochet in chain-3 space. Repeat the following procedure to end of row. * Chain 3. In the next single crochet, do this 3 times: put yarn over hook, insert hook, and pull through a loop about ½ inch (1.3 cm) long. Then place yarn over hook and draw through 7 loops. Chain 1, forming cluster. Chain 3. Make 1 single crochet in chain-3 space. * End row with 1 double crochet in last stitch. Chain 1 and turn.

For the **third row,** make a single crochet in the double crochet. Repeat the following procedure to end of row. * Chain 2. Make 1 double crochet, 3 chains, and 1 double crochet in single crochet. Chain 2. Take 1 single crochet in cluster. * End row with a single crochet in third stitch of chain stitch of chain-6. Chain 6 and turn.

Repeat the **second and third rows** until work is completed.

Fan Cluster Pattern

Wavy rows of fanlike clusters add special design interest to this lacy stitch pattern. Start with a foundation chain the required length, using a multiple of 8 stitches plus 1, with an additional chain stitch.

For the **first row,** make a single crochet in second chain from hook. Then repeat the following procedure to end of row. * Start by making 3 chain stitches. Then skip 3 chains. In next chain, take 1 double crochet, 3 chains, and 1 double crochet. Follow with 3 chains. Skip 3 chains. Make 1 single crochet in next chain. * At the end of the row, chain 1 and turn.

For the **second row,** work with right side toward you. Make a single crochet in first single crochet. Repeat the following procedure to end of row. * Take 3 single crochets in chain loop. Then make 1 single crochet in next double crochet. Make 5 single crochets in next chain loop. Continue with 1 single crochet in next double crochet, 3 single crochets in next chain loop, and 1 single crochet in next single crochet. * At end of row, chain 3 and turn.

For the **third row,** skip 5 single crochets. Repeat the following procedure to the end of row. * Put yarn over hook. Insert hook in next stitch. Pull up a loop about ½ inch (1.3 cm) long. Do this 3 times. Put yarn over hook. Draw through first 6 loops. Place yarn over hook again and pull through remaining 2 loops to make a cluster. Follow with 3 chain stitches and a cluster in next single cro-

chet. Do this until 5 clusters have been made. Then skip 4 single crochets. Make a treble crochet in next single crochet. Skip 4 single crochets. * End row with 1 treble crochet in last stitch. Chain 1 and turn.

For the **fourth row,** begin with 1 single crochet in first treble crochet. Repeat the following procedure to end of row. * Chain 4. Skip next chain loop. Make 1 single crochet in next chain loop. Chain 3. Take 1 single crochet in following chain loop. Skip next chain loop. Chain 4. Make 1 single crochet in next treble crochet. * At end of row, take 1 single crochet in top of turning chain. Then chain 1 and turn.

For the **fifth row,** make a single crochet in first single crochet. Repeat the following procedure to end of row. * Chain 3. Skip the chain-4 loop. In next chain-3 loop, make 1 double crochet, 3 chains, and 1 double crochet. Then chain 3. Skip next chain-4 loop. Take 1 single crochet in next single crochet. * At end of row, chain 1 and turn.

Repeat the **second through fifth rows** until work is completed.

LACY EFFECTS

Crocheting has always been identified with delicate needlework. At one time, it was regarded as a form of American lace. Some of the stitch patterns that you can use to create fabrics of cobwebby fineness are mentioned here.

Open Stripes

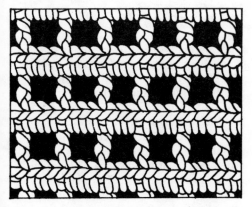

Rows of open squares create an allover eyelet effect in a striped design. Ribbon can be run through a row of eyelets as if it were an insertion. Begin with a foundation chain the required length. Use an even number of stitches.

For the **first row,** make a double crochet in fourth chain from hook. Repeat the following procedure to end of row. * Chain 1. Skip 1 stitch. Make a double crochet in next stitch. * Turn.

For the **second row,** chain 2. Make a half double crochet in each space and in each double crochet of previous row until row is completed. Turn.

For the **third row,** chain 3. Skip 1 stitch. Double crochet in next stitch. Repeat the following procedure to end of row. * Chain 1. Skip 1 stitch. Double crochet in next stitch. * At end of row, turn.

Repeat the **second and third rows** until work is completed.

Zigzag Stripes

This lacy design forms rows of stitches in a zigzag pattern to produce a striped

effect. Begin with a foundation chain the required length. Use a multiple of 4 stitches plus 1, with an additional 1 chain.

For the **first row,** take 1 single crochet in second chain from hook. Then make a single crochet in each chain to end of chain. Chain 7 and turn.

For the **second row,** skip 3 stitches. Take a single crochet in next stitch. Repeat the following procedure to end of row. * Chain 7. Skip 3 stitches. Take 1 single crochet in next stitch. * At the last 3 stitches, chain 3. Make 1 treble crochet in turning chain. Chain 1 and turn.

For the **third row,** take 1 single crochet in first stitch. Chain 3. Make 1 single crochet in fourth stitch of the first chain-7. Repeat the following procedure. * Chain 3. Make 1 single crochet in fourth stitch of next chain-7. * At the last chain-7, chain 3. Make a single crochet in fourth and fifth stitches of last chain. Chain 1 and turn.

For the **fourth row,** take a single crochet in second single crochet. Repeat the following procedure to end of row. * Make 3 single crochets in chain-3 space. Take 1 single crochet in next single crochet. * End with 1 single crochet in last single crochet. Make 1 single crochet in top of turning chain. Crochet 7 and turn.

Repeat the **second through fourth rows** until work is completed.

Clam Stitch

Frieze Pattern

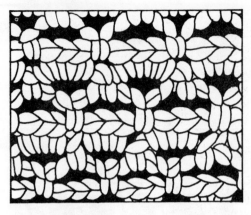

Tiny eyelets defining a small motif add interest to this textured stitch. Begin with a foundation chain the required length. Use a multiple of 16 stitches plus 11.

For the **first row,** take a double crochet in second chain. Repeat across row. At the end, turn.

For the **second row,** chain 3 stitches which take the place of the first double crochet. Make a double crochet in the next 10 stitches. Repeat the following procedure. * Skip 2 stitches. In the next stitch, take 1 double crochet, 1 chain, 1 double crochet, 1 chain, and 1 double crochet. Then skip 2 stitches. Double crochet in next 11 stitches. * Turn.

For the **third row,** chain 3. Work a double crochet in each stitch to end of row. Turn.

For the **fourth row,** chain 3. Double crochet in 3 stitches. Repeat the following procedure. * Skip 2 stitches. In next stitch, make 1 double crochet, 1 chain, 1 double crochet, 1 chain, and 1 double crochet. Skip 2 stitches. Double crochet in next 10 stitches. * End row by skipping 2 stitches. In next stitch, take 1 double crochet, 1 chain, 1 double crochet, 1 chain, and 1 double crochet. Then skip 2 stitches. Make a double crochet in the last 4 stitches. Turn.

For the **fifth row,** chain 3. Take a double crochet in each stitch to end of row.

Repeat the **second through fifth rows** until work is completed.

The arrangement of stitches for this design produces a border effect with openwork details. Begin with a foundation chain the required length. Use a multiple of 3 stitches plus 1.

For the **first row,** chain 1. Make 1 half double crochet in each stitch to end of row. Turn.

For the **second row,** chain 1. Then repeat this procedure to end of row. * Start with 1 single crochet and 3 chains. Then skip 2 stitches. * End the row with a single crochet. Turn.

For the **third row,** repeat the following procedure to end of row. * Chain 3. Make 1 single crochet in chain-3 space. * End the row with 2 chains and 1 single crochet. Turn.

For the **fourth row,** repeat the following procedure to end of row. * Begin by chaining 2. Then take 1 half double crochet in first space. Make 3 half double crochets in following spaces. * End with 2 half double crochets in last space.

Repeat the **second through fourth rows** until work is completed.

Bow Pattern

A combination of chain and single crochet stitches produces this design. Rows of chain stitches are bound together, creating the bow effect. Begin with a foundation chain the required length. Use a multiple of 10 stitches plus 4.

For the **first row,** take a single crochet in each stitch to end of row. Then chain 2 and turn.

For the **second row,** skip 1 stitch. Make 1 single crochet in next 3 stitches. Repeat the following sequence of stitches to end. * Chain 10. Take a single crochet in next 4 stitches. * End with 4 single crochets. Chain 2 and turn.

For the **third, fourth, and fifth rows,** use directions for second row.

For the **sixth row,** skip 1 stitch. Take a single crochet in next 3 stitches. Repeat the following sequence of stitches to end of row. * Chain 5. Make a single crochet going below 4 previously chained rows. Chain 4. Make a single crochet in 4 stitches. * End with 4 single crochets. Chain 2 and turn.

Repeat the **second through sixth rows** until work is completed.

Window Pattern

Two types of openwork squares alternate to give this stitch pattern an interesting lacy look. Each pattern requires 20 stitches. Multiply the number of squares by 20 stitches and then add 1 stitch.

Make a foundation chain the required length.

For the **first row,** make a double crochet in first 10 stitches. Chain 10. Skip 10 stitches. Take 1 double crochet in last stitch. Chain 2. Continue across row. Turn.

For the **second row,** chain 10. Skip 10 stitches. Take a double crochet in next 2 stitches. Chain 2. Skip 2. Take a double crochet in next 2 stitches. Chain 2. Double crochet in last 2 stitches. Chain 2 and turn.

For the **third row,** take a double crochet in second stitch and 2 double crochets in chain-2 space. Chain 2. Take 2 double crochets in next chain-2 space, and a double crochet in next 2 stitches. Chain 10. Skip 10 stitches. Make double crochet in next stitch. Chain 2. Turn.

For the **fourth row,** chain 4. Take 1 single crochet in linking together the 3 rows of chain-10 stitches. Chain 5. Make double crochet in next 2 stitches. Chain 2. Skip 2 stitches. Take 2 double crochets in chain-2 space. Chain 2. Take 2 double crochets in last 2 stitches. Chain 2 and turn.

For the **fifth row,** use directions for first row. However, the sequence of stitches should be arranged so that the second group of 10 stitches is made first. This creates the checkerboard effect.

For the **sixth, seventh, and eighth rows,** repeat the second, third, and fourth rows. The eight rows complete the design pattern.

Repeat the **first through eighth rows** until work is completed.

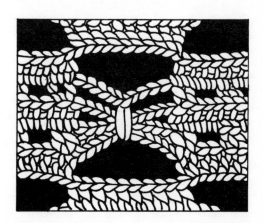

Picot Mesh Pattern

This mesh design is given a special decorative effect through the use of picots. Begin with a foundation chain the required length. Use a multiple of 4 stitches.

For the **first row,** repeat the following sequence of stitches. * Chain 5. Skip 3 stitches. In next stitch, take 1 single crochet, 3 chains, and 1 single crochet. * End with 5 chains. Skip 3 stitches. Make 1 single crochet, and turn.

For the **second row,** repeat the following sequence of stitches to end of row. * Chain 5. In the third stitch of the chain-5, make 1 single crochet, 3 chains, and 1 single crochet. * End with chain 5. Make 1 single crochet.

Repeat the **second row** to end of work.

Forget-me-not Stitch

This shell-like pattern creates a scalloped effect with a dainty floral design. Begin with a foundation chain the required length. Use a multiple of 3 stitches plus 1.

For the **first row,** chain 3. Then, in first stitch, take 1 double crochet, 2 chains, and 1 single crochet. Repeat the following procedure to end of row. * Start by skipping 2 stitches. Then, in next stitch, make 2 double crochets, 2 chains, and 1 single crochet. * At the row's end, turn.

For the **second row,** chain 2. Then, in chain-2 space, make 1 double crochet, 2 chains, and 1 single crochet. Repeat the following procedure to end of row. * Take 2 double crochets, 2 chains, and 1 single crochet in chain-2 space. * At end of row, turn.

Repeat the **second row** until work is completed.

Lacy Diamond Pattern

Open Squares

This stitch produces a geometric design with openwork spaces defining the lines. Begin with a foundation chain the required length. Use a multiple of 3 stitches plus 1, with an additional 1 chain.

For the **first row,** make a single crochet in second chain from hook. Take a single crochet in each chain to end of foundation chain. Chain 5 and turn.

For the **second row,** start with a treble crochet in first stitch, leaving 2 loops on hook. Skip 2 stitches. Make a treble crochet in next stitch, leaving 3 loops on hook. Put yarn over hook and draw through the 3 loops on hook. Chain 2. Repeat the following procedure to end of row. * Make 1 treble crochet in same stitch as last treble crochet, leaving 2 loops on hook. Skip 2 stitches. Take a treble crochet, leaving 3 loops on hook. Put yarn over hook and draw through 3 loops on hook. Chain 2. End with 1 treble crochet in last stitch, which was used for the last treble crochet. * Chain 3 and turn.

For the **third row,** skip first 3 stitches. Take 1 treble stitch in next stitch. Chain 2. Repeat the directions in second row from asterisk (*). Make last treble stitch in third stitch of turning chain. Chain 5 and turn.

Repeat the **second and third rows** until work is completed.

An interesting arrangement of stitches creates a series of squares, outlined with open spaces and moving in a diagonal direction. Begin with a foundation chain the required length. Use a multiple of 4 stitches plus 3.

For the **first row,** chain 3. In the fourth chain from the hook, take 3 double crochets, 3 chains, and 1 single crochet. Skip 1 stitch. Repeat the following sequence of stitches to end of row.
* Make 3 double crochets, 3 chains, and 1 single crochet in next stitch. Skip 1 stitch. * End with 3 double crochets and turn.

For the **second row,** chain 2. Then place 3 double crochets, 3 chains, and 1 single crochet in chain-3 space of each motif. End with 1 double crochet in last chain.

Repeat the **second row** to the end of work.

Web Pattern

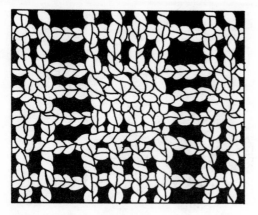

Rows of open motifs that seem to resemble a spider web produce a lacy effect. Start with a foundation chain the required length. Use a multiple of 11 stitches plus 1, with an additional 2 chains.

For the **first row,** take 1 double crochet in fourth chain from hook. Repeat the following procedure to end of row. * Begin by repeating this sequence of stitches 5 times: skip 1 chain, chain 2, and take 1 double crochet. Follow with a double crochet in next chain. * At end of foundation chain, chain 3 and turn.

For the **second row,** which is the right side of the work, skip first stitch. Repeat the following procedure to end of row. * Take 1 double crochet in next double crochet. Chain 4. Make 1 single crochet in each of next 4 double crochets. Chain 4. Take 1 double crochet in next double crochet. * End with 1 double crochet in top of turning chain. Chain 3 and turn.

For the **third row,** skip first stitch. Repeat the following procedure to end of row. * Make 1 double crochet in next double crochet. Chain 4. Take 1 single crochet in each of next 4 single crochets. Chain 4. Take 1 double crochet in next double crochet. * End with 1 double crochet in top of turning chain. Chain 3 and turn.

For the **fourth row,** skip first stitch. Repeat the following procedure to end of row. * Make 1 double crochet in next double crochet. Chain 4. Take 1 single crochet in each of next 4 single crochets. Chain 4. Make 1 double crochet in next double crochet. * End with 1 double crochet in top of turning chain. Chain 3 and turn.

For the **fifth row,** repeat directions for the fourth row.

For the **sixth row,** skip first stitch. Repeat the following procedure to end of row. * Take 1 double crochet in next double crochet. In next 4 single crochets, repeat this sequence of stitches; 2 chains and 1 double crochet in next double crochet. Then chain 2. Take 1 double crochet in next double crochet. * End with 1 double crochet in top of turning chain. Chain 3 and turn.

Repeat the **second through sixth rows** until work is completed.

Checkerboard Pattern

This stitch pattern can be used for soft, airy shawls. The lacy design forms a checkerboard of diamonds. Begin with a foundation chain the required length. Use a multiple of 10 stitches plus 1.

For the **first row,** chain 2 stitches. Make a double crochet in first stitch. Repeat the following procedure to end of row. * Chain 4. Skip 4 stitches. Take a single crochet in next stitch. To make 1 petal design, chain 7, take single crochet in same stitch. Repeat the preceding sequence of stitches twice. After making the petal design, chain 4. Skip 4 stitches. Take a double crochet in next stitch. * Turn.

For the **second row,** chain 1. Make a single crochet in double crochet of previous row. Repeat the following procedure to end of row. * Chain 1. Take a single crochet in first petal. Chain 3. Make a single crochet in second petal. Chain 3. Take a single crochet in third petal. Chain 1. Take a single crochet in double crochet of previous row. * Turn.

For the **third row,** chain 7. Take a single crochet in first stitch. Chain 7. Single crochet in same stitch. Chain 7. Single crochet in same stitch. Chain 4. Double crochet in single crochet of second petal. Repeat the following procedure. * Chain 4. Take single crochet in single crochet above double crochet. To make 3 petals, repeat this sequence of stitches 3 times: chain 7 and take a single crochet in the same stitch. * End with chain 7, a single crochet, chain 3, and a double crochet taken in the last stitch. Turn.

For the **fourth row,** chain 1. Make 1 double crochet in chain-3 space. Chain 3. Make double crochet in next petal. Repeat following sequence across row. * Chain 1. Single crochet in double crochet of previous row. Chain 1. Take single crochet in first petal. Chain 3. Make single crochet in second petal. Chain 3. Single crochet in third petal. * End row with chain 3 and single crochet in second petal. Turn.

For the **fifth row,** chain 2. Double crochet in first stitch. Repeat the following procedure. * Chain 4. Take 1 single crochet in single crochet above double crochet. To make petals, repeat this sequence of stitches 3 times: chain 7 and take a single crochet in same stitch. * End with chain 4 and a double crochet in single crochet above second petal of previous row.

Repeat the **second through fifth rows** until work is completed.

Butterfly Pattern

A miniature butterfly motif dots this lacy design. Begin with a foundation chain of the required number of stitches. Use a multiple of 16 stitches plus 6.

For the **first row,** chain 3 stitches. Make 3 double crochets in fourth stitch from hook. Repeat the following procedure. * Skip 5 stitches. Make 4 double crochets in next stitch. Chain 5. Skip 4 stitches. Make 1 single crochet in next stitch. Chain 5. Skip 4 stitches. Take 4 double crochets in next stitch. * End with skip 4 stitches and 1 double crochet in last stitch. Turn.

For the **second row,** chain 3. Make 4 double crochets in last double crochet of previous row. Skip 6 stitches. Take 4 double crochets in next stitch. Repeat the following sequence of stitches. * Chain 5. Make single crochet in single crochet of previous row. Chain 5. Make 4 double crochets in next double crochet of previous row. Skip 6 stitches. Make 4 double crochets in next double crochet of previous row. * End with 4 crochets in last double crochet. Turn.

For the **third row,** chain 3. Make 3 double crochets in first double crochet. Repeat the following procedure. * Skip 6 double crochets. Take 4 double crochets in next double crochet. Chain 5. Take 1 single crochet in the single crochet. Chain 5. * Make 4 double crochets in first double crochet. End with 1 double crochet in last stitch. Turn.

For the **fourth row,** chain 1. Take 1 single crochet in last stitch of previous row. Repeat the following procedure to end of row. * Chain 5. Skip 3 stitches. Take single crochet in next stitch. Chain 5. Make 4 double crochets in next stitch. Skip 6 stitches. Take 4 double crochets in next stitch. * End with chain 5. Take 1 double crochet at edge and turn.

For the **fifth row,** chain 6. Repeat the following procedure to end of row. * Make a single crochet in the double crochet. Chain 5. Skip 5 stitches. Take 4 double crochets in next stitch. Skip 6 stitches. Make 4 double crochets in next stitch. Chain 5. * End with a single crochet. Turn.

For the **sixth row,** chain 1. Make a double crochet in first stitch. Repeat the following procedure to end of row. * Chain 5. Take 1 single crochet in the single crochet. Chain 5. Make 4 double crochets in next stitch. Skip 6 stitches. Make 4 double crochets in next stitch. End with chain 5. * Make 1 double crochet in last stitch.

Repeat the **first through sixth rows** until work is completed.

Veil Stitch

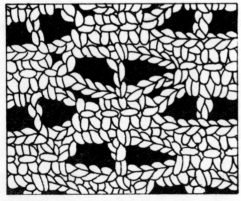

Motifs with an open circular feeling alternate to give this stitch pattern an airy look. For this lacy stitch, make a foundation chain the required number of stitches.

For the **first row,** take a single crochet in first stitch. Chain 1. Skip 2 stitches. Repeat the following sequence of stitches to end of row. * Make 3 single crochets. Chain 3. Skip 2 stitches. Take 3 single crochets, chain 3, skip 2 stitches. * End with 1 single crochet. Turn.

For the **second row,** chain 3. Skip 1 single crochet. Take 1 double crochet in next single crochet. Skip 1 single crochet. Chain 3. Repeat the following procedure to end of row. * Take 1 single crochet before the 3 single crochets of previous row, 1 single crochet in each single crochet, and 1 single crochet after the 3 single crochets. Chain 3. Take 1 double crochet in center of the next 3 single crochets. Chain 3. * End with chain 3 and 1 single crochet in last stitch. Turn.

For the **third row,** take 1 single crochet in first stitch. Chain 3. Repeat the following procedure to end of row. * Take 1 single crochet before the double crochet, 1 single crochet in the double crochet, and 1 single crochet after the double crochet. Chain 3. Skip 1 single crochet. Work single crochet in next 3 stitches. Skip next single crochet. Chain 3. * End with 1 single crochet before last stitch and 1 single crochet in last stitch. Turn.

For the **fourth row,** take 1 single crochet in first 2 stitches and another 1 in chain-3 space. Repeat the following procedure to end of row. * Chain 3. Skip 1 single crochet. Take double crochet in next stitch. Skip next single crochet. Chain 3. Make a single crochet before next 3 single crochets and then in all 3 stitches, and 1 single crochet after making them. * End with chain 3 and 1 double crochet in last stitch. Turn.

For the **fifth row,** take 1 single crochet in first stitch. Chain 3. Repeat the following procedure to end of row. * Skip 1 single crochet. Work single crochets in next 3 stitches. Skip 1 single crochet. Chain 3. Work 1 single crochet before the double crochet, 1 in the double crochet, and 1 after it. Chain 3. * End with single crochet in last 2 stitches.

Repeat the **second through fifth rows** until work is completed.

Viaduct Stitch

This stitch is frequently used for making a shawl. Begin with a foundation chain the required length.

For the **first row,** chain 1. Take 3 single crochets. Repeat the following procedure to end of row. * Chain 5. Skip 3 stitches. Take 5 single crochets. * End by making 5 chains and 3 single crochets. Turn.

For the **second row,** chain 2. Skip 2 single crochets. Make 1 single crochet in next stitch. Repeat the following procedure. * Make 9 treble crochets in chain-5 space. Take 1 single crochet in the first of the next 5 single crochets. Chain 2. Skip 3 stitches. Take 1 single crochet in the fifth single crochet. * End with 9 treble crochets in chain-5 space. Take 1 single crochet, 1 chain, and 1 single crochet in last single crochet. Turn.

For the **third row,** chain 6. Repeat the following procedure to end of row. * Make 3 single crochets in the 3 center treble crochets of motif in previous row. Chain 3. Take 1 treble crochet in chain-2 space of previous row. Chain 3. * End row with 3 chains and 1 treble crochet in turning chain of previous row. Turn.

For the **fourth row,** chain 3. Repeat the following procedure. * Take 1 single crochet in chain-3 space, before the first motif in the previous row. Make 1 single crochet in each of next 3 single crochets, and 1 single crochet in space following motif. This results in 5 single crochets. Then chain 5. Skip the treble crochet in the previous row. * End with 1 single crochet before the motif. Take 3 single crochets in motif. Chain 3. Make 1 single crochet in top of turning chain of previous row. Turn.

For the **fifth row,** chain 3. Make 4 treble crochets in first chain-3 space. Repeat the following sequence of stitches to end of row. * Take 1 single crochet in first of the 5 single crochets of previous row. Chain 2. Take 1 single crochet in the fifth single crochet and 9 treble crochets in next chain-5 space. * End with 1 single crochet, 2 chains, and 5 treble crochets in turning chain of previous row. Turn.

For the **sixth row,** chain 1. Make 1. Make 2 double crochets in the first 2 treble crochets. Repeat the following procedure. * Chain 3. Take 1 treble crochet in chain-2 space. Chain 3. Make 3 single crochets in the three center treble crochets of motif. * End with chain 3, 1 treble crochet, chain 3, and 2 single crochets in the last 2 treble crochets of previous row. Turn.

For the **seventh row,** follow directions for fourth row.

Repeat the **second through seventh rows** until work is completed.

LOOPED SURFACE

For added interest, loops of varying lengths can dot the surface. They can lie in different directions creating lovely textural patterns.

Brick Loop Pattern

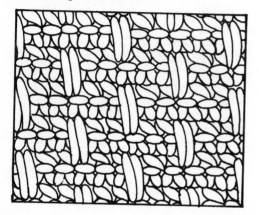

By using extended loops in an alternating design, it is possible to create the effect of laid bricks. To determine length of a row, use a multiple of 4 stitches plus 1 chain. Make a foundation chain the required length.

For the **first row,** make a single crochet in the second chain from hook. Then take a single crochet in each chain to the end. Chain 1 and turn.

For the **second row,** skip first stitch. Take 1 single crochet in each stitch of previous row, ending with 1 single crochet in turning chain. Chain 1 and turn.

For the **third row,** skip first stitch. Repeat the following procedure to end of row. * Make 1 single crochet in each of the next 3 stitches. Insert hook in first row. Chain directly below next stitch. Draw up a loop to make next stitch. * At the end of the row, chain 1 and turn.

For the **fourth row,** skip first stitch. Make 1 single crochet in each stitch to end of row. Chain 1 and turn.

For the **fifth row,** skip first stitch. Make a single crochet in next stitch. Repeat the following procedure. * Insert hook in stitch 2 rows below next stitch.

Draw up a long loop. Take a single crochet in each of the next 3 stitches. End the last repeat with 1 single crochet in each of last 2 stitches. * Then chain 1 and turn.

For the **sixth row,** repeat the fourth row.

Repeat the **fourth through sixth rows** until work is completed.

Looped Zigzag Pattern

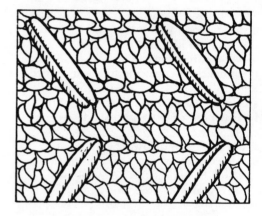

By alternating the direction of long loops, a zigzag design is created. Begin with a foundation chain the required length. Use a multiple of 5 stitches plus 1 chain.

For the **first row,** make a single crochet in second chain from hook. Take a single crochet in each chain to end of chain. Chain 3 and turn.

For the **second row,** skip first stitch. Take 1 double crochet in each stitch to end of row. Chain 1 and turn.

For the **third row,** skip first stitch. Take 1 single crochet in each stitch to end of row. Chain 3 and turn.

For the **fourth row,** use directions for second row.

For the **fifth row,** draw a loop, ½ inch (1.3 cm) long, between fifth and sixth double crochet of second row. Work this long loop as a single crochet. Skip first stitch on fourth row. Repeat the following procedure. * Take 1 single crochet in each of next 4 stitches. Skip 4 stitches in second row. Make a long loop between next 2 stitches. Skip 1 stitch in fourth row. * At last 4 stitches in fourth row, take a single crochet in each of the last 4 stitches. Chain 3 and turn.

For the **sixth, seventh, and eighth rows,** follow directions for second, third, and fourth rows.

For the **ninth row,** skip 2 stitches. Take a single crochet in each of next 3 stitches. Make a long loop between first and second stitches of sixth row. Repeat the following procedure to end of row. * Skip 1 stitch in eighth row. Take 1 single crochet in each of next 4 stitches. Skip 4 stitches in sixth row. Make a long loop between next 2 stitches. * At end of row, chain 3 and turn.

Repeat the **second through ninth rows** until work is completed.

Overlay Stripe Pattern

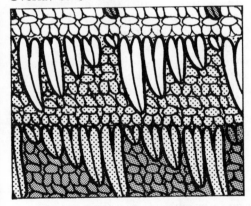

A series of graduated loops added to a background of single crochet creates an effective design, especially when worked in stripes of different colors. Begin with a foundation chain the required length. Use a multiple of 5 stitches plus 1. Crochet with yarn in 4 different colors: A, B, C, and D.

For the **first row,** work on the right side. Using yarn A, make a single crochet in second chain from hook. Repeat in each remaining chain. Chain 1 and turn.

For the **second through sixth rows,** single crochet in each single crochet to end of row.

For the **seventh row,** use yarn B. Re-

peat following procedure to end of row. * Single crochet in next crochet. Then, to make overlay stitches, take a long single crochet in next single crochet in second row below. Follow with 1 in the next stitch in third row below; next stitch, fourth row below; next stitch, fifth row below. * End row with a single crochet in last single crochet.

For the **eighth through twelfth rows,** continue to use yarn B. Make a single crochet in each single crochet to end of row.

For the **thirteenth row,** change to yarn C. Repeat the following procedure to end of row. * Begin with a long stitch in next single crochet in fifth row below. Follow with 1 in the next stitch, fourth row below; next stitch, third row below; next stitch, second row below. Single crochet in next single crochet. * End with a single crochet in last stitch.

For the **fourteenth through eighteenth rows,** continue to use yarn C. Single crochet in each single crochet to end of row.

For the **nineteenth through twenty-fourth rows,** follow the directions for the seventh through twelfth rows, using yarn D.

For the **twenty-fifth row,** repeat the thirteenth row, using yarn A.

For the remainder of the work, repeat the **second through twenty-fifth rows.**

Looped Chevron Stitch

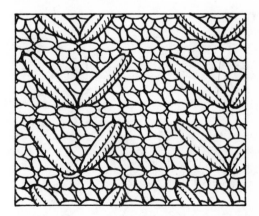

The design for this stitch pattern is developed by placing long loops diagonally on the surface of the crochet background. Make a foundation chain the required length. Use a multiple of 6 stitches plus 1 chain.

For the **first row,** make a single crochet in second chain from hook. Take a single crochet in each chain to end of foundation chain. Then chain 1 and turn.

For the **second row,** skip first stitch. Take 1 single crochet in each stitch of previous row. Chain 1 and turn.

For the **third and fourth rows,** repeat the second row.

For the **fifth row,** skip first stitch. Make 1 single crochet in next stitch. Then place yarn over hook and draw up a loop ½ inch (1.3 cm) long around first stitch in second row. The loop may be worked as a double crochet. Repeat the following procedure. * Skip the next 4 stitches in the second row. Make loop in next stitch. Skip next 2 stitches in fourth row. Take 1 single crochet in each of the next 4 stitches. Next make a loop in stitch in second row adjacent to last loop. * When the last 4 stitches are reached, make a loop in last stitch crocheted in second row. Skip next 2 stitches in fourth row. Make 1 single crochet in each of last 2 stitches. Chain 1 and turn.

Repeat the **second through fifth rows** until work is completed.

Looped Cross Stitch

The rows of zigzag loops seem to produce a cross stitch effect on the surface

of this stitch pattern. Start with a foundation chain the required length. Use a multiple of 6 stitches plus 1 chain.

For the **first row,** make a single crochet in second chain from hook. Then take a single crochet in each chain to end of foundation chain. Chain 1 and turn.

For the **second row,** skip first stitch. Make a single crochet in each stitch of previous row. Chain 1 and turn.

For the **third and fourth rows,** use directions for second row.

For the **fifth row,** skip first stitch. Make a single crochet in next stitch. To make a long loop, put yarn over hook. Pull up a loop, ½ inch (1.3 cm) long, around first stitch in second row. Work this loop as a double crochet, creating a long double crochet. Repeat the following procedure to the last 4 stitches at end of row. * Skip next 4 stitches in second row. Make another long double crochet in next stitch. Skip next 2 stitches in fourth row. Take a single crochet in each of the next 4 stitches. Make another long double crochet in stitch in second row next to the last long double crochet. * When the last 4 stitches are reached, take a long double crochet in last stitch. Skip next 2 stitches in fourth row. Make a single crochet in each of last 2 stitches. Chain 1 and turn.

For the **sixth and seventh rows,** use directions for second row.

For the **eighth row,** use directions for second row with this exception: omit chain 1 at end of eighth row.

For the **ninth row,** make a long double crochet in fourth stitch in sixth row. Skip first stitch in eighth row. Take a single crochet in each of the next 4 stitches. Make a long double crochet in stitch in sixth row next to last long double crochet. Repeat the following procedure. * Skip next 4 stitches in sixth row. Make a long double crochet in next stitch. Skip next 2 stitches in eighth row. Take 1 single crochet in each of next 4 stitches. * Make another long double crochet in stitch adjacent to last long double crochet in sixth row. Take a single crochet in last stitch. Chain 1 and turn.

Repeat the **second through ninth rows** until work is completed.

9

Styles and Types of Crochet

Although crocheting is generally worked in an allover stitch pattern, the type and style may change. The use of a different type of hook, a change in shape, and the introduction of color provide possibilities for creating different effects. Some ideas for this type of crocheting are shown on the following pages.

AFGHAN OR TUNISIAN

For a completely different look, try the afghan stitch, which is sometimes called tunisian. It is one of the two types of crocheting that is worked in a different manner. The results are lovely. The textural qualities are great for making coats, suits, and blankets. Many people feel it resembles knitting more than crocheting.

Construction Details

The work is done with a special hook. It looks like a knitting needle with the point replaced by a hook. The shaft is uniform in diameter. The knob at one end stops stitches from slipping off.

Basic Technique. The basic pattern is started with the usual foundation chain. But then the regular crocheting procedure changes. All of the stitches remain on the hook as you make the first row of stitches.

Two rows of stitches are needed to complete most afghan stitches. The first is sometimes referred to as the *pick-up* row because the stitches remain on the hook. The second row is called the *stitch* row. Here the stitches are worked off the hook one by one.

In crocheting the rows, you do not turn the work. Instead you work back and forth, first from right to left and then from left to right. But you must remember not to turn the crocheting. You always work on the same side. As you check each side, however, you will notice that each side has a different textural quality.

After making the foundation chain, insert the hook in the second chain from the hook. Put yarn over hook and draw a loop through the chain stitch. Continue this procedure to end of row, leaving all loops on the hook (A).

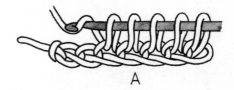

A

For the second row, do not turn work. Place yarn over hook. Draw a loop through first stitch on the hook. Then repeat this procedure until only 1 chain remains on the hook. Put the yarn over

111

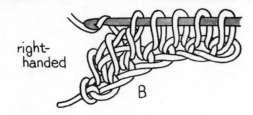

right-handed

B

the hook and draw it through 2 loops.
As you do this across the row, you will
remove the loops from the hook (B).

If you are *left-handed*, follow the same
stitch procedure, but instead of working
the first row from right to left, you will
crochet from left to right (C), and the
second row, you will work from right to
left (D).

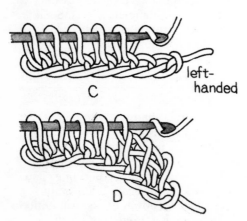

left-handed

C

D

Decrease a Stitch. When it is necessary
to decrease a stitch, put the hook under
2 vertical bars and pull up 1 loop. If
working at the right end of the row, join
the first and second stitches by pulling
up a loop in the second bar and then
bringing this loop through the first (A).

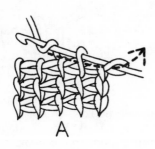

A

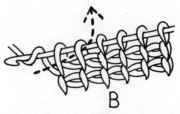

B

At the left end of the work, make the
decrease on the return row. Place the
yarn over the hook. Pull a loop through
2 loops, instead of the usual 1. This
makes the first stitch (B).

Increase a Stitch. The increases are always made in the first row—the one in
which loops are crocheted and kept on
the hook. Add a stitch by pulling up a
loop in the chain stitch between the vertical bars.

To make an increase at the beginning
of a row, work a loop in the first vertical
bar (A). At the opposite end, make a
loop between the last 2 vertical bars, entering the top part of the chain. Then
pick up a loop in the last vertical bar
(B).

Before you try the more unusual afghan stitch patterns, work with the basic
afghan stitch. The directions are given
here.

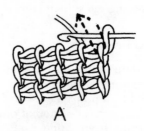

A

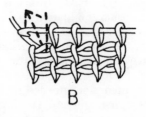

B

Basic Afghan Stitch

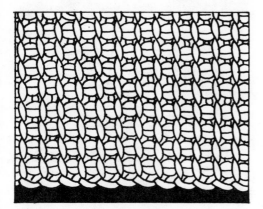

Crocheting made of afghan stitches is sometimes referred to as Tunisian Crochet. The stitches are made on a long hook that resembles a knitting needle. As one proceeds from right to left across a row, each stitch remains on the hook. The stitches are then worked off as the crocheting travels from left to right. Afghan stitches create an attractive, textured effect.

Begin with a row of chain stitches to form a foundation the required length.

For the **first row,** make a series of loops drawn through each stitch of the foundation chain. Leave all loops on the hook. To do this, insert the hook in the second chain from the hook. With yarn over the hook, draw a loop through the chain stitch. Continue the procedure to end of row.

For the **second row,** remove the loops from the hook without turning the work. Do this by placing the yarn over the hook. Draw a loop through first stitch on the hook. Then repeat the following procedure until only 1 chain remains on the hook. * Put the yarn over the hook and draw it through 2 loops. * At the end of the row, make 1 chain.

For the **third row,** leave the loops on the hook as for the first row. Working from right to left, insert the hook under the vertical stitch. Put yarn over hook. Draw through the loop. Continue this way to end of row.

For the **fourth row,** use the directions for the second row.

For the remainder of the work, repeat the **third and fourth rows.**

Many attractive textured effects are created by arranging the crocheted loops in different ways. They vary from the plain knitted look to the fancier ribbed designs. Experiment with the designs shown here until you create the look you want.

Knitted Afghan Stitch

For this afghan stitch, use a foundation chain of any number of stitches. The stitches produce a knitted effect.

For the **first row,** insert hook into second chain from hook. Put yarn over hook and pull through loop. Repeat this procedure, working in each chain to end of foundation chain. Keep all loops on hook. Do not turn work.

For the **second row,** put yarn over hook. Draw loop through first stitch on hook. Then place yarn over hook and pull through next 2 loops. Continue drawing the yarn through 2 loops until only 1 is left on hook. Chain 1.

For the **third row,** insert hook between the 2 double vertical stitches from front to back. Put yarn over hook. Pull through a loop. Continue to do this until row is completed.

For the **fourth row,** repeat the second row.

Repeat the **third and fourth rows** until work is completed.

Plain Tunisian Afghan Stitch

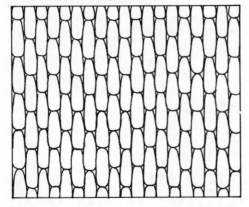

Purl Afghan Stitch

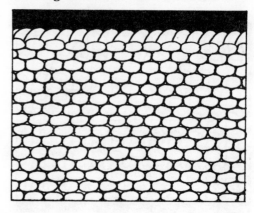

Make a foundation chain of the required number of stitches.

For the **first row,** make a series of loops drawn through each stitch of the foundation chain. Leave all loops on the hook. To do this, insert the hook in the second chain from the hook. With yarn over hook, draw loop through the chain stitch. Continue this procedure to end of row.

For the **second row,** remove the loops from the hook without turning the work. Do this by placing the yarn over the hook. Draw loop through first stitch on the hook. Then repeat the following procedure until only 1 chain remains on the hook. * Put the yarn over the hook and draw it through 2 loops. * At the end of the row, chain 1.

For the **third row,** repeat the following procedure to end of row. * Insert hook under the stitch between the vertical stitches of previous row. Put yarn over hook. Draw it through the loop. *

For the **fourth row,** use directions for the second row.

Repeat the **third and fourth rows** until work is completed.

For this afghan stitch, work a foundation chain the required length. Any number of stitches can be used.

For the **first row,** repeat the following sequence of stitches to end of row. * Hold yarn in front of work. Insert hook from back through chain with yarn under hook. Draw through a loop. * Keep all stitches on hook.

For the **second row,** put yarn over hook. Pull loop through first stitch on hook. Repeat the following procedure until 1 loop is left on hook. * Put yarn over hook and draw through 2 loops on hook. * Chain 1.

For the **third row,** repeat the following procedure. * With yarn in front of work, insert hook from right to left through vertical stitch of previous row. Put yarn over hook and draw through loop. * Keep all stitches on hook.

For the **fourth row,** use directions for the second row.

Repeat the **third and fourth rows** to end of work.

Crossed Tunisian Afghan Stitch

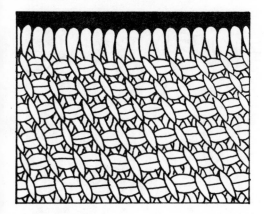

For this afghan stitch, make a foundation chain the required length.

For the **first row,** insert hook in the second chain from hook. Repeat the following procedure to end of row. * Put yarn over hook. Draw through a loop. Insert hook into next stitch. * Leave all loops on the hook. Do not turn work.

For the **second row,** put yarn over hook. Draw through a loop. Repeat the following procedure to end of row. * Put yarn over hook. Draw through 2 loops. *

For the **third row,** insert hook from right to left under the first vertical stitch. Put yarn over hook. Draw through a loop. Repeat the following procedure to end of row. * Insert hook from right to left under the third vertical stitch. Put yarn over hook. Draw through a loop. Repeat through second vertical stitch for crossed stitch. * This completes the first crossed stitch row.

For the **fourth row,** use the directions for second row with this exception: after the first loop, draw through 3 loops instead of 2, to the end of the row.

For the **fifth row,** follow directions for third row, continuing to work 1 stitch farther to the left for each alternating or crossed stitch row. This creates the diagonal or bias direction to the stitches.

Continue to work in this way, alternating the **second and third rows.**

Twill Afghan Stitch

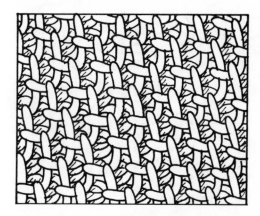

Begin with a foundation chain the required length. Use an even number of stitches.

For the **first row,** use the plain afghan stitch. Insert the hook into second chain from hook. Repeat the following procedure in each chain to end of row. * Put yarn over hook. Draw through a loop. * Keep loops on hook. Do not turn work.

For the **second row,** work off the loops by putting yarn over hook and pulling it through the first loop. Repeat the following procedure to end of row. * Put yarn over hook. Pull through next 2 loops. * End with 1 loop on hook. It is considered as the first stitch of the next row.

For the **third row,** skip the first vertical bar. Repeat the following procedure to end of row. * Pull up a loop under next vertical bar, making a plain stitch. Holding yarn with thumb in front and below hook, pull up a loop under next vertical bar, making a purl stitch. * End last stitch by inserting hook under last vertical bar and in loop at back of bar. Pull up 1 loop, making an edge stitch.

For the **fourth bar,** use directions for the second row.

For the **fifth row,** keeping all loops on hook, skip first vertical bar. Repeat the following procedure to end of row. * Make a purl stitch over a plain stitch. Make a plain stitch over a purl stitch. * End with an edge stitch.

Repeat the **fourth and fifth rows,** until work is completed.

Mesh Afghan Stitch

Ribbed Afghan Stitch

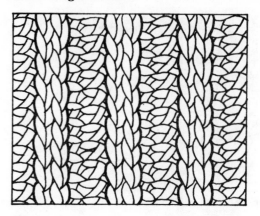

Begin with a foundation chain the required length. Use a multiple of 2 stitches plus 1.

For the **first row,** insert hook in third chain from hook. Put yarn over hook and draw through a loop. Repeat the following procedure to the end of row. * Chain 1. Skip 1 chain. Insert hook in next chain. Place yarn over hook and pull through a loop. * Keep all loops on hook. Do not turn work.

For the **second row,** put yarn over hook. Pull loop through first stitch on hook. Repeat the following procedure to end of row. * Chain 1. Place yarn over hook. Draw it through 2 loops. * At end of row, chain 1.

For the **third row,** insert hook through vertical stitch of previous row. Put yarn over hook and pull through a loop. Chain 1. Continue across row.

For the **fourth row,** use directions for the second row.

Repeat the **third and fourth rows** until work is completed.

This afghan stitch is started with a foundation chain, using a multiple of 4 stitches. Make a chain the required length. The stitches create a knitted effect.

For the **first row,** insert hook into second chain from hook. Repeat the following procedure to end of row. * Put yarn over hook. Draw through a loop. * Do this in each chain. Keep all loops on hook. Do not turn work to start second row.

For the **second row,** put yarn over hook. Pull loop through first stitch on hook. Repeat the following procedure to end of row. * Put yarn over hook. Draw through next 2 loops on hook. * At end of row, 1 loop remains on hook. Chain 1.

For the **third row,** repeat the following procedure. * Insert hook under vertical stitch from right to left. Put yarn over hook and draw through a loop; repeat. Then, with yarn in front of work, insert hook from right to left through vertical stitch of previous row. Put yarn over hook and draw through a loop. Do this twice. * Repeat the 4 stitches that have just been made to the end of the row.

For the **fourth row,** put yarn over hook and draw loop through first stitch on hook. Repeat the following procedure to end of row. * Put yarn over hook. Draw through next 2 loops. *

Repeat the **third and fourth rows** until work is completed.

Cluster Afghan Stitch

Make a foundation chain the required length. Use a multiple of 4 stitches plus 1.

For the **first row,** insert hook into second chain from hook. Repeat the following procedure to the end of the row.
* Place yarn over hook. Pull it through a loop. Do this in each chain to end of foundation chain, retaining all loops on hook. * Do not turn work.

For the **second row,** repeat the following procedure to end of row. * Chain 3. Put yarn over hook. Pull through 5 loops to make a cluster. Put yarn over hook. Draw through 1 loop. * At end of row, chain 1.

For the **third row,** repeat the following procedure to end of row. * Insert hook through top of cluster. Put yarn over hook. Pull through a loop. Insert hook in each chain stitch and draw through a loop. *

For the **fourth row,** use the directions for the second row.

Repeat the **third and fourth rows** to end of work.

Framed Squares Afghan Stitch

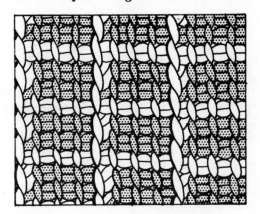

This stitch is made with a multiple of 4 stitches. It is most effective when worked in 2 colors. Begin with a foundation chain the required length.

For the **first row,** insert hook into second chain from hook. Repeat the following procedure to end of row. * Put the yarn over the hook. Pull through a loop. Then do the same thing in the next stitch. * Leave all loops on the hook. Do not turn work.

For the **second row,** put yarn over hook and pull through first loop. Place yarn over hook again and draw through 2 loops. Continue this way to end of row. Chain 1. Attach second color.

For the **third row,** repeat the first row, using second color.

For the **fourth row,** repeat the second row, using second color.

For the **fifth row,** repeat the third row.

For the **sixth row,** repeat the fourth row.

For the **seventh row,** use first color. Repeat the following procedure to end of row. * Pick up 3 loops. Put yarn over hook. Insert hook under vertical loop in second row. Place yarn over hook and pull through loop. Put yarn over hook and draw through 2 loops. *

For the **eighth row,** repeat second row, using first color.

Repeat the **second through seventh rows,** forming squares as described in the seventh row.

Bicolor Afghan Stitch

This use of yarns in 2 colors creates a tweedy look. Sometimes the stitch is referred to as Mock Rice. Begin this afghan stitch with a foundation chain the required length. Any number of stitches can be used. It should be remembered that the stitch can be made in 1 color.

For the **first row,** insert hook into the second chain from hook. Repeat the following procedure to end of row. * Put yarn over hook. Draw through a loop. Insert hook into next stitch and pull through another loop. * Leave all loops on hook. Do not turn work.

For the **second row,** put yarn over hook and draw through a loop. Repeat the following procedure to end of row. * Put yarn over hook. Draw through 2 loops. * At end of row, chain 1.

For the **third row,** change to a second color. Repeat the following procedure to end of row. * Insert hook from right to left of first vertical loop. Draw through a loop. Insert hook through vertical loop from left to right. Draw through a loop. With yarn in front, insert hook from right to left. Put yarn over hook and draw through a loop. With yarn in front, insert hook from left to right. Put yarn over hook and draw through a loop. *

For the **fourth row,** follow directions for the second row.

For the **fifth row,** follow directions for the first row.

For the **sixth row,** change back to first color. Follow directions for the second row.

Repeat from **third row,** displacing pattern by 2 loops for each repeat.

HAIRPIN LACE

Just as the afghan stitch produces a distinctive type of crocheting, so does hairpin lace. Although a hook is required, it is not employed in the usual way.

A special fork, loom, or staple is needed to make the lacy loops. Their size can vary, depending on the type of yarn or thread you use. It is thought that hairpin lace was first made on a hairpin.

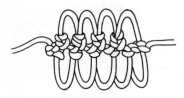

To make the lace, hold the fork in the left hand with the left prong between the thumb and first finger. The removable portion should be at the bottom so the lace can be removed.

Begin with a slip knot at end of yarn. Chain 1 stitch. Put the chain loop on the left-hand prong. Keep yarn in front of the work. Replace the bottom piece (A).

Return hook to slip-knot loop, drawing the loop to a center point between the 2 prongs. Wrap working yarn around right-hand prong. Hold yarn in back.

With the hook in the slip-stitch loop, insert it into the front of the loop on the left prong. Catch the working thread and make 1 single crochet (B).

Raise hook to a vertical position with hook end pointed downward. Turn the fork once, using a clockwise motion (C).

Bring hook into position in front of work. Insert it into the front loop to the left of the center. Put yarn over hook and make 1 single crochet (D).

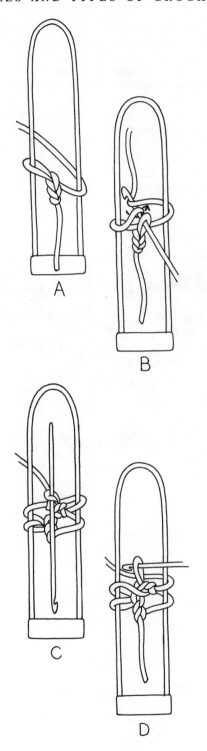

A

B

C

D

Continue to work in this way. Always keep yarn in back of lace.

The lace can be varied by replacing the single crochet stitches with double ones. Cluster and shell stitches can also be used. The important thing to remember is to keep the working thread in back of the work and the hook in a vertical position between the prongs so that it can be brought to the correct side of the lace after each turn.

When the fork is filled, remove lace except for the last 4 loops. Continue as before until required length is reached.

Linked Hairpin Lace

By joining 2 strips of hairpin lace, a decorative border trim with looped edges can be made. Be sure the 2 strips have the same number of loops, and that each can be divided evenly by number of loops to be used in the joining. For example, if the joining is to utilize 3 loops, then be sure that the number of loops can be divided by 3 in order to give an even appearance.

Arrange the 2 lace strips on a table with the beginning points of the strips opposite each other. Decide whether twisted loops or untwisted loops are to be used. Only one type should be employed. Care should also be taken to pick up each loop. Check the reverse side at regular intervals for missing ones. In case one has been skipped, rip work and correct mistake. Work upward.

To join the loops, place hook, pointing upward, through 3 loops on left-hand strip. Then put the hook through 3 loops on the right-hand strip. Keep the hook in the same position. Pull the second group of 3 loops through the first group. Pick up next 3 loops on the left-hand strip and pull these loops through the 3 loops on the hook. Continue working from side to side until the top of the strips is reached. This procedure creates a braided effect. After all the loops have been joined, fasten the last loops to the center with needle and yarn.

Hairpin Scalloped Edging

A strip of hairpin lace can be converted into an edging or insertion. The loops are joined, giving a scalloped effect to the trim. They can be twisted or untwisted, depending on the effect desired.

For the **lower edge** of this edging, attach yarn by passing it through the first 3 twisted loops. Make a single crochet in the same 3 loops. Repeat the following procedure across edge. Chain 3. Then make 1 single crochet in the next 3 loops. End with a single crochet.

BROOMSTICK LACE

Another type of crocheting that uses an unusual technique is this one. A knitting needle as well as a crochet hook is required. Sometimes this lacy stitch pattern is referred to as jiffy lace.

To make the stitch, use a multiple of five stitches for the foundation chain in the required length.

For the **first row,** pull up last loop. Put it on a large knitting needle, size 50, which is held in left hand. Insert hook in each chain. Pull yarn through and place on needle (A).

For the **second row,** repeat the following procedure the length of the foundation chain. * Insert hook in center of first 5 loops (B). Hold the loops together as 1 loop. Put yarn over hook and pull loops off the needle. Make 1 chain stitch. Follow with 5 single crochets in the same set of 5 loops. * Do not turn work at end of row.

For the **third row,** put the last stitch on knitting needle. Work in back loop. With crochet hook, pull yarn through each single crochet of previous row and place on knitting needle.

Repeat the **second and third rows** until work is completed.

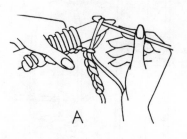

A

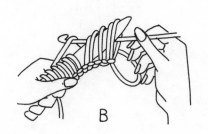

B

IRISH CROCHET

One of the most beautiful types of crocheting is Irish Crochet. A rose dominates the design. It creates a pretty three-dimensional effect with a dainty, lacy background. Irish crochet, which has a very distinctive look, can be used for an allover pattern or a medallion.

For the medallion shown here, begin at the center of the rose by chaining 8 stitches. Join with a slip stitch to form ring.

For the **first round,** chain 1. Make 18 single crochets in ring. Join with a slip stitch to first single crochet.

For the **second round,** make a single crochet in same place as last slip stitch. Repeat the following procedure to end of round. * Chain 5. Skip 2 single crochets. Single crochet in next single crochet. Mark this point with pin. * Six loops will have been made.

For the **third round,** take a slip stitch in first loop. In each of the 6 loops, make 1 single crochet, 1 half double crochet, 5 double crochets, 1 half double crochet, and 1 single crochet. This procedure creates 6 petals. Make a slip stitch in next stitch.

For the **fourth round,** repeat the following procedure to end of round. * Make 6 chains. Then make a single crochet in back of work in the next single crochet, which was marked with a pin in the second round. * This step makes 6 loops across the back of the petals.

For the **fifth round,** make a slip stitch in first loop. Then in each loop, make 1 single crochet, 1 half double crochet, 6 double crochets, 1 half double crochet, 1 single crochet. This procedure creates 6 petals behind the first layer of petals. Make a slip stitch in next stitch.

For the **sixth round,** repeat the following procedure to end of round. Chain 7. Make a single crochet in back of work in next single crochet of fourth round. This sequence of stitches makes 6 loops across back of petals.

For the **seventh round,** make a slip stitch in the first loop. Then work 1 single crochet, 1 half double crochet, 7 double crochets, 1 half double crochet, 1 single crochet in each loop. This procedure completes the rose motif, placing 6 petals behind the second layer of petals.

For the **eighth round,** make a slip stitch in each of the first 3 stitches of next petal. Then chain 1 and make a single crochet in same place as last slip stitch. Repeat the following procedure to end of round. * To make a picot, chain 5, and work a single crochet in fourth chain from hook. Then chain 7 and make a picot in fourth chain from hook. Follow with chain 1, skip 5 double crochets, make a single crochet in next double crochet, chain 5. Then make another picot and chain 7. Work another picot, chain 1, and make a single crochet in first double crochet of next petal. * This procedure creates 12 loops.

For the **ninth round,** make a slip stitch in each stitch, except picots, to the center of next loop. Then chain 3, make a double crochet in same place as last slip stitch, and chain 5. Make a picot, chain 7, and make another picot and chain 1. Holding back the last loop of each double crochet on hook, work 2 double crochets in same place where last double crochet was made. Put yarn over hook and draw through all 3 loops on hook. This completes a 2-double-crochet cluster and first corner loop. Repeat the following procedure. * Chain 5, make picot, chain 7, make picot, chain 1, make single crochet in center of next loop, chain 5, make single crochet in center of next loop, chain 5, make picot, chain 7, make picot, chain 1. Then work cluster in center of next loop, chain 5, make a picot, chain 7, make picot, chain 1. Work cluster in same place as last cluster, making a corner loop. * The preceding procedure is repeated 3 more times. End last repeat by joining last loop with slip stitch to top of first chain-3.

For the **tenth round,** begin with a slip stitch in each stitch to center of next loop at corner. Then chain 3. Make a double crochet in same place as last slip stitch. Chain 5. Make a picot. Chain 7. Make a picot. Chain 1. Work cluster in same place as last double crochet, placing a corner loop over corner loop. The following procedure is repeated 3 more

times. * Chain 5. Make a picot. Chain 7. Make a picot. Chain 1. Make single crochet in center of next loop. Chain 3 in next chain-5 loop. Work this sequence of stitches 3 times: 3 double-crochet clusters, 4 chains, and 1 picot. Follow with a 3-double-crochet cluster. Four clusters and 3 picots have been made over the loop. Then chain 3. Make a single crochet in center of next loop. Chain 5. Make a picot. Chain 7. Make a picot. Chain 1. Work a 2-double-crochet cluster in center of next loop. Chain 5. Make a picot. Chain 7. Make a picot. Chain 1. Again placing corner loop over corner loop, work a 2-double-crochet cluster in same place as last cluster. * After the preceding procedure has been repeated 3 times, end last repeat by joining last loop with a slip stitch to top of first chain-3.

FILET CROCHET

Filet is a type of crochet that allows for creativity. Designs can be copied if they lend themselves to a pattern made of a series of solid blocks and spaces. The blocks can be arranged in a simple checkerboard pattern or they can be arranged to form a definite design. The size of the blocks and spaces can vary in order to create a certain effect. In crocheting such a design, follow a chart worked in squares. This allows a design to be adapted for crocheting. Some examples of filet crochet are mentioned on the following pages.

Checkerboard Filet

Treble crochet with chain-3 blocks is used for this larger version of the checkerboard design shown in Chapter 7. Start with a foundation chain the required length. Use a multiple of 6 stitches plus 3, with an additional 3 chains.

For the **first row,** take 1 treble crochet in fifth chain from hook. Make another treble crochet in next chain. Repeat the following procedure to end of row. * Chain 3. Skip 3 chains. Take 1 treble crochet in each of next 3 chains. * Finish with 7 chains. Turn.

For the **second row,** repeat the following procedure to end of row. * Skip first 3 stitches. Take 1 treble crochet in each chain stitch. * At the last 3 stitches, chain 3. Skip 2 stitches. Make 1 treble crochet in top of turning chain. Chain 4 and turn.

For the **third row,** skip first stitch. Take 1 treble crochet in each of next 2 chains. Repeat the following procedure to end of row. * Chain 3. Skip 3 stitches. Take 1 treble crochet in each chain stitch. * End with 1 treble crochet in each of first 3 chains of turning chain. Chain 7 and turn.

Repeat the **second and third rows** until work is completed.

Design Filet

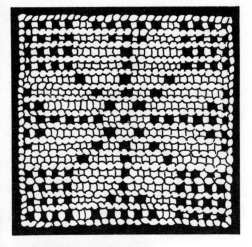

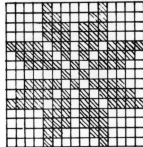

This type of crochet uses a double crochet with a chain-1 space. Designs are created by filling a space with a double crochet. Placing the design on graph paper makes the work easier to follow. Begin with a foundation chain the required length. Use an even number of stitches.

For the **first row,** make a double crochet in each chain stitch or every other chain.

The **following rows** require 4 chain stitches for turning; a double crochet in a double crochet of the previous row where an open mesh is needed; and a double crochet in a space where the design is needed. Each row is finished with a double crochet in the third chain of the chain-4 stitch at the beginning of the previous row.

Filet Crochet in Squares

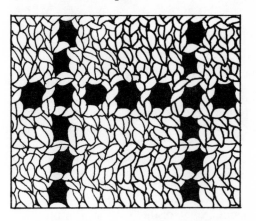

This pattern is worked so that spaces outline solid blocks of crochet. Begin with a foundation chain the required length. Use a multiple of 8 stitches plus 3 with an additional 2 chains.

For the **first row,** take 1 double crochet in fourth chain from hook. Then make a double crochet in each chain to end of foundation chain. At end of row, chain 4 and turn.

For the **second row,** skip first 2 stitches. Take a double crochet in next stitch. Repeat the following procedure to end of row. * Chain 1. Skip 1 stitch. Take 1 double crochet in next stitch. * End row with 1 double crochet in top of turning chain. Chain 4 and turn.

For the **third row,** skip first double crochet and 1 chain. Repeat the following procedure to end of row. * Take 1 double crochet in each of next 7 stitches. Chain 1. Skip 1 stitch. * Skip first stitch of turning chain. Make 1 double crochet in second stitch of turning chain. Chain 4 and turn.

For the **fourth and fifth rows,** repeat the third row.

Repeat the **second through fifth rows** until work is completed.

MEDALLIONS

This type of crocheting is a favorite one. The idea of making something small that is easy to handle and quick to construct is appealing. Also the possibilities for utilizing the medallions seem endless. By grouping them together, innumerable items can be created. Colorful afghans are among the most popular.

The medallions, which are sometimes called *motifs*, can be made in various shapes and sizes. Many of the stitch patterns can be adapted for this type of crocheting. Some of the many design possibilities are shown here. But remember that no matter which shape you are crocheting, you work in the round.

Granny Square

For many years this has been a very popular medallion. It can be made with yarns in different colors, providing you with a good opportunity to use bits of leftover yarn. One way of combining the colors is shown here. However, other color designs can be created, such as crossed diagonals, with the stitch pattern remaining the same. Begin by working 5 chain stitches. Make ring by joining stitches with a slip stitch.

For the **first round,** chain 3. Make 2 double crochets in ring. Chain 1. Follow with 3 double crochets in ring, repeating this step 3 times. End with 1 chain. Join with a slip stitch in third turning chain.

If different colors are being used, fasten off first color.

For the **second round,** attach second color in any chain-1 space. Chain 3. Make 2 double crochets in same space. Repeat the following procedure 3 times. * To make corner, take 3 double crochets, 1 chain, and 3 double crochets in next chain-1 space. * Ending with 3 double crochets, make 1 chain in beginning chain-1 space. Join with a slip stitch to top of chain-3. Fasten off second color.

For the **third round,** attach third color in any chain-1 space. Chain 3. Make 2 double crochets in same space. Repeat the following procedure 3 times. * Start with 3 double crochets in space between the next 2 groups of 3 double crochets. Take 3 double crochets in next chain-1 space. Chain 1. To make corner, make 3 double crochets in same space. * End round with 3 double crochets in space between next 2 groups of 3 double crochets. Chain 1 in beginning chain-1 space. Join round with a slip stitch to top of chain-3. Fasten off third color.

As each round is worked, continue to change colors. Three more rounds complete the design. In corners, work 3 double crochets, 1 chain, and another 3 double crochets. Take 3 double crochets between each 3-double-crochet group on the sides.

Cross Medallion

A cross of open spaces is the design pattern for this square medallion. Begin with a chain of 6 stitches. Join with a slip stitch to form circle.

For the **first round,** chain 3. Take 15 double crochets in circle. Slip stitch in top of chain 3.

For the **second round,** chain 3. Work two double crochets in same stitch. Repeat the following procedure twice. * Chain 2. Skip 1 double crochet. Make 1 double crochet in next double crochet. Chain 2. Skip 1 double crochet. Take 3 double crochets in next double crochet. * After this has been done, chain 2. Skip

1 double crochet. Make 1 double crochet in next double crochet. Chain 2. Slip stitch in top of chain 3.

For the **third round,** begin with chain 3. Repeat the following procedure 3 times. * Make 5 double crochets in next double crochet and 1 double crochet in next double crochet. Then chain 2 and take 1 double crochet in next double crochet. The preceding step should be repeated. * End last repeat with 1 double crochet and 2 chains. Slip stitch in top of chain 3.

For the **fourth round,** chain 3. Take 1 double crochet in each of next 2 double crochets. Repeat the following procedure 3 times. * Make 5 double crochets in next double crochet. Take 1 double crochet in each of next 3 double crochets. Chain 2. Make 1 double crochet in next double crochet. Chain 2. Make 1 double crochet in each of next 3 double crochets. * End last repeat with 1 double crochet. Chain 2. Slip stitch in top of chain 3.

For the **fifth round,** chain 3. Make 1 double crochet in first 4 double crochets. Repeat the following procedure 3 times. * Make 5 double crochets in the next double crochet. Take 1 double crochet in each of next 5 double crochets. * End with 2 chains. Slip stitch in top of chain 3. Fasten yarn and clip.

Popcorn Medallion

Begin with 5 chain stitches. Use a slip stitch to join, forming a circle.

For the **first round,** chain 3. Make 2 double crochets in circle. Repeat the following sequence of stitches 3 times. * Chain 3. Take 3 double crochets in circle. * Follow with 3 chain stitches. Join round with a slip stitch in third stitch of the chain-3 made at the beginning of the round.

For the **second round,** chain 3. Take a double crochet in next 2 double crochets. Pick up only back loop. Do this throughout work. Then take 2 double crochets in space. Repeat the following sequence of stitches to end of round. * Chain 3. Make 2 double crochets in space. Then take a double crochet in each of the next 3 double crochets. Make 2 double crochets in next space. * End with 3 chain stitches. Make 2 double crochets in space. Join round with a slip stitch in third stitch of the chain-3 made at the beginning of the round.

For the **third round,** chain 3. Take 5 double crochets in next double crochet. Remove loop from hook. Insert hook through the top of the first double crochet and the dropped loop. Pull the dropped loop through the stitch. Chain 1 to secure the popcorn motif. Then make a double crochet in each of the next 3 double crochets and 2 double crochets in next space. Repeat the following sequence of stitches to end of round. * Chain 3. Make 2 double cro-

chets in same space. Take double crochet in each of next 3 double crochets.
Make a popcorn in next double crochet.
Take double crochet in each of next 3
double crochets and 2 double crochets
in next space. * End with double crochet
in each of next 2 double crochets. Join
round with a slip stitch in the third
stitch of the chain-3 made at the beginning of the round.

For the **fourth round,** chain 3. Repeat
the following sequence of stitches to end
of round. * Make a double crochet in
next popcorn. Take another double crochet in next double crochet. Make a
popcorn in next double crochet. Then
make a double crochet in each of next 3
double crochets and 2 double crochets
in space. Chain 3. Make 2 double crochets in same space. Then take 1 double
crochet in each of next 3 double crochets. Make popcorn in next double crochet. Take 1 double crochet in next double crochet. * Join round with a slip
stitch in third stitch of the chain-3 made
at the beginning of the round.

For the **fifth round,** chain 3. Repeat
the following sequence of stitches to end
of round. * Make 1 popcorn in next
double crochet. Take a double crochet
in each of next 3 double crochets. Make
popcorn in next double crochet. Take a
double crochet in each of next 3 double
crochets and 2 double crochets in space.
Chain 3. Take 2 double crochets in same
space and a double crochet in each of
next 3 double crochets. Make a popcorn
in next double crochet. Make double
crochet in each of next 3 double crochets. * Join round with a slip stitch in
third stitch of the chain-3 made at the
beginning of the round.

For the **sixth and seventh rounds,**
continue to work in same way. Add corner stitches but place only 2 popcorn
stitches in each section.

For the **eighth round,** continue as before, adding corner stitches but placing
only 1 popcorn stitch in each section.

For the **ninth round,** continue to work
around medallion in double crochet. Increase at each corner as before, but do
not use any popcorn stitches.

The medallion can be made larger by

using increased stitches in the corners
and increasing the number of popcorns.
A reverse crochet stitch can be used to
finish the medallion.

Octagonal Medallion

Begin with 6 chain stitches. Form a circle by joining stitches with a slip stitch.

For the **first round,** chain 2. Take 23
double crochets in circle. Slip stitch in
top of chain-2.

For the **second round,** chain 4. Take
1 double crochet in same stitch. Chain 1.
Repeat the following sequence of
stitches 7 times. * Skip 2 stitches. Make
1 double crochet, 2 chains, and 1 double
crochet in next stitch. Chain 1. *
Slip-stitch in second stitch of chain-4.

For the **third round,** chain 2. In the
first chain-2 space, make 1 double crochet, 2 chains, and 2 double crochets.
Repeat the following sequence of
stitches 7 times. * Take 1 double crochet in chain-1 space. In next chain-2
space, make 2 double crochets, 2 chains,
and 2 double crochets. * End with 1
double crochet in last chain-1 space. Slip
stitch in top of chain-2.

For the **fourth round,** take 1 single
crochet in each stitch and 2 single crochets in each chain-2 space. Do this to
end of round. Slip stitch in first single
crochet. Fasten yarn and clip.

Pinwheel Medallion

Begin by making 4 chain stitches. To form a ring, join with a slip stitch.

For the **first round,** take 12 single crochets in center of ring.

For the **second round,** make a single crochet in first single crochet. Repeat the following sequence of stitches 6 times. * Chain 3. Skip next single crochet. Make a single crochet in next single crochet. * This procedure creates 6 spaces, each chain-3.

For the **third round,** make a single crochet in chain-3 space. Repeat the following sequence of stitches 5 times. * Chain 3. Single crochet in next single crochet. Follow with a single crochet in chain-3 space. * Chain 3. Skip next single crochet. Then single crochet in next single crochet.

For the **fourth round,** take 2 single crochets in chain-3 space. Repeat the following sequence of stitches 5 times. * Chain 3. Skip next single crochet. Take single crochet in next single crochet and then 2 single crochets in chain-3 space. * Chain 3. Skip next single crochet. Then make a single crochet in each of next 2 single crochets.

For the **fifth round,** make 2 single crochets in chain-3 space. Repeat the following sequence of stitches 5 times. * Chain 3. Skip next single crochet. Make single crochet in each of next 2 single crochets and 2 single crochets in chain-3 space. * Chain 3. Skip next sin-gle crochet. Make single crochet in each of next 3 single crochets.

For the **sixth round,** make 2 single crochets in chain-3 space. Repeat the following sequence of stitches 5 times. * Chain 3. Skip next single crochet. Single crochet in each of next 3 single crochets. Make 2 single crochets in chain-3 space. * Chain 3. Skip next single crochet. Single crochet in each of next 4 single crochets.

Continue in this way until the medallion is the desired size. Fasten yarn and clip.

Shell Octagon Medallion

Shell Square Medallion

Begin by making a foundation chain of 6 stitches. Join with a slip stitch to form circle.

For the **first round,** chain 2. Then take 23 double crochets in circle. Make a slip stitch in top of chain-2.

For the **second round,** chain 4. Take 1 double crochet in same stitch. Chain 1. Repeat the following sequence of stitches 7 times. * Skip 2 stitches. In next stitch, take 1 double crochet, 2 chains, and 1 double crochet. Chain 1. * Slip stitch in top of chain-2.

For the **third round,** chain 2. In first chain-2 space, take 1 double crochet, 2 chains, and 2 double crochets. Repeat the following procedure 7 times. * Chain 1. In next chain-2 space, make 2 double crochets, 2 chains, and 2 double crochets. * Chain 1. Slip stitch in top of chain-2.

For the **fourth round,** repeat the following procedure 8 times. * Make 7 double crochets in chain-2 space for shell. Then 1 single crochet in chain-1 space. * Slip stitch in first stitch. Fasten yarn and clip.

Begin by chaining 6 stitches. Join with a slip stitch to form circle.

For the **first round,** chain 2. Take 1 double crochet in circle. Repeat the following 4 times in circle: chain 1 and 4 double crochets. Chain 1. Take 2 double crochets in circle.

For the **second round,** take slip stitch in first chain-1 space. In first chain-1 space, chain 2, make 2 double crochets, chain 2, and make 3 double crochets. In each of the next 3 chain-1 spaces, make 3 double crochets, 2 chains, and 3 double crochets. Take a slip stitch in top of chain-2.

For the **third round,** make slip stitch in first chain-2 space. In the first chain-2 space, chain 3, make 3 treble crochets, chain 3, and finally take 4 treble crochets. In each of the next 3 chain-2 spaces, make 4 treble crochets, 3 chains, and 4 treble crochets. Take slip stitch in top of chain-2.

For the **fourth round,** take 1 single crochet in each stitch and 4 single crochets in each chain-3 space to end of round. Make slip stitch in first single crochet. Fasten yarn and clip.

10

Importance of Fit

The smartness of a crocheted fashion can be destroyed if it does not fit properly. A look that is too loose or too tight, too long or too short, destroys good proportion. The figure seems dwarfed or exaggerated. It is an unpleasing result that should be avoided. To ensure that it is, several factors should be considered.

Personal measurements and the way one crochets should be given careful consideration. The importance of gauge cannot be stressed too much. Too often one does not give enough attention to the fact that an article can be made larger or smaller than the directions indicate because the stitches are looser or tighter than intended.

CONSIDER THE SIZE

When you read directions for a certain project, you will notice that size and measurements are listed. To select the right one, you will need to know the bust or chest and hip measurements of the person for whom the garment is intended. Measurements should be taken precisely. This is most important. Unless they are taken accurately, they will be of little use.

Note Body Measurements

Before starting a garment, you should check certain measurements. This may seem unnecessary. But remember that body measurements do change. Waistlines thicken, hips bulge, arms become flabby. Such fluctuations can have frustrating results.

Misses', Women's, and Teens'. It is best to take the measurements when wearing the undergarments one intends to wear beneath the crocheted garment. Have someone take the measurements for you. They will be more accurate if they are taken from the back. Stand with your weight evenly distributed on both feet.

Start by recording your *height*. Knowing it, you will be able to crochet a sweater or garment to the correct length. In your stocking feet, stand against a wall in a natural position. Put a ruler on top of the head. At the point where the ruler touches the wall, place a mark. Measure the distance to the floor to get the height measurement.

Another length measurement that is handy to have is the *back waist length*. Take it from the top of the prominent bone at the base of the neck to the natural waistline, and then to the floor or to the point where the finished length will be, such as a hem line.

The *bust* measurement should be taken over the fullest part, well up under

Type	Size	Bust/ Chest	Waist	Hip	Height
Children's	6 mos.	19"	19"	20"	22"
	1	20	19½	21	25
	2	21	20	22	29
	3	22	20½	23	31
	4	23	21	24	33
Girls'	6	24	22	26	37
	8	27	23½	28	41
	10	28½	24½	30	45
	12	30	25½	32	49
	14	32	26½	34	53
Young Junior/	7/8	29	23	32	5'3"
Teens	9/10	30½	24	33½	
	11/12	32	25	35	
	13/14	33½	26	36½	
Misses'	6	30½	22	32½	5'6"
	8	31½	23	33½	
	10	32½	24	34½	
	12	34	25½	36	
	14	36	27	38	
	16	38	29	40	
	18	40	31	42	
Women's	38	42	34	44	5'7"
	40	44	36	46	
	42	46	38	48	
	44	48	40½	50	
	46	50	43	52	
	48	52	45½	54	
Boys'	1	20	19½	20	25"
	2	21	20	21	29
	3	22	20½	22	31
	4	23	21	23	33
	6	24	22	25	37
	8	26	23	27	41
	10	28	24	29	45
	12	30	25½	31	49
	14	32	27	33	53
	16	34	29	35½	55
Men's	34	34	30		5'9"
	36	36	32		
	38	38	34		
	40	40	36		
	42	42	38		
	44	44	40		

the arms, and straight across the back. Be sure that the tape measure is not pulled too tight, but keep it parallel to the floor.

The *waist* measurement should be taken snugly around the smallest part of the figure at a point between the ribs and hips. This is the natural waistline.

The *hip* measurement should be taken over the fullest part of the figure. For an adult, this is usually 7 to 9 inches (17.5–22.5 cm) below the natural waistline; for a child the distance is about 4 to 6 inches (10–15 cm).

Men's and Boys'. The chest measurement is the one you will need. Measure around the fullest part of the chest with the tape measure held loosely.

Children's. Again the chest measurement is the important one. Take it over the undergarments the child will be wearing. Children's garments are designed for an easy fit so be careful not to handle the tape measure too loosely or snugly.

Check the Sizing Chart

Before deciding on the correct size, examine the charts shown here, remembering that the measurements are given in inches. Choose the size that most nearly duplicates the body measurements of the person for whom the garment is to be made. If none of the measurements match exactly, select the size by the bust measure. Adjustments to the design are easier to make at the waist and hips than to the shoulder and bust area.

Sometimes the sizing is listed as small, medium, or large. Such a designation indicates two size ranges. Because of this, the finished garment will not fit as precisely as when the design is made for one size.

To complicate your selection, remember that this type of sizing is not always the same. For instance, a small size may be stated as a $\%$ or as an $\frac{8}{10}$. These differences can make a variation in the fit of the finished garment.

Remember Ease

This is most important. Too often one forgets that body measurements do not duplicate those of a pattern. A bit of ease is built into the design so that the body can move within the garment. A fashion that is too tight or too large is unattractive to see and uncomfortable to wear. The amount of ease depends on the type of garment and the look the designer is trying to create. For example, a camisole top needs less ease than a pullover.

Crocheting instructions allow for the needed amount of ease for each size. Sometimes the body measurements for which the garment has been designed are listed at the beginning of the directions. By checking the gauge you can determine just how much ease has been allowed.

Always study the picture of the fashion you are thinking of crocheting. Usually it portrays how the designer wants the garment to look on you. You can decide whether it creates the right image.

Also give some thought to how you will wear the garment. If it is to be worn over other fashions for a layered look then maybe you should choose a larger size.

IMPORTANCE OF GAUGE

Too often the gauge is ignored. This is too bad because the size and fit of a garment are destroyed unless the correct gauge is used.

Gauge applies to the number of stitches and rows that are produced by crocheting with a specific size hook and yarn. No doubt you have noticed that at the beginning of the instructions there is a statement about gauge. Usually it is given as the number of stitches per inch, such as "4 sts = 1 inch (2.5 cm); 7 rows = 1 inch using a size J (6 mm) crochet hook."

This indicates that if the item you are crocheting is to duplicate the size as intended by the instructions, 4 stitches in your crocheting should make 1 inch (2.5 cm) of horizontal stitches and 7 rows should make 1 inch (2.5 cm) of vertical stitches in rows.

Sometimes, however, the gauge refers to the stitch pattern—1 shell = 1 inch on size I hook—or perhaps you might find the gauge stated as "4 patterns = 3 inches on size H hook" or "7 sc = 2 inches on size E hook." Whichever way the gauge is stated, you will be wise to interpret it accurately.

The number of stitches varies depending on the yarn and the size of the hook you use. Study the accompanying drawing. Immediately you can see how the size of the hook can change the appearance of the crocheting when the identical yarn is used. As smaller hooks are used, the sample grows smaller. Also notice that the stitches seem to close up, changing the texture of the crocheting. The larger hooks produce a more open-work fabric, whereas the smaller hooks create a more solid effect.

The way you crochet also affects the gauge. Some people crochet more loosely than others. Of course it will be easier to duplicate the stated gauge if you crochet with a moderate tension. Take time to develop this skill if you do not have it. Your crocheting will be more pleasing if you do.

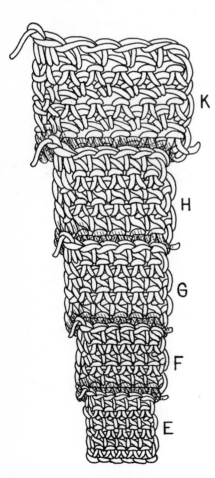

Test the Gauge

Before starting a new project, you should check the stitch gauge. This makes it possible for you to compare your work with the necessary gauge. Although this procedure may seem time-consuming, it really can prevent a catastrophe. Making something too large or too small can be most annoying.

Start by making a chain about 4 inches (10 cm) long using the required yarn and needles. Crochet in the specified pattern stitch for 3 inches (7.5 cm).

When the swatch is completed, block it. Do this by smoothing it out on a firm surface, but do not stretch it. Pin it in place along the four edges and steam press. With a ruler, measure off 1 inch (2.5 cm) crosswise. Mark ends with pins. Then measure an equal distance lengthwise and mark. Some people feel that a 2-inch (5 cm) measure gives a more accurate gauge.

Count the stitches and rows between the pins. Even if the gauge varies by only part of a stitch, do not ignore it. This tiny variation can make your garment several inches too small or too large. In analyzing the variation between the required gauge and your work, remember that if you crocheted more stitches to the inch, then you are crocheting too tightly. But if you crocheted fewer stitches to the inch, then you are crocheting too loosely. To correct the situation, try a hook one size larger if there were too many stitches; one size smaller if there were too few.

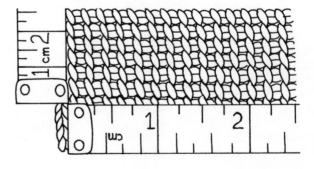

THINK ABOUT ADJUSTMENTS

If you sew, you know how often a pattern must be altered in order to produce a more pleasing look and better fit. The same situation may exist for crocheting. Shortening or lengthening a garment is a simple adjustment to make, whereas altering the width requires more skill. If a change is necessary, be sure to plan it before starting the project.

Shortening or Lengthening

Start by noting the height of the person for whom the fashion is being crocheted. Compare this measurement with the one given in the sizing chart for that size range. Designs are made for the average figure having the stated measurements. If you are crocheting for someone taller or shorter than the average, then it seems best to shorten or lengthen the garment as it is being crocheted.

Begin by considering how many inches may need to be added or subtracted using the measurements for height as a guide. Check this measurement by interpreting the directions. Some instructions direct you to crochet a certain number of inches before making a change in shaping. Others ask you to crochet a certain number of rows. Whichever method is employed, add the mentioned numbers for a total dimension. If the count is by rows, use the stated row gauge for determining the number of inches.

Decide on the Place. No doubt you have noticed on sewing patterns printed lines that indicate where adjustments should be made. It is a good guideline for you to use in crocheting. If you study a pattern, you will notice that the lines are marked where there is little or no shaping in the design. Remember that the adjustments should be made to both the front and back sections as well as both sleeves. Forgetting to do this is easy.

For a sweater or top, adjust between the lower edge and the shaping for the armhole. Sometimes if you are short-waisted, you may want to bring the neckline into its correct position by removing a small amount below the shoulderline. A gapping neckline is not attractive.

For sleeves, make the adjustment above and below the elbow for long sleeves; above the lower edge of a short sleeve.

For a skirt, change the directions between the lower edge and the place where the shaping for the hipline begins.

Decide on the Amount. Use the row gauge as your guide. If you need to lengthen the garment by 1 inch (2.5 cm) and the row gauge indicates that 4 rows equal 1 inch (2.5 cm), then you know that you must add 4 rows to the directions. If instead you need to remove rows in order to shorten the garment 1 inch (2.5 cm), then remove 4 rows from the directions.

Make the Adjustment. In crocheting, this is not as simple an operation as it is in sewing. You do not have a paper pattern to tuck or spread and test before you begin to make the article. Instead the adjustments are made as you crochet. You have to rely on your ruler to indicate where the alteration should be made. When you reach the correct row, make the adjustment by adding or subtracting rows to give the proper effect.

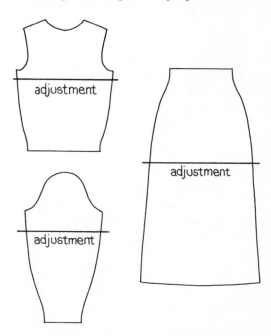

You may find it helpful to draw a pattern to use as a guide. Sometimes a basic paper pattern can prove useful in testing the sizing of the garment you are making.

Consider the Stitch Pattern. There are some stitch patterns that cannot be altered. Simple stitch patterns cause no problem, but if the design has a large repeat, adjusting may not be possible. Removing a complete repeat may shorten the garment too much or may be not quite enough. Consult the gauge for the stitch pattern before making a decision.

Note the Width

Generally an alteration to the width is not needed. The wide range of sizes eliminates this problem. These measurements, however, should not be forgotten. Width is so important to the correct fit of the garment.

Again it is the stitch gauge that must be checked. It tells you how many stitches there are to the inch. Then note the number of chain stitches that make the foundation. Be sure to add the numbers for back and front together. Divide the total by the number of stitches per inch. The result should correspond to a personal measurement. For instance, if your hips measure 36 inches (90 cm) and the stitch gauge is 6 stitches to the inch (2.5 cm), then you know that you will need to chain 216 stitches, depending on the type of yarn. Sometimes a few extra stitches are needed as an ease allowance. The garment should not look stretched over the bust and abdomen, which would give the garment a skimpy effect.

Before making a change in stitch numbers, you may want to try larger or smaller needles. A larger needle will increase the size; a smaller one, decrease it. Of course you should make a stitch gauge before beginning your project to avoid a mistake.

Change of Size

If you find a design you like, but the directions are not given for the size you need, you can alter the directions to make it a size larger or smaller. Start by reading the information at the beginning of the directions. For example, you may find this type of copy:

"These directions are for size 8. Changes for sizes 10, 12, and 14 are in parentheses.

"Back: Chain 60 (62-64-66) sts."

Notice that there is a difference of 2 stitches between the sizes. If you decided to make a size 16, you would chain 2 more stitches than the size 14 requires to create the new size. Of course, if you make such an alteration, be sure to adjust the remaining directions accordingly.

Making a simple drawing or diagram of each piece before beginning to crochet can simplify the construction process. On the diagram show specific details such as the number of stitches to chain, the distance to crochet before decreasing to shape armhole, the amount to decrease, width of shoulder, depth of armhole, shoulder shaping, and neckline. For many people, this visual aid is easier to follow than reading the directions.

Check the Yarn and Stitch Pattern

Yarns behave in different ways. Some stretch more than others. This characteristic does influence the fit of a crocheted garment. Knitted fabrics stretch more than woven ones, and so do yarns and crocheted stitch patterns. Analyze this characteristic by checking the give in the gauge swatch you make. Too little or too much stretch will cause fitting problems.

THE EFFECT OF CONSTRUCTION DETAILS

Often one forgets that the fit of a garment can be changed by the placement of certain construction details such as a buttonhole or a seam. Construction details also influence the look of the garment. Because of this, you should give special attention to how these features are being handled. Make certain that the detail is correctly positioned before you begin to crochet. Unless it is, the completed article can be a disappointment.

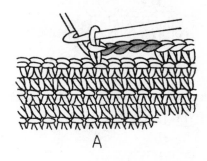

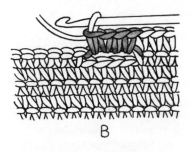

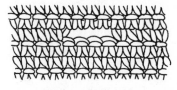

Check for Buttonholes

Generally, crocheted garments are closed with buttons and buttonholes or loops. Before starting your project, check the placement of the buttonholes to be sure they fall in the right spot. Determine where the article should be fastened at the neckline, the fullest part of the bust, and at a point just above the lower edge. The other buttonholes should be spaced evenly between these points.

In planning the placement of the buttonholes, also consider the button. The upper edge of a vertical buttonhole should be one row above the button. The end of the horizontal buttonhole which is closest to the edge should extend one stitch beyond the button.

Although the instructions you are using will tell you how to make the buttonholes, there may be times when you want to add an extra one to the design. This can be done in various ways. However, the type you choose should relate to the project and the desired effect.

Horizontal Buttonholes. Two ways of making this type of buttonhole are described below. One is used with single crochet, the other with double crochet.

When using *single crochet* stitches, chain the correct number of stitches at the point where the buttonhole begins. Usually 1 to 5 stitches are needed to accommodate the diameter of the button. Continue working in the pattern stitch, skipping the number of stitches for which you have made chain stitches (A).

For the next row, crochet to the point where the chain stitches begin. Then make single crochet stitches over the chain. Crochet the same number of stitches as there are chain stitches (B). Continue to crochet in pattern stitch.

When working with *double crochet* stitches, maneuver the hook in this manner at the point where the buttonhole is to start. Put the hook under the diagonal strand of the stitch that has just been completed. Do this about halfway down the stitch (A).

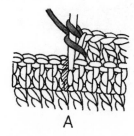

A

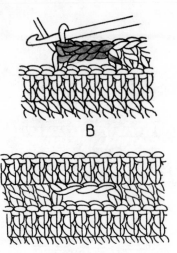

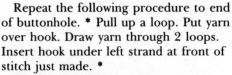

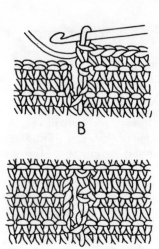

Repeat the following procedure to end of buttonhole. * Pull up a loop. Put yarn over hook. Draw yarn through 2 loops. Insert hook under left strand at front of stitch just made. *

When the required number of stitches have been crocheted, draw up a loop to complete the buttonhole. Be sure to skip the same number of stitches as you made for the buttonhole. Put the hook in next stitch. Draw up a loop and complete a double crochet (B).

Vertical Buttonhole. This type of buttonhole can be used with any stitch. On the right side of the garment, mark the point where the buttonhole should begin. Crochet to this place. Turn the work and continue to crochet this portion until the depth of the buttonhole has been attained.

If you have crocheted an *odd number of rows* for the buttonhole, clip yarn and fasten (A). When you have completed the work, weave the yarn into the back of the article.

For an *even number of rows,* leave yarn at the side of the article. Attach another strand of yarn to the edge of the buttonhole. Crochet the second half to match the first.

To complete the buttonhole, start the next row at the side edge. Crochet in pattern stitch across both sections, closing the end of the buttonhole (B).

Buttonhole Loop. Single crochet stitches are used for this popular fastener. It can be used on knitted garments also.

Crochet to the place where the loop will be worked on the right side of the garment. Make a chain the length of the buttonhole. Carry it back to the beginning of the buttonhole so it can be joined to the garment. Remove hook from chain carefully. Then insert the hook from front to back through top of stitch. Pick up chain and draw it through work. Insert hook in next stitch to the right. Put yarn over (A). Draw a loop through stitch and chain.

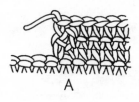

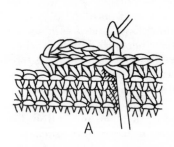

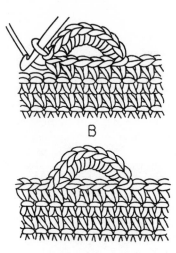

B

Finish loop by working single crochet stitches over chain. At the starting point of the loop, make a slip stitch (B). Continue work in the pattern stitch across the row.

Join the Parts

After the pieces have been blocked and you are sure they are the correct size, they are ready to be attached to each other. The pieces can be joined as in seaming or placed side by side so the edges touch. In Chapter 5 various methods are discussed.

Be sure to select the method that will create the best results for a given situation. A seam with right sides together produces a firm, neat look. It must be used when edges are uneven. Take great care to maintain the correct width of the seam. If you don't, the sizing of your garment can be altered.

An edge to edge joining produces a flat finish. It can only be used when the edges are even and an identical number of stitches has been used on each edge. It is an especially good finish to use for joining medallions and ribbing.

One method of joining that has not been mentioned works nicely when the article is made of a bulky yarn. A slip stitch is combined with a chain stitch. This combination of stitches allows more stretch in the seaming.

Begin by placing the right sides of the two pieces together. Then make a slip stitch through two corresponding stitches. Use this procedure to the end of the row, alternating a slip stitch with chain stitches. The number of stitches depends on the height of the row. Make a slip stitch at the beginning of the next row.

Whichever type of seam you make, avoid pulling the stitches tight. You do not want the seam to have a puckered effect. To prevent this situation, stretch out the seam gently after each stitch.

Steam press the seam for a smooth finish. To do this, put the seam on a padded surface. Wet a press cloth and place it over the seam. Move a hot iron over the cloth to produce steam, but be sure you do not let the weight of the iron rest on the cloth. You do not want to flatten the yarn and the seam.

Measure the Border

Crocheting lends itself to many interesting edgings and border treatments. Several are mentioned in Chapter 11. No doubt you will want to try some of them. But when you do, be sure to include the decorative detail in your garment measurements. Frequently one forgets to do this with the result that a jacket can look too long or too big. Naturally you do not want that to happen.

Also select an edging or border in proportion to the article and to your figure. When a design detail is out of proportion, an illusion of poor fit is created.

A crocheted edging produces a firm edge. It should remain flat with no puckering or curling, reinforcing the shape with a definite outline. A trim look is a desired feature.

BLOCK FOR GOOD FIT

Blocking is an important part of crocheting. It helps to shape a piece of crocheting to the intended form and sizing. Just as pressing confers a professional finish to sewing so does blocking to crocheting. A certain unevenness in the work is smoothed out. Sometimes a beautifully crocheted article can have an unprofessional look if it is not blocked correctly. Good blocking adds a certain smartness to a garment and helps it to fit properly.

Before the parts are joined, each one should be blocked separately. The method depends on the stitch pattern and yarn. Be sure to read the label on the yarn for blocking tips. Then test the reaction of the yarn and stitch pattern to the procedure by using a sample swatch before you actually begin the blocking.

Consult the Labels

Sometimes the preferred blocking method is suggested by the yarn manufacturer. Of course if the label lists the caution "do not block," you won't. Certain types of yarn, such as acrylics and some blends, are not improved by blocking.

Each yarn and stitch pattern have definite characteristics. These features may be affected differently by blocking. Be sure to give them some attention before beginning. For example, the fluffy appearance of angora yarn can be destroyed if it is pressed flat. Also you may find that mohair pieces shrink in length, but not in width. This may mean that you will have to stretch the piece slightly lengthwise.

Certain loosely crocheted articles and extra heavy yarns seem to stretch in length. They measure more when held up than when placed flat on the blocking board. To counterbalance this effect, block the pieces wider and shorter.

Some stitch patterns require an opening up of the design to create the proper effect. Blocking them 1 or 2 inches (2.5–5 cm) wider can prove helpful. It allows for the correct return to the original shape. Lacy patterns are included in this group.

Note the Measurements

Two sets of measurements should be studied before the blocking begins. First, there are the measurements of the person for whom the article is being made, and secondly, those of the finished item. It is also advisable to study the picture accompanying the instructions. Observe where the seamlines and fashion details fall. Note the features that influence the fit, such as blousing.

At the beginning of the directions, you will usually find the measurements for the garment listed. Sometimes blocking or finished measurements are given also. If they do not appear, it is wise to compile your own list. Use the stitch gauge as a guide. Write down the number of stitches and also the number of inches for the needed measurements. Include the lower edges, hip, waist, bust, shoulder, and underarm measurements.

Compare these measurements with those of the person for whom the garment is being made. For instance, if you have crocheted 24 rows before beginning to shape the armhole and if the gauge is 2 rows to the inch, then you know that the side seam edge should measure 12 inches (30.5 cm) when blocked. If you have worked 42 stitches for the shoulder and the stitch gauge is 7 stitches equals 2 inches (5 cm), then you know that the shoulder should be blocked to 12 inches (30.5 cm). After compiling such information, you can determine whether any alterations are needed.

If you want to make a slight change in the article, dampen it. Dampened yarn can be manipulated. Usually a change in size is limited to making the garment one size larger. Decreasing the size is difficult. The actual amount of decrease will be controlled by the fiber content of the yarn and how tightly it is spun. Yarns made of natural fibers are usually easier to adjust than most synthetics. The amount of adjustment is also influenced by the type of stitch pattern. Open designs stretch more than closed ones do.

Prepare the Crocheted Piece

Usually the piece is left with dangling ends of yarn. These should be concealed. Thread a blunt-pointed needle with the yarn and weave it into the edge for about 2 inches (5 cm). If you are working with a bulky yarn, it may be wise to split it and run each end separately through the stitches.

In case the crocheting has become soiled, wash it according to the label directions. Work gently. Squeeze out the water. Do not wring. Lay piece flat on a towel, smoothing it out. Arrange each piece so it measures no more than the required measurements. If the piece seems to stretch too much, keep the outline of the piece in position, but push the stitches together producing a puckered look. The unevenness will disappear as the piece dries. The piece can be dried and then blocked or it can be blocked and then allowed to dry. For some synthetic yarns and highly textured pattern stitches, this method gives better results.

Gather the Tools

A flat, padded surface is the most important piece of equipment for blocking. It should provide a large enough surface so the piece can be spread out completely. You may want a special board if you do a lot of crocheting. If not, a dressmaker's cutting board or a carpeted floor can be used. Of course you should protect the surface with a layer of plastic.

Whichever surface you decide to use, cover it with a piece of mattress covering or rug padding. Place a piece of muslin or a sheet over it. The layers should be fastened tautly in place for the best results.

To do the actual blocking, you will need rustproof pins, tape measure, firmly woven cheesecloth for pressing, and a steam iron.

Pinning

Pin the smoothed out piece to the board with the wrong side up. Keep the list of required measurements in front of you.

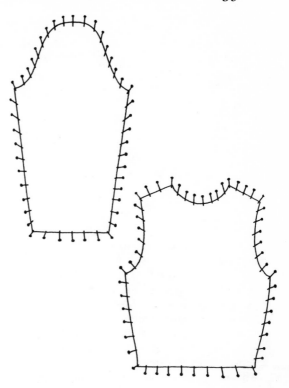

Make sure that the stitches and rows are straight. You know how important it is to keep the grain of fabric in perfect alignment. When the edges seem to be in the correct position, put a pin at each corner. Then continue pinning along the edges. Place the pins close enough together so that the edge does not become scalloped. The heads of the pins should fall away from the crocheting.

Pressing

Pressing can be done in two ways. One method allows the iron to rest on the crocheting and is called flat pressing. The other method does not allow the iron to touch the work and is referred to as steam pressing. The one you use will depend on the yarn, the stitch pattern, and the look desired. For example, if you wish to preserve a fluffy look, you should not press the crocheting flat, just as you would not want to flatten the effect of a puffy popcorn stitch by pressing it.

For flat pressing, cover the pinned piece with a press cloth. Lower the steam iron

so it comes in contact with cloth. Lower and raise the iron. Never shove it back and forth in an ironing stroke. When the piece has been completely pressed, allow it to remain in place until it is thoroughly dry. Then remove the pins.

In case there is another piece to be blocked to the identical measurements, replace pins in original position. They will provide an outline so the duplicate piece can be pinned in the same size and shape.

For steam pressing, hold the iron as close to the piece as possible without touching it. Move the iron slowly. You want the steam to penetrate the material. You can use a damp press cloth in order to produce extra steam if the yarn is very heavy. Continue to press until the crocheting is uniformly damp. Do not remove the pins until the piece is completely dry. It may need to be pressed very lightly.

Wet Blocking

When the crocheting needs to be washed or the pieces seem to be stretched out of shape, you may want to use this method. Wash the piece, handling it gently. Squeeze and roll in a turkish towel to remove moisture. Then place the piece on the blocking board. Pin in position. Allow it to dry thoroughly before removing it from the board.

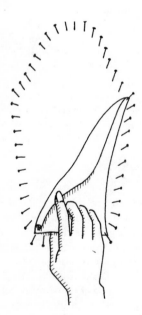

11

Decorative Details

Crocheting is decorative. The simplest stitch creates an interesting texture. Because of this, crocheted articles do not usually require embellishment except for an edging. But the ornamental feature of crocheting allows it to be used on other articles or as a trim. No doubt you have read about the designers who add an edging, a braid, a button for a special detail. You too can do this. However, when planning these decorative touches, it is most important that they seem to be a part of the basic design.

THE IMPORTANT EDGE

Crocheted edgings come in a variety of designs. Some are very simple; others, elaborate. Not only do they provide a decorative trim, but they also add firmness to the edge and give a definite definition to the outline.

When adding an edging directly to a garment, be sure the sections have been joined before beginning the crocheting at one of the seams. Of course the edging can be worked separately and then sewed to crocheted, knitted, or woven fabrics. The edging can be made of any type of yarn as long as it seems appropriate for the material to which it is to be applied.

Single Crochet

This is the easiest edging to crochet. It can be used to finish knitted or fabric articles as well as those that are crocheted. A row of single crochet stitches produces a firm edge with a chain stitch finish. It works equally well on a straight or curved edge.

To begin a single crochet edging, work with the right side toward you. Insert the hook at the right-hand edge. Put yarn around the hook and draw through to right side, leaving a short end free. Hold both ends together at the back as you insert the hook into the next stitch. Place both ends of yarn around the hook and draw through loop. This secures the thread, making a double stitch that will be counted as one on the next row. Complete the single crochet in the usual

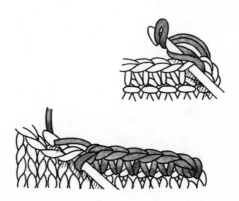

manner. Then continue across the edge taking one single crochet into each stitch. To turn a corner work two or three stitches into the corner stitch.

You may have to crochet into every other stitch or make a chain stitch between the stitches. It all depends on the thickness of the yarn in the article. You want to be sure the edge is flat and the stitches are not pulled together giving the work a curled look. Spacing the stitches correctly will avoid this situation.

Tailored Edging

To give an edge a corded finish, work **first row** of single crochet with right side of work facing the crocheter. Without turning, make the **second row,** crocheting from left to right. Note that this reverses the usual direction for working. Chain 1. Take 1 single crochet in each stitch of previous row.

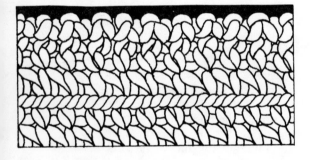

Cluster Edging

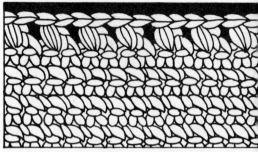

A row of cluster stitches provides a decorative but tailored trim to an edge. Work with the right side toward you. Join yarn at side edge. Crochet along edge to be trimmed by beginning with 3 chain stitches. Repeat the following procedure to end of edge. * Start by putting yarn over hook and drawing a loop through the next stitch. Do this 4 times. Then put yarn over hook and draw it through the 9 loops. Place yarn over hook and draw through last loop to form a cluster. Skip 1 stitch. * End row with a cluster in last stitch.

Shell Edging

This stitch is worked with a multiple of 5 stitches. Start with the wrong side of work toward you. Attach the yarn at side edge.

For the **first row,** work a foundation row of single crochet. Chain 4 and turn.

For the **second row,** begin with a double crochet in the first stitch. Repeat the following procedure. * Start by skipping 4 stitches. Then make a shell by taking 1 double crochet and 1 chain 3 times, following with a double crochet in same stitch. * When the last 5 stitches are reached, skip 4 stitches. Then in the last stitch, take 1 double crochet, 1 chain, and 1 double crochet.

Pineapple Stitch Edging

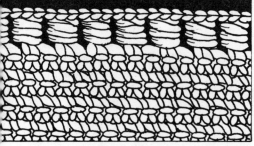

Many crochet stitches can be used for a decorative trim. This is one that gives a puffy effect along the edge. Attach the yarn at the right-hand edge with the right side of material facing you. Chain 2. Repeat the following procedure to the end of row. * Make 1 half double crochet. Then put yarn over hook, insert hook behind half double crochet, place yarn over hook again, and draw through a loop. Do this step 3 times. After this process has been completed, put yarn over hook. Draw through the 7 loops on hook. Chain 1 and skip 1 stitch. * After repeating these directions to end of work, finish with 1 half double crochet.

Popcorn Stitch Edging

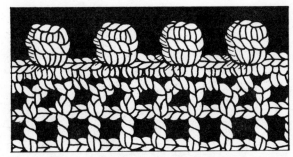

The popular popcorn stitch creates a pleasing ball-like trim. Before beginning the edging, make 1 foundation row of single crochet along edge. Then, with right side of work toward you, attach yarn at the point where foundation row begins. Take a single crochet in first 5 single crochets in foundation row. Repeat the following procedure to end of edge to be trimmed. * Chain 3. Take 5 double crochets in third chain of the just worked chain-3. Remove hook from loop. Insert it into the top of the first double crochet stitch. Pick up dropped loop and draw it through stitch. Chain 1 stitch to fasten the popcorn. Then chain 3. At the base of the popcorn, make a slip stitch in the top of the single crochet. Take a single crochet in the next 5 stitches. * Repeat until the edge is trimmed.

Fan Edging

An edge can be given a dainty scalloped trim when this edging is used. Make 1 double crochet. Chain 3. Follow with a slip stitch in third chain from hook for picot. Do this 3 times. Then make a single crochet in next stitch. Skip 2 stitches. Make 1 single crochet in next stitch.

Ruffle Edging

This attractive edging is started with the wrong side facing you. Attach the yarn at the side edge. Crochet along edge to be trimmed.

For the **first row,** chain 4. Repeat the following procedure to end of edge. * Skip 2 stitches. Take 1 double crochet in next stitch. Chain 2. * End with 1 double crochet in last stitch. Turn.

For the **second row,** work this way to construct the ruffle. Use the length of the stitch instead of the usual top of each stitch. It is known as a post. Work 5 double crochets around first post, working downward. Repeat the following sequence of stitches to end of row. * Chain 1. Work 5 double crochets down each post. * Fasten yarn and clip.

In case a wider ruffle is needed, use treble crochet in first row instead of double crochet and work 7 double crochets down each post.

SEPARATE EDGING

Strips of crocheting are often made to decorate household articles such as curtains, sheets, pillowcases, tablecloths, and place mats. Sometimes a matching insertion is also crocheted. The edging usually has one decorative edge and one straight one, whereas the insertion has two straight edges parallel to each other. Examples of both types of crocheting are given here.

In making a separate edging, the crocheting is done back and forth from the straight edge to the decorative one. This allows you to make a piece as long as is necessary.

Filet Edging

To crochet the design shown here, begin by making a chain of 32 stitches.

For the **first row,** take a double crochet in the eighth stitch from hook. Then repeat the following procedure 7 times. * Chain 2. Skip 2 chains. Make 1 double crochet in next stitch. * Chain 5 stitches and turn.

For the **second row,** make a double crochet in the first double crochet of the previous row. Repeat the following procedure 3 times. * Chain 2. Skip 2 chains. Take a double crochet in next stitch. * Then make a double crochet in next 3 stitches. Chain 2. Skip 2. Make a double crochet in next 4 stitches. Chain 2. Skip 2. Take a double crochet in last stitch. Chain 5 and turn.

For the **third row,** make a double crochet in first double crochet of previous row. Then chain 2. Skip 2. Make a double crochet in next 4 stitches. Repeat the following procedure to end of the row. * Chain 2. Skip 2. Take a double crochet in next stitch. * At end of row, chain 5 and turn.

For the **fourth row,** repeat the second row.

For the **fifth row,** make a double crochet in first double crochet of previous row. Repeat the following procedure across the row. * Chain 2. Skip 2. Take a double crochet in next stitch. * Chain 5 and turn.

For the **sixth row,** repeat the fifth row, decreasing one space at end of row and ending with a double crochet.

For the **seventh row,** decrease one space at the beginning of the row. Turn the work. Make a slip stitch in the 2 chain stitches. Chain 4. Make a double crochet in the next stitch. Chain 2. Skip 2. Double crochet in next stitch. Chain 2. Skip 2. Double crochet 4 stitches. Chain 2. Skip 2. Double crochet 4. Chain 2. Skip 2. Double crochet in last stitch. Chain 5 and turn.

For the **eighth row,** take a double crochet in first double crochet of previous row. Chain 2. Skip 2. Make 4 double crochets. Repeat the following procedure twice. * Chain 2. Make a double crochet in next stitch and decreasing row by one space. * Turn the work.

For the **ninth row,** increase one space at the beginning of the row by making a 5-stitch chain. Then take a double crochet in first stitch of previous row. Chain 2. Skip 2. Double crochet in next stitch. Chain 2. Skip 2. Double crochet in next 4 stitches. Chain 2. Skip 2. Double crochet in next 4 stitches. Chain 2. Skip 2. Finally make a double crochet in last stitch. Chain 5 and turn.

For the **tenth row,** make a double crochet in first double crochet of previous row. Repeat the following procedure across the row. * Chain 2. Skip 2. Double crochet in next stitch. * Increase 1 space at end by making a chain of 5 stitches. Make a slip stitch in same stitch as last double crochet. Turn the work. Take slip stitches in 3 chain stitches.

For the **eleventh row,** chain 5 stitches. Make a double crochet in third slip stitch, increasing work by 1 space. Repeat the following procedure across the row. * Chain 2. Skip 2. Take a double crochet in next stitch. *

Repeat the second through eleventh rows until you have crocheted a length of edging the required length.

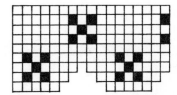

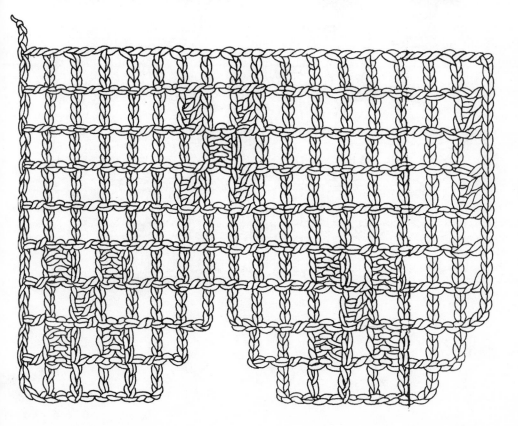

Matching Insertion

Start by making 26 chain stitches.

For the **first row,** work 1 double crochet in the eighth stitch from hook. Then repeat the following procedure 5 times. * Chain 2. Skip 2 chain stitches. Double crochet in next chain. * End by chaining 4 stitches. Then turn.

For the **second row,** work 1 double crochet in first double crochet of previous row. Make a double crochet in next 4 stitches. Repeat the following procedure to end of row. * Chain 2. Skip 2. Double crochet in next stitch. * End by making 4 chain stitches and turn.

For the **third row,** work 1 double crochet in first double crochet of previous row. Repeat the following procedure twice. * Chain 2. Skip 2. Double crochet in next stitch. * Then make a double crochet in the next 3 stitches. Continue by repeating the following procedure to end of row. * Chain 2. Skip 2. Double crochet in next stitch. * Chain 4 stitches and turn.

For the **fourth row,** repeat row 2.

For the **fifth row,** work 1 double crochet in first double crochet of previous row. Repeat the following procedure to end of row. * Chain 2. Skip 2. Double crochet in next stitch. * Chain 4 and turn.

For the **sixth row,** repeat the fifth row.

Continue to crochet this pattern by repeating the second through the sixth rows until the required length is reached.

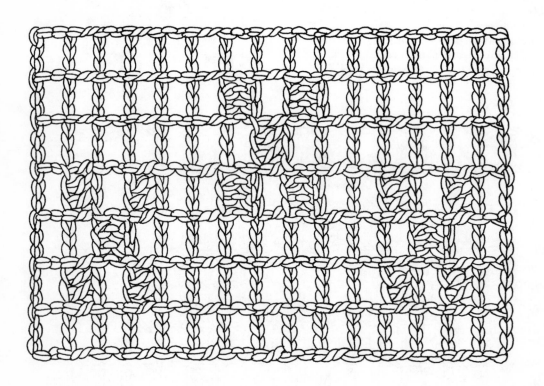

Filet Frill

This decorative piece of crocheting might be considered a wide edging. It creates a lovely lacy collar that can be most flattering.

To make the frill, chain the desired number of stitches for the foundation.

For the **first row,** work a single crochet in each chain.

For the **second row,** turn the work and then repeat the following procedure. * Chain 5. Skip 1 single crochet. Take a single crochet in next single crochet. * End with a chain-2 and a double crochet in the first single crochet you made.

For the **third row,** after turning the work, repeat the following procedure. * Chain 5. Make a single crochet in next loop. * End with a chain-2 and a double crochet in last loop.

For the **fourth and fifth rows,** repeat the third row.

For the **sixth row,** turn the work and then repeat the following procedure. * Chain 6. Make a single crochet in the first loop. * End with a chain-2 and a double crochet in the last loop.

For the **seventh, eighth, and ninth rows,** repeat the sixth row.

For the **tenth row,** turn the work and then repeat the following procedure. * Chain 7. Make a single crochet in first loop. * End with a chain-2 and a double crochet in last loop.

For the **eleventh, twelfth, and thirteenth rows,** repeat the tenth row.

FRINGED EDGE

Fringe always seems to add a festive air to an edge. It can be made in several ways. A few are mentioned here.

Tassel Fringe

This is probably the easiest fringe to make. Each tassel is made separately. A series of tassels creates the fringed effect. The spacing depends on the effect you wish to produce. The length and thickness of the tassel can also vary depending on the fashion or appropriateness to the item you are embellishing.

To make the fringe, cut strands of yarn to the desired length. When estimating the length, remember each strand will be folded in half and that a certain amount of the length will be taken up as it is looped through the material. It is best to make a sample tassel before cutting all of the strands of yarn.

Pick up the required number of strands for a tassel. Fold strands in half. Insert a crochet hook in one of the edge stitches (A). Draw the folded end of the strands through the stitch. Then draw the yarn ends through the loop (B). Pull ends to tighten, forming a knot. Repeat the procedure along the edge using the desired spacing. If the fringe does not seem to be even in length when finished, cut the ends.

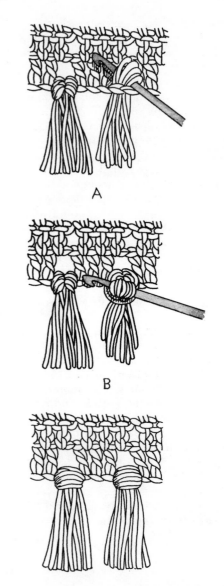

A

B

Chain Fringe

This method for making fringe produces a series of sturdy cords along the edge. To prepare edge for fringe, work with wrong side toward you. Attach yarn at side edge.

For the **first row,** work a row of single crochet along edge. Chain 1 and turn.

For the **second row,** slip stitch in first stitch. Repeat the following procedure to end of row. * Start by chaining 12 stitches. Turn. Crochet back along chain, working 1 slip stitch in each chain stitch. Slip stitch in next stitch. *

The length of the fringe can be changed by varying the number of chain stitches.

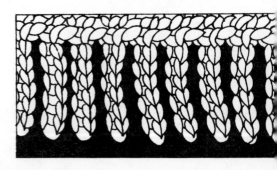

Looped Fringe

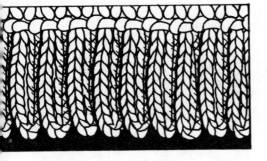

Crocheted chains are looped to form this decorative trim. Attach yarn at side edge with the wrong side facing you.

For the **first row,** work a row of single crochet along edge to be trimmed. Chain 1 and turn.

For the **second row,** make a single crochet in first stitch. Repeat the following procedure to end of row. * Begin by making 18 chain stitches. Take 1 single crochet in next stitch. *

The length of the fringe can be changed by varying the number of stitches in chain.

SCALLOPED EFFECT

No extra stitches are needed to create this curving edge. It just happens as you crochet this stitch pattern.

Scallop Pattern

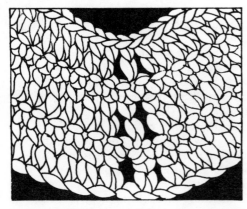

Begin this wavy design with a foundation chain the required length. Use a multiple of 14 stitches plus 13, with an additional 1 chain.

For the **first row,** make a double crochet in fourth chain from hook. Follow with a double crochet in each of next 3 chains. Repeat the following sequence of stitches. * Make 3 double crochets in next chain and 1 double crochet in each of next 5 chains. Skip 1 chain. Take 1 double crochet in next chain. Skip 1 chain. Make 1 double crochet in each of next 5 chains. * At last 6 chains, take 3 double crochets in next chain. Then 1 double crochet in each of last 5 chains. Turn.

For the **second row,** chain 1. Skip first 2 stitches. Take 1 single crochet in each of next 4 stitches. Repeat the following sequence of stitches. * Make 3 single crochets in next stitch and 1 single crochet in each of next 5 stitches. Skip one stitch. Take a single crochet in next stitch. Skip 1 stitch. Make a single crochet in each of next 5 stitches. * At the last 7 stitches, make 3 single crochets in next stitch. Then take 1 single crochet in each of next 4 stitches. Skip 1 stitch. Make 1 single crochet in top of turning chain. Turn.

For the **third row,** chain 3. Skip first 2 stitches. Take 1 double crochet in each of next 4 stitches. Repeat the following sequence of stitches. * Make 3 double crochets in next stitch and 1 double crochet in each of next 5 stitches. Skip 1 stitch. Take 1 double crochet in next stitch. Skip 1 stitch. Make 1 double crochet in each of next 5 stitches. * At the last 7 stitches, take 3 double crochets in next stitch. Make 1 double crochet in each of next 4 stitches. Skip 1 stitch. Take 1 double crochet in top of turning chain. Turn.

Repeat the **second and third rows** until work is completed.

RIB THE EDGE

When you first look at this ribbing you may think it has been knitted. The ridges are definite, providing an interesting finish when a firm but somewhat elastic one is needed. One of the easiest ribbings to make is the Ridge Stitch.

Ridge Stitch Ribbing

In making the ribbing, the work is done horizontally, then turned, and the pattern stitch is crocheted along one side edge, producing the vertical effect.

For the foundation chain, use the number of chains needed to produce ribbing of the desired depth.

For the **first row,** skip 1 chain and then repeat the following procedure. * Make 1 single crochet in each chain. * Chain 1 and turn.

For the **second row,** repeat the following procedure. * Make 1 single crochet in the back loop of each stitch. * Chain 1 and turn.

Repeat the second row to make the pattern. Continue until ribbing is the required length for the garment edge on which it is to be used. Secure the yarn. Then sew the ends of the ribbing together and crochet the pattern stitch along one side of the ridge pattern.

Afghan Ribbing

This pattern stitch seems to produce a softer ribbing with ridges that are less distinct. It is worked in afghan stitch, making it appropriate for a garment made with this type of crocheting.

Begin by using a foundation chain the required length. Use a multiple of 2 stitches.

For the **first row,** use a basic afghan stitch. Skip 1 chain. Then repeat the following procedure. * Insert hook in next chain and draw up a loop. * Leave loop on hook.

For the **second row,** put yarn over hook. Draw through 1 loop. Repeat the following procedure. * Put yarn over hook. Draw through 2 loops. *

For the **third row,** chain 1. Then insert the hook through the next vertical stitch loop and draw up a loop. Repeat the following procedure. * Insert hook in next chain and draw up a loop. Put yarn over hook. Draw through 2 loops. * This sequence of stitches creates a knit-purl look.

For the **fourth row,** put yarn over hook. Draw through 1 loop. Then repeat the following procedure. * Place yarn over hook. Draw through 2 loops. *

Repeat the **third and fourth rows** for the required depth of ribbing.

BRAIDS AND TRIMS

Braid adds a decorative touch to an otherwise plain texture. When it is crocheted it can produce an interesting effect. Braids can be made in various ways. A few are mentioned here.

Double Chain Stitch Braid

This stitch can be used in a variety of ways. It makes an excellent foundation when a firm one is required. Or it can be used for a narrow braid or cord, making an attractive trimming. Single and chain stitches are combined.

After making a slip knot, chain 2 stitches. Then work a single crochet in the second chain from the hook. Repeat the following procedure. * Insert the hook under the left loop of the single crochet. Put yarn over hook (A). Draw it through the loop, leaving 2 loops on the hook (B). Put yarn over hook and draw through the 2 loops (C). * Continue until the required length is crocheted.

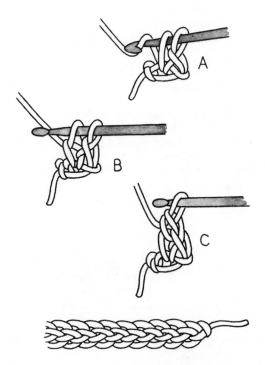

Twisted Braid

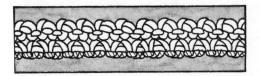

This trim does have an interesting twisted look. To attain the effect the hook is manipulated in a different way.

For the **foundation row,** use any number of chain stitches.

For the **first row,** skip the first stitch. Then repeat the following procedure. * Insert hook in the next chain. Draw up a loop. Then twist hook horizontally and clockwise for 1 complete turn. Put yarn over hook. Draw through 2 loops. * At end of row, chain 1. Continue around opposite side of chain. Repeat the directions between asterisks in each loop on that side. When completed, fasten the thread.

Woven Braid

An entirely different look in crocheting is found in this trim. The surface has a textural quality that resembles fabric.

To make the braid, start with 6 chain stitches.

For the **first row,** repeat the following procedure. * Insert hook in the first stitch. Put yarn over hook. Draw through a loop. * Keep all loops on hook.

For the **second row,** do not turn work. Repeat the following procedure. * Put yarn over hook. Draw through 2 loops, inserting hook under each horizontal strand. * For last loop, insert hook horizontally under last vertical strand.

Repeat the **first and second rows.**

Sawtooth Braid

For a more decorative braid this one could be used. It resembles rickrack braid.

Begin with 3 chain stitches.

For the **first row,** make a treble crochet and a double crochet in first chain stitch. Turn work.

For the **second row,** make 2 chains. Then in double crochet of previous row work a treble crochet and a double crochet. Turn work.

Repeat second row until the required length of braid has been made.

Crescent Braid

This braid creates a pretty, scalloped effect dotted with eyelets. It could add an interesting touch to an otherwise plain article.

Start with 5 chain stitches. Join with a slip stitch to form a ring.

In ring, work 6 double crochets, 4 chains, and 1 double crochet.

Then repeat the following procedure. * Turn work. In 4-chain space, work 6 double crochets, 4 chains, and 1 double chain. * Continue this way until braid is the required length.

Ring Trim

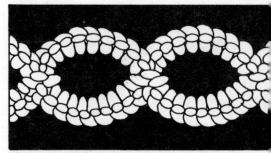

This trim might be considered a type of braid. Its openness allows it to be used for a decorative effect. It is an easy-to-make trim that can be made in varying sizes depending on how the yarn is wound. For a small size, wrap yarn around top of left thumb 3 times. This becomes the foundation for the ring. Then make single crochet stitches into center of ring until one half is covered. Remove ring from thumb so that the second ring can be started. Do not break yarn. Make the second and remaining rings in the same way. When the required length is reached, crochet completely around last ring. Continue to crochet around unfinished half of each ring until starting point is reached. Take a slip stitch in first single crochet. Fasten yarn and clip.

Covered Rings

Plastic rings can be covered for a decorative effect. A single ring or a series of rings can be used. Holding the yarn in back of the ring, pull the yarn through the ring, forming a loop. Work single crochet stitches over the ring. As the stitches are made, also cover the end of the yarn.

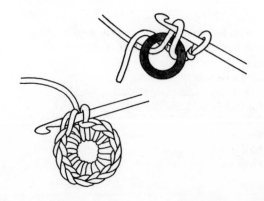

For **one ring,** continue until ring is completely covered. Slip stitch in first single crochet. Fasten yarn and clip.

For a **series of rings,** cover half of the first ring. Do not fasten yarn. Instead continue single crochet around one half of the ring and as many other rings as required. On the last ring, continue completely around, covering it. Then work over the uncovered half of each ring. When all rings are covered, make a slip stitch in the first single crochet that was made over first ring.

Motif for Appliqué

Another interesting way to use crochet is in a motif that can be applied to an article. Motifs can be made in many designs, sizes, and shapes. They seem to create a three-dimensional effect that contributes a gayness to the article they embellish. Directions for one design are given here.

Floral Motif

Begin with a 5-stitch chain. To form the foundation circle, join with a slip stitch.

For the **first round,** make 2 chain stitches. Then take 11 half double crochet stitches in circle. Follow with a slip stitch in top of the second chain.

For the **second round,** repeat the following sequence of stitches 5 times. * Chain 7. Take 1 half double crochet in second chain from hook. Follow with 1 half double crochet in each of the next 4 chains. Then slip stitch in bottom of chain. Also slip stitch in back loop only of next 2 stitches. * Each sequence of stitches produces one petal.

For the **third round,** repeat the following sequence of stitches around each petal. * Take one single crochet in each chain of petal. At top of petal, take 5 single crochet stitches in each half double crochet along other side of petal. Slip stitch in stitch between petals. * Continue around each petal. End with slip stitch in stitch between first and last petal. Fasten yarn. Run yarn through flower so it is inconspicuous. Clip end.

Tassels and Pompons

Another bit of decoration that adds a finishing touch is the tassel and pompon. No doubt you have seen a scarf or stole that needed something to produce the right look. A pompon on a beret or a row of tassels at the ends of a scarf can add the missing touch.

To make a tassel, cut two pieces of yarn about 7 inches (18 cm) long to use as a tie. Take a 4-inch (10 cm) piece of cardboard and wrap yarn around it as many times as required. At one end, draw one of the short pieces of yarn under the wrapped yarn. Tie it securely, pulling the strands together. Cut the yarn at the other edge. Wrap the remaining short piece of yarn around the looped end twice and tie securely. If necessary, trim the ends evenly.

To make a pompon, follow the directions for winding the yarn for a tassel. Remember the pompon is fuller than a tassel so there will be many more wrappings of the yarn. Then slip a piece of yarn under the wrapped yarn and tie it tightly. Cut the yarn at the other end and you have a pompon. Shake it so that each strand stands up. Trim the ends for a rounded effect.

DECORATIVE BUTTONS

Crocheted buttons can add a fashion touch. They look attractive on fabric as well as on knitted and crocheted garments. Sometimes they create a new look on an article that needs rejuvenation. Two versions are shown here. One duplicates the popular ball button.

Ball Button

The size and thickness of the button depends on the weight of the yarn. Experiment until you get the right three-dimensional effect.

Begin by making 3 chain stitches. To form the foundation circle, join the chain with a slip stitch.

For the **first round,** chain 1. Make 8 single crochets in ring. Slip-stitch to begin chain.

For the **second round,** chain 1. Repeat the following procedure 4 times.
* Take 1 single crochet in next stitch. Then 2 single crochets in next stitch. *
Then slip-stitch to begin chain. Pull the short end of yarn up through the center hole.

For the **third round,** chain 1. Repeat the following procedure 16 times.
* Then insert the hook through center hole. Pull up a long loop (A). Put yarn over hook and draw through 2 loops. *
End with a slip stitch to begin chain.

For the **fourth round,** begin with 1 single crochet in every other stitch (B).

To finish the button, clip yarn, leaving an end about 12 inches (30.5 cm) long. With a tapestry needle, take an overcast stitch in each outside loop. Then draw stitches toward center. Tie together the 2 ends of yarn. In order to be able to sew the button to an article, add some stitches to the back, forming an X.

Ring Button

To make a flatter button, begin with a plastic ring. Select one that is ⅛ inch (3 mm) smaller than you want the finished button to be.

Begin by making a slip knot. The stitches are made by inserting the hook through the ring so they can be made around the ring. Then work around the ring until it is completely covered. To close the ring, take a slip stitch in first stitch.

To finish the button, clip yarn, leaving an end about 12 inches (30.5 cm) long. With a tapestry needle, take an overcast stitch in each outside loop. Then draw stitches toward center. Tie together the 2 ends of yarn. In order to be able to sew the button to an article, add a yarn shank by making some stitches in the form of an X.

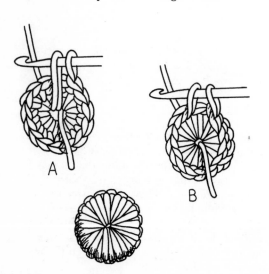

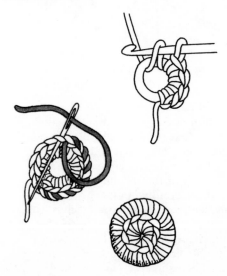

MULTICOLOR CROCHET

One of the most fascinating ways to add a decorative touch is through the use of color. Combining colors for a beautiful effect makes one feel so creative. If you haven't experienced this, please do. You will be surprised how exciting it can be.

By working a stitch pattern in different colors, you can create interesting effects. Several suggestions, using 2 or 3 colors, are mentioned.

Multicolor Strands

The easiest way to combine colors is by using several together as if they were one. This works nicely with one of the finer threads or cords. Recently I saw a place mat in which 14 different threads were used. They were beautifully blended so that the allover effect was lovely.

The actual crocheting was done with three strands of thread using single crochet. One color remained constant with the other 2 strands changed at random, one at a time. You can decide when you want to change colors. It all depends on the effect you are creating.

When changing one of the color threads, insert the hook in the next single crochet to be worked. Then put the 3 strands around the hook and draw up a loop. Bring the color strand to be changed to back, and cut it off 6 inches (15 cm) from hook. Then put the remaining 2 strands around the hook. Lay the new color strand across the hook leaving a 6-inch (15 cm) end at back. Pull the 3 strands through both loops on the hook.

Tricolor Stripes

Begin with a foundation chain the required length. Use a multiple of 4 stitches plus 1, with an additional 1 chain. Work with 3 colors—dark (A), medium (B), light (C), using each for alternating 2-row bands.

For the **first row,** use the dark color (A). Take 1 single crochet in second chain from hook. Make another single crochet in each chain to end of row. Turn.

For the **second row,** continue with the

same color. Begin by making 3 chains. Take 1 double crochet in first stitch. Repeat the following procedure to end of row. * Skip 3 stitches. Take 3 double crochets in next stitch. * At the last 4 stitches, skip 3 stitches. Take 2 double crochets in last stitch. Turn.

For the **third row,** attach medium color (B). Chain 2. Repeat the following procedure to end of row. * Make 3 double crochets in center of 3 stitches skipped in previous row. * End with 1 half double crochet in center of chain-3. Turn.

For the **fourth row,** continue with the same color. Chain 3. Take 1 double crochet in space between half double crochet and next group of double crochets. Insert hook in center of double-crochet group 2 rows below. Make 3 double crochets between each double-crochet group. End with 2 double crochets in space between last group and chain. Turn.

For the **fifth row,** attach light color (C). Chain 2. Take 3 double crochets in center of double-crochet group 2 rows below. End with 1 half double crochet in center of chain 3. Turn.

For the **sixth row,** follow directions for the fourth row, continuing to use the light color (C).

For the **seventh row,** follow directions for the fifth row, using dark color (A).

For the **eighth row,** follow directions for the fourth row, using the dark color (A).

For the **ninth row,** return to the medium color (B), using the directions for the fifth row.

Repeat the **fourth through ninth rows** until work is completed, retaining the same sequence of colors.

Tricolor Zigzag Pattern

The ripple pattern is most effective when worked in 3 colors. After deciding on color scheme, make a foundation chain the required length with 1 color (A). Use a multiple of 14 stitches plus 13, with an additional 1 chain.

For the **first row,** continue with color (A). Make 1 double crochet in fourth chain from hook. Then make 1 double

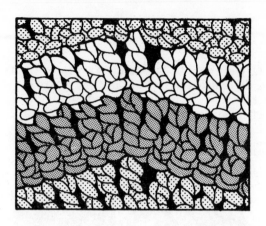

crochet in each of next 3 chains. Repeat the following sequence of stitches.
* Take 3 double crochets in next chain and 1 double crochet in each of next 5 chains. Skip 1 chain. Make 1 double crochet in next chain. Skip 1 chain. Take 1 double crochet in each of next 5 chains.
* At the last 6 chains, take 3 double crochets in next chain and 1 double crochet in each of last 5 chains. Turn.

For the **second row,** continue with same color (A). Chain 1. Skip 2 stitches. Take one single crochet in each of next 4 stitches. Repeat the following sequence of stitches. * Take 3 single crochets in next stitch. Make 1 single crochet in each of next 5 stitches. Skip 1 stitch. Make 1 single crochet in next stitch. Skip 1 stitch. Take 1 single crochet in each of next 5 stitches. * At last 7 stitches, take 3 single crochets in next stitch and 1 single crochet in each of next 4 stitches. Skip 1 stitch. Take 1 single crochet in top of turning chain. Chain 3. Turn.

For the **third and fourth rows,** change to second color (B). Use directions for first and second rows.

For the **fifth and sixth rows,** change to first color (A). Use directions for first and second rows.

For the **seventh and eighth rows,** change to third color (C). Use directions for first and second rows.

For the **ninth and tenth rows,** change to color (A). Use directions for first and second rows.

Continue in this way until work is completed. The width of the stripes can be adjusted to create different effects.

Woven Crochet

Chain Stitch Overlay

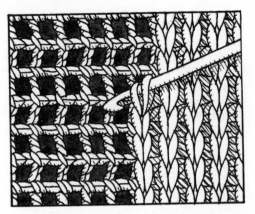

By interlacing yarn through a crochet mesh, a woven effect is created. It may be varied using different colors, size of mesh and width of stripes. A mesh made of double crochet stitches and chain-1 space is suggested. Begin with a foundation chain the required length. Use a multiple of 2 stitches plus 1, with an additional 2 chains.

For the **first row,** make 1 double crochet in fifth chain from hook. Repeat the following procedure to end of row. * Chain 1. Skip 1 chain. Make 1 double crochet in next chain. * Chain 4 and turn.

For the **second row,** skip 2 stitches. Repeat the following procedure to end of row. * Make 1 double crochet in next double crochet. Chain 1. * End with 1 double crochet in third stitch of turning chain. Chain 4 and turn.

Repeat **second row** until mesh is completed.

If a striped effect is required, introduce a different color at the beginning of an appropriate row.

For the weaving, use 3 strands of yarn. Weave over and under the chain bars, alternating from row to row. Use a blunt needle.

In this pattern stitch, color can be introduced not only in the background but also in the chained overlay. This allows you to create both striped and plaid designs. You can decide which one you prefer, but do plan the color pattern before you begin.

The resulting fabric can be used for various articles such as place mats, rugs, pillow covers, or skirts. It all depends on the weight and type of yarn you select.

Begin by preparing the mesh background. To do this, you can use the directions for the mesh for woven crochet.

For the **first row** of overlay chains, work with two strands of yarn. Make a slip knot. Then with the right side of the mesh facing you and the yarn held in back of it, pull a loop through the first space in the lower right corner. Follow by inserting the hook in the space directly above it. Draw a loop through the space and the loop on the hook. Continue crocheting this way to the top of the mesh.

For the **second row** of chain stitch, begin again at the lower edge, and continue upward as you did for the first row.

You can make as many chained rows as you wish, but be careful to maintain an even tension throughout. If you don't, the background may be pulled out of shape.

Patterned Crochet

This type of crocheting is often referred to as jacquard crocheting. A definite design is crocheted. Although it is possible to create or reproduce different designs such as flowers, the results are not always the most satisfying. Simple geometric patterns seem more effective, especially when worked in single crochet stitches.

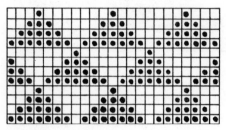

Sometimes a *graph chart* is used instead of the usual directions. Each square equals a stitch; each line, a row. Usually a vacant square indicates the background color with symbols or colored squares denoting the contrasting colors. A key accompanies the chart, which you use as a guide in interpreting the design.

To *follow a chart*, begin at the lower edge and read from right to left for the right-side rows, and from left to right for wrong-side rows. In case you see a cross stitch or other needlework design you like, be sure to make a sample before you attempt a full-scale project. Designs of this type do not adapt well to crochet because of the elongated nature of the stitch.

Although this type of crocheting is easy as far as the making of the stitch, you may have a problem handling the strand of yarn that isn't to be worked with. To alleviate this situation, study the special techniques mentioned here.

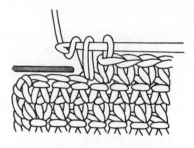

To introduce a color at beginning of row, lay the yarn over the last few stitches of the row below. Continue to work with the first color, covering the end of the new yarn. Crochet with the first color to the last two loops of the final stitch. Then pull the new color through these two loops.

To introduce a color in mid-row, use the same method. Lay the end of the new yarn over the row below. Do this a few stitches before you need to use the new color (A). Continue to work with the first color, covering the end of the new color. Use the first color until you are ready to crochet the last 2 loops of the final stitch. Then pull the new color through these two loops (B).

One advantage to using this method is that the crocheting has a neat finish. No dangling ends to thread through the work.

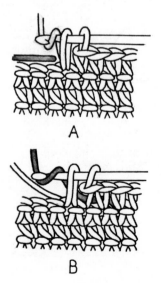

A

B

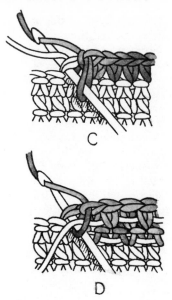

C

D

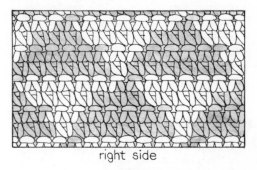

Drop the first color so it is in back and to the left of the second color. Put yarn over hook and draw through 2 loops with the second color.

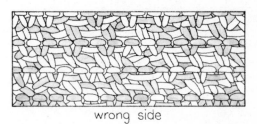

right side

wrong side

To work over more than 3 stitches, catch the unused yarn into the crocheting at every other stitch. This creates a very neat finish. The strands are less likely to be snagged or pulled. Also it is easier to keep the tension even, but do be careful not to exert any extra tension to the yarn. You do not want the work to be puckered.

When working on a *right-side row,* put hook into the stitch, then under the yarn you are not working with, and finally catch the working yarn (C). Pull up a loop. Complete the stitch.

When working on a *wrong-side row,* put hook under the yarn that you aren't working with. Then pass it through stitch. Pick up working yarn with the hook (D). Pull up a loop and finish stitch.

The look of the back of the crocheting should always be considered. The method you use for treating the different yarns depends on whether the back will be seen. For instance, if you are making a pillow cover, the back finish is not as important as if you are making an unlined jacket.

When you are creating a jacquard pattern and the finish is not important, you can work in this manner.

To change color on a right-side row, crochet with the first color to the last two loops of the final stitch in the design.

To change color on a wrong-side row, use first color to the final 2 loops of the last stitch. Drop first color on front and to the right of second color. Put second color around hook and draw through 2 loops.

If you decide to make a reversible-type fabric, then you will want to use the different yarns in another way. But before deciding to use this finish, remember that more yarn is needed than if you cut and wove the ends through the work, and the finished product will be heavier. However, it is much quicker to do. Another thing to remember is that although the yarn that is carried across the back is covered, it can be seen on the right side between the stitches. Sometimes this produces an unattractive effect, depending on the design and colors you are using. In order to accommodate the bulk of the unused yarn, it is best to use a hook one size larger than the directions suggest.

To carry the unused yarn for a reversible effect, place it on top of the previous row as you crochet stitches in the contrasting color.

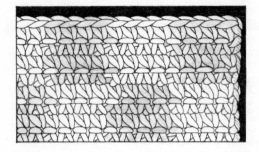

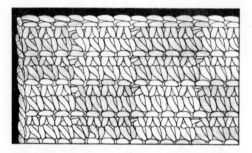

the stitches that can be used this way is the cross stitch. Applied to a basic afghan stitch fabric, it can be most effective. However, the attractiveness of the motif depends on the regularity of the stitches. Be sure the length and slant of the stitches are even.

In working the stitches, make 2 separate rows of single diagonal stitches. Do this by bringing up the needle just below the crossbars of the afghan stitch at the lower left-hand corner of the design line. Pull through the yarn leaving an end about 4 inches (10 cm) long. Insert the needle, coming up behind both crossbars of the stitch. Keep the needle in a vertical position. Continue until the row of single slanting stitches is completed.

Then, working from right to left, make a second row of diagonal stitches, crossing those in first row. Insert the needle at the ends of the stitches in the first row.

To make the next row, thread the needle through the fabric behind the crossbars. Continue until the design is completed.

Clip the yarn. Weave ends into the fabric. Be sure the stitches do not show on the back.

To change colors, pull a loop of the second color through the last 2 loops of the final stitch in the first color.

To discontinue a color, crochet it to the last 2 loops of the final stitch. Draw up a loop with the new color. Leaving a 6-inch (15 cm) end, clip the first color. Thread the yarn end through 4 to 6 stitches of the color that matches it, when the article is completed. Cut off the remaining end close to the work.

If you decide not to carry a color from design to design, the method previously mentioned can be used. It is frequently used when unused yarn must be carried for some distance, the color change is made at the end of a row, or for motifs with an irregular outline. In threading the yarn through the stitches, make sure it does not show on the right side.

Embroidered Detail

Another way of introducing color to a design is through the use of embroidery. A simple touch of color can create interest in an otherwise plain fabric. One of

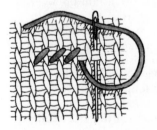

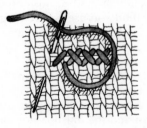

12

Crocheting for Everyone

If variety is the spice of life, certainly crocheting contributes to it. With a simple hook and some thread, hundreds and hundreds of items can be created. They can range from the frivolous to the practical, the beautiful to the bizarre. A wacky toy, a colorful pot holder, a fragile shawl, a sturdy rug, a luxurious jacket, a weather-defying poncho are just a few of the articles you can create. It is this versatility that produces pleasurable moments for so many.

Crocheting can produce something for everyone from the baby to the grandfather or even the pet dog. The article can look as right in the morning as in the evening; as appropriate at school and office as at a festive occasion. It can provide a decorative touch as well as a protective covering. Although in the past crocheting has probably been thought of more frequently in connection with household articles, it now has a place in fashion. Crocheted jackets, tops, and accessories can be found in the smartest shops. But whatever way a crocheted article is to be used, it is important that the design, the yarn, and the stitches seem appropriate for the wearer or the house in which it is to be seen.

On the following pages, you will find a variety of articles to crochet. Some are easy to make whereas others require more skill. Some can be crocheted quickly; others are more time-consuming, although they may still be simple to construct. Whichever grouping they are in, all of them have been selected to make your crocheting experience a pleasure.

In order that your crocheting will have satisfying results, be sure to follow the directions carefully. They have been prepared by various yarn manufacturers with great effort to provide you with accurate and complete instructions. However, they caution you that they cannot be responsible for variations in the work of individual crocheters or for typographical errors. They warn you to check the gauge carefully and to substitute any size hook that will give the required stitch gauge. If you don't heed this admonition the results of your crocheting may be less than gratifying.

SWEATER WITH STRIPES

Stripes give this classic design a new look. Of course if you wish, you can make the sweater in a solid color.

Information to Check Before You Start

Sizing: Directions are written for Small (8–10). Changes for Medium (12–14) and Large (16) are in parentheses.
· Finished Measurement at Underarm:
—Approx. 35 (37, 39) inches
Materials: The sweater is made of Unger's Roly Sport Yarn in 1¾ oz. balls. You need:
—5 (6, 7) balls, White (A)
—2 (2, 3) balls, Blue (B)
—1 (1, 2) balls, Gold (C)
Tool: Aluminum Crochet Hook—Size G
Gauge: 4 dc = 1 inch
2 dc rows = 1 inch

Directions to Follow

Back. Lower Border: NOTE that border is worked from seam edge to seam edge. With A, ch 17.

Row 1: Hdc in 4th ch from hook, hdc in each ch—15 hdc, counting turning ch. Ch 2, turn.

Row 2: Ch 2 on turn is counted as first hdc, * Post hdc around next st (Post hdc—Phdc—yo hook, insert hook in space before st, going from front to back; bring hook across back of st and out in space after st, going from back to front; draw up a loop and work off as a hdc); rep from * to within last st, hdc in last st. Ch 2, turn. Rep Row 2 until there are 26 (28, 30) ribs, or desired size for waistband—it should meas approx. 26 (28, 30) inches.

Body. Row 1: Ch 3 (counts as 1 dc) and work 71 (75, 79) dc along row edge of lower border—72 (76, 80) dc. Ch 3, turn.

Row 2: Ch 3 on turn counts as first dc, dc in each dc. Ch 3, turn. Rep Row 2 until piece meas 15 inches from beg, or desired length.

Beg **Stripe Pat** as follows: This starts the armhole. **Row 1:** Right side. With B, work dc in each st. Ch 2, turn.

Row 2: With B, ch 2 on turn counts as first st, work Phdc across, end hdc in end st, drawing through C when working off last 2 lps of last st. Ch 2 C, turn.

Row 3: With C, hdc in each st, end draw through A when working off last 2 lps of last st. Ch 2 A, turn.

Row 4: With A, hdc in each st. Draw through B. Ch 2 B, turn.

Row 5: With B, hdc in each st. Draw through A. Ch 3 A, turn.

Row 6: With A, dc in each st. Draw through C. Ch 2 C, turn.

Row 7: With C, hdc in each st. Draw through B. Ch 2 B, turn.

Row 8: With B, hdc in each st. Draw through C. Ch 2 C, turn.

Row 9: With C, hdc in each st. Draw through A. Ch 3 A, turn.

Row 10: With A, dc in each st. Draw through C. Ch 2 C, turn.

Row 11: With C, hdc in each st. Ch 2, turn.

Row 12: With C, as Row 2.

Row 13: With B, as Row 3.

Row 14: With A, as Row 4.

Row 15: With C, as Row 5.

Row 16: With A, as Row 6.

Row 17: With B, as Row 7.

Row 18: With C, as Row 8.

Row 19: With B, as Row 9.

Row 20: With A, as Row 10.

NOTE: Always work turning ch with the next color to be used. Rep these 20 rows for Stripe Pat until armhole meas 7½ (8, 8½) inches. Fasten off.

Front: Work same as back until 2 rows less than back to start of Stripe Pat—72, (76, 80) sts.

Shape Neck: Work 33 (35, 37) sts, dec 1 st over next 2 sts (neck dec—yo draw up a lp in next st, retain on hook, draw up a lp in next st, yo draw through all lps on hook). Work on left front side only. Turn. Dec 1 st at neck edge, complete row.

Change to Stripe Pat and dec 1 st at neck edge on Rows 3, 5, 7, 9, 11, 13, 15, 17, 19 (11 neck decreases in all)—24 (26, 28) sts. Work even in pat to shoulder as for back. Fasten off. Skip 2 center sts at neck, attach yarn and work other side to correspond, reversing shaping.

Sleeves: With A, ch 12. **Row 1:** Hdc in 4th ch from hook, hdc in each ch. Ch 2, turn—10 hdc, counting turning ch. Work in Phdc as for lower back border until there are 12 (13, 14) ribs. Ch 2 and work 38 (40, 42) dc along row edge of cuff rib.

Next row, work in dc, inc 8 sts evenly spaced—46 (48, 50) sts. Work with A in dc and inc 1 st each end every 1½ inches for 4 (5, 6) times—54 (58, 62) sts.

At the same time, when 11 inches from beg (this includes cuff), change to Stripe Pat. Work even until 19 inches from beg, or desired length. Fasten off.

Finishing: Weave shoulder seams.

Weave straight edge of sleeves to armholes. Weave side and undersleeve seams.

Neckband: With B, ch 8. Row 1: Hdc in 4th ch from hook, hdc in each ch. Ch 2, turn. Work even in Phdc on 6 sts as for lower back border until piece meas from center back of neck to within the 2 center sts of front V (stretch slightly when measuring).

Shape V: Row 1: Work ch 2 on turn and 3 Phdc, 1 post sc in next st, sl st in last st, turn, sl 1, post sc, Phdc to end. Ch 2, turn. Work even in Phdc to correspond to other side of V to center back of neck. Fasten off.

Sew band to neck, making sure shaped V is at center of V. Weave both ends of band at center back.

DO NOT BLOCK. Wet block. (Wet with cold water. Lay on a towel to measurements. Dry away from heat and sun.)

COPYRIGHT © 1981 WILLIAM UNGER & CO., INC.

CREW NECK PULLOVER

This sweater, with its simple lines, takes on a new look when it is crocheted. The textural quality of the stitches provides the interest.

Information to Check Before You Start

Sizing: Directions are for Size 8. Changes for Sizes 10, 12, and 14 are in parentheses.

Material: For this sweater, Susan Bates® Sport Yarn in 2 oz. skeins is used. You need 6 (6, 7, 7) in color desired.

Tool: Crochet Hook in Size G or 6 (4¼ mm).

Gauge: 4 dc = 1 inch
3 rows = 1½ inches

Directions to Follow

Back: Ribbing—Ch 12. Sc in 2nd ch from hk and in ea ch across, ch 1, turn.

Next Row: Working thru *back lp only*, sc in ea st across, ch 1, turn. Rep last row until piece measures 15¼ (15¾, 16½, 17½) inches. Do not turn.

Next Row: Ch 3 (counts as 1st dc), working along long side of ribbing, work 66 (68, 71, 75) dc evenly spaced across, turn.

Next Row: Ch 3 (counts as 1st dc), dc in 2nd dc and in ea dc across, end dc in top of ch 3, turn. Rep last row on 67 (69, 72, 76) sts until piece measures 15 (15, 16, 16) inches from beg, or desired length to underarm.

Shape Raglan: Sl st across 1st 4 (4, 5, 5) sts, work across to within last 4 (4, 5, 5) sts, ch 3, turn. Work 1 row even, then dec 1 st ea end every row 20 (21, 21, 22) times. Tie off.

Front: Work same as back until there are 31 (31, 32, 34) sts.

Shape Neck: Keeping decs at arm edge, work across 1st 10 (10, 10, 11) sts, turn. Dec 1 st at neck edge and arm edge every row until 1 st rems. Tie off. Sk center 11 (11, 12, 12) sts of last long row. Attach yarn in next st, ch 2, then complete row, dec'ing at arm edge. Dec 1 st at neck edge and arm edge every row until 1 st rem. Tie off.

Sleeves: Ribbing—ch 12 and work ribbing, same as for back, until piece measures 7½ (8, 8½, 9) inches. Do not turn.

Next Row: Ch 3 (counts as 1st dc), working along long side of ribbing, work 37 (39, 41, 43) dc evenly spaced across, turn. Inc. 1 st ea end on next row, then every 4 (4, 4½, 4½) inches 3 times. Work even on 46 (48, 50, 52) sts until sleeve measures 17 (17½, 18, 18) inches from beg, or desired length to underarm.

Shape Raglan: Sl st across 1st 4 (4, 5, 5) sts, work across to within last 4 (4, 5, 5) sts, ch 3, turn. Work 1 row even. Dec 1 st ea end on next and every other row 4 (4, 5, 5) times, then every row until 6 (6, 8, 8) sts rem. Tie off.

Finishing: Sew side seams. Sew raglan seams of sleeves to body, keeping top 6 (6, 8, 8) sts of sleeves free. Sew sleeve seams.

Neckband: Ch 5 and work ribbing same as for back until piece fits around neckline, slightly stretched to lie flat. Tie off. Sew in place.

CLASSIC CARDIGAN

Fashions in sweaters change but the classic cardigan always seems to be in style. The dropped shoulderline and striped effect create interest.

Information to Check Before You Start

Sizing: Directions are written for Size 8. Changes for Sizes 10, 12, and 14 are in parentheses.

Materials: This sweater is made in Susan Bates® Knitting Worsted using 4 oz. skeins. Select any color you wish. You need:

—5 (5, 6, 6) skeins

—Six ¾-inch buttons

Tool: Crochet Hook I or 9 (5½ mm).

Gauge: 7 dc = 2 inches
2 rows = 1 inch

Directions to Follow

Body: Beg at bottom edge of both fronts and back, ch 114 (118, 124, 132).

Row 1: Sc in 2nd ch from hk and in ea st of ch. Mark this side for right side. Turn.

Row 2: Ch 3 (counts as 1 dc), sk 1st sc, dc in next sc and in ea sc across, turn—113 (117, 123, 131) dc.

Row 3: Ch 3 (counts as 1 dc), sk 1st dc, dc in next dc and in ea dc across, end dc in top of turning ch, turn. Rep Row 3 until piece measures 14 (15, 15, 16) inches from beg or desired length to underarm, end right side. Tie off.

Back: With wrong side facing attach yarn in 32nd (33rd, 35th, 37th) st from end, ch 3 (counts as 1 dc). Work across next 50 (52, 56, 58) dc, turn. Continue in established pat on 51 (53, 57, 59) sts for 6½ (7, 7, 7½) inches.

Shape Shoulders: Work across 1st 17 (18, 19, 20) sts. Tie off. Sk next 17 (17, 19, 19) sts. Attach yarn in next st and work to end. Tie off.

Left Front: With wrong side facing, attach yarn at front edge, ch 3. Dc in ea of next 24 (25, 26, 29) sts, turn. Continue in established pat until armhole measures 2″ less than back, end at arm edge.

Shape Neck: Work across to within last 6 (6, 7, 8) sts, turn. Dec 1 st at neck edge every row 2 (2, 1, 2) times. Work even on rem 17 (18, 19, 20) sts until armhole measures same as back. Tie off.

Right Front: With wrong side facing, attach yarn in 25th (26th, 27th, 30th) st from end of last long row. Ch 3 and work to front edge. Complete to correspond to left front, reversing shaping.

Sleeves: Ch 26 (29, 31, 33). Work same as body until piece measures 2 (2½, 2½, 2½) inches. Inc 1 st ea end on next row then every 3rd row until there are 45 (48, 50, 52) sts. Work even until sleeve measures 17 (17½, 18, 18) inches. Tie off.

Finishing: Sew shoulder seams. Sew top edge of sleeves to armhole. Sew sleeve edges across 6 sk'd sts of body, then sew remainder of sleeve seam.

Border: With right side facing, beg at lower right edge, work 1 row sc, evenly spaced, along right front, around neck edge, and down left front, working 3 sc at ea neck edge corner, ch 1, turn. Work 1 more row in same manner. Mark position for bottom of 6 buttonholes, evenly spaced, on right edge.

Next Row: * Sc to next marker, ch 2, sk 2 sts; rep from * across to beg of neck, then complete row as before, ch 1, turn.

Next Row: Sc in ea sc and ch of last row, working 3 sc in corners, ch 1, turn. Work 1 more row sc. Tie off. Sew on buttons. Steam lightly.

COPYRIGHT © C. J. BATES, INC.

HIS AND HER SWEATERS

This classic design has been made in a variety of sizes and has been adapted so it can be crocheted both as a vest and a cardigan. Another feature is its versatility, for it looks equally attractive on both men and women.

Information to Check Before You Start

Sizing: The directions are written for Size 34. Changes for Sizes 36, 38, 40, 42, and 44 are in parentheses.
Material: The sweaters are made of Brunswick Fore 'N Aft® Sport Yarn using 50 gram balls.
For the cardigan, you need 7 (8, 8, 9, 9, 10) balls of No. 6024 Cardinal.
For the vest, you need 5 (6, 6, 7, 7, 8) balls of No. 6035 Camel.
Tool: Aluminum Crochet Hook— Size 4 or E
Gauge: 4½ dc = 1 inch
—Approx. 2 rows dc = 1 inch

Directions to Follow

CARDIGAN

Pocket Facings: Make 2. Chain loosely 21 sts, turn, dc in 3rd st from hook, then dc in each st across. Ch'ing 3 to turn each time, work 9 more rows dc. Fasten off.

Bottom Ribbing: Chain loosely 11 sts, turn, sc in 2nd st from hook, then sc in each st across. Turn, ch 1, then sc in back loop of each st across. Repeat this last row until there are 45 (47, 49, 51, 53, 55) ridges. Ch 2, then work, evenly spaced across top of ridges 148 (158, 166, 176, 184, 194) dc.

Begin Pocket Design: NOTE—Always ch 2 at beg of each row and count as 1 dc. Work dc across 6 (6, 6, 8, 8, 8) sts, mark each side of next 20 sts. On these 20 sts work as follows; dc in each of next 2 sts, * make post st by working dc around post of next dc of previous row, dc in each of next 2 sts; rep from * across, dc around to within 26 (26, 26, 28, 28, 28)

sts of end, repeat pattern on next 20 sts as before, dc to end. Work dc across all sts of wrong side row. Repeat these last 2 rows 4 more times.

Pocket Opening: On right side work dc across 6 (6, 6, 8, 8, 8) sts, place 1 pocket facing under next 20 sts of sweater (facing will hang down on inside with last row dc even with last pattern row), work next dc through next st of sweater and first st of facing tog, then work dc across next 18 sts of facing only, then skipping 18 sts of sweater, work dc through next st of sweater and last st of facing tog, work dc around to within 26 (26, 26, 28, 28, 28) sts of other end, repeat as for other pocket, work dc to end. Work even in dc until piece meas from bottom of ribbing 12 (12, 12½, 12½, 13, 13) inches, ending on wrong side.

Begin V-Neck Shaping: Dec 1 st each end of following, then every other row 3 times in all. Work 1 row even.

Shape Right Front: On right side ch 2, dec on next 2 sts, dc across next 23 (25, 27, 30, 32, 34) sts, dec on next 2 sts, turn, and working on sts of right front only, at arm edge dec 1 st every row 4 more times. *At the same time* at neck edge (beg of row), dec 1 st every other row (counting from last dec) 6 (6, 6, 7, 7, 7) more times. This will be a total of 5 armhole decs, and 10 (10, 10, 11, 11, 11) neck edge decs. When armhole measures 7½ (7¾, 8, 8¼, 8½, 8¾) inches.
Shape Shoulder: If you ended at arm edge slip st across 6 (7, 8, 9, 10, 11) sts, sc in next st, hdc in next st, dc across last 8 (9, 10, 11, 12, 13) sts. If at neck edge, ch 2, dc across next 7 (8, 9, 10, 11, 12) sts, hdc in next st, sc in next st, slip next st, fasten off. There will be for each shoulder 16 (18, 20, 22, 24, 26) sts.

Left Front: Attach yarn at underarm in 28th (30th, 32nd, 35th, 37th, 39th) st from left front edge. Ch 2, dec on next 2 sts, work to within 2 sts of front edge, dec on last 2 sts. Working on sts of front only dec as for right front. NOTE— Neck decs will be made on last 2 sts on right side each time, to reverse shaping.

Back: Skipping 10 sts at underarm, attach yarn on right side and dec 1 st each side every row 5 times, when armholes meas same as front.

Shape Shoulder: Slip st across 6 (7, 8, 9, 10, 11) sts, sc in next st, hdc in next st, dc across next 8 (9, 10, 11, 12, 13) sts, dc across next 24 (26, 26, 26, 26, 28) sts of back of neck, then dc across next 8 (9, 10, 11, 12, 13) sts of other shoulder, hdc in next st, sc in next st, slip next st. Fasten off.

Sleeves: Work ribbing same as for cardigan until there are 12 (13, 14, 15, 17, 17) ridges. Turn, ch 2, then work, evenly spaced across top of ridges, 40 (42, 44, 46, 48, 48) dc. Now repeat the post st pattern as for pocket design on next 8 rows. NOTE—Do not work post st on last st, just work dc. Work now in dc, inc'ing 1 st each side in next, then every 3rd row until there are 56 (58, 60, 62, 64, 66) sts. When sleeve meas from beg 17 (17½, 17½, 18, 18, 19) inches or desired length to underarm.

Shape Cap: Slip st across 5 sts, ch 2, dec on next st, work across to within 7 sts of other end, dec on last 2 sts. Now dec 1 st each side every row 3 (4, 5, 6, 7, 8) times, then dec 2 sts each side every row—4 times. Fasten off.

Finishing: Weave or sew shoulder and sleeve seams. Sew sleeves in place. Sew pocket facings in place on wrong side. Work 5 rows sc around entire neckline, easing in to lie flat, making buttonholes in 3rd row on left side for men and right side for women. To make buttonholes ch 2, then skip 2 sc. In following row work 2 sc in each buttonhole. Have top buttonhole at beg neck shaping and space them about 3 inches apart. Sew buttons to correspond.

VEST

Work same as cardigan, omitting sleeves and working 7 decs in armhole shaping instead of 5. Make armholes ½ inch deeper than for cardigan. Each shoulder will be 2 sts narrower than cardigan. Finish as for cardigan, working 2 rows sc around armholes.

DECORATIVE VEST

Fashion touches highlight this vest. The bobbled edging, variegated coloring, and blouson effect give added interest to the design.

Information to Check Before You Start

Sizing: Directions are written for Size 8. Changes for Sizes 10, 12, 14, and 16 are in parentheses.
· Finished Measurements:
Bust—35 (36, 38, 39½, 40½) inches
Width of back at underarm—
17½ (18¼, 19, 19¾, 20½) inches
Width of each front, excluding border—
7¾ (8¼, 8¾, 9¼, 9¾) inches
Materials: The vest is made of Columbia-Minerva Glimmerfluff using 3 oz. balls. You may substitute Nantuk 4-ply, Shannon, or Performer yarn if you wish. You need 4 (4, 5, 5, 6) balls.
Tools: Crochet Hooks—Size H and Size I
Gauge: Using Size I hook—3 sc = 1 inch; 2 rows = 1 inch

Directions to Follow

Back. Row 1 (right side): With Size I hook, ch 54 (56, 58, 60, 62), sc in 2nd ch from hook and each ch across; 53 (55, 57, 59, 61) sc.
Row 2: Ch 1, turn, sc in each sc across. Rep row 2 until 5 inches from beg, end with right side row.
Bobble Row: Ch 1, turn, sc in first sc, * [yo hook and draw up a lp] 4 times all in next sc, yo and thru 8 lps on hook, yo and thru rem 2 lps (bobble st), sc in next sc; rep from * across.
Next Row: Ch 1, turn, sc in each st across. Work even in sc until 13 inches from beg or desired length to underarm.
Shape Armholes. Row 1: Ch 1, turn, sl st in first 5 sc, sc to within last 5 sc.
Row 2: Ch 1, turn, draw up a lp in each of first 2 sc, yo and thru all 3 lps on hook (dec), sc to within last 2 sc, dec over last 2 sc. Rep last row twice more; 37 (39, 41, 43, 45) sc. Work even until 7½ (7½, 8, 8, 8½) inches above beg of armhole.

Shape Shoulders. First Shoulder.
Row 1: Ch 1, turn, sl st in first 3 sc, sc in next 7 (7, 8, 9, 9) sc.
Row 2: Ch 1, turn, dec over first 2 sc, sc to end. Fasten off.
Second Shoulder: Turn, sk center 17 (19, 19, 19, 21) sc, join yarn in next sc, sc in same st, sc in next 6 (6, 7, 8, 8) sc.
Row 2: Ch 1, turn, sc to within last 2 sc, dec over last 2 sc. Fasten off.

Left Front: With Size I hook, ch 24 (26, 28, 30, 32). Work same as back to underarm; 23 (25, 27, 29, 31) sc.
Shape Armhole: At armhole edge, take off 5 sc once. Dec 1 sc every row 3 times; 15 (17, 19, 21, 23) sc. Work even until 4 (4, 4½, 4½, 5) inches above beg of armhole.
Shape Neck: At neck edge take off 4 (5, 5, 6, 7) sc once. Dec 1 sc every row 2 (3, 4, 4, 5) times; 9 (9, 10, 11, 11) sts. Work even until same length as back to shoulder.
Shape Shoulder: At armhole edge, take off 3 sts once. Work 1 row even. Fasten off.

Right Front: Work to correspond to left front, reversing shaping.

Finishing: Sew shoulder and side seams.
Front and Neck Borders: Right side facing, with Size H hook join yarn at lower right front corner, work 54 sc evenly along front edge to neck edge, 3 sc in corner, work about 17 (18, 19, 19, 20) sc to shoulder seam, work 17 (19, 19, 19, 21) sc across back neck edge, 17 (18, 19, 19, 20) sc along opposite side edge, 3 sc in corner, 54 sc to lower edge.
Next Row: Rep bobble row. Work 1 row sc. Fasten off.
Armhole Edging: Right side facing, join yarn at underarm seam, work 56 (58, 60, 62, 64) sc evenly around armhole, join in first sc.

Rnd 2: Ch 1, turn, sc in joining, * bobble in next st, sc in next sc; rep from * around, end bobble in last sc, join.

Rnd 3: Ch 1, turn, sc in each st around, join. Fasten off.

Cord: With Size I hook, ch 156, sl st in 2nd ch from hook, and in each ch to end. Fasten off. Weave cord thru bobble row at waist.

Ties: Make 2. With Size I hook, ch 45, finish same as cord. Sew ties to front neck corners.

DRESSY PULLOVER

The openwork stitches give this classic design a dressy look. For someone who likes fancy clothes, this is great.

Information to Check Before You Start

Sizing: Directions are written for Size 8. Changes for Sizes 10, 12, 14, and 16 are in parentheses.
· Finished Measurements:
Bust—36 (38, 39½, 40½, 42) inches
Width of back or front at underarm—
18¼ (19, 19¾, 20¼, 21) inches
Width of sleeves at underarm—
11½ (12¼, 13, 13¾, 14¼) inches

Materials: The pullover is made of Columbia-Minerva Glimmerfluff yarn using 3 oz. balls. If you wish you may substitute Nantuk 4-ply, Shannon, or Performer yarns. You need 5 (5, 6, 6, 7) balls.

Tools: Crochet Hooks—Size H and Size I

Gauge: Using Size I Hook—3 dc = 1 inch; 3 rows = 2 inches

Directions to Follow

Back. Base Row (right side): With Size I hook, ch 56 (58, 60, 62, 64), dc in 3rd ch from hook and each rem ch; 55 (57, 59, 61, 63) dc. (NOTE—Ch-3 at beg of row counts as 1 dc.)

Pat—Row 1: Ch 3, turn, dc in 2nd dc, dc in next 3 (4, 5, 6, 7) dc, * ch 2, sk 2 dc, sc in next dc, ch 2, sk next 2 dc, dc in each of next 5 dc; rep from * across, end dc in last 4 (5, 6, 7, 8) dc, dc in top of ch-3.

Row 2: Ch 3, turn, dc in 2nd dc, dc in next 3 (4, 5, 6, 7) dc, * ch 1, sc in next ch-2 sp, ch 2, sc in next ch-2 sp, ch 1, dc in next 5 dc; rep from * across, end as for row 1.

Row 3: Ch 3, turn, dc in 2nd dc, dc in next 3 (4, 5, 6, 7) dc, * work 5 dc in center ch-2 sp, dc in next 5 dc; rep from * across, end as in row 1. Rep Rows 1 thru 3 for pat. Work even until 10 inches from beg or 3 inches less than desired length to underarm, end with pat row 3.

Shape Armholes. Next Row: Ch 1, turn, sl st in each of first 4 sts, ch 3, work in pat to within last 3 sts. Dec 1 dc each side edge every row twice; 45 (47, 49, 51, 53) sts. Work even in pat until 7 (7½, 7½, 8, 8) inches above beg of armhole.

Shape Shoulders. Row 1: Ch 1, turn, sl st in first 7 (7, 8, 8, 8) sts, ch 3, work in pat to within last 6 (6, 7, 7, 7) sts.

Row 2: Ch 1, turn, sl st in first 7 (8, 8, 8, 9) sts, work in pat to within last 6 (7, 7, 7, 8) sts; 21 (21, 21, 23, 23) sts. Fasten off.

Front: Work same as back to underarm.

Shape Armholes and Neck. Row 1: Ch 1, turn, sl st in first 4 sts, ch 3, work in pat across next 23 (24, 25, 26, 27) sts, sk next st, join 2nd ball of yarn in next st, work in pat to within last 3 sts; 24 (25, 26, 27, 28) sts. Working each side separately, at each armhole edge dec 1 dc every row twice, *at same time,* at each neck edge dec 1 st in next row, then every other row 3 times, then every row 6 (6, 6, 7, 7) times; 12 (13, 14, 14, 15) sts. Work even until same length as back to shoulder.

Shape Shoulders: At each armhole edge, take off 6 (6, 7, 7, 7) sts once. Fasten off.

Sleeves: With Size I hook, ch 24 (24, 26, 26, 28), work base row same as back; 23 (23, 25, 25, 27) dc.

Pat Row 1: Ch 3, turn, dc in 2nd dc, dc in each of next 7 (7, 8, 8, 9) dc, ch 2, sk next 2 dc, sc in next dc, ch 2, sk next 2 dc, dc in next 8 (8, 9, 9, 10) dc, dc in top of ch-3. Working pat over center sts, inc 1 dc each side edge in next row, then every 1½ inches, 5 (6, 6, 7, 7) times more; 35 (37, 39, 41, 43) sts. Work even until 14 inches from beg or 3 inches less than desired length to underarm.

Shape Cap: Ch 1, turn, sl st in first 4 sts, ch 3, work to within last 3 sts, turn. Dec 1 st each side edge every row 9 (10, 10, 11, 11) times; 11 (11, 13, 13, 15) sts. Dec 2 sts each side edge in next row. Fasten off.

Finishing: Sew shoulder, side, and sleeve seams; sew in sleeves.

Lower Edge Ribbing. Row 1: With Size H hook, ch 14, sc in 2nd ch from hook and each rem ch; 13 sc.

Row 2: Ch 1, turn, working in front lps only, sc in each sc across.

Row 3: Ch 1, turn, working in back lps only, sc in each sc across. Rep Rows 2 and 3 until 25 (26, 26, 27, 27, 28) inches from beg. Fasten off. Sew ends tog. Gather lower edge of pullover to fit and sew to ribbing. From right side, work 1 row sl st around lower edge of ribbing.

Sleeve Cuff Ribbing: Work same as for lower edge until 7 inches from beg or long enough to fit around wrist. Fasten off. Sew ends tog. Gather lower edge of sleeve and sew to ribbing. Sl st along lower edge of cuffs.

Neckband: Right side facing, with Size H hook, join yarn at right back neck corner, sc in each st across back neck, work about 27 (27, 28, 28, 29) sc along side edge, sc in center front st, work 27 (27, 28, 28, 29) sc along opposite side edge, join with sl st in first sc.

Rnd 2: Ch 1, sc in joining, sc in each sc to within 2 sc of center front sc, dec over next 2 sc, sc in center sc, dec over next 2 sc, sc to end, join. Rep last rnd twice. Fasten off. COPYRIGHT © 1981 COLUMBIA-MINERVA CORPORATION

RIPPLE STITCH PULLOVER

Attention-getting describes this sweater's interesting combination of stitches and lovely blending of colors. The ripple pattern emphasized with bobbles creates a fascinating textural effect.

Information to Check Before You Start

Sizing: Directions are written for Small (8–10). Changes for Medium (12–14) and Large (16–18) are in parentheses.
· Finished Measurement:
Bust—36 (39½, 43) inches
Materials: This sweater was made of Caron Glencannon using 3 oz. skeins. You need 4 (4, 5) skeins of each color, A (Poppy), B (Fisherman), and C (Ginger Spice).
Tool: Crochet Hook—Size I
Gauge: 3 sc = 1 inch
    3 rows = 1 inch
    1 chevron pat = 4½ (4¾, 5) inches

Directions to Follow

Back. Row 1 (right side): With A, ch 58 (66, 74), draw up lp in 2nd ch from hook, draw up lp in next ch, yo and thru 3 lps on hook (1 sc dec), * sc in next 5 (6, 7) ch, 3 sc in next ch, sc in next 5 (6, 7) ch, draw up lp in each of next 3 ch, yo and thru 4 lps on hook (2 sc dec); rep from * 3 times more, end draw up lp in last 2 ch, yo and thru 3 lps on hook; 57 (65, 73) sts—4 pats.
  Row 2: Ch 1, turn, sc in each sc across.
  Row 3: Ch 1, turn, 1 sc dec over first 2 sc, * sc in next 5 (6, 7) sc, 3 sc in next sc, sc in next 5 (6, 7) sc, 2 sc dec over next 3 sc; rep from * 3 times more, end 1 sc dec over last 2 sc. Rep Rows 2 and 3 for pat. Work in pat until 9 rows from beg are completed, end with Row 3. Fasten off A, join B.
  Bobble St Row (wrong side): Ch 1, turn, sc in first sc, * yo hook, draw up lp in next sc, (yo hook, draw up lp in same sc) 3 times, yo and thru 8 lps on hook, yo and thru rem 2 lps on hook (Bobble

St), sc in next sc; rep from * across. Fasten off B, join C. Beg with Row 3, rep rows 2 and 3 for 9 rows. Fasten off C, join B. Rep Bobble St Row once. Fasten off B, join A. Rep last 20 rows once. Fasten off B, join A. Beg with Row 3, work even in pat for 4 rows.

Shape Sleeves. Row 1: With A, ch 8 (9, 10), 2 sc in 2nd ch from hook, sc in each of next 5 (6, 7) ch, draw up lp in next ch and each of next 2 sc, yo and thru 4 lps, work in pat to within last 2 sc, drop lp from hook, join 2nd strand of A in last sc, ch 7 (8, 9), fasten off; pick up dropped lp, draw up lp in last 2 sc and first ch, yo and thru 4 lps, sc in next 5 (6, 7) ch, 2 sc in last ch.
  Row 2: Ch 8 (9, 10), sc in 2nd ch from hook and each ch and sc to within last sc, drop lp from hook, join 2nd strand of A in last sc, ch 7 (8, 9), fasten off; pick up dropped lp, sc in last sc and each ch to end.
  Row 3: Ch 8 (9, 10), draw up lp in 2nd ch from hook, draw up lp in next ch, yo and thru 3 lps, sc in next 5 (6, 7) ch, 3 sc in next sc, work in pat to within last sc, drop lp from hook, join 2nd strand of A in last sc, ch 7 (8, 9), fasten off; pick up dropped lp, 3 sc in last sc, sc in next 5 (6, 7) ch, draw up lp in each of last 2 ch, yo and thru 3 lps.
  Row 4: Rep Row 2.
  Row 5: Rep Row 1.
  Row 6: Ch 8 (9, 10), sc in 2nd ch from hook and next 6 (7, 8) ch, fasten off A, join B, * sc in next sc, Bobble St in next sc; rep from * to within last sc, drop lp from hook, join strand of A in last sc, ch 7 (8, 9), fasten off; pick up dropped lp of B, draw up lp in last sc, drop B, draw lp of A thru 2 lps on hook, with A sc in each ch to end; 141 (161, 181) sts. Fasten off A and B, join C. Work even in pat for 9 rows. Join B, work 1 row in Bobble St pat. Join A, work 1 (3, 3) row in pat.
Shape Sleeve Top and Shoulders.
Row 1: Ch 3, turn, dc in 2nd sc, hdc in next 2 (2, 3) sc, sc in next 2 (3, 3) sc, sl

st in each of next 3 sc, sc in next 2 (3, 3) sc, hdc in next 2 (2, 3) sc, dc in next 2 sc—mark last dc—sc in each sc across to within last 15 (17, 19) sts, dc in next 2 sc—mark first dc—hdc in next 2 (2, 3) sc, sc in next 2 (3, 3) sc, sl st in each of next 3 sc, sc in next 2 (3, 3) sc, hdc in next 2 (2, 3) sc, dc in last 2 sc. Fasten off.

Row 2: Turn, with lp of C on hook, draw up lp in marked dc and next sc, yo and thru 3 lps, work across in pat to within 1 st of last marked dc, draw up lp in next sc and marked dc, yo and thru 3 lps.

Row 3: Ch 1, turn, sk first st, hdc in next 3 (3, 4) sc, sc in next 2 (3, 3) sc, sl st in each of next 3 sc, sc in next 2 (3, 3) sc, hdc in next 2 (2, 3) sc, dc in next 2 sc—mark last dc—work in pat to within last 15 (17, 19) sts, dc in next 2 sc—mark first dc—hdc in next 2 (2, 3) sc, sc in next 2 (3, 3) sc, sl st in each of next 3 sc, sc in next 2 (3, 3) sc, hdc in next 3 (3, 4) sc, sl st in last st. Fasten off. Rep Rows 2 and 3 twice more for Rows 4 through 7.

Row 8: Rep Row 2; 27 (31, 35) sts.

Neck Edge. Row 9: Ch 1, turn, sk first st, hdc in next 3 (3, 4) sc, sc in next 2 (3, 3) sc, sl st in next 3 sc, sc in next 2 (3, 3) sc, hdc in next 2 (2, 3) sc, dc in next 3 sc, hdc in next 2 (2, 3) sc, sc in next 2 (3, 3) sc, sl st in next 3 sc, sc in next 2 (3, 3) sc, hdc in next 3 (3, 4) sc, sl st in last st. Fasten off.

Front: Work same as back to first row of sleeve top and shoulder shaping.

Shape Sleeve Top, Neck, and Shoulder. Row 1: Work as for back across first 15 (17, 19) sts, sc in next 48 (55, 62) sts.

Row 2: Ch 1, turn, dec 1 sc over first 2 sc, sc in next 4 (5, 6) sc, work in pat to end, finish as for row 2 of back. Shape shoulder edge as for back, at neck edge dec 1 st every row 5 (4, 3) times, then 0 (2, 2) sts every row 0 (1, 2) times. Fasten off. Sk center 15 (17, 19) sts, join C in next st, sc in same st and next 47 (54, 61) sts, finish row same as end of row 1 of back. Finish 2nd half to correspond to 1st half, reversing shaping.

Finishing: Sew shoulder and top of sleeve seams.

Collar. Rnd 1: Wrong side facing, join B at left shoulder seam, work 28 (32, 36) sc across back neck edge, 11 (12, 13) sc along side neck, 15 (17, 19) sc across front neck edge, 12 (13, 14) sc along side neck, join in first sc; 66 (74, 82) sc.

Rnd 2: Ch 1, turn, sc in each sc, join. Rep Rnd 2 twice more. Inc 11 sc evenly spaced in next rnd; 77 (85, 93) sc. Work even until 10 inches from beg. Fasten off. Along each underarm edge of sleeves, work 1 row of filling st as for back neck edge. Sew side and sleeve seams.

Sleeve Cuff: Right side facing, join B at underarm seam, work 24 (28, 32) sc evenly spaced around sleeve edge, join. Work 9 rnds of sc. Fasten off.

Lower Edge: Right side facing, join A in side seam, work 1 sc in each foundation ch st around lower edge, join. Fasten off.

TUNIC TOP

This tunic has been given dressmaker touches that add a certain softness to the design. The yoked neckline, the nipped-in waistline, and push-up sleeves contribute to this look.

Information to Check Before You Start

Sizing: Directions are written for Size 8. Changes for Sizes 10, 12, 14, and 16 are in parentheses.

· Finished Measurements:
Bust—34 (35, 36, 38, 40) inches
Materials: The tunic is made of Caron Dazzle-aire in 3 oz. skeins. You need 6 (6, 7, 8, 9) skeins.
Tools: Crochet Hooks—Size H and Size I
Gauge: Pat st made with Size I hook— 3 sts = 1 inch 5 rows = 2 inches

Directions to Follow

Back. Row 1 (right side): With Size I hook, ch 57 (59, 61, 63, 67) loosely, sc in 2nd ch from hook, dc in next ch, * sc in next ch, dc in next ch; rep from * across; 56 (58, 60, 62, 66) sts.

Row 2: Ch 1, turn, sc in first dc, * dc in next sc, sc in next dc; rep from * across, end dc in last sc. Rep Row 2 for pat. Work even in pat until 8½ inches from beg, end with right side row.

Dec Row 1: Ch 1, turn, work in pat across first 6 (6, 8, 8, 8) sts, * draw up lp in each of next 2 sts, yo and thru 3 lps on hook, yo hook, draw up lp in each of next 2 sts, yo and thru 3 lps on hook, yo and thru 2 lps on hook (pat dec), work in pat across next 6 sts; rep from * 4 (4, 4, 4, 5) times more, end last rep work in pat to end; 46 (48, 50, 52, 54) sts.

Dec Row 2: Ch 1, turn, work in pat across first 6 (6, 8, 4, 4) sts, * work pat dec over next 4 sts, work in pat across next 6 sts; rep from * 3 (3, 3, 4, 4) times more, end last rep work in pat to end; 38 (40, 42, 42, 44) sts. Change to Size H hook.

Waistband. Row 1 (wrong side): Ch 2, turn, hdc in 2nd st and each st across. (NOTE—Ch 2 at beg counts as 1 hdc.)

Row 2: Ch 2, turn, sk first hdc, yo hook, from front of work insert hook around vertical bar of next hdc, yo, and draw up lp, yo and thru 3 lps on hook (Post hdc—Phdc), * hdc in next hdc, Phdc in next hdc; rep from * across, hdc in top of ch-2.

Row 3: Ch 2, turn, sk first hdc, hdc in next hdc, * yo hook, from back of work insert hook around next Phdc, yo, and draw up lp, yo and thru 3 lps on hook, hdc in next hdc; rep from * across, hdc in top of ch-2.

Row 4: Rep Row 2. Change to Size I hook.

Next Row: Ch 1, turn, sc in first st, * dc in next st, sc in next st; rep from * across, dc in last st.

Inc Row 1: Ch 1, turn, 1 sc and 1 dc in each of first 2 sts (pat inc), work in pat to within last 2 sts, 1 sc and 1 dc in each of last 2 sts. Work 3 rows even. Rep last 4 rows 2 (2, 2, 3, 3) times more; 50 (52, 54, 58, 60) sts. Work even

until 9 inches above end of waistband or desired length to underarm.

Shape Armholes. Row 1: Turn, sl st in each of first 3 sts, dc in next st, work in pat to within last 3 sts.

Row 2: Ch 1, turn, draw up a lp in each of first 2 sts, yo and thru 3 lps on hook (dec), work in pat to within last 2 sts, dec over last 2 sts. Rep Row 2, 2 (2, 2, 3, 3) times more; 38 (40, 42, 44, 46) sts. Work even until 2½ inches above beg of armholes, end with right-side row.

Yoke. Row 1: Work same as waistband. Rep rows 2 and 3 of waistband until 6 (6, 6½, 6½, 7) inches from beg of armholes.

Shape Neck and Shoulders. Next Row: Ch 2, turn, sk first st, work in rib pat across next 9 (10, 11, 11, 12) sts; 10 (11, 12, 12, 13) sts. Work 1 row even. Fasten off. Turn, sk center 18 (18, 18, 20, 20) sts, join yarn in next st, ch 2, work in rib to end. Work 1 row. End off.

Front: Work as back until armholes 4 (4, 4½, 4½, 5) inches.

Shape Neck and Shoulders: Work as for back, working even on 10 (11, 12, 12, 13) sts until same as back shoulder. Fasten off.

Sleeves. Row 1 (right side): With Size H hook, ch 21 (21, 23, 23, 25), hdc in 3rd ch from hook and each rem ch; 20 (20, 22, 22, 24) sts.

Row 2: Rep Row 3 of waistband.

Row 3: Rep Row 2 of waistband. Rep last 2 rows once. Change to Size H hook.

Inc Row: Ch 1, turn, sc in first st, * dc in next st, 1 sc and 1 dc in next st, sc in next st; rep from * 5 (5, 5, 5, 7) times more, work in pat to end; 26 (26, 28, 28, 32) sts. Work 6 rows even. Inc 1 st each side edge in each of next 2 rows. Rep last 8 rows once; 34 (34, 36, 36, 40) sts. Work even until 17 inches from beg.

Shape Cap: Turn, sl st in each of first 3 sts, work in pat to last 3 sts. Dec 1 st each side edge every row 9 (9, 10, 10, 11) times; 10 (10, 10, 10, 12) sts.

Next Row: Turn, sl st in first 2 sts, work in pat to last 2 sts, sl st in last 2 sts. End off.

Finishing: Sew seams. Sew in sleeves.

TEXTURED PULLOVER

Puffy stitches give a new look to this classic design. They create a certain prettiness that is most attractive.

Information to Check Before You Start

Sizing: The directions are written for Small Size (8–10), Medium Size (12–14), and Large Size (16–18).

Materials: The sweater is made of Bernat Cassino using 50 gram pull pouches. You need 7 (8, 8) pouches.

NOTE —All sizes are made on the same number of stitches using the hook suggested for the correct gauge.

Tools: Crochet Hooks (Bernat U.S.) in one of three sizes:

For the Small-Size sweater—Size H (5 mm)

For the Medium-Size sweater—Size I (5.5 mm)

For the Large-Size sweater—Size J (6 mm)

Gauge: 3 puff sts and 3 hdc = 2 inches on Size H hook

3 puff sts and 2 hdc = 2 inches on Size I hook

2 puff sts and 3 hdc = 2 inches on Size J hook

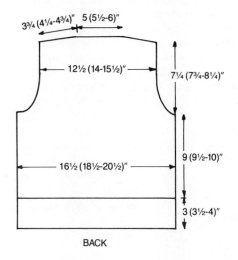

BACK

Directions to Follow

Back: Ch 47 sts very loosely.

Row 1: Yo, insert hook in 4th ch from hook, yo, draw up a lp, yo, pull through 2 lps on hook, (yo, insert hook in same st, yo, draw up a lp, yo, pull through 2 lps on hook) twice, yo, pull through all 4 lps on hook, * 1 hdc in next st of ch, yo, insert hook in next st, yo, draw up a lp, yo, pull through 2 lps on hook, (yo, insert hook in same st, yo, draw up a lp, yo, pull through 2 lps on hook) twice, yo, pull through all 4 lps on hook (puff st made), rep from *, ending 1 hdc in last st of ch, ch 1, turn—22 puff stitches.

Row 2: 1 hdc in each puff st and in each hdc, 1 hdc in top of turning ch, ch 1, turn.

Row 3: 1 hdc in first hdc, * 1 puff st in next st, 1 hdc in next st, rep from * across row, ch 1, turn.

Row 4 and all even rows through **Row 20:** Rep Row 2.

Row 5 and all odd rows through **Row 21:** Rep Row 3.

Shape Armholes: Row 22: Sl st over first 2 sts, sl st in next st, 1 hdc in same st, 1 hdc in each st to last 2 sts, turn.

Row 23: Sl st in first hdc, 1 hdc in each of next 2 hdc, * 1 puff st in next st, 1 hdc in next st, rep from * to last 3 sts, 1 hdc in each of next 2 sts, turn.

Row 24: Sl st in first st, ch 1, 1 hdc in next hdc, 1 hdc in each remaining st to last st, ch 1, turn—37 sts.

Row 25 and all odd rows through **Row 39:** Rep Row 3.

Row 26 and all even rows through **Row 40:** Rep Row 2.

Shape Left Shoulder. Row 41: Sl st over first 3 sts, 1 sc in each of next 3 sts, 1 hdc in next st, 1 puff st in next st, 1 hdc in next st, 1 puff st in next st, 1 hdc in next st. Fasten off.

Shape Right Shoulder: Skip next 15 sts, join yarn in next st and work to correspond to left shoulder, reversing all shaping.

Front: Ch 47 sts very loosely. Work Rows 1 through 29 as for back.

Shape Left Front. Row 30: 1 hdc in each of first 12 sts, turn.

Row 31: Sl st in first st, 1 hdc in next st, work Row 3 of pat st for back to end of row, ch 1, turn.

Rows 32 and all even rows through **Row 40:** Rep Row 2.

Rows 33 and all odd rows through **Row 39:** Rep Row 3. Fasten off.

Shape Right Front: Work in same manner as left front, reversing all shaping. Fasten off.

Sleeves: Ch 39 sts very loosely.

Rows 1 through 5: Work Rows 1 through 5 as for back on 37 sts.

Row 6: Sl st over first 2 sts, sl st in next st, 1 hdc in same st, 1 hdc in each st to last 2 sts, turn.

Row 7: Sl st in first hdc, 1 hdc in each of next 2 sts, * 1 puff st in next st, 1 hdc in next st, rep from * to last 3 sts, 1 hdc in each of next 2 sts, turn.

Row 8: 1 hdc in each st, turn.

Row 9: Sl st in first hdc, * 1 hdc in next st, 1 puff st in next st, rep from * across row to last 2 sts, 1 hdc in next st, ch 1, turn.

Row 10: Rep Row 8.

Row 11: Rep Row 7.

Row 12: Rep Row 8.

Row 13: Rep Row 9.

Row 14: Rep Row 10.

Row 15: Rep Row 9.

Row 16: Sl st in first st, ch 1, 1 hdc in each st to last st, turn.

Row 17: Rep Row 7.

Row 18: Rep Row 16.

Row 19: Rep Row 17.

Row 20: Rep Row 16. Fasten off.

Finishing: Sew shoulder seams. Set in sleeves. Sew underarm and sleeve seams.

Ribbing. Rnd 1: Working around lower edge, join yarn in st at underarm seam, ch 1, 1 hdc in each st around, join with a sl st, ch 1, turn.

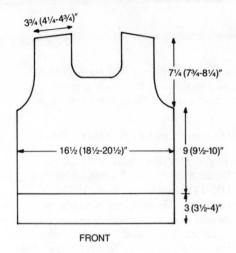

FRONT

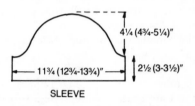

SLEEVE

Rnd 2: Skip first st, * yo, insert hook from *front to back* of next st and working around post of same st, work 1 hdc (F hdc), yo, insert hook from *back to front* of next st and working around post of same st, work 1 hdc (B hdc), rep from * around, join with a sl st in top of turning ch, ch 1, turn.

Rnd 3: * 1 F hdc in next st, 1 B hdc in next st, rep from * around, join with a sl st to top of turning ch, ch 1, turn.

Rnds 4 and 6: Rep Rnd 2.

Rnds 5 and 7: Rep Rnd 3, but do not ch at end of Rnd 7. Fasten off.

Neck Edging: Join yarn at left shoulder seam and work 1 sc in each st around neck edge, join. *Do not turn.* Working from *left* to *right*, work 1 sc in each st, join. Fasten off. Work same edging around sleeve edges.

CARDIGAN AND HAT

These two articles can be worn together or separately. The V-neckline and center closing of the sweater creates a slenderizing effect and the hat adds a certain perkiness to an outfit.

Information to Check Before You Start

Sizing: Directions are written for Size 8. Changes for Sizes 10, 12, 14, and 16 are in parentheses. · Finished Measurements:
Bust—34 (35, 36, 38, 40) inches with cardigan closed
Width of back at underarm—17 (17½, 18, 19, 20) inches
Width of each front at underarm (including band)—9½ (9¾, 10, 10½, 11¼) inches
Width of sleeve at underarm—12 (12½, 13, 13¾, 14¼) inches
Materials: The two pieces are made with Columbia-Minerva Monique in 1 oz. balls. You need 9 (10, 11, 12, 13) balls. You'll also need plastic rings—4 in ¾-inch size
Tools: Afghan Hooks—Size G and Size H, 14 inches
Crochet Hooks—Size E and Size J
Gauge: Using Size H Afghan Hook—
5 sts = 1 inch
9 rows = 2 inches
Using Size J Crochet Hook for Hat—
3 sc = 1 inch
3 sc rows = 1 inch

Directions to Follow

CARDIGAN

Back: With Size G Afghan Hook, ch 85 (88, 90, 95, 100).
Afghan St Ribbing—Row 1, 1st Half: Bring yarn to front of work and hold below 2nd ch from hook, insert hook in same ch, yo, and draw lp thru (P st), * with yarn at back, draw up a lp in next ch (K st), with yarn in front draw up a lp in next ch; rep from * across ch; 85 (88, 90, 95, 100) lps on hook. **2nd Half:** Yo hook and thru 1st lp, * yo and thru 2

lps; rep from * across until 1 lp rems on hook. (NOTE—Lp on hook is 1st lp of next row and forms vertical edge st.)
Row 2, 1st Half: Holding yarn in front, below 1st vertical bar from edge, yo and draw up lp in same vertical bar (P st), * holding yarn in back, draw up lp in next vertical bar (K st), holding yarn in front, draw up lp in next vertical bar; rep from * across. **2nd Half:** Work off lps same as for 2nd half of row 1. Rep Row 2 for ribbing until 2½ inches from beg. Change to Size H Hook.
Plain Afghan St—Row 1, 1st Half: With yarn at back of work, draw up a lp in each vertical bar across. **2nd Half:** Work off lps same as before. Work in plain afghan st until 12 inches from beg or desired length to underarm.
Shape Armholes. Row 1: Sl st in each of 1st 5 vertical bars, draw up a lp in next bar and each bar to within last 5 bars; 75 (78, 80, 85, 90) lps on hook. **2nd Half:** Work off lps as before.
Dec Row, 1st Half: Insert hook under 1st 2 bars, yo and draw lp thru (dec), draw up a lp in each bar to within last 3 bars, draw up 1 lp under next 2 bars, draw up lp in last bar. **2nd Half:** Work off lps as before. Dec 1 st each side edge every row 4 (4, 4, 5, 7) times more; 65 (68, 70, 73, 74) sts. Work even until 7 (7½, 8, 8½, 9) inches above beg of armhole.
Shape Neck and Shoulders. Next Row, 1st Half: Draw up a lp in each of first 18 (19, 20, 21, 21) bars, dec over next 2 bars; 20 (21, 22, 23, 23) lps on hook. **2nd Half:** Work off lps as before. Work 1 row even.
Next Row: Sl st in each bar across. Fasten off. Join yarn in st after dec and before next free bar on last full row; sl st in 1st bar and next 23 (24, 24, 25, 26) bars, dec over next 2 bars, draw up a lp in each bar to end. Work off lps. Work 1 row even. Sl st in each bar. Fasten off.

Left Front: With Size G Afghan Hook, ch 47 (48, 50, 53, 56). Work ribbing same as back. Change to Size H Afghan Hook.

Next Row, 1st Half: Work in plain afghan st to within last 7 bars, work in ribbing across last 7 bars. **2nd Half:** Work off lps. Rep last row until 9 rows less than back to underarm, end at underarm edge.

Shape Neck and Armhole. Next Row: Work to within last 9 bars, dec 1 bar, rib to end; work off lps. At front edge, dec 1 bar before ribbing sts every 4th row 9 (9, 10, 11, 12) times more, *at the same time,* when same length as back to underarm, at side edge shape armhole same as right armhole of back; 27 (28, 29, 30, 30) sts. Work even until same length as back to shoulder.

Last Row: Sl st in each bar to within last 6 bars, rib to end; 7 lps on hook. Work in ribbing for 6 (6, 6, 6¼, 6¼) inches or until long enough to fit across back neck edge to right shoulder. Sl st in each bar across. Fasten off. Mark position of 4 buttons evenly spaced on front band, having lower one on 4th row from lower edge and top one 4 rows below first neck edge dec.

Right Front: Work as for left front, reversing band, shaping and working buttonholes opposite markers as follows: Rib in first 2 bars, sl st in next 3 bars, rib across next 2 bars, work to end. Work off lps, working ch 2 over buttonhole. In next row, draw up lps in each bar and ch. At shoulder sl st across all bars.

Sleeves: With Size G Afghan Hook, ch 43 (45, 45, 47, 47). Work ribbing same as back. Change to Size H Afghan Hook. Work in plain afghan st for 5 rows. Inc 1 st each side edge in next row, then every 6th row 8 (8, 9, 10, 11) times more; 61 (63, 65, 69, 71) sts. *(To inc,* draw up a lp in st between edge st and 1st bar, at end of row draw up a lp in st between last 2 bars.) Work even until 17 inches from beg desired length to underarm.

Shape Cap: Sl st in 1st 5 bars, draw up a lp in each bar to within last 5 bars; work off lps. Dec 1 st each side edge every row 14 (15, 16, 17, 18) times, then dec 2 sts each side edge in next row; 19 (19, 19, 21, 21) sts. Sl st in each bar across.

Finishing: Leaving right front band sts free, sew shoulder, side, and sleeve seams. Sew in sleeves. Weave end of left neckband to right front band sts, sew lower edge of band to back neck.

Buttons: Make 4. With Size E crochet hook, work about 24 sc around ring to cover. Fasten off, leaving a 10 inch end. Thread end in tapestry needle and weave through tops of sc, drawing sc up tightly and pushing to center of ring. Fasten securely and sew on button.

HAT

NOTE—Use 2 strands of yarn held tog as 1 throughout.

Crown: With Size J hook, ch 3, join with sl st in first ch to form ring.

Rnd 1: Ch 1, work 6 sc in ring. With contrasting thread, mark last sc for end of rnd. Carry up marker at end of each rnd.

Rnd 2: 2 sc in each sc around; 12 sc.

Rnd 3: * Sc in next sc, 2 sc in next sc; rep from * around; 18 sc. Continue inc 6 sc evenly spaced every rnd until crown measures 6 inches in diameter.

Body. Rnd 1: Sc in 1st sc, dc in same sc, * skip next sc, 1 sc and 1 dc in next sc; rep from * around, end skip last sc.

Rnd 2: Work 1 sc and 1 dc in 1st sc, * skip dc, 1 sc and 1 dc in next sc; rep from * around. Rep rnd 2 until 8 inches from end of crown. Join with sl st at end of last rnd. Fasten off. Roll brim as desired.

Woven Jacket and Scarf
(See page 258)

Smart Cardigan
(See page 244)

Textured Pullover
(See page 248)

Sunny Top
(See page 251)

Belted Tunic
(See page 252)

Coat and Shell
(See page 247)

dspread or Afghan
e page 263)

Granny Afghan
(See page 262)

DRESSY BLOUSE

An allover design creates a pretty effect. The results are light and lovely with a definite fashion look.

Information to Check Before You Start

Sizing: The directions are written for Small (6–8). Changes for Medium (10–12) and Large (14) are in parentheses.
· Finished Measurement at Underarm:
—Approx. 34 (36, 38) inches

Materials: The blouse is made of Unger's Angel Spun in 1.7 oz. balls. You need:
5 (5, 6) balls
1 yard of ¼-inch elastic

Tools: Aluminum Crochet Hooks—Size F and Size G

NOTE 1: Gauge is not given. Measurements are listed for individual piece throughout.

NOTE 2: Peplum is added onto back and front when pieces are completed.

NOTE 3: LDC—Abbreviation for Long Double Crochet, a dc that is pulled up to ¾ inch high.

Directions to Follow

Back: With larger hook, ch 53 (53, 60) loosely.

Foundation Row: Dc in 4th ch from hook, dc in each ch across—51 (51, 58) dc, counting turning ch. Turn.

Row 1: Ch 2, sc in next dc, * skip 2 dc, work 7 LDC in next dc (shell), skip 2 dc, sc in next dc, ch 2, sc in next dc; rep from *, end last rep ch 1, hdc in next dc—7 (7, 8) shells. Turn.

Row 2: Ch 3 (counts as 1 dc), work 3 LDC in ch-1 sp, * skip 3 LDC, sc in sp between 3rd and 4th LDC, ch 2, sc in sp between 4th and 5th LDC, work 7 LDC in ch-2 sp; rep from *, end last rep 4 LDC in last ch-2 sp—6 (6, 7) shells plus a half shell at each end. Turn.

Row 3: Ch 2, sc in sp between 1st and 2nd LDC, work 7 LDC in ch-2 sp, rep from * of Row 2, ending skip 3 LDC, sc in sp between 3rd and 4th LDC, ch 1, hdc in top of turning ch (ch 1, hdc counts as ch-2)—7 (7, 8) shells—to meas approx. 17 (17, 19) inches. Rep Rows 2 and 3 for pat until approx. 12 inches from beg, ending with Row 3.

Next Row: Ch 3, 3 LDC in ch-1 sp, sc in 4th LDC of shell, 7 LDC in next ch-2 sp, work pat across to last full 7 LDC shell, sc in 4th LDC, 4 LDC in last ch-2 sp. Turn.

Shape Armholes: Sl st across 4 LDC, sc and 3 LDC in ch-2 sp, sc in sp between 3rd and 4th LDC, ch 2, sc in sp between 4th and 5th LDC, pat st to last shell, hdc in sp between 3rd and 4th LDC, ch 1, hdc in sp between 4th and 5th LDC. Continue in pat, having 4 (4, 5) shells plus a half shell at each end on one row and 5 (5, 6) shells on other row—should meas approx. 13½ (13½, 14½) inches across in width. Work even until armhole meas approx. 6½ (6½, 7½) inches, ending with a pat Row 2.

Shape Neck: Work pat until 2 7-LDC shells are completed, end sc in 4th LDC, turn; sl st across 4 LDC, pat to end, turn. Work pat and in 1st ch-2 sp work 7 LDC, shortening LDC gradually to the 4th LDC, then lengthening LDC for the 5th, 6th, 7th LDC, making top edge of shell even, sc in 4th LDC. Fasten off. Attach yarn in sc at neck edge of last full

row, work pat, working 1 (1, 2) shells for even edge (shortening and lengthening LDC), sc in 4th LDC, work pat to end—2 shells. Turn.

Next Row: Work pat until 1 LDC shell is completed, sc in 4th LDC; turn; sl st in 4 LDC, work straight-edge shell, sc in last LDC. Fasten off.

Peplum: With smaller hook, beg on opposite edge of dc row and work Row 1 of pat as for back—7 (7, 8) shells. Work pat for 2½ inches. Change to larger hook and continue in pat until 6 inches from beg, ending with Row 3 of pat.

Last Row: Omit ch-2 of first and last lp and work a sc only, work rem of row in pat. Fasten off.

Front: Ch 53 (60, 67) loosely. Work Foundation Row as for back—51 (58, 65) dc, counting turning ch. Beg with Pat Row 1—7 (8, 9) shells. Work same as back to underarm. Piece should meas approx. 17 (19, 21) inches across in width. Work the row before armhole shaping and armhole shaping as for back. Work even until armhole meas approx. 5½ (5½, 6½) inches, ending with Row 2 of pat.

Shape Neck: Shape neck as on back. When shaping is complete, work straight edge shell as for back. Work 2 (2, 3) straight-edge shells for front neck and work other side to correspond.

Peplum: Work same as for back, starting with 7 (8, 9) shells.

Sleeves: Ch 47 (58, 58) loosely.

Row 1: Sc in 3rd ch from hook, * skip 4 chs, 7 LDC in next ch, skip 4 chs, sc in next ch, ch 2, sc in next ch; rep from * across—4 (5, 5) shells.

Beg with **Pat Row 2** and work even in pat until approx. 5 inches from beg, ending with **Pat Row 3.**

NOTE—First inc will be at beg of row and 2nd inc will be made at end of row.

1st Inc: Work 7 LDC in first ch-1 sp (inc—place a marker), work pat even to end.

Next Row: Work pat even to last shell, sc in sp between 3rd and 4th LDC, ch 2, sc in sp between 4th and 5th LDC, work 4 LDC in last LDC.

Work pat as established until 12 (12, 9) inches from beg, ending ready to work from side of marker for first inc.

2nd Inc: Work pat as established to end, working 7 LDC in last ch-2 sp. Turn.

Next Row: Ch 3, 3 LDC in 1st LDC, sc in sp between 3rd and 4th LDC, ch 2, sc in sp between 4th and 5th LDC, complete row in pat as established—5 (6, 6) shells on 1 row, 4 (5, 5) shells plus a half shell at each end on other row. Piece to meas approx. 12 (13½, 13½) inches across in width. For small and medium, work even until 17 inches from beg, ending with Row 3. For large, work 1 more complete inc, working first inc when 12 inches from beg and 2nd inc at 15 inches from beg—7 shells on 1 row and 6 shells plus a half shell at each end on other row. Piece should meas approx. 15 inches across in width. Work even until 17 inches from beg, ending with Row 3.

Shape Cap: Sl st same as for back armhole, sc in sp between 3rd and 4th LDC, ch 2, sc in sp between 4th and 5th LDC, work pat as established to last shell, sc in sp between 3rd and 4th LDC, ch 1, hdc in sp between 4th and 5th LDC, turn. Work pat as established until cap meas approx. 4½ (4½, 5½) inches, ending with Row 3.

Next Row: Work pat, omitting ch 2 at beg and end of row. Turn.

Dec Row 1: Sl st in 4 LDC, pat st across as established, end sc in 4th LDC. Rep last row once.

Next Row: Sl st in 4 LDC, * work straight-edge shell, sc in 4th LDC; rep from *. Fasten off.

Belt: With larger hook, ch 15 loosely.

Row 1: 3 LDC in 4th ch from hook, skip 4 chs, sc in next ch, ch 2, sc in next ch, skip 4 chs, 4 LDC in last ch. Turn.

Row 2: Ch 2, sc in sp between 1st and 2nd LDC, work 7 LDC in ch-2 sp, sc in sp between 3rd and 4th LDC, ch 1, hdc in top of turning ch. Turn.

Row 3: Ch 4, 3 LDC in ch-1 sp, sc in sp between 3rd and 4th LDC, ch 2, sc in sp between 4th and 5th LDC, 4 LDC in last ch sp.

Rep Rows 2 and 3 until belt is desired length, ending with Row 2. Work Row 3 of pat, working 1 sc in 4th LDC instead of sc, ch 2, sc. Fasten off.

Finishing: Weave shoulder seams. With smaller hook, work 1 row of sc around neck, shaping to fit. Be careful not to draw in too tightly. Weave side and sleeve seams. Sew in sleeves.

DO NOT BLOCK. Run elastic through dc row for blouson look. Cut elastic to desired size and sew short ends of elastic tog.

COPYRIGHT © 1982 WILLIAM UNGER & CO., INC.

PATTERNED BLOUSE

A combination of shell and V stitches creates an interesting textural look for this sweater. Although the effect seems a bit dressy, this garment can be worn for a variety of occasions.

Information to Check Before You Start

Sizing: Directions are written for Small (8–10). Changes for Medium (12–14) are in parentheses.
· Finished Measurement at Underarm:
—Approx. 35 (38) inches
Materials: This blouse is made of Unger's Fluffy Yarn in 1¾ oz. balls. You need 7 (8) balls

Tools: Aluminum Crochet Hooks—
   Sizes G and H (G and I)
Gauge: With H Hook—
   1 shell and V st = 2 inches
I Hook—
   1 shell and V st = 2½ inches

Directions to Follow

Lower Back Band: With G hook, ch 7.
   Row 1: Hdc in 3rd ch from hook, hdc in each ch—6 hdc, counting turning ch. Ch 2, turn.

Row 2: Ch 2 on turn counts as first hdc, * post hdc around next st (yo hook, insert hook in sp before next st, bring hook across back of st and out in sp after the st, draw up a lp, and work off the 3 lps as a hdc); rep from * to last st, hdc in last st. Ch 2, turn. Rep Row 2 until piece meas 15 (16) inches. Do not break yarn.

Body: Change to H (I) hook and working along side edge of band, work 51 sc (make sure to center work so you have 25 sc on each side of center st). Ch 3, turn.

Row 1: Ch 3 on turn always counts as first dc, dc in next st, * skip 2 sc, 5 dc in next st (shell), skip 2 sc, dc, ch 1, dc all in the next st (V st); rep from *, end skip 2, 5 dc in next st, skip 2, 1 dc in each of last 2 sts. Ch 3, turn.

Row 2: Dc in next st, * 1 dc in each of 5 dc of shell, V st (dc, ch 1, dc) under ch-1 of V st; rep from *, end 1 dc in each of last 2 sts. Ch 3, turn.

Row 3: Repeat Row 2.

Row 4: Dc in next st, * V st in 3rd dc of group of 5, 5 dc for shell under ch-1 of V st; rep from *, end 1 dc in each of 2 sts. Ch 3, turn.

Row 5: Dc in next st, * V st under ch-1 of V st, 1 dc in each of 5 dc of shell; rep from *, end V st, 1 dc in each of 2 sts. Ch 3, turn.

Row 6: As Row 5.

Row 7: Dc in next st, * 5 dc (shell) under ch-1 of V st, V st in 3rd dc of group of 5 dc; rep from *, end 1 dc in each of 2 sts. Ch 3, turn. Rep Rows 2 through 7 for pat. Work even until 7 complete patterns (a pat is 3 rows) plus 2 rows of the 8th pat (side edges have 2 dc, V st, then 5 dc). Fasten off.

Front: Work same as for back.

Sleeves: Make 2. With G hook, ch 11. Work as for lower back band on 10 sts until cuff meas 7 (7½) inches. Do not fasten off. Change to H (I) hook and work 45 sc along side edge of cuff. Work pat st as for back until 2 rows of 9th pat are completed (side edges have 2 dc, then 5 dc).

Yoke. Rnd 1: Starting with back, leave off first 7 sts for armhole (2 dc, dc, ch 1, dc of V st, and 2 dc of shell), attach yarn

in 3rd dc of group of 5 dc. Ch 3 (counts as a dc), 1 dc in next 2 sts, work pat across to within last 7 sts for armhole, ending 1 dc in 3 sts.

Join Sleeve as Follows: Leave off 5 sts of sleeve for armhole (2 dc and 3 dc of group of 5), dc in each of 2 sts, work pat across to within last 5 sts (end with 2 dc).

Join Front as Follows: Leave off 7 sts for armhole, 1 dc in each of 3 sts, work to within last 7 sts, ending 1 dc in 3 sts.

Join Second Sleeve as Follows: Leave off 5 sts for armhole, 1 dc in 2 sts, work pat across to last 5 sts, ending 1 dc in 2 sts. Join with a sl st to top of starting ch. NOTE—At each armhole joining you have 2 dc coming from sleeve and 3 dc from back and front, making a complete pat.

Rnd 2: Ch 5, dc back in same st for a V st, * 5 dc in next V st, V st in center dc of next shell, 3 dc in next V st, V st in center of next shell; rep from * around, end 3 dc in V st, join with a sl st in 4th ch of starting ch.

Rnds 3 and 4: Work pat as established on Rnd 2.

Rnd 5: Change pat and work all shells with 3 dc.

Rnds 6 and 7: Follow pat as established on Rnd 5.

Rnd 8: Change pat and work every other shell with 3 dc and the alternate shell with 1 dc.

Rnds 9 and 10: Work even in pat as established on Rnd 8.

Rnd 11: Change pat and work 1 dc in each shell.

Rnds 12 and 13: Work even in pat as established on Rnd 11. Join with a sl st and fasten off.

Finishing: With G hook and right side facing, work 1 rnd of sc around neck, taking in slightly for fit. Fasten off.

Neckband: With G hook, ch 5. Work pat as for lower back band to meas around neck. Fasten off. Weave band to neck edge, placing seam at center back of neck.

Weave undersleeve and side seams.

DO NOT BLOCK. Wet block. (Wet with cold water. Lay on a towel to measurements. Dry away from heat and sun.)

TUNIC TOP IN FILET

The use of filet stitches turns a classic design into a fashion item. On a warm day, this would be the perfect thing to wear.

Information to Check Before You Start

Sizing: Instructions are for Size 6–8. Changes for Sizes 10–12 and 14–16 are in parentheses.
· Finished Measurements:
Bust—35 (37, 39½) inches
Back at Underarm—17½ (18½, 19¼) inches
Material: The top is made of Bucilla Tempo using 2 oz. skeins. You need 8 (9, 10) skeins.
Tool: Steel Crochet Hook—Size I
Gauge: 7 dc and 6 ch-1 sps =
    2 inches
    3 rows = 1 inch

Directions to Follow

Back—Ch 114 (122, 130) for lower edge border.

Row 1—right side—Work 1 sc in 2nd ch from hook and each rem ch across; 113 (121, 129) sc.

Row 2—Ch 1, turn, 1 sc in each sc across. Rpt row 2 twice more.

Mesh Pat—Row 1—right side—Ch 4, turn, skip 1st 2 sc, 1 dc in next sc, * ch 1, skip next sc, 1 dc in next sc; rpt from * across; 57 (61, 65) dc and 56 (60, 64) ch-1 sps—113 (121, 129) sts.

NOTE: Ch 4 counts as 1 dc and 1 ch-1 sp.

Row 2—Ch 4, turn, 1 dc in 2nd dc, * ch 1, 1 dc in next dc; rpt from * across.

Rpt row 2 for pat until 40 mesh rows have been completed, about 14 inches from beg, end on wrong side.

Raglan Shaping—Sl st into 1st 5 (5, 7) sts, ch 4, work pat to within 4 (4, 6) sts of end; 105 (113, 117) sts.

Next Row—Dec Row—Ch 3, yo, draw up a loop in next ch-1 sp, yo and through 2 loops on hook, yo, draw up a loop in next dc, yo and through 2 loops on hook, yo and through all 3 loops on hook—a dec made—work pat to within last 3 sts, work a dec on next dc and next ch-1 sp, 1 dc in last dc; 103 (111, 115) sts.

Continue to dec 1 st each side every row 21 (23, 25) times more; 61 (65, 65) sts.

Work 1 row even in mesh. Fasten off.

Front—Work 4 rows border and 4 rows mesh pat same as for back, end on wrong side.

Filet Pat—Row 1—Ch 4, turn, * 1 dc in next dc, ch 1 *; rpt between *'s 5 (7, 9) times, †[1 dc in next dc, 1 dc in ch-1] twice, 1 dc in next dc, ch 1; rpt between *'s 7 times †; rpt between †'s 3 times, [1 dc in next dc, 1 dc in ch-1] twice; rpt between *'s across, end 1 dc in last dc.

Row 2—Ch 4, turn, * 1 dc in next dc, ch 1 *; rpt between *'s 4 (6, 8) times, † 1 dc in next dc, 1 dc in next sp, 1 dc in each of next 2 dc, ch 1, skip next dc, 1 dc in each of next 2 dc, 1 dc in ch-1 sp; rpt between *'s 6 times †; rpt between †'s 4 times; rpt between *'s 0 (2, 4) times, 1 dc in last dc.

Row 3—Ch 4, turn, * 1 dc in next dc, ch 1 *; rpt between *'s 5 (7, 9) times, † ‡ [1 dc in next dc] twice, 1 dc in ch-1 sp, [1 dc in next dc] twice, ‡ ch 1; rpt between *'s 7 times †; rpt between †'s 3 times; rpt between ‡'s once, work pat to end.

Rows 4, 5, 6, 7, and 8—Ch 4, turn, work mesh pat across.

Row 9—Ch 4, turn, * 1 dc in next dc, ch 1 *; rpt between *'s 0 (2, 4) times; rpt between †'s of row 1, 5 times, [1 dc in next dc, 1 dc in ch-1 sp] twice; rpt between *'s 2 (4, 6) times, 1 dc in last dc.

Row 10—Ch 4, turn, * work 1 dc in next dc, ch 1 *; rpt between *'s 0 (2, 4) times; rpt between †'s of row 2, 5 times, 1 dc in next dc, 1 dc in ch-1 sp, 1 dc in each of next 2 dc, ch 1, skip next dc, 1 dc in each of next 2 dc, 1 dc in ch-1 sp; rpt between *'s across, end 1 dc in last dc.

Row 11—Ch 4, turn, * 1 dc in next dc, ch 1 *; rpt between *'s 0 (2, 4) times; rpt between †'s of row 3, 5 times, [1 dc in next dc] twice, 1 dc in ch-1 sp, [1 dc in next dc] twice; rpt between *'s 2 (4, 6) times, 1 dc in last dc.

Rows 12, 13, 14, 15, and 16—Ch 4, turn, work mesh pat across. Rpt last 16 rows for pat, working until same length as back to underarm, end on wrong side.

NOTE: Discontinue pat at armhole edges when working raglan shaping. Keeping pat, work raglan shaping same as for back. Work 1 row even. Fasten off.

Sleeves—Ch 92 (94, 96) for lower edge.

Row 1—Work 1 sc in 2nd ch from hook and each rem ch across; 91 (93, 95) sts.

Row 2—Ch 4, turn, 1 dc in 3rd sc, * ch 1, skip next sc, 1 dc in next sc; rpt from * across.

Row 3—Ch 4, turn, 1 dc in 2nd dc, * ch 1, 1 dc in next dc; rpt from * across.

Rpt row 3 for pat until 18 inches from beg, end on wrong side.

Raglan Shaping—Work same as back. Work 1 row even. Fasten off.

Neck Cord—Make a ch 52 inches long. Work a sl st in 2nd ch from hook and each rem ch across. Fasten off.

Sleeve Cords—Make a ch 18 inches long. Work a sl st in 2nd ch from hook and each rem ch. Fasten off.

Finishing—Sew raglan seams. Sew side and sleeve seams. Draw neck cord through top mesh row and gather as illustrated. Draw sleeve cords through first mesh row and gather.

Steam lightly.

LACY CAMISOLE

A delicate diamond design gives a dressy feeling to an otherwise simple camisole, which combines beautifully with a summery country skirt.

Information to Check Before You Start

Size: Instructions are for size 6–8. Changes for sizes 10–12 and 14–16 are in parentheses.
· Finished Measurements:
Bust—32½ (35, 37½) inches
Back at underarm—16¼ (17½, 18¼) inches
Material: The camisole is made of Bucilla Tempo using 2 oz. skeins. You need 4 (5, 5) skeins.
Tool: Steel Crochet Hook—Size I
Gauge: 6 dc = 1 inch
3 rows = 1 inch

Directions to Follow

Back—Ch 98 (106, 114) loosely for lower edge.
Row 1—right side—Work 1 sc in 2nd ch from hook and in each rem ch across; 97 (105, 113) sc.
Row 2—Ch 1, turn, 1 sc in each sc across.
Row 3—Ch 3, turn, skip 1st st, 1 dc in each of next 7 sts, * ch 1, skip next st, 1 dc in each of next 7 sts; rpt from * 10 (11, 12) times, end 1 dc in last st.
NOTE: Ch-3 at beg of row counts as 1 dc. Always skip 1st dc at beg of row. Ch-1 counts as 1 st.
Row 4—Ch 3, turn, 1 dc in each of next 6 dc, * ch 1, skip next dc, 1 dc in next st, ch 1, skip next dc, 1 dc in each of next 5 dc; rpt from * 10 (11, 12) times, end 1 dc in last 2 dc.
Row 5—Ch 3, turn, 1 dc in next dc, * ch 1, skip next dc, 1 dc in next 3 sts; rpt from * across, end 1 dc in last 2 sts.
Row 6—Ch 3, turn, 1 dc in next 2 sts, * ch 1, skip next dc, 1 dc in next st, ch 1, skip next st, 1 dc in each of next 5 sts; rpt from * 10 (11, 12) times, ch 1, skip next st, 1 dc in last 3 sts.
Row 7—Ch 3, turn, 1 dc in next 3 dc, * ch 1, skip next dc, 1 dc in each of next 7 sts; rpt from * 10 (11, 12) times, ch 1, skip next st, 1 dc in last 4 sts.
Row 8—Rpt row 6.
Row 9—Rpt row 5.
Row 10—Rpt row 4.
Rpt rows 3 through 10, 3 times more; row 3 once again; 35 rows from beg.
Row 36—Ch 1, turn, 1 sc in first st and each st across.
Next Row—Picot Row—Ch 1, turn, 1 sc in first sc, * ch 2, 1 sc in 2nd ch from hook—a picot—1 sc in each of next 2 sc; rpt from * across. Fasten off.

Front—Same as back.
Straps—Make 4—Make a ch 14 inches long, work 1 sc in 2nd ch from hook and each rem ch across. Fasten off.
Waist Cord—Make a ch 50 inches long, work 1 sc in 2nd and each rem ch. Fasten off.

Finishing—Sew side seams. Sew on straps as illustrated and tie into bow. Draw waist cord through first openwork row at waistline and tie as illustrated.
Steam lightly.

LACY BLOUSE AND TUBE

The dainty openwork design is reminiscent of Irish crochet. It creates a lovely lacy effect. Wear it over a tubelike camisole in a contrasting color for a smart effect.

Information to Check Before You Start

Sizing: Directions are written for Small (8–10). Changes for Medium (12–14) are in parentheses.
· Body Measurement at Underarm:
—Approx. 35–36 (37–38) inches
Materials: The blouse is made of Unger's Janet yarn in 1$\frac{4}{10}$ oz. balls. You need 10 (11) balls
Tool: Aluminum Crochet Hook— Size F (G)
Note: Body is worked all around to underarm. Because of the nature of the pattern, the measurement around body is given instead of a stitch gauge.

Directions to Follow

BLOUSE

Lower Rib: With F (G) hook, ch 21.
   Row 1: Hdc in 4th ch from hook, hdc in each ch across—19 hdc, including turning ch. Ch 2, turn.
   Row 2: Note—Ch 2 on turn is always counted as 1st st. * Hdc around post of next hdc (yo insert hook in space before st, going from front to back, bring hook across back of st and out in next space after the st, going from back to front, draw up a loop and work off as a hdc); repeat from * across, ending with hdc in last st. Ch 2, turn. Repeat Row 2 until there are 60 ribs (should measure approx. 25 (28) inches. Fasten off. Weave short ends of rib tog.

Body: Attach yarn at joining of rib. With F (G) hook, work 120 sc around side edge of rib. Join with a sl st. DO NOT TURN.
   Rnd 1: * Ch 3, skip 1 sc, sc in next st; repeat from * around, end ch 1, join with a dc in first ch-3 space (60 ch-3 spaces). DO NOT TURN.
   Rnd 2: * Ch 2, in next ch-3 space (sp) work 5 dc, remove hook and leave loop free, insert hook in 1st dc of group of 5, draw free loop through 1st st (popcorn made—PC), ch 2, sc in next ch-3 sp, (ch 3, sc in next ch-3 sp) 4 times; repeat from * around, ending (ch 3, sc in next ch-3 sp) 3 times, ch 1, dc in base of 1st ch-2. Turn.
   Rnd 3: (Ch 3, sc in ch-3 sp) 3 times, * ch 3, sc in ch-2 sp, ch 2, sc in next ch-2 sp, (ch 3, sc in next ch-3 sp) 4 times; repeat from *, ending ch 3, sc in ch-2 sp, ch 2, sc in ch-2 sp, ch 1, dc in base of first ch 3. Turn.
   Rnd 4: * Work 8 dc (shell) in ch-2 sp, sc in next ch-3 sp, (ch 3, sc in next ch-3 sp) 4 times; repeat from *, ending (ch 3, sc in next ch-3 sp) 3 times, ch 1, dc in same sp as turning. Turn.
   Rnd 5: (Ch 3, sc in ch-3 sp) 3 times, * (ch 3, skip 2 dc, sc in next dc) twice, (ch 3, sc in next ch-3 sp) 4 times; repeat from *, ending (ch 3, skip 2 dc, sc in next dc) twice, ch 1, dc in base of turning ch. Turn.
   Rnd 6: (Ch 3, sc in ch-3 sp) 3 times. Repeat from * of Rnd 2, ending ch 2, PC in next ch sp, ch 2, sc in ch-3 sp, ch 1, dc in base of first ch-3. Turn.
   Rnd 7: Work from * of Rnd 3, ending (ch 3, sc in ch-3 sp) 3 times, ch 1, dc in base of turning ch. Turn.
   Rnd 8: (Ch 3, sc in next ch-3 sp) 3 times. Work from * of Row 4, ending shell in ch-2 sp, sc in ch-3 sp, ch 1, dc in base of turning ch. Turn.
   Rnd 9: Repeat from * of Rnd 5, ending (ch 3, sc in ch-3 sp) 3 times, ch 1, dc in base of turning ch. Turn. Repeat Rnds 2 through 9 until piece measures 10 inches above rib, ending with completion of Rnd 5. Leave yarn attached and set aside.

Sleeves: With F (G) hook, ch 17. Work rib pattern as lower border until there are 14 (14) ribs (should measure approx. 6½ (7½) inches). Fasten off. Weave short ends tog. Attach yarn at rib joining.

Rnd 1: With F (G) hook, work 24 sc around side edge of rib. DO NOT TURN.

Rnd 2: * Ch 3, sc in next sc; repeat from *, ending ch 1, dc in same sp as first ch-3. Work pattern st as on body until piece measures 19 inches above rib, starting with Rnd 2 and ending with Rnd 9. Fasten off.

Joining of Body and Sleeves. Yoke: Beg working on body with Rnd 6, repeat from * once; ch 2, PC in next ch sp, ch 2, sc in next ch-3 sp, ch 3, sc in next ch-3 sp; ch 3, insert hook in next ch-3 sp on body (over a shell) and in the 4th ch-3 sp to the left of sleeve ending (over a shell), work sc through both loops, work across sleeve as follows: (ch 3, sc in next ch-3 sp) twice, continue from * of Rnd 6 across sleeve until 3 PC are completed, ch 2, sc in next ch-3 sp on sleeve, ch 3, sc in next ch-3 sp, ch 3, in-sert hook in next ch-3 sp on sleeve (over a shell), skip 5 ch-3 spaces on body and insert hook in next ch-3 sp on body (over a shell), sc through both loops, work across front of body as follows: (ch 3, sc in next ch-3 sp) twice, continue pattern across front as on Rnd 6, start-ing with ch 2, PC; work across until 4 PC are completed, ch 2, sc in next ch-3 sp, ch 3, sc in next ch-3 sp. **Attach sleeve as follows:** ch 3, insert hook in next ch-3 sp on body, insert hook in 4th ch-3 sp to left of sleeve ending (over a shell), work sc through both loops, work across sleeve as follows: (ch 3, sc in next ch-3 sp) twice, continue from * of Rnd 6 across sleeve until 3 PC are completed, ch 2, sc in next ch-3 sp, ch 3, sc in next ch-3 sp, ch 3, insert hook in next ch-3 sp on sleeve (over a shell), skip 5 ch-3 loops on body and insert hook in next ch-3 sp on body (over a shell), sc through both loops, complete pattern across back as follows: (ch 3, sc in next ch-3 sp) twice; repeat from * of Rnd 6 end ch 2, sc in ch-3 sp, ch 1, dc in base of starting ch-3. Turn. Work pattern around back, front, and sleeves, starting with Rnd 7, then work Rnds 8, 9, 2, 3, 4.

Yoke Shaping. Dec Rnd 1: * (Ch 3, sc in next ch-3 sp) 3 times, (ch 3, skip 2 dc, sc in next dc) 2 times, ch 1, sc in next ch-3 sp; repeat from *, end (ch 3, skip 2 dc, sc in next dc) 2 times, ch 1, dc in base of starting ch. Turn.

Rnd 2: (Ch 3, sc in next ch-3) 3 times, * ch 2, PC in next ch sp, ch 2, sc in next ch-3 sp, (ch 3, sc in next ch-3 sp) 3 times (NOTE—The ch-1 sp is skipped over); repeat from *, end ch 2, PC in next ch sp, ch 2, sc in next ch-3 sp, ch 1, join with a dc to base of starting ch. Turn.

Rnd 3: * Ch 3, sc in ch-2 sp, ch 2, sc in next ch-2 sp, (ch 3, sc in next ch-3 sp) 3 times; repeat from *, end ch 1, dc in base of starting ch. Turn.

Rnd 4: * (Ch 3, sc in ch-3 sp) 3 times, 8 dc in next ch-2 sp, sc in next ch-3 sp; repeat from *, end ch 1, dc in base of starting ch. Turn.

Rnd 5: * (Ch 3, skip 2 dc, sc in next dc) twice, (ch 3, sc in next ch-3 sp) 3 times; repeat from *, end ch 1, dc in base of 1st ch. Turn.

Rnd 6: * Ch 2, PC in next ch-3 sp, ch 2, sc in next ch-3 sp, (ch 3, sc in next ch-3 sp) 3 times; repeat from *, end ch 1, dc at base of 1st ch. Turn.

Rnd 7: * (Ch 3, sc in ch-3 sp) 3 times, ch 3, sc in next ch-2 sp, ch 2, sc in next ch-2 sp; repeat from *, end ch 2, sc in next ch-2 sp, ch 1, dc at base of starting ch. Turn.

Rnd 8: * 8 dc in 1st ch-2 sp (shell above popcorn), sc in next ch sp, (ch 3, sc in next ch-3 sp) 3 times; repeat from *, end last repeat (ch 3, sc in next ch-3 sp) 2 times, ch 1, dc in last sp. Join with a sl st. Turn.

Rnd 9: * (ch 3, sc in next ch-3 sp) 2 times, (ch 3, skip 2 dc, sc in next dc) twice, ch 1, sc in next ch-3 sp; repeat from *, end ch 1, sl st in joining. Turn.

Rnd 10: * (Ch 3, sc in next ch-3 sp) 2 times (the ch-1 sp is skipped), ch 2, PC in next ch-3 sp, ch 2, sc in next ch-3 sp; repeat from *, end ch 1, dc in base of starting ch. Turn.

Rnd 11: * Ch 3, sc in ch-2 sp, ch 2, sc in ch-2 sp, (ch 3, sc in ch-3 sp) twice; re-peat from *, end ch 1, dc in base of starting ch. Turn.

Rnd 12: * (Ch 3, sc in next ch-3 sp)

twice, 8 dc in next ch-2 sp (above PC), sc in next ch-3 sp; repeat from *, end ch 1, dc in base of starting ch. Turn.

Rnd 13: * (Ch 2, skip 2 dc, dc in next dc) twice, (ch 2, sc in next ch-3 sp) twice; repeat from *, end ch 1, dc at base of starting ch. Turn.

Rnd 14: * Ch 2, PC in next ch-2 sp, ch 2, sc in next ch-2 sp, (ch 2, sc in next ch-2 sp) 2 times; repeat from *, end ch 1, hdc at base of starting ch. Turn.

Rnd 15: * Ch 1, sc in ch-2 sp, repeat from *, end join with a sl st to first ch-1.

Rnd 16: Ch 1, work a hdc under each ch-1 sp around, end join with a sl st. DO NOT TURN.

Rnd 17: With right side facing, working backwards from left to right, ch 1, * sc in next st; repeat from * around. Join with a sl st. Fasten off.

Finishing: Weave open mesh under sleeve to body. DO NOT BLOCK.

TUBE

Information to Check Before You Start

Sizing: Directions are for Small (8–10). Changes for Medium (12–14) are in parentheses.

Materials: The tube is made of Unger's Janet yarn in 1$\frac{4}{10}$ oz. balls. You need 2 (3) balls.

Tool: Aluminum Crochet Hook—Size F

Gauge: 9 dc = 2 inches

Directions to Follow

Ch 142 (148) loosely.

Rnd 1: Dc in 4th ch from hook, dc in each ch—140 (146) dc, counting turning ch. Join with a sl st to first ch-3. Be careful not to twist. Turn.

Rnd 2: Ch 3 (always counted as 1 dc at beg of rnd), dc in each dc. Join with a sl st to top of ch-3. Turn.

Rnds 3, 5, 7: Ch 3, work in dc, decreasing 10 dc evenly spaced on rnd (to dec—yo draw up a loop in one st, retain 3 loops on hook, draw up a loop in next st, yo draw through 2 loops, yo draw through all loops on hook). Join with a sl st to top of ch-3. Turn.

Rnds 4, 6, 8, 9: Ch 3, dc in each st. Join with a sl st to top of ch-3—110 (116) dc. Turn.

Rnds 10, 12, 14, 16, 18, 20: Ch 3, work in dc, increasing 5 dc evenly spaced on rnd (to inc, work 2 dc in one st).

Rnds 11, 13, 15, 17, 19: Ch 3, dc in each st. Join with a sl st. After Rnd 20 is completed there are 140 (146) sts.

Bust Shaping. Row 1: Place a marker between the 70th and 71st (73rd and 74th) st (this is front). Starting at beg of row, work 4 sc, 4 hdc, dc across to within 8 sts of marker, work 4 hdc, 4 sc. Ch 1, turn.

Row 2: Sl st across 4 sts, work 4 sc, 4 hdc, dc across to within 12 sts of beg of row, work 4 hdc, 4 sc, 4 sl st. Ch 1, turn.

Rnd 21: From here on you will work dc around all sts as on previous rnd. Ch 3, dc in each st on rnd. Join with a sl st to top of ch 3. Ch 1, turn. Repeat Rnd 21 until 11½ inches from beg, or desired length.

Short Rnd: Work 5 hdc, 60 (63) dc, 15 hdc, 50 (53) sc, 10 hdc. Join with a sl st.

Next rnd: Attach tubular elastic. Work 1 rnd of sc over elastic. Fasten off elastic securely. DO NOT TURN.

Last rnd: With right side facing, working backwards from left to right, sc in each st. Fasten off. DO NOT BLOCK.
COPYRIGHT © 1980 WILLIAM UNGER & CO., INC.

FANCY SHAWL

An unusual combination of lacy motifs, bands, and edging is used for this lovely wrap. The result: a very decorative shawl to drape around your shoulders.

Information to Check Before You Start

Sizing: The directions are written for one size only.
Materials: The shawl is made of Bernat Berella® Sportspun in 50 gram balls. You need 7 balls.
Tools: Crochet Hook (Bernat U.S.)— Size G (4.5 mm)
Gauge: 5 dc and 4 ch-1 spaces = 2 inches; 3 rows = 1 inch

Directions to Follow

Ch 34 sts loosely.
Row 1: 1 dc in 6th ch from hook, (ch 1, skip next ch, 1 dc in next ch) 14 times—15 spaces.
Row 2: Ch 4, turn, 1 dc in 1st space, (ch 1, 1 dc in next dc) 7 times, 3 dc in next space, skip next dc, (ch 1, 1 dc in next dc) 6 times, ch 1, 1 dc, ch 1, 1 dc in last space.
Row 3: Ch 4, turn, 1 dc in 1st space, (ch 1, 1 dc in next dc) 7 times, 3 dc in next space, ch 3, skip next 4 dc, 3 dc in next space, 1 dc in next dc, (ch 1, 1 dc in next dc) 6 times, ch 1, 1 dc, ch 1, 1 dc in last space.
Row 4: Ch 4, turn, 1 dc in 1st space, (ch 1, 1 dc in next dc) 7 times, 3 dc in next space, ch 3, skip next 4 dc, 1 dc in next space, ch 3, skip next 4 dc, 3 dc in next space, 1 dc in next dc, (ch 1, 1 dc in next dc) 6 times, ch 1, 1 dc, ch 1, 1 dc in last space.
Row 5: Ch 4, turn, 1 dc in 1st space, (ch 1, 1 dc in next dc) 7 times, 3 dc in next space, ch 3, skip next 4 dc and 2 ch, 1 sc in next ch, 1 sc in next dc, 1 sc in next ch, ch 3, skip next 2 ch and 4 dc, 3 dc in next space, 1 dc in next dc, (ch 1, 1 dc in next dc) 6 times, ch 1, 1 dc, ch 1, 1 dc in last space.
Row 6: Ch 4, turn, 1 dc in 1st space, (ch 1, 1 dc in next dc) 7 times, 3 dc in next space, ch 3, skip next 4 dc and 2 ch, 1 sc in next ch, 1 sc in each of next 3 sc, 1 sc in next ch, ch 3, skip next 2 ch and 4 dc, 3 dc in next space, 1 dc in next dc, (ch 1, 1 dc in next dc) 6 times, ch 1, 1 dc, ch 1, 1 dc in last space.
Row 7: Ch 4, turn, 1 dc in 1st space, (ch 1, 1 dc in next dc) 7 times, 3 dc in next space, ch 1, skip next 3 dc, 1 dc in next dc, 3 dc in next space, ch 3, skip next sc, 1 sc in each of next 3 sc, ch 3, 3 dc in next space, 1 dc in next dc, ch 1, 3 dc in next space, 1 dc in next dc, (ch 1, 1 dc in next dc) 6 times, ch 1, 1 dc, ch 1, 1 dc in last space.
Row 8: Ch 4, turn, 1 dc in 1st space, (ch 1, 1 dc in next dc) 7 times, 3 dc in next space, ch 1, skip next 3 dc, 1 dc in next dc, ch 1, 1 dc in next dc, ch 1, skip next 2 dc, 1 dc in next dc, 3 dc in next space, ch 3, skip next sc, 1 dc in next sc, ch 3, 3 dc in next space, 1 dc in next dc, ch 1, skip next 2 dc, 1 dc in next dc, ch 1, 1 dc in next dc, ch 1, skip next 3 dc, 3 dc in next space, 1 dc in next dc, (ch 1, 1 dc in next dc) 6 times, ch 1, 1 dc, ch 1, 1 dc in last space.
Row 9: Ch 4, turn, 1 dc in 1st space, (ch 1, 1 dc in next dc) 7 times, 3 dc in next space, ch 1, skip next 3 dc, 1 dc in next dc, (ch 1, 1 dc in next dc) 3 times, ch 1, skip next 2 dc, 1 dc in next dc, 3 dc in next space, ch 1, 3 dc in next space, 1 dc in next dc, ch 1, skip next 2 dc, 1 dc in next dc, (ch 1, 1 dc in next dc) 3 times, ch 1, skip next 3 dc, 3 dc in next space, 1 dc in next dc, (ch 1, 1 dc in next dc) 6 times, ch 1, 1 dc, ch 1, 1 dc in last space.
Row 10: Ch 4, turn, 1 dc in 1st space, (ch 1, 1 dc in next dc) 7 times, 3 dc in next space, ch 1, skip next 3 dc, 1 dc in next dc, (ch 1, 1 dc in next dc) 5 times, ch 1, skip next 2 dc, 1 dc in next dc, 2 dc in next space, 1 dc in next dc, ch 1, skip next 2 dc, 1 dc in next dc, (ch 1, 1 dc in next dc) 5 times, ch 1, skip next 3 dc, 3 dc in next space, 1 dc in next dc, (ch 1, 1 dc in next dc) 6 times, ch 1, 1 dc, ch 1, 1 dc in last space.

Row 11: Ch 4, turn, 1 dc in 1st space, (ch 1, 1 dc in next dc) 7 times, 3 dc in next space, ch 1, skip next 3 dc, 1 dc in next dc, (ch 1, 1 dc in next dc) 6 times, 3 dc in next space, ch 3, skip next 4 dc, 3 dc in next space, 1 dc in next dc, (ch 1, 1 dc in next dc) 6 times, ch 1, skip next 3 dc, 3 dc in next space, 1 dc in next dc, (ch 1, 1 dc in next dc) 6 times, ch 1, 1 dc, ch 1, 1 dc in last space.

Row 12: Ch 4, turn, 1 dc in 1st space, (ch 1, 1 dc in next dc) 7 times, 3 dc in next space, ch 1, skip next 3 dc, 1 dc in next dc, (ch 1, 1 dc in next dc) 6 times, 3 dc in next space, ch 3, skip next 4 dc, 1 dc in next dc, ch 3, skip next 4 dc, 3 dc in next space, 1 dc in next dc, (ch 1, 1 dc in next dc) 6 times, ch 1, skip next 3 dc, 3 dc in next space, 1 dc in next dc, (ch 1, 1 dc in next dc) 6 times, ch 1, 1 dc, ch 1, 1 dc in last space.

Row 13: Ch 4, turn, 1 dc in 1st space, (ch 1, 1 dc in next dc) 7 times, 3 dc in next space, ch 1, skip next 3 dc, 1 dc in next dc, (ch 1, 1 dc in next dc) 6 times, 3 dc in next space, ch 3, skip next 4 dc and 2 ch, 1 sc in next ch, 1 sc in next dc, 1 sc in next ch, ch 3, skip next 2 ch and 4 dc, 3 dc in next space, 1 dc in next dc, (ch 1, 1 dc in next dc) 6 times, ch 1, skip next 3 dc, 3 dc in next space, 1 dc in next dc, (ch 1, 1 dc in next dc) 6 times, ch 1, 1 dc, ch 1, 1 dc in last space.

Row 14: Ch 4, turn, 1 dc in 1st space, (ch 1, 1 dc in next dc) 7 times, 3 dc in next space, ch 1, skip next 3 dc, 1 dc in next dc, (ch 1, 1 dc in next dc) 6 times, 3 dc in next space, ch 3, skip next 4 dc and 2 ch, 1 sc in next ch, 1 sc in each of next 3 sc, 1 sc in next ch, ch 3, skip next 2 ch and 4 dc, 3 dc in next space, 1 dc in next dc, (ch 1, 1 dc in next dc) 6 times, ch 1, skip next 3 dc, 3 dc in next space, 1 dc in next dc, (ch 1, 1 dc in next dc) 6 times, ch 1, 1 dc, ch 1, 1 dc in last space.

Row 15: Ch 4, turn, 1 dc in 1st space, (ch 1, 1 dc in next dc) 7 times, 3 dc in next space, ch 1, skip next 3 dc, 1 dc in next dc, (ch 1, 1 dc in next dc) 6 times, 3 dc in next space, ch 1, skip next 3 dc, 1 dc in next dc, 3 dc in next space, ch 3, skip next sc, 1 sc in each of next 3 sc, ch 3, 3 dc in next space, 1 dc in next dc, ch 1, skip next 3 dc, 3 dc in next space, 1 dc in next dc, (ch 1, 1 dc in next dc) 6 times, ch 1, skip next 3 dc, 3 dc in next space, 1 dc in next dc, (ch 1, 1 dc in next dc) 6 times, ch 1, 1 dc, ch 1, 1 dc in last space.

Row 16: Ch 4, turn, 1 dc in 1st space, (ch 1, 1 dc in next dc) 7 times, 3 dc in next space, ch 1, skip next 3 dc, 1 dc in next dc, (ch 1, 1 dc in next dc) 6 times, 3 dc in next space, ch 1, skip next 3 dc, 1 dc in next dc, ch 1, 1 dc in next dc, ch 1, skip next 2 dc, 1 dc in next dc, 3 dc in next space, ch 3, skip next sc, 1 dc in next sc, ch 3, skip next sc, 3 dc in next space, 1 dc in next dc, ch 1, skip next 2 dc, 1 dc in next dc, ch 1, 1 dc in next dc, ch 1, skip next 3 dc, 3 dc in next space, 1 dc in next dc, (ch 1, 1 dc in next dc) 6 times, ch 1, skip next 3 dc, 3 dc in next space, 1 dc in next dc, (ch 1, 1 dc in next dc) 6 times, ch 1, 1 dc, ch 1, 1 dc in last space.

Row 17: Ch 4, turn, 1 dc in 1st space, (ch 1, 1 dc in next dc) 7 times, 3 dc in next space, ch 1, skip next 3 dc, 1 dc in next dc, (ch 1, 1 dc in next dc) 6 times, 3 dc in next space, ch 1, skip next 3 dc, 1 dc in next dc, (ch 1, 1 dc in next dc) 3 times, ch 1, skip next 2 dc, 1 dc in next dc, 3 dc in next space, ch 1, skip next dc, 3 dc in next space, 1 dc in next dc, ch 1, skip next 2 dc, 1 dc in next dc, (ch 1, 1 dc in next dc) 3 times, ch 1, skip next 3 dc, 3 dc in next space, 1 dc in next dc, (ch 1, 1 dc in next dc) 6 times, ch 1, skip next 3 dc, 3 dc in next space, 1 dc in next dc, (ch 1, 1 dc in next dc) 6 times, ch 1, 1 dc, ch 1, 1 dc in last space.

Row 18: Ch 4, turn, 1 dc in 1st space, (ch 1, 1 dc in next dc) 7 times, 3 dc in next space, ch 1, skip next 3 dc, 1 dc in next dc, (ch 1, 1 dc in next dc) 6 times, 3 dc in next space, ch 1, skip next 3 dc, 1 dc in next dc, (ch 1, 1 dc in next dc) 5 times, ch 1, skip next 2 dc, 1 dc in next dc, 2 dc in next space, 1 dc in next dc, ch 1, skip next 2 dc, 1 dc in next dc, (ch 1, 1 dc in next dc) 5 times, ch 1, skip next 3 dc, 3 dc in next space, 1 dc in next dc, (ch 1, 1 dc in next dc) 6 times, ch 1, skip next 3 dc, 3 dc in next space, 1 dc in next dc, (ch 1, 1 dc in next dc) 6 times, ch 1, 1 dc, ch 1, 1 dc in last space.

Row 19: * Ch 4, turn, 1 dc in 1st space, (ch 1, 1 dc in next dc) 7 times, 3 dc in next space, ch 1, skip next 3 dc, 1 dc in next dc, (ch 1, 1 dc in next dc) 6 times, 3 dc in next space, ch 1, skip next 3 dc, 1 dc in next dc, (ch 1, 1 dc in next dc) 6 times, 3 dc in next space *, ch 3, skip next 4 dc, ** 3 dc in next space, 1 dc in next dc, (ch 1, 1 dc in next dc) 6 times, ch 1, skip next 3 dc, 3 dc in next space, 1 dc in next dc, (ch 1, 1 dc in next dc) 6 times, ch 1, skip next 3 dc, 3 dc in next space, 1 dc in next dc, (ch 1, 1 dc in next dc) 6 times, ch 1, 1 dc, ch 1, 1 dc in last space **.

NOTE—Rows 20 through 61: Work between *'s of Row 19, then work center sts following directions as given for row being worked, then end as between **'s of Row 19.

Row 20: Ch 3, skip next 4 dc, 1 dc in next space, ch 3.

Row 21: Ch 3, skip next 4 dc and 2 ch, 1 sc in next ch, 1 sc in next dc, 1 sc in next ch, ch 3, skip next 2 ch and 4 dc.

Row 22: Ch 3, skip next 4 dc and 2 ch, 1 sc in next ch, 1 sc in each of next 3 sc, 1 sc in next ch, ch 3, skip next 2 ch and 4 dc.

Row 23: Ch 3, skip next 3 dc, 1 dc in next dc, 3 dc in next space, ch 3, skip next sc, 1 sc in each of next 3 sc, ch 3, skip next sc, 3 dc in next space, 1 dc in next dc, ch 3.

Row 24: Ch 3, skip next 4 dc, 1 dc in next space, ch 3, skip next 4 dc, 4 dc in next space, ch 3, skip next sc, 1 dc in next sc, ch 3, 4 dc in next space, ch 3, skip next 4 dc, 1 dc in next space, ch 3.

Row 25: Ch 3, skip next 4 dc and 2 ch, 1 sc in next ch, 1 sc in next dc, 1 sc in next ch, skip next 2 ch and 4 dc, (ch 3, 4 dc in next space) twice, ch 3, skip next 4 dc and 2 ch, 1 sc in next ch, 1 sc in next dc, 1 sc in next ch, ch 3.

Row 26: Ch 3, skip next 4 dc and 2 ch, 1 sc in next ch, 1 sc in each of next 3 sc, 1 sc in next ch, ch 3, skip next 2 ch and 4 dc, 4 dc in next space, ch 3, skip next 4 dc and 2 ch, 1 sc in next ch, 1 sc in each of next 3 sc, 1 sc in next ch, ch 3, skip next 2 ch and 4 dc.

Row 27: Ch 3, 4 dc in next space, ch 3, skip next sc, 1 sc in each of next 3 sc, (ch 3, 4 dc in next space) twice, ch 3,

skip next sc, 1 sc in each of next 3 sc, ch 3, 4 dc in next space, ch 3.

Row 28: (Ch 3, 1 dc in next space, ch 3, 4 dc in next space, ch 3, skip next sc, 1 dc in next sc, ch 3, 4 dc in next space) twice, ch 3, 1 dc in next space, ch 3.

Row 29: (Ch 3, skip next 4 dc and 2 ch, 1 sc in next ch, 1 sc in next dc, 1 sc in next ch, ch 3, skip next 2 ch and 4 dc, 4 dc in next space, ch 3, 4 dc in next space) twice, ch 3, skip next 4 dc and 2 ch, 1 sc in next ch, 1 sc in next dc, 1 sc in next ch, ch 3.

Row 30: (Ch 3, skip next 4 dc and 2 ch, 1 sc in next ch, 1 sc in each of next 3 sc, 1 sc in next ch, ch 3, skip next 2 ch and 4 dc, 4 dc in next space) twice, ch 3, skip next 4 dc and 2 ch, 1 sc in next ch, 1 sc in each of next 3 sc, 1 sc in next ch, ch 3, skip next 2 ch and 4 dc.

Row 31: (Ch 3, 4 dc in next space, ch 3, skip next sc, 1 sc in each of next 3 sc, ch 3, 4 dc in next space) 3 times, ch 3.

Row 32: (Ch 3, 1 dc in next space, ch 3, 4 dc in next space, ch 3, skip next sc, 1 dc in next sc, ch 3, 4 dc in next space) 3 times, ch 3, 1 dc in next space, ch 3.

Row 33: (Ch 3, skip next 4 dc and 2 ch, 1 sc in next ch, 1 sc in next dc, 1 sc in next ch, ch 3, skip next 2 ch and 4 dc, 4 dc in next space, ch 3, 4 dc in next space) 3 times, ch 3, skip next 4 dc and 2 ch, 1 sc in next ch, 1 sc in next dc, 1 sc in next ch, ch 3, skip next 2 ch and 4 dc.

Row 34: (Ch 3, skip next 4 dc and 2 ch, 1 sc in next ch, 1 sc in each of next 3 sc, 1 sc in next ch, ch 3, skip next 2 ch and 4 dc, 4 dc in next space) 3 times, ch 3, skip next 4 dc and 2 ch, 1 sc in next ch, 1 sc in each of next 3 ch, 1 sc in next ch, ch 3, skip next 2 ch and 4 dc.

Row 35: (Ch 3, 4 dc in next space, ch 3, skip next sc, 1 sc in each of next 3 sc, ch 3, 4 dc in next space) 4 times, ch 3.

Row 36: (Ch 3, 1 dc in next space, ch 3, 4 dc in next space, ch 3, skip next sc, 1 dc in next sc, ch 3, 4 dc in next space) 4 times, ch 3, 1 dc in next space, ch 3.

Row 37: (Ch 3, skip next 4 dc and 2 ch, 1 sc in next ch, 1 sc in next dc, 1 sc in next ch, ch 3, skip next 2 ch and 4 dc, 4 dc in next space, ch 3, 4 dc in next space) 4 times, ch 3, skip next 4 dc and 2 ch, 1 sc in next ch, 1 sc in next dc, 1 sc in next ch 3, skip next 2 ch and 4 dc.

Row 38: (Ch 3, skip next 4 dc and 2 ch, 1 sc in next ch, 1 sc in each of next 3 sc, 1 sc in next ch, ch 3, skip next 4 dc, 4 dc in next space) 4 times, ch 3, skip next 4 dc and 2 ch, 1 sc in next ch, 1 sc in each of next 3 sc, 1 sc in next ch, ch 3.

Row 39: (Ch 3, 4 dc in next space, ch 3, skip next sc, 1 sc in each of next 3 sc, ch 3, 4 dc in next space) 5 times, ch 3.

Row 40: (Ch 3, skip next 4 dc, 1 dc in next space, ch 3, skip next 4 dc, 4 dc in next space, ch 3, skip next sc, 1 dc in next sc, ch 3, 4 dc in next space) 5 times, ch 3, 1 dc in next space, ch 3.

Row 41: (Ch 3, skip next 4 dc and 2 ch, 1 sc in next ch, 1 sc in next dc, 1 sc in next ch, ch 3, skip next 2 ch and 4 dc, 4 dc in next space, ch 3, 4 dc in next space) 5 times, ch 3, skip next 4 dc and 2 ch, 1 sc in next ch, 1 sc in next dc, 1 sc in next ch, ch 3, skip next 2 ch and 4 dc.

Row 42: (Ch 3, skip next 4 dc and 2 ch, 1 sc in next ch, 1 sc in each of next 3 sc, 1 sc in next ch, ch 3, skip next 2 ch and 4 dc, 4 dc in next space) 5 times, ch 3, skip next 4 dc and 2 ch, 1 sc in next ch, 1 sc in each of next 3 sc, 1 sc in next ch, ch 3.

Row 43: (Ch 3, 4 dc in next space, ch 3, skip next sc, 1 sc in each of next 3 sc, ch 3, 4 dc in next space) 6 times, ch 3.

Row 44: (Ch 3, 1 dc in next space, ch 3, 4 dc in next space, ch 3, skip next sc, 1 dc in next sc, ch 3, 4 dc in next space) 6 times, ch 3, 1 dc in next space, ch 3.

Row 45: (Ch 3, skip next 4 dc and 2 ch, 1 sc in next ch, 1 sc in next dc, 1 sc in next ch, ch 3, skip next 2 ch and 4 dc, 4 dc in next space, ch 3, 4 dc in next space) 6 times, ch 3, skip next 4 dc and 2 ch, 1 sc in next ch, 1 sc in next dc, 1 sc in next ch, ch 3.

Row 46: (Ch 3, skip next 4 dc and 2 ch, 1 sc in next ch, 1 sc in each of next 3 sc, 1 sc in next ch, ch 3, skip next 2 ch and 4 dc, 4 dc in next space) 6 times, ch 3, skip next 4 dc and 2 ch, 1 sc in next ch, 1 sc in each of next 3 sc, 1 sc in next ch, ch 3, skip next 2 ch and 4 dc.

Row 47: (Ch 3, 4 dc in next space, ch 3, skip next sc, 1 sc in each of next 3 sc, ch 3, 4 dc in next space) 7 times, ch 3.

Row 48: (Ch 3, 1 dc in next space, ch 3, 4 dc in next space, ch 3, skip next sc, 1 dc in next sc, ch 3, 4 dc in next space) 7 times, ch 3, 1 dc in next space, ch 3.

Row 49: (Ch 3, skip next 4 dc and 2 ch, 1 sc in next ch, 1 sc in next dc, 1 sc in next ch, ch 3, skip next 2 ch and 4 dc, 4 dc in next space, ch 3, 4 dc in next space) 7 times, ch 3, skip next 4 dc and 2 ch, 1 sc in next ch, 1 sc in next dc, 1 sc in next ch, ch 3, skip next 2 ch and 4 dc.

Row 50: (Ch 3, skip next 4 dc and 2 ch, 1 sc in next ch, 1 sc in each of next 3 sc, 1 sc in next ch, ch 3, 4 dc in next space) 7 times, ch 3, skip next 4 dc and 2 ch, 1 sc in next ch, 1 sc in each of next 3 sc, 1 sc in next ch, ch 3, skip next 2 ch and 4 dc.

Row 51: (Ch 3, 4 dc in next space, ch 3, skip next sc, 1 sc in each of next 3 sc, ch 3, 4 dc in next space) 8 times, ch 3.

Row 52: (Ch 3, 1 dc in next space, ch 3, 4 dc in next space, ch 3, skip next sc, 1 dc in next sc, ch 3, 4 dc in next space) 8 times, ch 3, 1 dc in next space, ch 3.

Row 53: (Ch 3, skip next 4 dc and 2 ch, 1 sc in next ch, 1 sc in next dc, 1 sc in next ch, ch 3, skip next 2 ch and 4 dc, 4 dc in next space, ch 3, 4 dc in next space) 8 times, ch 3, skip next 4 dc and 2 ch, 1 sc in next ch, 1 sc in next dc, 1 sc in next ch, ch 3.

Row 54: (Ch 3, skip next 4 dc and 2 ch, 1 sc in next ch, 1 sc in each of next 3 sc, 1 sc in next ch, ch 3, skip next 2 ch and 4 dc, 4 dc in next space) 8 times, ch 3, skip next 4 dc and 2 ch, 1 sc in next ch, 1 sc in each of next 3 sc, 1 sc in next ch, ch 3.

Row 55: (Ch 3, 4 dc in next space, ch 3, skip next sc, 1 sc in each of next 3 sc, ch 3, 4 dc in next space) 9 times, ch 3.

Row 56: (Ch 3, 1 dc in next space, ch 3, 4 dc in next space, ch 3, skip next sc, 1 dc in next sc, ch 3, 4 dc in next space) 9 times, ch 3, 1 dc in next space, ch 3.

Row 57: (Ch 3, skip next 4 dc and 2 ch, 1 sc in next ch, 1 sc in next dc, 1 sc in next ch, ch 3, skip next 2 ch and 4 dc, 4 dc in next space, ch 3, 4 dc in next space) 9 times, ch 3, skip next 4 dc and 2 ch, 1 sc in next ch, 1 sc in next dc, 1 sc in next ch, ch 3, skip next 2 ch and 4 dc.

Row 58: (Ch 3, skip next 4 dc and 2 ch, 1 sc in next ch, 1 sc in each of next 3 sc, 1 sc in next ch, ch 3, skip next 2 ch and 4 dc, 4 dc in next space) 9 times, ch 3, skip next 4 dc and 2 ch, 1 sc in next ch, 1 sc in each of next 3 sc, 1 sc in next ch, ch 3, skip next 2 ch and 4 dc.

Row 59: (Ch 3, 4 dc in next space, ch 3, skip next sc, 1 sc in each of next 3 sc, ch 3, 4 dc in next space) 10 times, ch 3.

Row 60: (Ch 3, 1 dc in next space, ch 3, 4 dc in next space, ch 3, skip next sc, 1 dc in next sc, ch 3, 4 dc in next space) 10 times, ch 3, 1 dc in next space, ch 3.

Row 61: (Ch 3, skip next 4 dc and 2 ch, 1 sc in next ch, 1 sc in next dc, 1 sc in next ch, ch 3, skip next 2 ch and 4 dc, 4 dc in next space, ch 3, 4 dc in next space) 10 times, ch 3, skip next 4 dc and 2 ch, 1 sc in next ch, 1 sc in next dc, 1 sc in next ch, ch 3, skip next 2 ch and 4 dc. When Row 61 has been completed, DO NOT FASTEN OFF.

Edging: Work left side, lower, and right side edges as follows:

Row 1: Ch 2, 2 dc in same space, ch 1, * 2 dc in next space, ch 1, repeat from * to corner space, 2 dc, ch 1, 2 dc in same space, ch 1, ** 2 dc in next space, ch 1, repeat from ** across lower edge to next corner space, 2 dc, ch 1, 2 dc in same space, ch 1, *** 2 dc in next space, ch 1, repeat from *** across row, ending 2 dc in last space at right neck edge, ch 1, 1 dc in turning ch.

Row 2: Ch 4, turn, 2 dc in 1st space, ch 1, * 2 dc in next ch-1 space, ch 1, repeat from * across row to corner space, ch 1, 2 dc, ch 1, 2 dc in same space, ch 1, ** 2 dc in next space, ch 1, repeat from ** to next corner space, 2 dc, ch 1, 2 dc in same space, *** ch 1, 2 dc in next space, repeat from *** to last space, ch 1, 2 dc in same space, ch 1, 1 dc in turning ch. Repeat Row 2 once more. DO NOT FASTEN OFF. Work across neck edge of shawl as follows: * Ch 5, sl st in 4th ch from hook (picot made), ch 1, skip 2 sts, 1 sc in next space, repeat from * across row. Fasten off.

Edging: Ch 17 sts loosely.

Row 1: 1 dc in 8th ch from hook, (ch 2, skip next 2 ch, 1 dc in next ch) 3 times—4 spaces.

Row 2: Ch 3, turn, * 2 dc in next space, ch 3, sl st in 3rd ch from hook (picot made), 2 dc in same space, repeat from * 3 times more.

Row 3: Turn, sl st to 1st picot, 1 sc in same picot, ch 5, 1 sc in next picot.

Row 4: Ch 3, turn, work 9 dc in ch-5 space.

Row 5: Ch 4, turn, skip 1st dc, 1 sc in next dc, (ch 4, 1 sc in next dc) 7 times, ch 3, 1 sc in next picot.

Row 6: Turn, (ch 2, 1 dc in next ch-4 space) 8 times, 1 dc in last st of Row 2 of preceding pattern.

Row 7: Ch 3, turn, 1 dc in next space, work a picot, 2 dc in same space, (2 dc in next space, work a picot, 2 dc in same space) 7 times, 1 dc in next picot. Repeat Rows 3 through 7 fifty-two times more. Fasten off. Starting at beg of starting ch of edging, join yarn in first space, ch 3, work 2 dc, picot, 2 dc in same space, (2 dc, picot, 2 dc in next space) 3 times, work 2 dc, picot, 2 dc in top of each of next 2 dc, in next space, and in next picot—8 motifs. Work along side edge of motifs as follows:

Row 1: * Ch 3, 1 dc in next picot, ch 3, 1 dc in next picot, (ch 3, 1 sc in next picot) twice, repeat from * across row, ending ch 3, 2 tr in next picot where motifs are joined, ch 3, 2 tr in next picot, 1 dc in next picot.

Row 2: Ch 4, turn, skip 1st dc, 1 dc in space between next 2 tr, ch 1, 1 dc in ch-3 space between next 2 tr, ch 1, 1 dc in next space between next 2 tr, * (ch 1, 1 dc, ch 1, 1 dc in next space) 3 times, ch 1, 1 dc in next space, repeat from * across row, ending (ch 1, 1 dc, ch 1, 1 dc in next space) 3 times, ch 1, skip 1 dc, 1 dc in next dc. Fasten off. Sew last row of edging to shaped edges of shawl. Steam lightly. COPYRIGHT © 1976 BERNAT YARN & CRAFT CORPORATION

FILET CAMISOLE AND STOLE

This pretty twosome seems perfect for a warm evening. Although it is lacy, the geometric pattern seems to give the design a trim, tailored look.

THE CAMISOLE

Information to Check Before You Start

Sizing: Directions are written for Small Size (8–10). Changes for Medium Size (12–14) and Large Size (16–18) are in parentheses.

Materials: This camisole is made of Bernat Saluki using 50 gram balls. You need: 5 (6, 6) balls

Tool: Crochet Hook (Bernat U.S.)— Size E (3.5 mm.)

Gauge: 9 sts = 2 inches

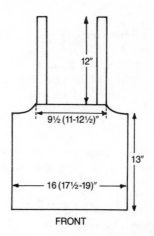

FRONT

Directions to Follow

Pattern Stitch No. 1—Row 1: 1 dc in 3rd dc, * ch 1, skip 1 dc, 1 dc in next dc, repeat from *, ending ch 2, turn.

Row 2: * 1 dc in next ch 1 space, 1 dc in next dc, repeat from *, ending ch 2, turn.

Row 3: 1 dc in each of next 2 dc, * ch 1, skip 1 dc, 1 dc in each of next 3 dc, repeat from *, ending ch 2, turn.

Row 4: 1 dc in each of next 2 dc, * 1 dc in next ch-1 space, 1 dc in each of next 3 dc, repeat from *, ending ch 3, turn.

Pattern Stitch No. 2—Row 1: 1 dc in ch 1 space, 1 dc in next dc, * ch 1, skip next ch-1 space, 1 dc in next dc, (1 dc in next ch-1 space, 1 dc in next dc) 3 times, repeat from *, ending ch 1, skip next ch 1 space, 1 dc in next dc, 2 dc in top of turning ch, ch 2, turn.

Row 2: 1 dc in each of next 2 dc, * ch 1, 1 dc in each of next 3 dc, ch 1, skip next dc, 1 dc in each of next 3 dc, repeat from *, ending ch 1, 1 dc in each of next 3 dc, ch 2, turn.

Row 3: 1 dc in each of next 2 dc, * ch 1, 1 dc in each of next 3 dc, 1 dc in next ch-1 space, 1 dc in each of next 3 dc, repeat from *, ending ch 1, 1 dc in each of next 3 dc, ch 2, turn.

Front: Ch 80 (88, 96) sts. 1 dc in 3rd ch from hook, 1 dc in each remaining st of ch, ch 3, turn 79 (87, 95) sts. Work Rows 1 through 4 of pattern st No. 1 3 times, then work Row 1 of same pattern st and mark this row for waistline, ch 2, turn. Now work in pattern st No. 2 once, then repeat Rows 2 and 3 of same pattern st 7 times more. Work Rows 1 through 4 of pattern st No. 1 once, then work Rows 1 and 2 of same pattern st once, omitting turning ch at end of last row.

Shape Armholes. Row 1: Sl st over next 5 sts, 1 sc in next st, 1 dc in next st, * ch 1, skip next st, 1 dc in each of next 3 sts, repeat from * to last 8 sts, ch 1, skip next st, 1 dc in next st, 1 sc in next st, turn.

Row 2: Sl st over next 4 sts, ch 2, 1 dc in each of next 2 sts, * 1 dc in next ch-1 space, 1 dc in each of next 3 sts, repeat from * to last 3 sts, turn.

Row 3: Sl st over next 3 sts, ch 3, skip next st, 1 dc in next st, * ch 1, skip next st, 1 dc in next st, repeat from * to last 2 sts, turn.

Row 4: Sl st over next 3 sts, ch 2, * 1 dc in next ch-1 space, 1 dc in next st, repeat from * to last ch 3, turn.

Row 5: Sl st over next 3 sts, ch 3, skip next st, 1 dc in each of next 3 sts, * ch 1, skip next st, 1 dc in each of next 3 sts, repeat from * to last 4 sts, ch 1, skip next dc, 1 dc in next st, turn.

Row 6: Sl st over next 3 sts, ch 2, 1 dc in each of next 2 sts, * 1 dc in next ch-1 space, 1 dc in each of next 3 sts, repeat from * to last ch 3, ch 2, turn—47 (55, 63) sts.

Right Shoulder Strap. Row 1: 1 dc in each of next 2 dc, ch 1, skip 1 dc, 1 dc in each of next 3 dc, ch 2, turn.

Row 2: 1 dc in each of next 2 dc, ch 1, skip next ch-1 space, 1 dc in each of next 3 dc, ch 2, turn. Repeat Row 2 until strap measures 12½ inches. Fasten off.

Left Shoulder Strap: Join yarn and work to correspond to right shoulder strap.

Back: Work to correspond to front to beg of armhole shaping.

Shape Armholes: Work Rows 1 through 4 of front. Fasten off.

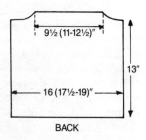

9½ (11-12½)"

13"

16 (17½-19)"

BACK

Finishing: Sew underarm seams.

Edging. Round 1: With right side facing you, starting at shoulder strap, join yarn and work 1 round sc around neck and shoulder strap edges, join.

Round 2: 1 sc in first st, * ch 3, 1 sc in 3rd st of ch (picot made), skip next sc, 1 sc in each of next 3 sc, repeat from * around, join. Fasten off. Work same edging around armhole and lower edges.

Tie: Using yarn double, make a ch to measure approximately 45 inches. Fasten off. Weave through waistline. Knot each end and tie.

THE STOLE

Information to Check Before You Start

Sizing: Approximately 24 × 56 inches excluding fringe

Materials: The stole is made of Bernat Saluki yarn using 50 gram balls. You need 10 balls.

Tool: Crochet Hook (Bernat U.S.)— Size F (4 mm)

Gauge: 9 sts = 2 inches

Directions to Follow

Ch 105 sts.

Row 1: 1 dc in 5th ch from hook, ch 1, skip next st, 1 dc in next st, ch 1, skip next st, * 1 dc in each of next 7 sts, (ch 1, skip next st, 1 dc in next st) twice, ch 1, skip next st, repeat from *, ending 1 dc in last st, ch 3, turn. Always count turning ch as first st.

Row 2: * 1 dc in next dc, ch 1, 1 dc in next dc, ch 1, 1 dc in each of next 3 dc, ch 1, skip next st, 1 dc in each of next 3 dc, ch 1, repeat from *, ending 1 dc in next dc, (ch 1, 1 dc in next dc) twice, ch 3, turn.

Row 3: * 1 dc in next dc, ch 1, 1 dc in next dc, ch 1, 1 dc in each of next 3 dc, 1 dc in next ch 1 space, 1 dc in each of next 3 dc, ch 1, repeat from *, ending 1 dc in next dc, (ch 1, 1 dc in next dc) twice, ch 3, turn. Repeat Rows 2 and 3 for pattern st until piece measures 56 inches, ending with Row 3 of pattern st. Fasten off.

Finishing. Edging—Round 1: With right side facing you, join yarn in any st and work 1 round sc, join.

Round 2: * Ch 3, 1 sc in 3rd st of ch (picot made), 1 sc in each of next 3 sts, repeat from * around, join. Fasten off.

Fringe: Cut strands of yarn 15 inches long. Knot 6 strands in each picot st across each short end. Trim ends.

EMBROIDERED AFGHAN

This afghan seems to have a pretty daintiness about it. The floral designs and the lightness of the stitches seem to contribute to this feeling.

Information to Check Before You Start

Sizing: Approximately 52 × 53 inches
· Finished Measurements:
Narrow Panel—5½ × 60 inches
Wide Panel—14 × 60 inches
Smocked Panel—6¼ × 60 inches

Materials: The afghan is made of Columbia-Minerva Performer in 3 oz. balls. You may substitute Nantuk 4-ply or Shannon yarn if you wish. You need 17 balls of White (Color A)
—For embroidery, you need
1 ball each of Peony Pink, Claret, Kelly Green, Light Green, and Light Pink.
Tool: Afghan Hook—Size G
Gauge: 3 sts = 1 inch
3 rows = 1 inch

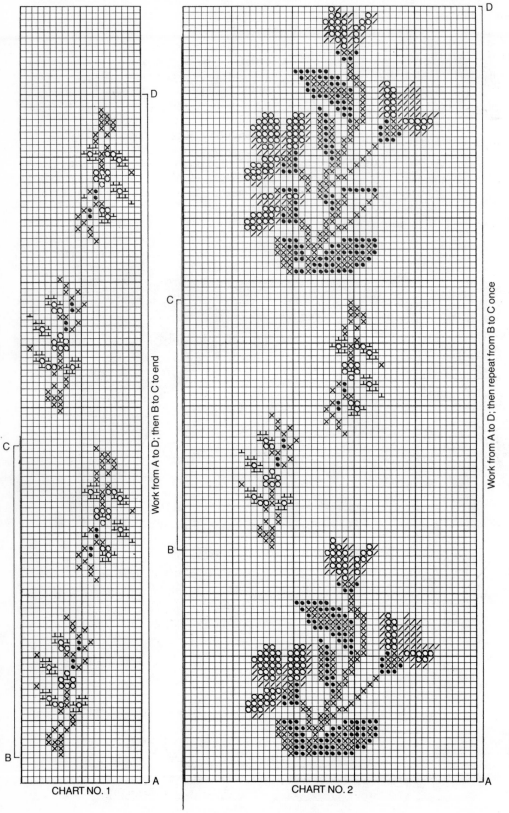

Work from A to D; then B to C to end

Work from A to D; then repeat from B to C once

CHART NO. 1

CHART NO. 2

☒ KELLY GR
☒ CLARET
● LIGHT GR
○ PEONY PI
⊞ LIGHT PIN

Directions to Follow

Narrow Panel: Make 2. With A, ch 20.

Row 1, 1st Half: Draw up a lp in 2nd ch from hook and each rem ch—20 lps on hook. **2nd Half:** Yo hook and draw thru first lp, * yo hook and thru 2 lps; rep from * across.

Row 2, 1st Half: Draw up a lp in each vertical bar across—20 lps on hook. **2nd Half:** Work off lps same as for 2nd half of Row 1. Rep Row 2 for plain afghan st until 160 rows from beg are completed.

Last Row: Sl st in each bar across. Fasten off.

Wide Panel: Make 2. With A, ch 48. Work same as Narrow Panel.

Smocked Panel: Make 3. With A, ch 24. Work **Row 1** same as for Narrow Panel.

Row 2, 1st Half: Draw up a lp in 2nd vertical bar, * bring yarn to front of work and hold below next bar, draw up a lp in same bar, draw up a lp in regular manner in next bar; rep from * across—24 lps. **2nd Half:** Work off lps as for plain st.

Row 3, 1st Half: Holding yarn in front below 2nd bar, draw up lp in same bar, * draw up lp in next bar in regular manner, holding yarn in front below next bar, draw up a lp in same bar; rep from * across. **2nd Half:** Work off lps as for plain afghan st. Rep rows 2 and 3 for pat until 160 rows from beg are completed.

Last Row: Sl st in each bar across. Fasten off.

Embroidery: Work all embroidery in cross st, working each cross st over 1 row and between vertical bars. Follow Chart 1 for Narrow Panel and Chart 2 for Wide Panel.

Finishing: Having a Narrow Panel at each side edge and a Smocked Panel between each embroidered panel, crochet panels tog with 1 row sc worked from right side.

Border: Right side facing, work 1 row sc around entire edge of afghan, working 3 sc in corners to turn. Fasten off. Along each long side edge, work 1 row more of sc.

Fringe: Wind A around a 5 inch piece of cardboard; cut at 1 end. Use 2 strands of yarn for each fringe, fold strands in half and knot 1 fringe in each st across each short end.

ARAN ALGHAN

Contrasting panels, each featuring an interesting arrangement of stitches, make this cover outstanding. The raised diamond pattern adds a new dimension to the design.

Information to Check Before You Start

Sizing: Approximately 56 × 69 inches

Materials: The afghan is made of Columbia-Minerva Performer Yarn in 3 oz. balls. If you wish you can substitute Nantuk 4-ply or Shannon yarn. You need 22 balls

Tools: 14-inch Afghan Hook—Size I
Crochet Hook—Size I

Gauge: 7 sts = 2 inches
3 rows = 1 inch

Directions to Follow

Chevron Panel and Star Stitch Border: Make 4. With afghan hook, ch 9.

   Row 1, 1st Half: Draw up lp in 2nd ch from hook and each rem ch—9 lps on hook. **2nd Half:** Yo and thru first lp, * yo and thru 2 lps; rep from * across.

   Row 2, 1st Half: (NOTE—Lp on hook counts as 1st lp and forms 1st vertical bar.) Draw up a lp in 2nd and each vertical bar across—9 lps on hook. **2nd Half:** Work off lps same as for Row 1.

   Row 3: Rep Row 2.

   Row 4, 1st Half: Draw up a lp in each of first 3 bars (4 lps on hook), yo hook 3 times, draw up a lp in 2nd vertical bar 3 rows below, [yo and thru 2 lps on hook]

3 times (tr), yo hook 3 times, draw up a lp in 8th vertical bar 3 rows below, [yo and thru 2 lps on hook] 4 times—(5 lps on hook), sk center vertical bar of row being worked, draw up a lp in each of last 4 bars—9 lps on hook. **2nd Half:** Work off lps in same manner as before.

Row 5: Rep Row 2. Rep Rows 4 and 5 for pat until 195 rows from beg are completed, end with Row 5.

Last Row: Sl st in each bar across. Fasten off. Mark 1st row for lower edge.

Star Stitch Border: Work border on long side edges only as follows: On left side edge of 1 panel for right edge of afghan and on the right side edge of 1 panel for left edge of afghan; work along both side edges of rem 2 panels.

Row 1: Right side facing, join yarn with crochet hook in corner st at one end of panel, ch 2, draw up ⅝ inch lp in 2nd ch from hook (NOTE—draw up all lps to same height), draw up a lp in corner st of panel, draw up a lp in end st of 1st row, draw up a lp in end st of next row, yo and thru all 5 lps on hook (star st), ch 1 to form eye of star, * draw up a lp in eye st, draw up a lp in back thread of last lp of last star st, draw up a lp in end st of each of next 2 rows, yo and thru all 5 lps on hook, ch 1; rep from * across side edge, end with hdc in same st as last lp; 98 star sts.

Row 2: Ch 2, turn, hdc in eye of each star across, hdc in top of ch-2. Fasten off.

Picot Panel: Make 3. With afghan hook, ch 34. Work **Row 1** same as for Chevron Panel.

Row 2, 1st Half: Draw up a lp in each vertical bar across—34 lps. **2nd Half:** Work off first 5 lps, ch 4 for picot, * work off next 6 lps, ch 4 for picot; rep from * 3 times more, work off rem lps.

Row 3, 1st Half: Holding picots to front of work, draw up a lp in each vertical bar—34 lps. **2nd Half:** * Work off 4 lps, picot, work off 2 lps, picot; rep from * 4 times more, work off rem 4 lps.

Row 4, 1st Half: Work as for Row 3. **2nd Half:** Work off 3 lps, picot, * work off 4 lps, picot, work off 2 lps, picot; rep

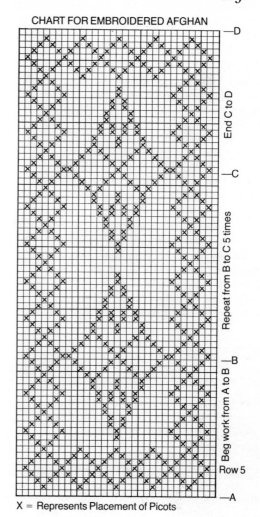

CHART FOR EMBROIDERED AFGHAN

—D

End C to D

—C

Repeat from B to C 5 times

—B

Beg work from A to B

Row 5

—A

X = Represents Placement of Picots

from * 4 times more, end last rep work off 3 lps.

Row 5, 1st Half: Work as for Row 3. **2nd Half:** Work off 2 lps, picot, * work off 6 lps, picot; rep from * 4 times more, work off last 2 lps. Complete panel following chart for picot pattern. Work 1 row plain afghan st when picot pat is complete; 195 rows.

Last Row: Sl st in each bar across. Fasten off. Mark lower edge. Work Star Stitch border along both side edges of each Picot Panel same as for Chevron Panel.

Finishing: Alternating Chevron and Picot panels, with all marked ends at same end, join bordered edges as follows: Holding wrong sides together, join yarn in 1st st of both borders, on right side, working thru both lps of hdcs of each panel, sc in each st across side edge matching stars. Fasten off.

Afghan Border. Rnd 1: Right side facing, join yarn in lower corner st at right hand side edge. †Work Star Stitch pat along side edge to next corner, end with star st in corner st (98 star sts), * draw up lp in eye st, draw up 1 lp in back thread and 1 lp in front thread of last lp of last star st, draw up lp in corner st, yo and thru all 5 lps, ch 1 *; rep between *'s once, work Star Stitch pat along end of afghan, end with star st in corner st, rep between *'s twice; rep from † once, join with sl st in top of ch-2.

Rnd 2: Ch 2, turn, hdc in 1st eye st, * 2 hdc in each eye st to corner eye st, 6 hdc in corner eye st; rep from * around, join with sl st in top of ch-2. Fasten off.

PUFF STITCH AFGHAN

The textural quality of this afghan is outstanding. Stripes of puffy stitches mingle with bands of lacy ones.

Information to Check Before You Start

Sizing: Approximately 48 × 60 inches without edging
Materials: This afghan is made of Columbia-Minerva Nantuk Sports yarn in 2 oz. balls. You need:
8 balls Terra Cotta (A)
8 balls Orange (B)
Or if you wish you can substitute any sport weight yarn using about 16 oz. of each color.
Tool: Crochet Hook—Size G
Gauge: 7 dc = 2 inches
7 rows = 5 inches
NOTE: When changing colors work off last 2 lps of last st of a color with a new color. Cut color when not needed.

Directions to Follow

With A ch 172 to measure approximately 49 inches.

Row 1 (right side): Dc in 4th ch from hook and in each ch to end (169 dc, counting ch-3 at beg of row as 1 dc). Ch 3, turn.

Row 2: Sk 1st dc, dc in each dc, dc in top of tch, working off last 2 lps with B. Cut A. Ch 1, turn.

Row 3: Sc in first st, * ch 2, draw up a ¾ inch lp, yo, insert hook in 1st ch of ch-2, draw up a lp, yo and thru 2 lps on hook, [yo, draw up a lp in same ch, yo and thru 2 lps] 3 times yo and thru 5 lps on hook (popcorn—PO), sk 2 sts, sc in next st; rep from * to end, working off last sc with A (56 PO). Ch 1, turn. Cut B.

Row 4: Sc in first sc, * ch 3, sc in sc between PO; rep from *, end sc in last sc. Ch 3, turn.

Row 5: 2 dc in 1st ch-3 lp, * dc in next sc, 2 dc in next lp; rep from *, end dc in last sc (169 dc). Ch 3, turn.

Rows 6–9: Rep Rows 2–5, working off last 2 lps of last dc with B. Cut A.

Row 10: Rep Row 2, working off last 2 lps with A.

Row 11: Rep Row 3, working off last 2 lps with B.

Rows 12 and 13: Rep Rows 4 and 5.

Rows 14–17: Rep Rows 10–13, working off last 2 lps of last dc with A. Rep Rows 2–17 seven times more. Rep Rows 2–9 once. Do *not* cut A. Ch 3, turn.

Last Row: With A, rep Row 2. Fasten off.

Edging: Working from right side, join B in 1st dc of last row, sc in same st with joining, * ch 10, work PO in 2nd ch from hook. Ch 1 tightly, ch 2 more, PO in 2nd ch from hook, sl st in same ch as 1st PO, ch 8, sk 6 sts, sc in next st; rep from *, end sc in last st. Fasten off. Work edging across other short end in same way.

AFGHAN OR COVERLET

If you have wanted to have an old-fashioned afghan or bedspread, then you will like this design. Worked in bands of contrasting stitches, this article has a lovely textured effect.

Information to Check Before You Start

Sizing: The directions are for a Small, personal-size afghan throw. Changes for a Medium-size coverlet (twin bed) and Large-size coverlet (double bed) are in parentheses.
—Small size measures 48 × 62 inches not including fringe.
—Medium size measures 66 × 102 inches not including fringe.
—Large size measures 76 × 102 inches not including fringe.
NOTE: Both coverlets have been fringed for use with a dust ruffle.
Materials: The article is made of Bernat Berella "4" using 4 oz. balls. You need 18 (21, 27) balls.
Tool: Crochet Hook (Bernat-Aero)— Size G (4.5 mm)
Gauge: 4 dc = 1 inch
NOTE—Entire afghan is worked in *back loop only.*

Pattern Stitch for Shell. Row 1: 1 dc in 4th ch from hook, 1 dc in same st, skip next 2 sts, 1 sc in next st, skip next 2 sts, * 5 dc in next st (shell), skip next 2 sts, 1 sc in next st, skip next 2 sts, repeat from * across row, ending 3 dc in last st (half shell)—29 (40, 45) shells and 2 half shells.
  Row 2: Ch 1, turn, working in *back loop only,* 1 shell in next sc, * 1 sc in 3rd dc of next shell, 1 shell in next sc, repeat from *, ending 1 sc in top of turning ch—30 (41, 46) shells.
  Row 3: Ch 3, turn, 2 dc in 1st st, * 1 sc in 3rd dc of next shell, 1 shell in next sc, repeat from *, ending 3 dc in top of turning ch—29 (40, 45) shells and 2 half shells. (Always count ch 3 as first dc.) Repeat Rows 2 and 3 for pattern stitch.

Pattern Stitch for Double Crochet. Row 1: Ch 3, turn, working in *back loop only,* 1 dc in each st across row—181 (247, 277) sts. Repeat Row 1 for pattern stitch.

Pattern Stitch for Bobble. Row 1: Ch 3, turn, working in *back loop only,* 1 dc in each of next 4 dc, * 5 dc in next st, remove hook from st, insert hook in *back loop* of 1st st of 5 dc just made and draw loop of last st through loop on hook (Back Loop Bobble), 1 dc in each of next 5 dc, repeat from *, ending Back Loop Bobble in next st, 1 dc in turning ch—30 (41, 46) bobbles.
  Row 2: Ch 3, turn, 1 dc in each of next 3 sts, * 5 dc in next st, remove hook from st, insert hook in *front loop* of first st of 5 dc just made and draw loop of last st through loop on hook (Front Loop Bobble), 1 dc in each of next 5 sts, repeat from *, ending Front Loop Bobble in next st, 1 dc in next st, 1 dc in turning ch. Bobbles will be on right side.
  Repeat Rows 1 and 2 for pattern stitch.

Directions to Follow

Ch 184 (250, 280) sts. Work in pattern st as follows:
  8 rows Shell Pattern
  8 rows Double Crochet Pattern
  8 rows Bobble Pattern
  8 rows Double Crochet Pattern
Repeat these 32 rows 3 times more for small-size afghan *only.* DO NOT FASTEN OFF. For medium- and large-size coverlets *only,* repeat these 32 rows 4 times more, ending 8 rows Shell Pattern, 9 rows Double Crochet Pattern. DO NOT FASTEN OFF.
  Edging (for All Sizes): With right side facing you, * 5 dc in turning ch of next row (shell), 1 sc in last st of next row, skip 1 row, repeat from * to 1st corner, working 1 shell in corner st. Work same edging on remaining lower and side edges. Fasten off.
  Fringe: Cut strands of yarn 10 inches long, knot 10 strands in space between 2nd and 3rd st of shell st on 3 sides of afghan. Trim ends. Steam lightly.

BABY BLANKET

Not only is this blanket pretty, but it also can be made quickly and easily. It is a perfect gift for the new baby.

Information to Check Before You Start

Sizing: Approximately 33 × 38 inches
Materials: The blanket is made of Bernat Berella #4® using 4 oz. balls. You need:
3 White (A)
2 Pastel Ombre (B)
Tool: Crochet Hook—Size Q
Gauge: 3 sc = 2 inches
NOTE: 1 strand each of Colors A and B is used throughout

Directions to Follow

Ch 53 sts loosely.
Row 1: 1 sc in 2nd ch from hook, 1 sc in each remaining st of ch, ch 1, turn—52 sts.
Row 2: 1 sc in each st, ch 1, turn. Repeat Row 2 until 50 rows have been completed. Fasten off.
Finishing. Edging: Using Color A double, with right side facing you, join yarn in any st and working from *left* to *right,* 1 sc in each st around all edges and 2 sc in corner sts, join. Fasten off.

LACY BABY SET

A shell stitch pattern gives this lovely sacque, bonnet, blanket, and soakers an interesting textured look. It is the perfect baby gift.

Information to Check Before You Start

Sizing: Directions are written for Infant Size. Changes for 6-month and 1-year. Sizes are in parentheses.

· Finished Measurements:

Sacque: Chest—20 (21, 22) inches
 Width of sleeve at underarm—
 7½ (8, 8½) inches

Bonnet: Width across front edge—
 10 (11, 12) inches
 Width across back—3 (3, 4) inches

Blanket: Approximate size 29 × 30 inches

Soakers: Waist—20 (21, 22) inches
 Width of back or front—10 (10½, 11) inches

Materials: The set is made of Columbia-Minerva Monique using 1 oz. balls. You need 11 (11, 12) balls.

—24 inches of ¼ inch wide elastic

Tool: Crochet Hook—Size G

Gauge: 1 shell = 1 inch
 2 rows = 1 inch

Directions to Follow

Pattern Stitch: Multiple of 4 sts.

Row 1 (right side): 3 dc in 4th ch from hook, sk next 3 ch, sc in next ch, * ch 3, 3 dc in same ch as last sc (shell), sk next 3 ch, sc in next ch; rep from * across, end 1 sc in last ch.

Row 2: Ch 3, turn, 3 dc in 1st sc, sc in next ch-3 sp of previous row (side of shell), * ch 3, 3 dc in same ch-3 sp, sc in next ch-3 sp; rep from * across, end sc in last ch-3 sp. Rep Row 2 for pat.

BLANKET

Ch 120. Work in pat st until about 30 inches from beg; 29 shells. Fasten off.

Edging: Right side facing, join yarn in any corner st, 3 sc in corner. * 3 sc in next ch-3 sp, sc in next sc; rep from * around, working 3 sc in each corner st, end, join with sl st in 1st sc.

Rnd 2: Ch 1, sc in joining, * 3 sc in corner st, sc in each sc to next corner; rep from * around, join with sl st in 1st sc. Fasten off.

SACQUE

Body: Ch 76 (80, 88). Work in pat st for 12 (12, 14) rows; 19 (20, 22) shells.

Divide for Right Front. Row 1: Ch 3, turn, work 5 (5, 6) shells, end sc in next ch-3 sp. Work even for 3 rows more.

Next Row-Dec Row: Ch 3, turn 3 dc in 1st sc, draw up lp in each of next 2 ch-3 sps, yo and thru 3 lps on hook, ch 3, 3 dc in last ch-3 sp (1 shell dec), sc in next ch-3 sp, work in pat to end; 4 (4, 5) shells.

Work 1 (3, 3) rows even.

Rep dec row once; 3 (3, 4) shells. Work 2 (1, 2) rows even. Fasten off.

Back. Row 1: Join yarn in last sc of Row 1 of right front, ch 3, 3 dc in same ch-3 sp, sc in next ch-3 sp, work 9 (10, 10) shells. Work even for 8 (9, 10) rows more. Fasten off.

Left Front: Join yarn in last sc of Row 1 of back, ch 3, 3 dc in same ch-3 sp, work to end in pat; 5 (5, 6) shells. Work 3 rows even.

Dec Row: Ch 3, turn, work 3 (3, 4) shells, dec 1 shell over last 2 shells; 4 (4, 5) shells. Work 1 (3, 3) rows even. Rep

dec row, working 1 shell less before dec; 3 (3, 4) shells. Work 2 (1, 1) rows even. Fasten off. Sew shoulder seams, leaving center back sts free.

Sleeves: Right side facing, join yarn at underarm. Work 9 (10, 11) shells around armhole edge.

Row 2: Ch 3, turn, work in pat across. Work even for 4 (4, 5) rows. Dec 1 shell each side edge in next row; 7 (8, 9) shells. Work 4 rows even.

Cuff. Row 1: Ch 1, turn, sc in 1st sc, * ch 2, sc in next ch-3 sp; rep from * across.

Row 2: Ch 1, turn, sc in 1st sc, * in ch-2 sp, sc in next sc; rep from * across.

Rows 3, 4, and 5: Ch 1, turn, sc in each sc. Fasten off.

Finishing: Sew sleeve seams.

Edging: Right side facing, join yarn at 1 shoulder seam, sc evenly around neck, front, and lower edges, working 3 sc in corners to turn, end join with sl st in 1st sc. Fasten off.

Tie: Make 2. With yarn double, ch 19. End off. Attach at front edges.

BONNET

Front Section: Ch 36 (40, 44). Work even in pat st until 4½ (5, 5½) inches from beg; 9 (10, 12) shells. Fasten off.

Back Section: Turn, sk 1st 3 (3, 4) shells, join yarn in ch-3 sp of last sk shell, sc in same sp, ch 3, 3 dc in same sp. Work 2 (3, 3) shells more; 3 (4, 4) shells. Work even until back is same length as adjacent edge of front section. Fasten off.

Finishing: Sew side edges of back to corresponding edges of front section.

Neck Edging: Right side facing, join yarn at front neck edge, sc evenly across neck edge having an uneven number of sc.

Beading Row: Ch 2, turn, dc in first sc, * ch 1, sk next sc, dc in next sc; rep from * across. Fasten off.

Cord: Make a ch 24 inches long, sl st in 2nd ch from hook and each rem ch, fasten off. Weave cord thru Beading Row.

SOAKERS

Back. Row 1 (right side): With Size G hook and A, ch 9 (10, 11), sc in 2nd ch from hook and each rem ch; 8 (9, 10) sc. Working in sc, inc 1 st each side edge every row 14 (15, 16) times; 36 (39, 42) sc. Work even until 8 (8½, 9) inches from beg. Fasten off.

Front: Right side of back facing, sc in each st along opposite side of foundation ch. Working in sc, inc 1 st each side edge in next row, then every other row 3 times more, then every row 4 (5, 6) times.

Next Row: Ch 7, sc in 2nd ch from hook and each rem ch, sc in each sc across.

Next Row: Rep last row; 36 (39, 42) sc. Work even until same as back. Fasten off.

Finishing: Sew side seams. At top edge, fold last 3 rows to wrong side for casing, sew loosely in place leaving a 1-inch opening. Thread elastic thru casing, adjust to desired length and sew ends tog. Work edging around leg openings same as for neck edge of sweater.

MATCHING BABY FASHIONS

This set of hooded sweater, pants, and mittens with coordinating blanket makes an excellent baby gift. Each article is something a young child can use.

Information to Check Before You Start

Sizing: Directions are for Size 6 months. Changes for 12 months and 18 months are in parentheses.

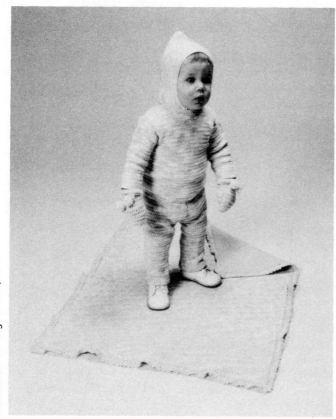

Materials: The set is made in Susan Bates® "Softura" Baby Yarn (50 gram balls) or "Softura" Pompadour Yarn (50 gram balls) in No. 1230 Rainbow. You need

—5 (5, 6) balls of the Baby Yarn or
—6 (6, 7) balls of the Pompadour Yarn

Tools: Crochet Hook (Susan Bates)—Size D or 3 (3¼ mm) Pom-Pon Maker, a Susan Bates® Adjustable "Trim-Tool"™

Separating lightweight zipper—18 (18, 20) inches

½ yd ¾-inch elastic

Gauge: 5 sts = 1 inch
9 rows = 2 inches

Directions to Follow

Pattern Stitch. Row 1 (right side): sc in ea st across, ch 1, turn.

Row 2: Hdc in ea st across, ch 1, turn. Rep Rows 1 and 2 for Pat St.

SWEATER

Beg at bottom edge of front and backs, loosely ch 101 (105, 109).

Row 1: Sc in 2nd ch from hk, sc in ea st across, ch 1, turn—100 (104, 108) sc.

Row 2: Sc in ea st across, ch 1, turn.

Work even in Pat St until piece measures 6½ (7, 7¼) inches, or desired length to underarm, end wrong side.

Left Back: Keeping in Pat, work across 23 (24, 25) sts, turn (underarm). Working on these sts only, dec 1 st at beg of next row, then at same edge every other row once. NOTE—[To dec: (Insert hk into next st, yo, and pull up a lp) twice, yo and thru all lps on hk]. Work even on 21 (22, 23) sts until armhole measures 3¼ (3¾, 4) inches from underarm. Tie off.

Right Back: With right side facing, work 1 row in pat across last 23 (24, 25) sts of last long row. Work to correspond to left back, reversing armhole shaping.

Front: With right side facing, work 1 row in pat across center 48 (50, 52) sts of last long row. NOTE—3 sts on ea side of front sts are left unworked for underarm. Dec 1 st ea end every other row twice. Work even on 44 (46, 48) sts until

piece measures 2¼ (2¾, 3) inches from underarm.

Shape Neck: Work across 14 sts, turn. Dec 1 st at neck edge every other row twice. Work even until armhole measures same as back. Tie off. Work other side in same manner leaving center 16 (18, 20) sts free. Sew shoulder seams leaving 9 (10, 11) sts of ea back neck edge free for hood.

Hood: Beg at front edge ch 73 (77, 81).

Row 1: Sc in 2nd ch from hk and in ea st across, ch 1, turn. Work 3 more rows in sc.

Next Row: Work in sc, inc'ing 12 sts evenly spaced—84 (88, 92) sts. Work even in Pat St, beg with Row 2, until piece measures 7 (7¼, 7½) inches. Tie off.

Fold in half crosswise and sew short sides to neck edge, easing in fullness, and placing front edges at center front of body, leaving back edges free for zipper.

Sleeves: Ch 29 (31, 33).

Row 1: Sc in 2nd ch from hk and in ea st of ch, ch 1, turn. Work even in Pat St for 5 rows. Keeping in Pat, inc 1 st ea end on next row, then every 5th row until there are 36 (38, 42) sts. Work even until piece measures 7½ (8½, 9) inches, or desired length to underarm, allowing for a 1-inch hem.

Shape Cap: Sl st in 1st st, work in Pat to within 1 st of end, turn.

Next Row: Sl st across 1st 2 sts, work in Pat to within last 2 sts, turn. Rep last row until 14 (16, 16) sts rem. Tie off.

Finishing: Sew sleeve seams. Turn under 1 inch hem and tack in place. Sew sleeves to body. With right side facing, work 1 row sc along entire back edge of body and hood. Sew zipper in place along back edge of hood and body, having zipper pull at top of hood when closed.

Doll Tassel: With Trim-Tool™ make a 3-inch tassel. Place 15 3-inch strands of yarn between long strands of tassel for arms. Tie under arm strands and at end of ea arm. Divide long strands in half and tie at ea end for legs. Attach tassel to zipper pull.

PANTS

1st Side: Beg at bottom of leg, loosely ch 43 (45, 47).

Row 1: Sc in 2nd ch from hk in ea ch across—42 (44, 46) sts. Work even in Pat St until piece measures 7½ (8½, 9½) inches.

Shape Crotch and Body: Keeping in Pat St, inc 1 st ea end every row until there are 62 (64, 66) sts, then dec 1 st ea end every other row until there are 48 (50, 52) sts. Work even until piece measures 8½ (9, 9½) inches from beg of decs. Tie off. **2nd Side:** Make same as 1st side.

Finishing: Sew both leg seams to crotch, then sew both pieces tog at center front and back. Fold 1 inch to inside at waist and tack in place, inserting elastic before closing. Fold under 1-inch hem of leg and tack in place.

MITTENS

Ch 31 (33, 33). **Row 1:** Sc in 2nd ch from hk and in ea st across, ch 1, turn.

Row 2: Hdc in ea st across, ch 1, turn.

Row 3: Work in sc dec'ing 4 sts evenly spaced, ch 1, turn—26 (28, 28) sts.

Row 4: Hdc in ea st across, ch 1, turn.

Row 5–Beading Row: * Hdc in next st, ch 1, sk 1 st; rep from *, end hdc in last 2 sts, ch 1, turn.

Next Row: Sc in ea hdc and ch of last row, ch 1, turn. Work even in Pat St for 8 (10, 12) rows.

Shape Top: Continue in Pat St, dec'ing 4 sts evenly spaced every other row 3 times—14 (16, 16) sts.

Next Row: Work 2 sts tog all across. Tie off, leaving a long end for sewing.

Finishing: Gather sts at top tog, then sew side seam. Ch 60 for tie. Lace thru beading row, having ends at center of top. With Pom-Pon Maker, make 2 small pompons and attach at ea end of tie. Make other mitten the same.

REVERSIBLE BABY BLANKET

Information to Check Before You Start

Size: Approximately 30 × 34 inches
Materials: The blanket is made in Susan Bates® "Softura" Baby Yarn (50 gram balls) or "Softura" Pompadour Yarn (50 gram balls). You need
—5 balls each No. 0120 Blue(A) and No. 1230 Rainbow(B) of the Baby Yarn or
—6 balls each No. 0120 Blue(A) and No. 1230 Rainbow(B) of the Pompadour Yarn
Tool: Crochet Hook (Susan Bates)—Size G or 6 (4¼ mm.)
Gauge: 5 sc = 1 inch
10 rows (both sides) = 1 inch

Directions to Follow

With A ch 141 to measure 28 inches.

Row 1: Sc in 2nd ch from hk and in ea st across. With B, ch 1, turn. Cut A leaving a 3-inch end.

Row 2: Insert hk thru *back loop* of 1st sc and thru foundation ch and complete 1 sc. Sc in this manner across row. With A, ch 1, turn. Cut B leaving a 3-inch end.

Row 3: Insert hk thru *back loop* of 1st sc and thru free lp of sc 2 rows before and complete sc. Sc in this manner all across. With B, ch 1, turn. Cut A leaving a 3-inch end.

Rep Row 3 for pattern but alternate colors A and B.

NOTE—Ends may be worked in as work progresses. See FINISHING.

Work even in pattern until piece measures 32 inches, working the last row as follows: Sc across by inserting hk thru *both loops* of sc and thru free lp of sc 2 rows before. Tie off.

Finishing: Weave in loose ends by tying 2 ends tog in a square knot, then run back thru 4 sts.

Border. Rnd 1: Attach A in any corner (hdc, ch 2, hdc) for corner, * ch 1, sk 1 st, hdc in next st; rep from * to next corner, then work rem 3 sides in same manner, join with sl st in top of 1st hdc. Cut A.

Rnds 2 and 3: With B, work same as Rnd 1, placing hdc in ea ch sp. Cut B.

Rnd 4: With A, * (sc, ch 3, sc) in next ch space, ch 1; rep from * around. Join. Tie off.

V-NECK SWEATER

This sweater with its bulky look seems so right for the young athlete. The design details add a grown-up feeling that a small child will love.

Information to Check Before You Start

Sizing: The directions are written for Toddler's Size 1. Changes for Sizes 2, 3, and 4 are in parentheses.

Materials: The sweater is made of Bernat Berella Sportspun in 2 oz. balls or Saluki in 50 gram balls. You need:
—3 (3, 4, 4) balls Berella Sportspun or
—4 (4, 5, 5) balls Saluki

Tools: Crochet Hooks (Bernat U.S.)—Size G (4.5 mm) and Size I (5.5 mm)

Gauge: 4 sts = 1 inch on Size I (5.5 mm) hook

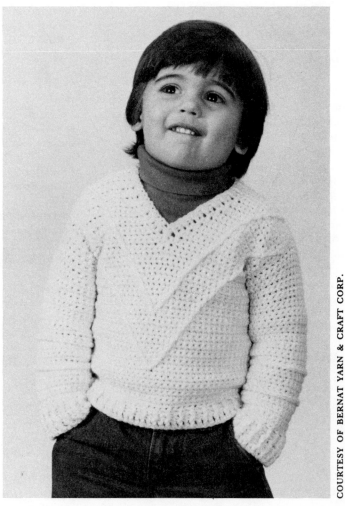

COURTESY OF BERNAT YARN & CRAFT CORP.

Directions to Follow

Back: Using smaller hook, ch 42 (44, 46, 48) sts.

Row 1: 1 dc in 3rd ch from hook, 1 dc in each remaining st of ch, ch 2, turn—41 (43, 45, 47) sts. Turning ch counts as 1st st.

Row 2: Skip 1st st, * yo, insert hook from *front* to *back* and working around post of next dc, work 1 dc (*front* dc), yo, insert hook from *back* to *front* and working around post of next dc, work 1 dc (*back* dc), repeat from *, ending 1 *front* dc in next st, 1 hdc in top of turning ch, ch 2, turn.

Row 3: Skip 1st st, * 1 *back* dc in next st, 1 *front* dc in next st, repeat from *, ending 1 *back* dc in next st, 1 hdc in top of turning ch, ch 1, turn.

Change to larger hook.

Row 1: 1 sc in each st, ch 1, turn—41 (43, 45, 47) sts. Work even in sc until piece measures 7 (7½, 8, 9) inches. Put a marker at each end of last row to mark start of armhole. Continue to work even in sc until armholes measure 3¾ (4, 4¼, 4½) inches above markers. Do not ch at end of last row.

Shape Shoulders. Row 1: Sl st in 1st 3 (3, 4, 4) sts, ch 1, work in sc to last 3 (3, 4, 4) sts, turn.

Row 2: Repeat Row 1.

Row 3: Sl st each of 1st 3 (3, 4, 4) sts, work in sc to last 3 (3, 4, 4) sts. Fasten off.

Front: Work to correspond to back until 12 (14, 16, 18) rows have been worked in sc. Put a marker in center st.

Row 13 (15, 17, 19): 1 sc in each of 1st 19 (20, 21, 22) sts, 1 *front* dc in center st 2 rows below, skip st behind *front* dc, 1 sc in center st, 1 *front* dc in same center st 2 rows below, skip 1 st behind *front* dc, 1 sc in each of last 19 (20, 21, 22) sts, ch 1, turn.

Row 14 (16, 18, 20) and all even rows: 1 sc in each st, ch 1, turn—41 (43, 45, 47) sts.

Row 15 (17, 19, 21): 1 sc in each of 1st 18 (19, 20, 21) sts, 1 *front* dc in *front* dc of row below, skip 1 st, 1 sc in each of next 3 sts, 1 *front* dc in *front* dc of row below, skip 1 st, 1 sc in each of last 18 (19, 20, 21) sts, ch 1, turn.

Row 17 (19, 21, 23): 1 sc in each of 1st 17 (18, 19, 20) sts, 1 *front* dc in *front* dc of row below, skip 1 st, 1 sc in each of next 5 sc, 1 *front* dc in *front* dc of row below, skip 1 st, 1 sc in each of last 17 (18, 19, 20) sts, ch 1, turn. Continue in this manner to work 2 more sc between *front* dcs and 1 less st at each arm edge every right side row until there are 13 sc between *front* dcs, ending with a wrong-side row.

On the **next row,** work 1 sc in each of 1st 13 (14, 15, 16) sts, 1 *front* dc in next st, skip 1 st, 1 sc in each of next 5 sts, 1 *front* dc in center st 2 rows below, skip 1 st, 1 sc in center st, 1 *front* dc in same

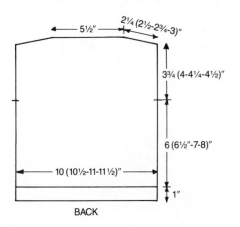

BACK

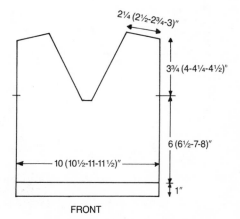

FRONT

center st 2 rows below, skip 1 st, 1 sc in each of next 5 sts, 1 *front* dc in next st, skip 1 st, 1 sc in each of last 13 (14, 15, 16) sts, ch 1, turn. Continue in this manner to work 2 more sc between each group of *front* dcs and 1 less sc at each arm edge every other row in same manner as before until piece measures 6½ (7, 7½, 8½) inches, ending with a wrong-side row.

Shape Neck: Work in pattern st on 1st 19 (20, 21, 22) sts, draw up a loop in each of next 2 sts, yo and draw through 3 loops (dec). Working on left side of front *only* and continuing in pattern st, dec 1 st at neck edge every other row 9 times more and then *every row* twice more, and *at the same time,* when piece measures 7 (7½, 8, 9) inches, put a marker in each end of last row to mark start of armhole. Work even, if necessary, on remaining 9 (10, 11, 12) sts until armhole is same length as back.

Shape Shoulder: At arm edge, sl st in each of 1st 3 (3, 4, 4) sts twice and 3 (3, 4, 4) sts once. Join yarn at center st, dec 1 st and work right side of front to correspond to left side, reversing all shaping.

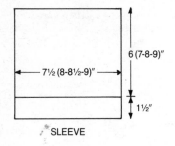

SLEEVE

7½ (8-8½-9)"

6 (7-8-9)"

1½"

Sleeves: Using smaller hook, ch 31 (33, 35, 37) sts.

Row 1: 1 dc in 3rd ch from hook, 1 dc in each remaining st of ch, ch 2, turn—30 (32, 34, 36) sts.

Row 2: Skip 1st st, * 1 *front* dc in next st, 1 *back* dc in next st, repeat from *, ending 1 hdc in top of turning ch, ch 2, turn.

Rows 3 through 5: Repeat Row 2, ending last row ch 1, turn.

Change to larger hook.

Row 1: 1 sc in each st, ch 1, turn—30 (32, 34, 36) sts.

Rows 2 through 5: Repeat Row 1, ending last row ch 2, turn.

Row 6 (right side): 1 hdc in next st, 1 hdc in each remaining st, ch 2, turn.

Row 7: Skip first st, * yo, insert hook from *front* to *back* and working around post of next hdc, work 1 hdc (*front* hdc), repeat from *, ending 1 hdc in top of turning ch, ch 1, turn.

Rows 8 through 11: Repeat Row 1, ending last row ch 2, turn.

Row 12: Repeat Row 6.

Row 13: Repeat Row 7. Work even in sc until piece measures 7½ (8½, 9½, 10½) inches. Fasten off.

Finishing: Sew shoulder seams. Sew sleeves to front and back armholes between markers. Sew underarm and sleeve seams.

Neckband: Using smaller hook, with right side facing you, starting at center back, work **1 round** dc around neck edge, dec 1 st at center front, join, ch 2, do not turn.

Round 2: Work in *front* dc, *back* dc ribbing pattern st, dec 1 st at center front, join. Fasten off.

BATH-MITT PUPPETS

Children will find scrubbing much more fun when they use these happy aids. They offer a great incentive for keeping clean.

Information to Check Before You Start

Sizing: Mitts measure 6½ inches long and 3¾ inches wide.

Materials: The bath-mitts are made of Coats & Clark's O.N.T. "Speed-Crosheen" Mercerized Cotton, Art. C. 44. You need:

—For the Pig:
 1 ball of No. 46-A MidRose (Main Color)
 5 yards of No. 34-C American Beauty

—For the Rabbit:
 1 ball of No. 1 White (Main Color)
 15 yards of No. 4 Blue

—For the Elephant:
 1 ball of No. 122 Watermelon (Main Color)
 1 ball of No. 34-C American Beauty

—For the Dog:
 1 ball of No. 10-A Canary Yellow (Main Color)
 1 ball of No. 131 Fudge Brown
 1 yard of No. 46-A MidRose

Tools: Steel Crochet Hook—No. 1 Tapestry Needle, No. 18 (J. & P. Coats)

Gauge: 11 sc = 2 inches
 13 rows = 2 inches

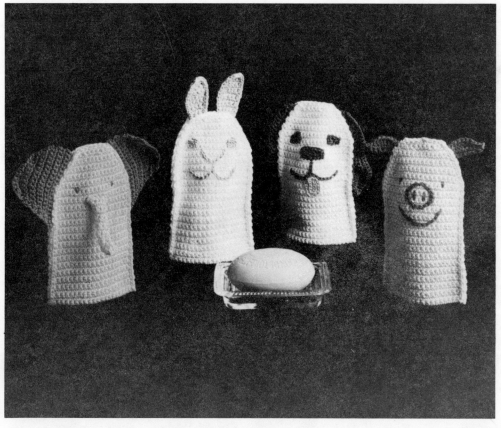

Directions to Follow

PIG

Mitt Panel (make 2): Starting at lower edge, with Main Color ch 22 to measure 4 inches.

Row 1 (wrong side): Sc in 2nd ch from hook and each ch across—21 sc. Ch 1, turn.

Row 2: Sc in each sc across. Ch 1, turn.

Rows 3–32: Repeat Row 2.

Row 33: Skip 1st sc—dec made at beg of row; sc in each sc to last 2 sc, skip next sc, sc in last sc—dec made at end of row. Ch 1, turn.

Row 34: Work even. Ch 1, turn. Repeat last 2 rows 3 more times—13 sc on last row.

Next 2 Rows: Making a dec at each end of row, sc in each st across. Ch 1, turn. Break off and fasten.

Ear (make 2): With American Beauty, ch 10.

Row 1: Sc in 2nd ch from hook and each ch across—9 sc. Ch 1, turn.

Row 2: Sc in 1st 2 sts, hdc in next st, dc in next st, (2 dc in next st) twice; hdc in next st, sc in next st, sl st in last st. Ch 1, turn.

Row 3: Sl st in each st across. Break off and fasten.

Tail: With American Beauty, ch 21.

Row 1: Sl st in 2nd ch from hook and in every other ch st across, end with sl st in last ch. Break off and fasten.

Features for Front Panel: With wrong side of 1 mitt panel facing, using American Beauty and tapestry needle, with Chain Stitch embroider a circular snout, having top of snout 1¾ inches from top edge. With Straight Stitch make 2 nostrils inside of snout and 1 eye at either side in line with top edge of snout, 1 inch from side edge of panel. With Chain Stitch, make 2¼-inch curved line ½ inch below snout for mouth.

With right side of other panel (back panel) facing, sew tail to center of panel, 1 inch above lower edge.

Hanging Loop: Attach Main Color at center of back panel, 1½ inches from top edge, pull up a loop and ch 14. Break off and pull end of thread through crocheted piece where thread was attached and secure.

Joining Panels: With undecorated side of panels facing each other, pin panels together, inserting ears at the top, 2 inches apart, with curved edge up. With front of mitt facing and working through both thicknesses, attach Main Color to lower right corner, sl st evenly around, leaving lower edge open. Break off and fasten.

RABBIT

With Main Color, make 2 Mitt Panels as for Pig.

Ear (make 2): Starting at lower edge with Blue, ch 4.

Row 1: Sc in 2nd ch from hook and in next 2 ch—3 sc. Ch 1, turn.

Row 2: Sc in each sc across. Ch 1, turn.

Row 3: Sc in 1st sc, 2 sc in next sc—1 sc increased; sc in last sc. Ch 1, turn.

Rows 4–5: Repeat Row 2.

Rows 6–9: Repeat Rows 3 and 2 twice.

Row 10: Sc in 1st 2 sc, draw up a loop in each of next 2 sc, thread over and draw through all 3 loops on hook—1 sc decreased; sc in last 2 sc. Ch 1, turn.

Row 11: Repeat Row 2.

Row 12: Sc in 1st sc, dec 1 sc, sc in last 2 sc. Ch 1, turn.

Row 13: Repeat Row 2.

Row 14: Skip first sc, sc in next 2 sc. Do not work in remaining sc. Ch 1, turn.

Row 15: Sc in first sc, sl st in next sc. Break off and fasten. Attach thread to lower corner of ear and sl st evenly around entire outer edge. Join with sl st to 1st sl st. Break off and fasten.

Features on Front Panel: With wrong side of a mitt panel facing, with Blue and tapestry needle, embroider eyes in Chain Stitch 1 inch down from top edge and ½ inch in from side edge, working in a circular pattern until each eye is ½ inch in diameter. With Chain Stitch make a U-shaped nose between lower part of eyes. For mouth, work U shapes to both right and left of lower center of nose.

On other panel (back panel) embroider a 1 inch in diameter tail, centered 1 inch above lower edge, in same manner as eye. Make hanging loop as for Pig.

Joining Panels: Join as for Pig, placing ears between panels at top edge, ½ inch apart.

ELEPHANT

With Main Color make 2 Mitt Panels as for Pig.

Ear (make 2): Starting at lower edge with American Beauty, ch 17.

Row 1: Sc in 2nd ch from hook, sc in next 6 ch, (in next ch make sc and h dc) twice; sc in next 7 ch—18 sts. Ch 1, turn.

Row 2: Sc in each st across to last st, make 2 sc in last st—19 sts. Ch 1, turn.

Row 3: Sc in each sc across to last sc. Do not work in last sc. Ch 1, turn.

Row 4: Skip first sc, sc in next sc and in each sc across—17 sc. Ch 1, turn.

Row 5: Sc in sc across to last sc. Do not work in last sc. Ch 1, turn.

Row 6: Skip 1st sc, sc in next 4 sc, (2 sc in next sc) twice; sc in next 9 sc—17 sc. Ch 1, turn.

Row 7: Repeat Row 5.

Row 8: Skip 1st sc, sc in each st across to last sc. Do not work in last sc. Ch 1, turn.

Row 9: Skip 1st sc, sc in next 6 sc, (2 sc in next sc) twice; sc in next 4 sc. Do not work in last sc. Ch 1, turn.

Row 10: Repeat Row 8.

Row 11: Skip 1st sc, sc in next 4 sc, hdc in next sc, dc in next sc, hdc in next sc, sc in next 3 sc. Do not work in last sc. Ch 1, turn.

Row 12: Sl st in 1st 2 sts, sc in next 2 sts, 2 sc in next st, sc in next 3 sts, sl st in next 2 sts. Break off and fasten.

Tail: With American Beauty, ch 8. Sl st in 2nd ch from hook and in next 2 ch; sc in next 3 ch, sl st in last ch. Break off and fasten.

Trunk: With Watermelon, ch 6.

Row 1: Sc in 2nd ch from hook and in each ch across—5 sc. Ch 1, turn.

Rows 2–16: Sc in each sc across. Ch 1, turn. At end of last row, break off, leaving a 12-inch length. Sew side edges of trunk together, leaving last 2 rows free.

Features on Front Panel: With American Beauty, make eyes as for Pig. Center trunk 2 inches down from top edge, and sew free end sts to panel between lower part of eyes.

On other panel (back panel), center tail and sew in place 1 inch above lower edge. Make hanging loop as for Pig.

Joining Panels: Join as for Pig, inserting ears with curved sides up, 2 inches apart at center top, and lower edges between side edges of panels.

DOG

With Main Color make 2 Mitt Panels as for Pig.

Ear (make 2): Starting at lower edge with Brown, ch 21.

Row 1: Sc in 2nd ch from hook and in each ch across—20 sc. Ch 1, turn.

Row 2: Skip 1st sc, hdc in next 8 sc, (2 sc in next sc) twice; sc in next 4 sc, (2 dc in next sc, dc in next sc) twice; 2 dc in last sc. Ch 2, turn.

Row 3: Make 2 dc in 1st st, (dc in next st, 2 dc in next st) twice; 2 hdc in next st, sc in next 17 sts. Do not work in last st. Ch 1, turn.

Row 4: Skip 1st st, sc in next 7 sts, 2 sc in next st, sc in next 10 sts, 2 sc in next st, sc in next 6 sts, sl st in last st. Break off and fasten.

Features on Front Panel: With Brown, embroider eyes and mouth as for Rabbit. With Chain Stitch make a rectangular nose 1 inch wide by ½ inch high above mouth, working back and forth to fill in space. With MidRose embroider a 1 by 1 inch oval tongue with Chain Stitch below mouth, working back and forth to fill in space. On other panel (back panel) make a hanging loop as for Pig.

Joining Panels: Join as for Pig, inserting ears with short sides up, 2 inches apart at center top, and lower edge between side edges of panels.

CUTE DOG

Here is a pet for everyone. Its low-slung features seem to add a humorous touch to this stuffed toy.

Information to Check Before You Start

Sizing: Directions are written for a toy about 16½ inches long, excluding the tail.

Materials: The dog is made of Coats & Clark Red Heart® in a 4-ply Hand-knitting Yarn, Art. E. 231. You need:

—3 oz. of No. 653 Avocado
—2 oz. of No. 360 Wood Brown
—1 oz. of No. 251 Vibrant Orange
—1 oz. of No. 602 Dark Gold
—1 oz. of No. 1 White
—1 oz. of No. 12 Black
—Polyester stuffing

Tool: Crochet Hook—Size 1

Gauge: 7 sts = 2 inches
  7 sc rounds = 2 inches

Directions to Follow

Head: Starting at front, with Avocado ch 2.

  Rnd 1: Make 6 sc in 2nd ch from hook. Join with sl st to 1st sc.

Rnd 2: Ch 1, 2 sc in joining, 2 sc in next 5 sc. Join as before—12 sc.

Rnd 3: Ch 1, sc in joining; 2 sc in next sc—inc made; (sc in next sc, inc in next sc) 5 times. Join—18 sc.

Rnd 4: Ch 1, sc in joining, sc in next sc, inc in next sc, * sc in next 2 sc, inc in next sc. Rep from * around. Join—24 sc.

Rnd 5: Ch 1, sc in joining, sc in next 2 sc, inc in next sc, * sc in next 3 sc, inc in next sc. Rep from * around. Join—30 sc.

Rnd 6: Ch 1, sc in joining; increasing 6 sc evenly spaced, sc in each sc around. Join—36 sc.

Rnds 7–11: Ch 1, sc in joining and in each sc around. Join.

Rnd 12: Ch 1, sc in joining and in each sc around; drop Avocado, with Orange sl st in 1st sc to join—color change made. Always change colors this way.

Rnds 13–14: With Orange work even, changing to White at end of Rnd 14.

Rnds 15–18: With White work even.

Rnd 19: With White work as for Rnd 5—45 sc.

Rnds 20–23: Working even, use 1 rnd White, 2 rnds Gold.

Rnd 24: With Avocado ch 1, sc in joining, sc in next 2 sc; draw up a loop in each of next 2 sc, yarn over and draw through all loops on hook—dec made; * sc in next 3 sc, dec over next 2 sc. Rep from * around. Join—36 sc.

Rnds 25–30: Working even, use 1 rnd Gold, 2 rnds Avocado, 1 rnd Gold. As work progresses stuff head firmly.

Rnds 31–34: Ch 1, sc in joining; decreasing 6 sc evenly spaced, sc in each sc around. Join—12 sc on last rnd.

Rnd 35: Ch 1, dec over joining and next sc; (dec over next 2 sc) 5 times. Join. Break off and draw end through sts, pull together; secure.

Body: Starting at neck, with Gold ch 2.
Rnds 1–7: Work as for Head.
Rnd 8: Work as for Rnd 5 of Head—45 sc.
Rnds 9–34: Working even, use 6 rnds White, 14 rnds Brown, 6 rnds Orange.
Rnd 35: With Orange work as for Rnd 24 of Head—36 sc. Stuff body firmly as work progresses.
Rnds 36–40: Work as for Rnds 31–35 of Head. Complete same as Head.

Leg (make 4): Starting at bottom, with Avocado ch 9.
Rnd 1: Make 2 sc in 2nd ch from hook, sc in next 6 ch, 4 sc in last ch; working along opposite side of starting chain, sc in next 6 ch, 2 sc in 1st ch used. Join—20 sc.
Rnd 2: Ch 1, 2 sc in joining, sc in 8 sc, inc in each of next 2 sc; sc in 8 sc, inc in last sc. Join—24 sc.
Rnd 3: Ch 1, sc in joining, inc in next sc, sc in 8 sc, inc in next sc, sc in 2 sc, inc in next sc, sc in 8 sc, inc in next sc, sc in last sc. Join—28 sc.
Rnds 4–6: Work even.
Rnd 7: Ch 1, sc in joining, dec over 2 sc, sc in 8 sc, dec over 2 sc, sc in 2 sc, dec over 2 sc, sc in 8 sc, dec over 2 sc, sc in last sc. Join—24 sc.
Rnd 8: Ch 1, dec over joining and next sc, sc in 8 sc, (dec over 2 sc) twice; sc in 8 sc, dec over last 2 sc. Join—20 sc.
Rnd 9: Ch 1, dec over joining and next sc, sc in 6 sc, (dec over 2 sc) twice; sc in 6 sc, dec over last 2 sc. Join—16 sc.

Rnds 10–11: Ch 1, dec over joining and next sc, sc in each sc around to last 2 sc; dec over last 2 sc. Join. Break off. Stuff firmly and close opening to make a flat edge.

Sew head to body, see photograph. Sew flat edge of legs to body as shown, tack inner leg to body 1 inch below flat edge.

Nose: Starting at center, with Black ch 2.
Rnds 1–3: Work as for Head—18 sc.
Rnds 4–7: Work even. Break off, leaving a 10 inch end. Stuff firmly and sew in place.
Eye (make 2): With Black, ch 4. Join with sl st to form ring.
Rnd 1: Ch 1, make 2 sc in joining and in each ch around. Join. Break off, leaving a 10 inch end; sew in place.

Ear (make 2): Starting at lower edge, with Brown ch 11.
Row 1: Dc in 4th ch from hook, dc in each ch to last ch, 2 dc in last ch—10 dc, counting ch-3 as 1 dc. Ch 3, turn.
Row 2: Dc in first dc—inc made at beg of row; dc in each dc to ch-3; 2 dc in top of ch-3—inc made at end of row—12 sts. Ch 3, turn.
Rows 3–5: Dc in next 10 dc, dc in top of ch-3. Ch 3, turn.
Row 6: Holding back on hook last loop of each dc, dc in next 2 dc, yarn over and draw through all 3 loops on hook—dec made; dc in each dc to last 2 dc and ch-3; dec over next 2 dc, dc in top of ch-3—10 sts. Ch 3, turn.
Row 7: Work as for Row 6.
Row 8: Work even.
Row 9: Work as for Row 6—6 sts.
Row 10: Work even. Do not turn. Ch 1; keeping work flat, make 3 sc in each of the 4 corners, sc evenly around outer edge. Join. Break off, leaving a 10 inch end. Sew in place.

Tail: Starting at end, with Orange ch 4. Join to form ring.
Rnd 1: Ch 1, 4 sc in ring. Do not join rnd.
Rnd 2: Sc in each sc around. Rep last rnd for 4 inches. Break off, leaving a 10 inch end. Sew in place.

DECORATIVE PILLOWS

Pillows have their place in home fashions. Here are two that produce a different decorative touch. Only the front is crocheted.

POPCORN PILLOW FRONT

Information to Check Before You Start

Sizing: Directions are written for a Pillow Front that is 14¼ inches square.

Materials: The front is made of Coats & Clark Red Heart® LusterSheen, Art. A. 94, in 2 oz. skeins. You need
—2 skeins of No. 262 Coral Crush
—A 15-inch square pillow, color of your choice

Tool: Steel Crochet Hook—No. 5

Gauge: 7 sts = 1 inch
10 rounds = 3 inches

Directions to Follow

Starting at center, ch 5. Join with sl st to form ring.

Rnd 1: Ch 3, make 2 dc in ring, (ch 3, make 3 dc in ring) 3 times; ch 1, hdc in top of ch-3 to form last loop.

NOTE—Always count ch-3 as 1 dc.

Rnd 2: Ch 3, dc in loop just made, (dc in next 3 dc; in next loop make 2 dc, ch 3, and 2 dc) 3 times; dc in next 3 dc, 2 dc in 1st loop used at beg of rnd, ch 1, hdc in top of ch-3.

Rnd 3: Ch 3, dc in loop just made, * dc in next 3 dc; make 4 dc in next dc, drop loop from hook, insert hook from front to back in 1st dc of the 4-dc group and draw dropped loop through—pc st made; dc in next 3 dc; in next loop make 2 dc, ch 3, and 2 dc. Rep from * around, end last rep with 2 dc in 1st loop used, ch 1, hdc in top of ch-3.

Rnd 4: Ch 3, dc in loop just made, * (dc in next 3 sts, pc st in next dc) twice; dc in next 3 dc; in next loop make 2 dc, ch 3, and 2 dc. Rep from * around, end last rep with 2 dc in 1st loop used, ch 1, hdc in top of ch-3.

Rnd 5: Ch 3, dc in loop just made, * (dc in next 3 sts, pc st in next dc) 3 times; dc in next 3 dc; in next loop make 2 dc, ch 3, and 2 dc. Rep from * around, end as before.

Rnd 6: Ch 3, dc in loop just made, * (dc in next 3 sts, pc st in next dc) 4 times; dc in next 3 dc; in next loop make 2 dc, ch 3, and 2 dc. Rep from * around, end as before.

Rnd 7: Ch 3, dc in loop just made, * dc in next 2 dc, ch 7, dc in next 5 sts, (pc st in next dc, dc in next 3 sts) twice; pc st in next dc, dc in next 5 sts, ch 7, dc in next 2 dc; in next loop make 2 dc, ch 3, and 2 dc. Rep from * around, end as before.

Rnd 8: Ch 3, dc in loop just made, * dc in next 2 dc, ch 3, sc in next ch-7 loop, ch 3, skip next 2 dc, dc in next 5 sts, pc st in next dc, dc in next 3 sts, pc st in next dc, dc in next 5 sts, ch 3, sc in next ch-7 loop, ch 3, skip next 2 dc, dc in next 2 dc; in next loop make 2 dc, ch 3, and 2 dc. Rep from * around, end as before.

Rnd 9: Ch 3, dc in loop just made, * dc in next 2 dc, ch 3, sc in next ch-3 loop, sc in sc, sc in next ch-3 loop, ch 3, skip next 2 dc, dc in next 5 sts, pc st in next st, dc in next 5 sts, ch 3, sc in next ch-3 loop, sc in sc, sc in next ch-3 loop, ch 3, skip next 2 dc, dc in next 2 dc; in next loop make 2 dc, ch 3, and 2 dc. Rep from * around, end as before.

Rnd 10: Ch 3, dc in loop just made, * dc in next 2 dc, ch 3, sc in next loop, sc in next 3 sc, sc in next loop, ch 3, skip next 2 dc, dc in next 7 sts, ch 3, sc in next loop, sc in next 3 sc, sc in next loop, ch 3, skip next 2 dc, dc in next 2 dc; in next loop make 2 dc, ch 3, and 2 dc. Rep from * around, end as before.

Rnd 11: Ch 3, dc in loop just made, * dc in next 2 dc, ch 3, sc in next loop, sc in next 5 sc, sc in next loop, ch 3, skip next 2 dc, dc in next 3 dc, ch 3, sc in next loop, sc in next 5 sc, sc in next loop, ch 3, skip next 2 dc, dc in next 2 dc; in next loop make 2 dc, ch 3, and 2 dc. Rep from * around, end as before.

Rnd 12: Ch 3, dc in loop just made, * dc in next 4 dc, 2 dc in next loop, ch 3, skip 1 sc, sc in next 5 sc, ch 3, 2 dc in next loop, dc in next 3 dc, 2 dc in next loop, ch 3, skip 1 sc, sc in next 5 sc, ch

3, 2 dc in next loop, dc in next 4 dc; in next loop make 2 dc, ch 3, and 2 dc. Rep from * around, end as before.

Rnd 13: Ch 3, dc in loop just made, * dc in next 8 dc, 2 dc in next loop, ch 3, skip 1 sc, sc in next 3 sc, ch 3, 2 dc in next loop, dc in next 7 dc, 2 dc in next loop, ch 3, skip 1 sc, sc in next 3 sc, ch 3, 2 dc in next loop, dc in next 8 dc; in next loop make 2 dc, ch 3, and 2 dc. Rep from * around, end as before.

Rnd 14: Ch 3, dc in loop just made, * dc in next 12 dc, 2 dc in next loop, ch 3, skip 1 sc, sc in next sc, ch 3, 2 dc in next loop, dc in next 11 dc, 2 dc in next loop, ch 3, skip 1 sc, sc in next sc, ch 3, 2 dc in next loop, dc in next 12 dc; in next loop make 2 dc, ch 3, and 2 dc. Rep from * around, end as before.

Rnd 15: Ch 3, dc in loop just made, * dc in next 16 dc, (2 dc in next loop) twice; dc in next 15 dc, (2 dc in next loop) twice; dc in next 16 dc; in next loop make 2 dc, ch 3, and 2 dc. Rep from * around, end as before.

Rnd 16: Ch 3, dc in loop just made, * dc in next dc, ** ch 1, skip next dc, dc in next dc. Rep from ** to next corner loop; in next loop make 2 dc, ch 3, and 2 dc. Rep from * around, end as before.

Rnd 17: Ch 3, dc in loop just made, * dc in each dc and in each ch-1 across to next corner loop; in next loop make 2 dc, ch 3, and 2 dc. Rep from * around, end as before.

Rnd 18: Ch 3, dc in loop just made, * dc in next 3 dc, (pc st in next dc, dc in next 3 dc) 16 times; in next loop make 2 dc, ch 3, and 2 dc. Rep from * around, end as before.

Rnd 19: Ch 3, dc in loop just made, * dc in next 3 dc, (pc st in next dc, dc in next 3 dc) 17 times; in next loop make 2 dc, ch 3, and 2 dc. Rep from * around, end as before.

Rnd 20: Ch 3, dc in loop just made, * dc in each st to next corner loop; in next loop make 2 dc, ch 3, and 2 dc. Rep from * around, end as before.

Rnd 21: Rep Rnd 16.

Rnd 22: Rep Rnd 17.

Rnd 23: Ch 3, dc in loop just made, * dc in each dc to next corner loop; in next loop make 2 dc, ch 3, and 2 dc. Rep from * around, end with 2 dc in 1st loop used at beg of rnd, ch 3. Join to top of ch-3.

Rnd 24: Ch 1, sc in joining, * sc in each st to next corner loop; sc in next ch, 2 sc in following ch, sc in next ch. Rep from * around. Join. Fasten off.

Do not press.

Leaving the sts of last rnd free, sew to front of pillow.

FILET PILLOW FRONT

Information to Check Before You Start

Sizing: Directions are written for a pillow front that is 18 inches square excluding border.

Material: The front is made of Coats & Clark Red Heart® LusterSheen, Art. A. 94, in 2 oz. skeins. You need
—4 skeins of No. 805 Natural
—An 18 inch square pillow; color of your choice

Tool: Steel Crochet Hook—No. 5

Gauge: 3 sps or bls = 1 inch
3 rows = 1 inch

Directions to Follow

Ch 114, having 6 ch sts to the inch.

Row 1: Starting at A on Chart, dc in 6th ch from hook; * ch 1, skip 1 ch, dc in next ch—sp made. Rep from * across—55 sps. Ch 4, turn.

Row 2: Skip 1st sp, dc in next dc—starting sp over sp made; * dc in next sp, dc in next dc—bl over sp made; make 1 more bl; ch 1, skip next sp, dc in next dc—sp over sp made. Rep from * to last 3 sps, make 2 bls; ch 1, skip next ch, dc in next ch—end sp over sp made. Ch 4, turn.

Row 3: Make starting sp; dc in next 2 dc—bl over bl made; make 1 more bl, * make 1 sp and 2 bls. Rep from * to last sp, make 1 end sp. Ch 4, turn.

Row 4: Make starting sp over sp; * (ch 1, skip next dc, dc in next dc—sp over bl made) twice; make sp over sp. Rep from * across, end with end sp over sp. Ch 4, turn.

NOTE—Follow every even-numbered row on Chart from left to right and every odd-numbered row from right to left.

Row 5: Follow Row 5 on Chart.

Row 6: Make starting sp, 2 bls, 1 sp, 1 bl; (ch 2, skip next 2 dc, dc in next dc) twice—2 long sps over 3 bls made, start of long sp pattern; make 1 bl, 1 sp, 2 bls, 14 sps, 3 bls, 14 sps, 2 bls, 1 sp, 1 bl, 2 long sps, 1 bl, 1 sp, 2 bls, 1 end sp. Ch 4, turn.

Row 7: Make starting sp and 3 sps, 1 bl; ch 2, sl st in next dc, ch 2, dc in next dc—2 loops over 2 long sps made; make 1 bl, 14 sps, 2 bls, 1 sp, 3 bls, 1 sp, 2 bls, 14 sps, 1 bl; 2 loops over next 2 long sps; 1 bl, 3 sps, 1 end sp. Ch 4, turn.

Row 8: Starting sp, 2 bls, 1 sp, 1 bl; ch 2, dc in same place where next sl st

was made, ch 2, dc in next dc—2 long sps over 2 loops made; make 1 bl, 14 sps, 3 bls, 1 sp, 1 bl, 1 sp, 3 bls, 14 sps, 1 bl; 2 long sps over next 2 loops; 1 bl, 1 sp, 2 bls, 1 end sp. Ch 4, turn.

Row 9: Starting sp, 2 bls, 1 sp, 1 bl; (dc in next 2 ch, dc in next dc) twice—3 bls over 2 long sps made, long sp pattern completed; make 1 bl, 15 sps, 7 bls, 15 sps, 1 bl; 3 bls over next 2 long sps; 1 bl, 1 sp, 2 bls, 1 end sp. Ch 4, turn. Starting with Row 10, follow Chart to C, then follow same Chart from B back to A. At end of last row ch 1, turn.

Border. Rnd 1: Make 2 sc in corner sp, * sc in next st, (sc in next sp, sc in next st) 13 times; skip next sp, sc in next st, (sc in next sp, sc in next st) 25 times; skip next sp, sc in next st, (sc in next sp, sc in next st) 13 times; 3 sc in corner sp. Rep from * around remaining 3 sides, end with sc in 1st corner sp used at beg of rnd. Join with sl st to first sc.

Rnd 2: Ch 1, sc in joining, * (ch 7, skip 3 sc, sc in next sc) 26 times; ch 7, skip 3 sc; in corner sc make sc, ch 7, and sc. Rep from * around remaining 3 sides, end with ch 7, sc in 1st sc used, ch 3, tr in same sc—112 loops.

Rnd 3: Ch 1, sc in loop just formed, * ch 2, 7 dc in next loop, ch 2, sc in next loop. Rep from * around, end with ch 2. Join to 1st sc.

Rnd 4: Sl st in next sp, ch 1, sc in same sp, * ch 7, sc in next ch-2 sp. Rep from * around, end with ch 3, tr in 1st sc.

Rnd 5: Ch 3, 5 dc in loop just made, * (ch 2, sc in next loop, ch 2, 7 dc in next loop, ch 2) 13 times; sc in next loop, ch 2, 10 dc in next corner loop. Rep from * around, end with ch 2, make 4 dc in 1st corner loop used. Join to top of ch-3.

Rnd 6: Sl st in next dc; in next dc make sl st, ch 1, and sc; * (ch 7, sc in next ch-2 sp) 28 times; ch 7, skip 3 dc, sc in next dc, ch 7, skip next 2 dc, sc in next dc. Rep from * around, end with ch 7. Join to 1st sc.

Rnd 7: Sl st to center of next loop, ch 1, sc in same loop, ch 2, * 7 dc in next loop, ch 2. Rep from * around. Join to 1st sc.

Rnd 8: Sl st to next dc, ch 1, * sc in

CHART

Row 10

A   Row 5   B   C

☐ sp
☒ bl

Long sp pattern

next 7 dc, ch 2. Rep from * around. Join to 1st sc.

Rnd 9: Ch 1, skip joining, * sc in next sc, (ch 5, sc in next sc) 4 times; ch 5, sc in next ch-2 sp, ch 5, skip next sc. Rep from * around, end with ch 5. Join. Fasten off.

DO NOT PRESS.

Leaving the 9 rnds of border free, sew crocheted front to pillow.

EDGING FOR PLACE MAT

Although this edging is shown on a place mat, it can be adapted for other purposes. It adds a pretty touch to a plain piece of linen.

Information to Check Before You Start

Sizing: The directions are written for an edging 1¾ inches wide and for a finished mat that measures 12 × 18 inches.

Materials: The edging is made of Coats & Clark Red Heart® LusterSheen, Art. A. 94, in 2 oz. skeins. You need 2 skeins of No. 805 Natural to make the edging for 3 place mats
—Each place mat requires a 10 × 16 inch piece of fabric of your choice.

Tool: Steel Crochet Hook—No. 1

Directions to Follow

Inner Border—First Side: Ch 6.

Row 1: Dc in 4th ch from hook, dc in next 2 ch. Ch 5, turn.

Row 2: Skip next 2 dc, dc in top of ch-3. Ch 3, turn.

Row 3: Dc in next 3 ch. Ch 5, turn.

Row 4: Skip next 2 dc, dc in top of ch-3. Ch 5, turn.

Row 5: Skip next 2 ch, dc in following ch. Ch 3, turn.

Rows 6–9: Rep Rows 3, 2, 3, and 4.

Row 10: Rep Row 5.

Rows 11–12: Rep Rows 3 and 2. Now rep Rows 3 through 12 once; then rep Rows 3 and 4 once more, end with ch 5, turn.

Now make **1st corner** as follows: Skip next 2 ch, dc in following ch, ch 5, do not turn; dc in same place where last dc was made—corner completed. Ch 3, turn.

Now work **2nd side** as follows: Rep Rows 3 and 2 once; then rep Rows 3 through 12 3 times and then rep Rows 3 through 9 once, end with ch 5, turn. Work next corner same as 1st corner.

Now work **3rd side** as follows: Rep Rows 3 and 2 once; then rep Rows 3 through 12 twice and then rep Rows 3 and 4 once, end with ch 5, turn.

Now work **3rd corner** as follows: Skip next 2 ch, dc in next ch, ch 1, turn; sl st in next 3 ch; ch 5, do not turn; dc in base of ch-5 made on previous row—corner completed. Ch 3, turn.

Now work **4th side** as 2nd side was made; then work next corner as for 1st corner. Do not ch 3 at end. Fasten off.

Being careful not to twist border, sew narrow ends together matching sts.

—

Outer Border—Rnd 1 (right side): Working along outer edge of inner border, attach yarn to 1st sp between 2 blocks following any corner, ch 4, in same sp make 2 tr, ch 4, and 3 tr; * sc in next sp, sc in st between sps, sc in next sp; in next sp make 3 tr, ch 4, and 3 tr. Rep from * to next 3-sp corner group; sc in next sp; in corner sp make dc, 2 tr, ch 6, 2 tr, and dc; sc in next sp; in next sp make 3 tr, ch 4, and 3 tr. Now work along remaining sides in same way. Join with sl st to top of ch-4. DO NOT TURN.

Rnd 2: Sl st in next 2 tr and in next ch-4 sp, ch 7, sl st in 4th ch from hook, in same ch-4 sp make (2 tr; ch 3, sl st in top of last tr made—picot made) 4 times; ch 1; * in next ch-4 sp make tr, picot, and (2 tr, picot) 4 times; ch 1. Rep from * to next ch-6 corner sp; in ch-6 sp make tr, picot, and (2 tr, picot) 6 times; ch 1. Now work along remaining sides in same way. Join last ch-1 to 4th ch of ch-7. Fasten off.

DO NOT PRESS.

Finishing: Measure inside opening of edging; then add 1 inch to width and length measurements and cut linen. Fold under ¼ inch twice on all sides for hem and baste. Blind stitch hem; then sew edge of inner border in place on linen.

COPYRIGHT © 1980 COATS & CLARK, INC.

RECTANGULAR AND OVAL DOILIES

These filet pieces are versatile and pretty. They can be used as place mats, decorative doilies, and pillows. The dainty floral design remains the same for both shapes.

Information to Check Before You Start

Sizing: Directions are written for
—Rectangular Doily measuring 11½ × 14½ inches
—Oval Doily measuring 13½ × 16½ inches
Materials: Both shapes are made of Clark's Big Ball Mercerized Cotton, Art. B. 34, Size 30.
—For rectangle, you need 2 balls of No. 122 Watermelon.
—For oval, you need 2 balls of No. 43 Dk. Yellow.
Tool: Steel Crochet Hook, No. 10
Gauge: 5 bls or sps = 1 inch
   5 rows = 1 inch

Directions to Follow

RECTANGLE

With Watermelon and starting at A on Chart 1, ch 224 having 15 ch sts to 1 inch.

Row 1: Dc in 8th ch from hook; * ch 2, skip 2 ch, dc in next ch—sp made. Rep from * across—73 sps in all. Ch 5, turn.

Row 2: Skip 1st sp, dc in next dc—starting sp over sp made; * 2 dc in next sp, dc in next dc—bl over sp made. Rep from * to last sp; ch 2, skip 2 ch, dc in next ch—end sp over sp made. Ch 5, turn.

Row 3: Make starting sp; dc in next 3 dc—bl over bl made; make 8 more bls; ch 2, skip 2 dc, dc in next dc—sp over bl made; make 10 more sps, 11 bls, 9 sps, 11 bls, 11 sps, 9 bls, 1 end sp. Ch 5, turn.

NOTE—Follow every even-numbered row on Chart from left to right; every odd-numbered row from right to left.

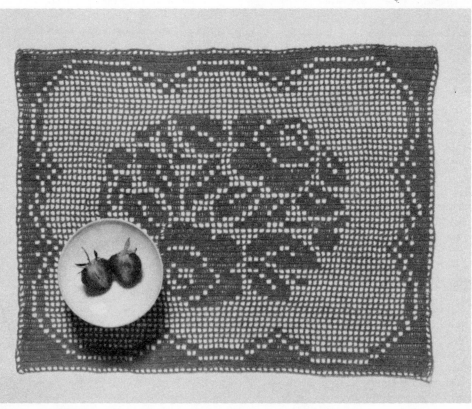

CHART 1

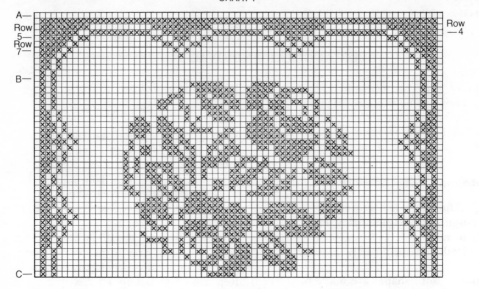

Rows 4–5: Follow Rows 4 and 5 on Chart.

Row 6: Make starting sp, 5 bls, 1 sp, 1 bl, 2 sps; ch 2, skip 2 ch, dc in next dc—sp over sp made; make 12 sps, 2 bls, 1 sp, 1 bl, 1 sp, 2 bls, 13 sps, 2 bls, 1 sp, 1 bl, 1 sp, 2 bls, 15 sps, 1 bl, 1 sp, 5 bls, end sp. Ch 5, turn. Starting with Row 7, follow Chart to C, then follow Chart from B back to A. Break off and fasten.

Starch lightly and press.

OVAL

With Dk. Yellow and starting at A on Chart 2, ch 38 having 15 ch sts to 1 inch.

Row 1: Dc in 8th ch from hook; * ch 2, skip 2 ch, dc in next ch—sp made. Rep from * across—11 sps in all. Ch 16, turn.

Row 2: Dc in 8th ch from hook, (ch 2, skip 2 ch, dc in next ch) twice; ch 2, dc in next dc—4 sps increased at beg of row; ch 2, dc in next dc—sp over sp made; 2 dc in next sp, dc in next dc—bl over sp made; make 8 more bls, 1 sp, ch 2; thread over twice, draw up a loop in same place as last dc was made, thread over and draw through 2 loops, thread over and draw through 1 loop for ch-1 at base of new sp, now work off remaining 3 loops as for 1 dc—inc sp at end of row made; (ch 2, thread over twice; draw up a loop in ch-1 at base of previous inc sp and complete another inc sp as be-

fore) 3 times—4 inc sps made at end of row. Ch 16, turn.

Row 3: Make 4 inc sps at beg of row, 1 sp, 4 bls; dc in next 3 dc—bl over bl made; make 12 bls, 1 sp, 4 inc sps at end of row. Ch 13, turn.

Row 4: Make 3 inc sps, 1 sp, 25 bls, 1 sp, 3 inc sps at end of row. Ch 10, turn.

Row 5: Make 2 inc sps, 1 sp, 5 bls; ch 2, skip 2 dc, dc in next dc—sp over bl made; 5 sps, 9 bls, 6 sps, 5 bls, 1 sp, 2 inc sps. Ch 10, turn.

NOTE—See NOTE in Rectangle Directions.

Rows 6–8: Follow Rows 6 through 8 on Chart. At end of last row ch 7, turn.

Row 9: Make 1 inc sp, then follow Row 9 on Chart to last sp, make 1 inc sp. Ch 7, turn.

Rows 10–17: Follow Chart. At end of last row ch 5, turn.

Row 18: Skip 1st sp, dc in next dc—end sp over end sp made; then follow Row 18 of Chart. Ch 5, turn.

Rows 19–38: Follow Chart. At end of last row, turn.

Row 39: Sl st in next 2 ch, sl st in next dc—1 sp decreased at beg of row; ch 5, dc in next dc—starting sp made; follow Row 39 to end; do not work over last sp of previous row—1 sp decreased at end of row. Ch 5, turn.

Starting with **Row 40,** follow Chart to B. Break off and fasten.

Starch lightly and press.

COPYRIGHT © 1978 COATS & CLARK, INC.

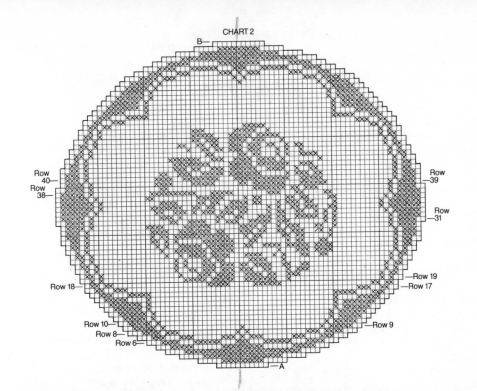

CHART 2

OCCASIONAL RUG

A geometric design gives this rug an interesting textural look. The rug can be used in a variety of places.

Information to Check Before You Start

Sizing: Directions are written for a rug 26 × 37 inches.

Materials: The rug is made of Coats & Clark's Craft & Rug Yarn, Art. C. 207, in 3-ply skeins. You need 12 skeins of No. 243 Mid Orange.

Tool: Crochet Hook—Size K

Gauge: 2 sc = 1 inch
  8 rows = 3 inches

NOTE: Use 2 strands held together throughout.

Directions to Follow

Starting at narrow edge, with 2 strands held tog ch 52, having 2 ch sts to the inch.

Row 1 (wrong side): Sc in 2nd ch from hook and in each remaining ch across—51 sc. Ch 1, turn.

Row 2: Sc in 1st 2 sc, (ch 5, sc in next sc) 14 times; * sc in next 3 sc, (ch 5, sc in next sc) 14 times. Rep from * once more, sc in last sc. Ch 1, turn.

Row 3: Keeping all loops in back of work, sc in each sc across—51 sc. Ch 1, turn.

Rows 4–5: Rep Rows 2 and 3.

Row 6: Sc in 1st 2 sc, (ch 5, sc in next sc) twice; * sc in next 10 sc, (ch 5, sc in next sc) twice; sc in next 3 sc, (ch 5, sc in next sc) twice. Rep from * once more, sc in next 10 sc, (ch 5, sc in next sc) twice; sc in last sc. Ch 1, turn.

Rows 7–9: Rep Rows 3, 6, and 3.

Row 10: Sc in 1st 2 sc, (ch 5, sc in next sc) twice; * sc in next 3 sc, (ch 5, sc in next sc) 4 times; sc in next 3 sc, (ch 5, sc in next sc) twice; sc in next 3 sc, (ch 5, sc in next sc) twice. Rep from * once more, sc in next 3 sc, (ch 5, sc in next sc) 4 times; sc in next 3 sc, (ch 5, sc in next sc) twice; sc in last sc. Ch 1, turn.

Row 11: Rep Row 3.

Rows 12–15: Rep Rows 10 and 3 twice.

Rows 16–19: Rep Rows 6 and 3 twice.

Rows 20–23: Rep Rows 2 and 3 twice.

Rows 24–25: Sc in each sc across. Ch 1, turn. Rep Rows 2–25 twice, then rep Rows 2–24 once. At end of last row ch 1, turn.

Edging: With wrong side facing, keeping work flat and making 3 sc in each corner, sc around entire rug. Join with sl st to 1st sc. Fasten off. With wrong side facing, attach yarn to corner sc following a narrow edge, then sl st in each sc across next long edge to opposite corner. Fasten off. Work sl st across other long edge in same way.

Fringe: Cut 5 strands, each 12 inches long. Double these strands to form a loop. Insert hook from back to front in first st of one narrow edge and draw loop through. Draw loose ends through loop and pull up tightly to form a knot. Knot 5 strands as before in every other st across. Work fringe along opposite narrow edge in same way. Trim evenly.

GINGHAM POT HOLDERS

An array of brightly checked pot holders adds a cheery note to a kitchen. They are not only decorative, but also easy to make.

Information to Check Before You Start

Materials: The pot holders are made of Caron Heavy Rug Yarn in a 1.6 oz. skein. You need a total of 1 oz. of yarn for each pot holder. To create the checked effect, use a light color, a dark color, and white.

Tool: Crochet Hook—Size H

Gauge: 3 sc = 1 inch

Directions to Follow

With dark color ch 21. On each row work over color not in use.

Rows 1–4: * Dark color, work 4 sc, light color, 4 sc; rep from *, end dark color, 4 sc—20 sc. Ch 1, turn.

Rows 5–8: * Light color, work 4 sc, white, 4 sc; rep from *, end light color, 4 sc. Rep Rows 1–8 once, then Rows 1–4. At end of last row, ch 6 for hanging ring. Join, work 12 sc in ring.

OVEN MITT AND POT HOLDERS

It is always nice to add a touch to a kitchen that is both fun and practical. These accessories seem to do just that.

Information to Check Before You Start

Materials: Each item is made of Coats & Clark Craft and Rug Yarn, Art. C. 207, in 3-ply skeins. You need for the 3 items:
—2 oz., No. 282 Rust
—2 oz., No. 588 Amethyst
—2 oz., No. 814 Robin Blue
—2 oz., No. 848 Skipper Blue
—Small pieces of terry cloth for lining may be used if you wish.
Tool: Crochet Hook—Size K
Gauge: 11 sc = 4 inches
   3 sc rows = 1 inch

Directions to Follow

OVEN MITT

Starting at lower edge, with Amethyst ch 27.

Row 1 (wrong side): Sc in 2nd ch from hook and in each remaining ch—26 sc. Ch 1, turn.

Rows 2–4: Sc in each sc across. Ch 1, turn.

Row 5: Sc in each sc across. Fasten off Amethyst, attach Rust. Always change color in this way. Ch 1, turn. Rep Row 2 for stitch pattern, work 1 row Rust, 6 rows Robin Blue, 1 row Skipper Blue, 10 rows Rust, and 8 rows Skipper Blue.

To Shape Tip—Row 1: With Skipper Blue; (draw up a loop in next 2 sc, yarn over and draw through all loops on hook—1 sc dec; sc in 8 sc, dec 1 sc over next 2 sc) twice. Ch 1, turn.

Row 2: (Dec 1 sc over 2 sc, sc in 6 sc, dec 1 sc over 2 sc) twice. Ch 1, turn.

Row 3: (Dec 1 sc over 2 sc, sc in 4 sc, dec 1 sc over 2 sc) twice. Fasten off.

Thumb: Starting at base, with Skipper Blue ch 7.

Row 1: Sc in 2nd ch from hook and in next 5 ch. Ch 1, turn.

Rows 2–4: Make 2 sc in 1st sc, sc in each sc to last sc, 2 sc in last sc. Ch 1, turn.

Rows 5–7: Sc in each sc across. Ch 1, turn.

Row 8: Dec 1 sc at each end, sc in each sc across. Ch 1, turn.

Row 9: Dec 1 sc over every 2 sc. Fasten off.

Sew thumb seam. Inserting thumb in seam about 4½ inches from lower edge, sew side seam of mitt. Line mitt with terry cloth, if desired.

With right side facing, attach Amethyst at side seam. Working around lower edge and working from left to right, * sc in next st to the right. Rep from * around. Fasten off. For loop, attach Amethyst at lower edge of mitt opposite side seam, ch 8, sl st in same place. Ch 1, turn. Make 10 sc in loop; sl st in edge of mitt. Fasten off.

FISH POT HOLDER

Starting at mouth, with Robin Blue ch 6.

Row 1: Sc in 2nd ch from hook and in next 4 ch—5 sc.

Rows 2–5: Make 2 sc in 1st sc, sc in each sc to last sc, 2 sc in last sc. Ch 1, turn. There are 13 sc on Row 5.

Row 6: Sc in each sc across. Ch 1, turn.

Rows 7–8: Rep Rows 2 and 6—15 sc. At end of last row fasten off Robin Blue, attach Amethyst. Ch 1, turn.

Row 9: Rep Row 2—17 sc. Fasten off, attach Skipper Blue. Ch 1, turn.

Row 10: Rep Row 6. Ch 2, turn.

Row 11: Skip next sc; in next sc make 2 hdc, ch 1, and 2 hdc—shell made; (skip 1 sc, sc in next sc, skip 1 sc, shell in next sc) 3 times; skip 1 sc, hdc in last sc. Fasten off, attach Robin Blue. Ch 2, turn.

Row 12: In 1st hdc make hdc, ch 1, and 2 hdc; (sc in ch-1 sp of next shell, shell in next sc) 3 times; sc in sp of next shell, 2 hdc in top of ch-2. Fasten off, attach Skipper Blue. Ch 1, turn.

Row 13: Sc in 1st hdc, (shell in next sc, sc in center of next shell) 3 times; shell in next sc, skip 2 hdc, sc in next ch-1 sp, ch 1, hdc in top of ch-2. Fasten off, attach Amethyst. Ch 2, turn.

Row 14: In 1st ch-1 sp make hdc, ch 1, and 2 hdc; (sc in center of next shell, shell in next sc) 3 times; sc in center of next shell, hdc in last sc. Fasten off, attach Skipper Blue. Ch 2, turn.

Row 15: Shell in next sc, (sc in center of next shell, shell in next sc) 3 times; sc in last ch-1 sp. Fasten off, attach Robin Blue. Ch 1, turn.

Row 16: Sc in center of 1st shell, (shell in next sc, sc in next shell) 3 times. Turn.

Row 17: Sl st in 1st hdc, ch 2, skip next ch-1 sp, dec 1 sc over next 2 hdc, sc in next sc, sc in next 2 hdc, sc in next sp, sc in next 2 hdc, sc in next sc, dec 1 sc over next 2 hdc, skip next ch-1 and following hdc, hdc in next hdc. Ch 1, turn.

Rows 18–21: Rep Row 6. At end of last row fasten off, attach Skipper Blue. Ch 1, turn.

Edging—Rnd 1: Make 3 sc in corner, sc in next 9 sc, 3 sc in corner; keeping work flat sc evenly to 1st corner at mouth; 3 sc in corner, sc in next 3 sts, 3 sc in corner, sc evenly to shell row worked with Robin Blue, ch 3, skip ¼ inch along edge, sc evenly to beg of rnd. Join with sl st to 1st sc.

Rnd 2: Working from left to right, * sc in next st to right. Rep from * around including the ch-3. Join. Fasten off. With Skipper Blue embroider a circle for eye. Rep on other side.

ROUND POT HOLDER

Starting at center, with Rust ch 5. Join with sl st to form ring.

Rnd 1: Ch 3, make 15 dc in ring. Join with sl st to top of ch-3.

Rnd 2: Ch 1, sc in joining, ch 2, (skip 1 dc, sc in next dc, ch 2) 7 times. Join to 1st sc.

Rnd 3: Sl st in 1st ch-2 loop, ch 2, make 3 hdc in same loop, (ch 4, sc in top of last hdc made, 4 hdc in next loop) 7 times; ch 4, sc in top of last hdc made. Join to top of ch-2.

Rnd 4: Sl st in next hdc, ch 1, sc between last and next hdc; (make 4 hdc, ch 1, and 4 hdc in next loop—hdc-loop made; sc between 2nd and 3rd hdc of next 4-hdc group) 7 times; make 4 hdc, ch 1 and 4 hdc in next loop. Join to 1st sc. Fasten off, attach Robin Blue to horizontal strand in back of the 2nd hdc of hdc-loop.

Rnd 5: Ch 1, sc in same place, * (sc in horizontal strand in back of next hdc) 5 times; ch 2, skip next hdc and next sc and following hdc; sc in horizontal strand in back of next hdc. Rep from * around. Join. Fasten off, attach Robin Blue to ch-1 sp of the hdc-loop of Rnd 4.

Rnd 6: Ch 1, sc in same place, * make 6 dc in next ch-2 loop of Rnd 5, sc in ch-1 sp of the hdc-loop of Rnd 4. Rep from *, end with 6 dc in last ch-2 loop. Join to 1st sc. Fasten off, attach Amethyst.

Rnd 7: Ch 1, sc in joining, * sc in next 2 dc, 3 sc in each of next 3 dc, sc in next dc, sc in next sc. Rep from *, end with sc in last dc. Join to 1st sc. Then ch 8, sl st in joining for hanging loop. Ch 1, turn. Make 8 sc in ch-8 loop, sl st in next sc on holder. Fasten off.

GOLF CLUB COVERS

Give a drab golf bag a bright touch by using these covers. They also make a fun gift.

Information to Check Before You Start

Materials: The covers are made of Coats & Clark Red Heart® Fabulend ™ Wool Blend Worsted Yarn, Art. E. 235, in 4-ply skeins. You need:
—8 oz., No. 903 Devil Red
—8 oz., No. 848 Skipper Blue
—4 yards of white yarn for embroidery
Tool: Crochet Hook—Size J
Gauge: 10 sts = 3 inches
        7 rows = 2 inches

Directions to Follow

Cover (make 4): Starting at center back, with Blue ch 43.

Row 1: Sc in 2nd ch from hook and in each ch across—42 sc. Ch 1, turn.

Rows 2–7: Working in back loop only, sc in each sc across, Ch 1, turn.

Row 8: Working in back loop only, sc in next 22 sc; working through both loops, sc across remaining sts. Ch 1, turn. This is top of cover.

Row 9: Working through both loops, sc in next 20 sts; working in back loop only, sc across remaining sts. Ch 1, turn.

Rep Rows 8 and 9 alternately until there are 17 rows in all. Rep Row 2–7 once more. Fasten off, leaving an 18-inch length of yarn.

Making each number 1½ inches wide and 3 inches high and using the shapes illustrated, embroider a number onto flat section of sc at top of each cover with white yarn and a double line of couching: lay yarn along the line of the design. With another strand, attach it to the background with small stitches at even intervals.

Using the 18-inch length of yarn, sew center back seam of cover.

With another strand of Blue, pick up every other end st along top of cover,

pull up tightly, and fasten off securely. With crochet hook, attach a double strand of Blue to any st on back at top of cover, ch 4, sl st in same st where Blue was attached. Fasten off. With Red, work a row of sl st around bottom edge of cover.

Pompon (make 4): Cut 2 cardboard circles, each 6 inches in diameter. Cut a hole 1¼ inches in diameter in center of each circle. Place cardboard circles together and wind Red around the double circles, drawing yarn through center opening and over edge until hole is filled. Cut yarn around outer edge between circles. Double an 18-inch length of Red. Slip between the circles and tie securely around strands of pompon. Remove cardboard and trim ends evenly. Sew 1 pompon to top of each cover.

Cord: Using a double strand of Blue, make a chain 30 inches long. Fasten off. Thread cord through loops at top of covers and fasten ends of cord tog.

1 2
3 4

GLITTERY CHRISTMAS ANGEL

Here is an ornament that will make your Christmas tree sparkle. The little angel will add a pretty touch.

Information to Check Before You Start

Materials: The angel is made of gold or silver Kanagawa, Art. No. 614, metallic yarn. You need:
—Approximately 11 yards. (10 meters)
—Hook for hanging
Tool: Crochet Hook—Size 2

Directions to Follow

Ch 25.
  Row 1: Dc in 4th ch from hook and in ea ch across.
  Rows 2–6: Dc across working dec at beg and end of ea row.

WINGS

Ch 7, sl st in top of dc on row 4, ch 1, turn, over ch-7 make 1 sc, 2 hdc, 3 dc, 4 tr, end off.
  Attach yarn in 1st dc of row 6, ch 7, sl st in top of dc on row 4, repeat as for other side. End off.

HEAD

Ch 5, join with sl st to form ring.
  Row 1: Ch 3, 12 dc in ring, join with sl st to starting ch-3.
  Row 2: Ch 5, dc in next dc, * ch 2, dc in next dc, repeat from * around, ending with ch 2, sl st in 3rd ch of starting ch-5. End off.
  Sew 3 spaces of last row of head to center 7 dc of row 6 of body.
  Sew hanger to top of head.
  Block lightly.

CHRISTMAS BALL

If you have been wanting a new look for your Christmas tree, then here is an idea. Made of several motifs, the balls have a light, airy feeling.

Information to Check Before You Start

Sizing: Directions are for a ball that measures 4¾ inches in diameter.

Materials: The ball is made of J. & P. Coats "Knit-Cro-Sheen" Mercerized Cotton, Art. A. 64. You need:
—1 ball of No. 1 White
—Red ribbon for bow
—1 large round balloon

Tool: Steel Crochet Hook—No. 9

Directions to Follow

Pentagon Motif (make 12): Starting at center, ch 8. Join with sl st to form ring.

Rnd 1: Ch 3, (hdc in ring, ch 1) 9 times. Join to 2nd ch of ch-3.

Rnd 2: Sl st in next hdc, ch 1, (sc in next ch-1 sp, ch 8, sl st in 3rd ch from hook for picot, ch 5, skip next ch-1 sp) 5 times. Join to first sc.

Rnd 3: Ch 1, sc in joining, * sc in next 5 ch sts, 3 sc in next picot, sc in next 5 ch sts, sc in next sc. Rep from * around, end with sc in last 5 ch sts. Join to 1st sc.

Rnd 4: Sl st in each sc to center sc of next 3-sc picot group, ch 1, sc in center sc, (ch 15, sc in center sc of next 3-sc pi-

cot group) 4 times; ch 15. Join to 1st sc.

Rnd 5: Ch 1, sc in each ch st and in each sc around. Join. Fasten off.

Joining of Motifs: With a different color mark 1 motif. With wrong side of marked motif and wrong side of another motif together, join 1 side of the 2 motifs as follows: Make a loop on hook, working through both thicknesses sc in corner sc, sc in each sc to next corner. Do not break off. Join 1 motif to each of the 4 remaining sides of marked motif in same manner. Then join the adjacent sides of the 5 motifs to form one half of the ball. Join remaining 6 motifs in same manner to form second half of ball. Remove markers. Join the 2 halves in same manner, matching points on one half with inverted points on other half.

Sugar Starch: Dissolve 1 cup sugar in ½ cup of water over heat. When completely dissolved and about to simmer, remove from heat and allow to cool for 10 minutes.

Insert deflated balloon through a space of 1 motif. Blow up balloon until round in shape; secure balloon opening. Hang balloon by a string over a shallow dish, (apply a coat of sugar starch over it and allow to dry) 5 times. Pop balloon when last coat is completely dry.

Hanging Loop: Make a chain 10 inches long. Tie ends to a ring of a motif. Tie ribbon around base of hanging loop.

RECTANGULAR SHAWL

Stripes add a special interest to this easy-to-make wrap. Not only is it attractive, it is also functional, providing warmth to an outfit.

Information to Check Before You Start

Sizing: One size fits all. Approximate size 84 × 33 inches including fringe.
Materials: The shawl is made of Bucilla Machine Washable Win-Knit in 4 oz. paks or Knitting Worsted in 4 oz. balls. You need:
—5 of Color A
—1 of Color B
—2 of Color C
—1 of Color D
Tool: Crochet Hook—Size G
Gauge: 10 sts = 3 inches
5 rows = 3 inches

Directions to Follow

Row 1: With A, ch 228. Work 1 dc in 4th ch from hook, 1 dc in each rem ch to end; 226 dc.
Row 2: Ch 3, turn, 1 dc in 2nd dc and each dc to end.
Note—Ch 3 counts as 1 dc.
Rpt Row 2 twice more, drawing loop of B through last 2 loops of last dc to change color. Break A, rpt row 2 for pat, working 2 rows B, * 4 rows A, 4 rows C, 4 rows A, 2 rows D, * 4 rows A, 6 rows C, 4 rows A, 2 rows D, 4 rows A, 4 rows C, 4 rows A, 2 rows B, 4 rows A; 54 rows from beg. Fasten off.
Pockets (make 2): With B, ch 30. Rpt rows 1 and 2. Working row 2 for pat, rpt between *'s once. Fasten off.
Sew on pockets as illustrated, matching stripes.
Fringe: Wind yarn around a 9-inch cardboard, cut at one end. Knot a 3-strand fringe every 2nd row, matching color of fringe to color of stripe. Trim evenly.

SMART CARDIGAN

Although classic in styling this cardigan has a smart, fashionable look. It is an excellent choice for the extra jacket in your wardrobe.

Information to Check Before You Start

Sizing: Directions are written for Small Size (8–10). Changes for Medium Size (12–14) and Large Size (16–18) are in parentheses.
Materials: The cardigan is made of Bernat Linette using 50 gram pull pouches. You need 13 (15, 17).
Tool: Crochet Hook (Bernat U.S.)—Size F (4 mm)
Gauge: 4 dc = 1 inch
2 rows = 1 inch
Note: Always count turning ch as 1 dc.

Directions to Follow

Body: Ch 138 (142, 144) sts.
Row 1: 1 dc in 6th ch from hook, * ch 1, skip 1 st, 1 dc in next st, repeat from * across row.
Rows 2 through 7: Ch 3, turn, 1 dc in next dc, * ch 1, 1 dc in next dc, repeat from * across row.
Row 8: Ch 2, turn, 1 dc in 1st space, 1 dc in next dc, * 1 dc in next space, 1 dc in next dc, repeat from * across row—135 (139, 141) sts.
Rows 9 through 31: Ch 2, turn, 1 dc in each dc.

Divide for Front and Back—
Right Front—Shape Armhole.
Row 32: Turn, with right side facing you, 1 dc in each of next 30 (31, 32) sts, yo, insert hook in next st, draw up a loop, yo, pull through 2 loops on hook, yo, insert hook in next st, draw up a loop, yo, pull through 2 loops on hook, yo, pull through all 3 loops on hook (1 st dec).
Row 33: Turn, dec 1 st, 1 dc in each dc to end of row.
Rows 34 through 51: Turn, dec 1 st in same manner as before—12 (13, 14) sts remain.

Collar. Rows 52 through 61: Work even on 12 (13, 14) sts. Fasten off.

Left Front: With right side facing you, skip next 71 (73, 73) sts, join yarn in next st and work to correspond to right front, reversing all shaping.

Back: With right side facing you, skip 5 sts for underarm, join yarn in next st, dec 1 st, work in pattern as established on next 57 (59, 59) sts, dec 1 st, turn. Continue to dec 1 st each end of *every row* until 21 (23, 23) sts remain. Work 0 (2, 3) rows even in pattern as established. Fasten off.

Sleeves: Ch 56 (60, 64) sts.
Row 1: 1 dc in 6th ch from hook, * ch 1, skip 1 st, 1 dc in next st, repeat from * across row.
Rows 2 through 7: Ch 3, turn, 1 dc in next dc, * ch 1, 1 dc in next dc, repeat from * across row.
Row 8: Ch 2, turn, * 1 dc in ch-1 space, 1 dc in next dc, repeat from * across row—53 (57, 61) sts.
Rows 9 through 27: Ch 2, turn, 1 dc in each dc.
Shape Raglan Cap: Turn, sl st over 1st 3 sts, dec 1 st, 1 dc in each st to last 5 sts, dec 1 st, turn. Continue to dec 1 st each end of *every row* in same manner as on back until 5 (5, 7) sts remain. Fasten off.

Finishing: Sew sleeve seams. Sew sleeves to front and back armholes. Seam neckband and sew to back of neck.
Edging: With right side facing you, join yarn in any st at lower edge, ch 2, 1 dc in each st around lower, front, and collar edges, working 3 dc in each corner, join.
Round 2: Ch 1, turn, * yo, insert hook from *back* to *front* of next dc and working around post of same st of previous round, work 1 dc (B dc), yo, insert hook from *front* to *back* of next st and working around post of same st of previous round, work 1 dc (F dc), repeat from * around to center corner st, 1 dc in space before center corner st, 1 B dc in center corner st, 1 dc in space between center corner st and next st, 1 B dc in next st, continue to alternate 1 F dc, 1 B dc to next corner, work corner in same manner as before, then alternate 1 F dc, 1 B dc to end of round, join.
Round 3: Repeat Round 2, working 1 B dc in each B dc and 1 F dc in each F dc. Work corners as follows: 1 dc in space before center corner st, 1 F dc in center corner st, 1 dc in space between center corner st and next st, 1 F dc in next st, join at end of round. Fasten off.
Sleeve Edging: Omitting corners, work same edging around sleeve edges.

CASUAL VEST

A vest adds an extra dimension to one's wardrobe. It can be used in many ways, and at the same time produce a flattering effect.

Information to Check Before You Start

Sizing: Instructions are written for bust measurement 32 (34, 36, 38) inches (84 [87, 93, 99] cm.)

Materials: The vest is made of Phildar's Shoot Yarn in red (rouge). You need 8 (8, 9, 9) balls.

Tool: Crochet Hook—Size J or 4 (6 mm.)

Gauge: After steaming lightly, the swatch should measure
11 sts = 4 inches (10 cm)
7 rows = 4 inches (10 cm)

Stitches: St 1: Single Crochet
St 2: Double Crochet

NOTE: Figures shown on the diagrams are in centimeters.

Directions to Follow

Back: Using 6 mm hook ch 52 (54, 56, 60) and work in dc.

When back measures 17¾ inches (45 cm), **Shape Armholes:** Dec 4 sts on each side. 44 (46, 48, 52) sts remain. Cont. straight.

When back measures 27½ (27½, 28, 28¼) inches (70 [70, 71, 72] cm), fasten off.

Mark 20 central sts to denote neckline.

Front: Using 6 mm hook ch 27 (28, 29, 31) and work in dc.

When front measures 17¾ inches (45 cm), **Shape Armhole:** Wrong side facing, dec 4, work to end. 23 (24, 25, 27) sts remain. Cont. straight.

When front measures 24½ (24½, 24¾, 25) inches (62 [62, 63, 64] cm),

Shape Neck: Right side facing, Dec 11 sts, work to end. 12 (13, 14, 16) sts remain.

When front measures 27½ (27½, 28, 28¼) inches (70 [70, 71, 72] cm), fasten off.

Work 2nd front to match reversing shaping.

Finishing: Sew side and shoulder seams. Work 2 rows sc around armholes, along fronts, and around neck. Steam seams lightly.

COPYRIGHT © 1979 PHILDAR, INC.

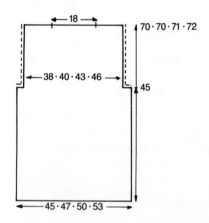

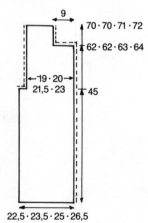

COAT AND SHELL

This beautifully coordinated coat and top, although fashionably smart, takes little effort to make. Worn together or separately they make a nice addition to a wardrobe.

Information to Check Before You Start

Sizing: Directions are for Size 8. Changes for Sizes 10, 12, 14, and 16 are in parentheses.
· Finished Measurements:
For Shell:
Bust—33½ (34½, 36, 37½, 39) inches
Width of front or back at underarm—
16¾ (17¼, 18, 18¾, 19½) inches
For Coat:
Bust—42 (43, 44, 45, 46) inches
Width of each front at underarm—
10¾ (11, 11⅔, 12⅓, 13) inches
Width of back at underarm—
21 (21½, 22, 22½, 23) inches
Width of sleeves at underarm—
15½ (16, 16½, 17, 17½) inches
Materials: The items are made in Columbia-Minerva Shannon in 3 oz. balls. If you wish, you can substitute Nantuk 4-ply or Performer yarn. You need:
For Shell—4 (4, 5, 6, 7) balls
For Coat—14 (14, 15, 16, 17) balls
Tools: Crochet Hooks—Size H, Size I, and Size J
Gauge: Shell using Size I hook—
7 sts = 2 inches
4 rows = 1 inch
Coat using Size J hook—
3 sc = 1 inch
3 rows = 1 inch

Directions to Follow

SHELL

Back. Row 1 (right side): With Size I hook, ch 59 (61, 65, 67, 69), sc in 3rd ch from hook, * ch 1, sk next ch, sc in next ch; rep from * across; 58 (60, 64, 66, 68) sts.

Row 2: Ch 2, turn, sc in 1st ch-1 sp, * ch 1, sc in next ch-1 sp; rep from * across, end ch 1, sc between last sc and ch-2. Rep Row 2 for pat. Work even until 15 inches from beg or desired length to underarm.

Shape Armholes. Row 1: Ch 1, turn, sl st in each of 1st 4 sts, ch 2, sc in next sp, work in pat to within last 4 sts.

Dec. Row: Ch 2, turn, draw up a lp in each of 1st 2 ch-1 sps, yo and thru all 3 lps on hook (pat dec), work in pat to within last 4 sts, dec 1 pat. Rep dec row once; 42 (44, 48, 50, 52) sts. Work even until 7 (7, 7½, 7¾, 8) inches above beg of armhole.

Shape Shoulders. Row 1: Ch 1, turn, sl st in each of first 6 sts, ch 2, sc in next ch-1 sp, [ch 1, sc in next sp] 2 (2, 3, 3, 3) times; fasten off: Sk next 9 (10, 10, 11, 12) sc, join yarn in next sp, ch 2, sc in next ch-1 sp, [ch 1, sc in next sp] 2 (2, 3, 3, 3) times. Fasten off.

Front: Work same as back until 4 (4, 4¼, 4½, 4½) inches above beg of armhole.

Shape Neck. Row 1: Ch 2, turn, sc in 1st sp, [ch 1, sc in next sp] 8 (8, 9, 9, 9) times; 18 (18, 20, 20, 20) sts. At neck edge, dec 1 pat every row 3 times. Work even until same length as back to shoulder.

Shape Shoulder: Work same as 1st half of shoulder of back. Fasten off. Sk center 3 (4, 4, 5, 6) sc on last full row of front, join yarn in next ch-1 sp, ch 2, sc in next ch-1 sp, work in pat to end. Finish to correspond to 1st half.

Finishing: Sew shoulder and side seams. From right side, with Size H hook, work 1 row sc around armhole edges and lower edge of shell.

Turtleneck. Rnd 1: Right side facing, with Size H hook join yarn in 1st sc at right back neck edge, ch 2, sc in next sp, work in pat across back neck, work 7 (7, 8, 8, 9) pats along side edge, work in pat across front neck, work 7 (7, 8, 8, 9) pats along side edge, join in 1st st; 52 (56, 60, 64, 72) sts.

Rnd 2: Ch 2, turn, work around in pat, join. Rep rnd 2 until 3 inches from beg.

Next Rnd: Ch 2, turn, in 1st ch-1 sp
work sc, ch 1, sc (pat inc), work around
in pat, inc 7 pats more evenly spaced; 68
(72, 76, 80, 88) sts. Work 2 rnds even.
Change to Size I hook. Work even until
7 inches from beg.

Last Rnd: Ch 1, turn, sc in each st
around, join. Fasten off.

COAT

Back. Row 1 (right side): With Size J
hook, ch 63 (65, 67, 69, 71), sc in 2nd
ch from hook and each rem ch; 62 (64,
66, 68, 70) sc.

Row 2: Ch 1, turn, sc in each sc
across. Rep row 2 until 25 inches from
beg or desired length to underarm. Mark
beg and end of last row for underarm.
Work even in sc until 8 (8, 8½, 8½, 9)
inches above markers. Fasten off. Mark
5¼ (5½, 6¼, 6½, 6¾) inches in from
each side edge for shoulders.

Fronts: Make 2. With Size J hook, ch 33
(34, 36, 38, 40). Work same as back.

Sleeves. Row 1: With Size J hook, ch 36
(36, 38, 38, 40), sc in 2nd ch from hook
and each rem ch; 35 (35, 37, 37, 39) sc.
Work even in sc until 5 inches from beg.
Inc 1 st each side edge in next row, then
every 1½ inches, 6 times more; 49 (49,
51, 51, 53) sc. Work even until 20
inches from beg or 3 inches more than
desired length to underarm, allowing for
3-inch cuff and drop shoulder. Fasten
off.

Finishing: Sew shoulder seams from side
edge to markers and side seams from
lower edge to underarm marker. Sew
sleeve seams, sew in sleeves.

Front and Neck Edging: Right side
facing, with Size H hook join yarn at
lower right front corner, sc evenly along
front edge to neck edge, 3 sc in corner
to turn, sc along neck edge, dec 5 sts
evenly spaced across back neck edge, 3
sc in left neck corner, sc evenly to lower
edge. Fasten off.

COPYRIGHT © 1981 COLUMBIA-MINERVA
CORPORATION

TEXTURED PULLOVER

A combination of stitches gives an interesting textured look to this classic design. The puffy stitches arranged in vertical lines produce a flattering effect.

Information to Check Before You Start

Sizing: Directions are written to fit a
   31½–32½-inch bustline. Changes for
   Bust Sizes 34–36, 38–40, and 42–44
   inches are in brackets.
   Working Measurements:
   —*Width of back or front at underarm*—
   16 [18, 20, 22] inches
   —*Width of sleeve at underarm*—
   12¼ [12¾, 13¼, 14¾] inches
Materials: The pullover is made of
   Coats & Clark Red Heart® Sport
   Yarn, Art. E. 281, in 2-ply skeins. You
   need:
   —12 [14, 14, 16] ounces, No. 920 Cranberry
   —4 Buttons
Tools: Crochet Hooks—Sizes D and G
Gauge: With Size G hook—4 sts = 1
   inch
   10 pattern rows = 3 inches

Directions to Follow

Back Ribbing: Starting at narrow edge,
with D hook ch 19, having 6 ch sts to 1
inch.

Row 1: Sc in 2nd ch from hook and in
each ch—18 sc. Ch 1, turn.

Row 2: Sc in back loop of each sc. Ch
1, turn. Rep Row 2 until ribbing slightly
stretched is 14 [16, 18, 20] inches.
Change to G hook.

Foundation Row: Ch 1, make 64 [72,
80, 88] sc evenly across adjacent long
edge. Ch 3, turn.

Next Row: Dc in next 20 [24, 28, 32]
sc, mark last 2 dc with a thread; dc in 26
sc, mark last 2 dc; dc in 17 [21, 25, 29]
sc—64 [72, 80, 88] dc, counting ch-3 at
1 dc. Ch 1, turn. Always count ch-3 as a
st.

Following Row: Sc in each st across.
Ch 3, turn.

Now work **pattern.**

Row 1 (right side): Dc in next 10 [14, 18, 22] sts; 4 dc in next st, drop loop from hook, insert hook in 1st dc of 4-dc group and draw dropped loop through, ch 1 to fasten—pc st made; dc in next 5 sts; (yarn over, insert hook from right to left under bar of 1st marked dc below, yarn over and draw up a long loop to height of previous dc, yarn over and draw through 2 loops on hook) twice, yarn over and draw through 2 loops on hook—raised st made; raised st around bar of next marked dc below; skip 2 sts behind raised sts, dc in 9 sts, pc st in next st, dc in 8 sts, pc st in next st, dc in 5 sts, (raised st around bar of next marked dc below) twice; skip 2 sts behind raised sts, dc in 9 sts, pc st in next st, dc in 9 [13, 17, 21] sts. Ch 1, turn.

Row 2: Sc in each st—64 [72, 80, 88] sc. Ch 3, turn.

Row 3: Dc in 8 [12, 16, 20] sts, pc st in next st, dc in 9 sts, (raised st around bar of next raised st below) twice; skip sts behind raised sts, dc in 5 sts, pc st in next st, dc in 8 sts, pc st in next st, dc in 9 sts, (raised st around bar of next raised st below) twice; skip sts behind raised sts, dc in 5 sts, pc st in next st, dc in 11 [15, 19, 23] sts. Ch 1, turn.

Row 4: Rep Row 2.

Row 5: Work as for Row 1, making each raised st around bar of corresponding raised st below. Ch 1, turn. Rep Rows 2–5 for pattern until total length is 13 [13, 13½, 14] inches, end on right side. Turn.

Armhole Shaping. Row 1: Sl st in 1st 4 [4, 5, 6] sts, ch 1, sc in each st to last 4 [4, 5, 6] sts; do not work remaining sts. Ch 3, turn.

Row 2: Holding back on hook last loop of each dc, dc in next 2 sts, yarn over and draw through all loops on hook—dc-dec made; work in pattern to last 3 sts, make dc-dec, dc in last st. Ch 1, turn.

Row 3: Sc in each st across. Ch 3, turn. Rep Rows 2 and 3 alternately 3 [4, 5, 5] more times—48 [54, 58, 64] sts. Work even until length from Row 1 of armhole shaping is 4 [4½, 5, 6] inches, end on wrong side. Ch 3, turn.

Back Opening. Row 1: Work until 24 [27, 29, 32] sts including ch-3 have been worked; do not work remaining sts. Ch 1, turn. Work even until length from Row 1 of armhole shaping is 7 [7½, 8, 9] inches, end at armhole. Turn.

Right Shoulder Shaping: Sl st in 1st 5 sts, hdc in 9 [11, 12, 13] sts, work across. Fasten off.

Attach yarn in next free st on last long row worked before back opening.

Row 1: Ch 3, dc in next st, work across. Ch 1, turn. Work as for other side to shoulder, end at center back. Ch 3, turn.

Left Shoulder Shaping: Work until 10 [11, 12, 14] sts including ch-3 are worked, hdc in 9 [11, 12, 13] sts, sl st in last 5 sts. Fasten off.

Front: Work as for Back until length from Row 1 of Armhole Shaping is 4 [4½, 4½, 5½] inches, end on wrong side. Ch 3, turn.

Neck Shaping. Row 1: Work until 16 [18, 19, 21] sts including ch-3 are worked, make dc-dec—17 [19, 20, 22] sts; do not work remaining sts. Ch 1, turn.

Row 2: Work even. Ch 3, turn.

Row 3: Work to last 2 sts, make dc-dec. Ch 1, turn. Rep last 2 rows alternately 2 [2, 2, 3] more times—14 [16, 17, 18] sts. Work even until length is same as back to shoulder, end at armhole. Turn.

Left Shoulder Shaping: Sl st in 1st 5 sts, hdc in 9 [11, 12, 13] sts. Fasten off.

Skip the 10 [12, 12, 14] center sts on last long row worked, attach yarn to next st.

Row 1: Ch 3, make dc-dec, work across. Ch 1, turn.

Row 2: Work even. Ch 3, turn.

Row 3: Make dc-dec, work across. Ch 1, turn. Rep last 2 rows alternately 2 [2, 2, 3] more times—14 [16, 17, 18] sts. Work as for other side to shoulder, end at neck. Ch 2, turn.

Right Shoulder Shaping: Hdc in 8 [10, 11, 12] sts, sl st in last 5 sts. Fasten off.

Sleeves. Ribbing: With D hook, ch 17. Work ribbing as for Back over 16 sc until piece slightly stretched is 7½ [8,

8½, 9] inches. Change to G hook.

Foundation Row: Ch 1, make 35 [37, 39, 39] sc evenly across adjacent long edge. Ch 3, turn.

Next Row: Dc in next 10 [11, 12, 12] sc, mark last 2 dc; dc in 17 sts, mark last 2 dc; dc in 7 [8, 9, 9] sc—35 [37, 39, 39] sts, counting ch-3 as 1 dc. Ch 1, turn.

Following Row: Sc in each dc, sc in top of ch-3. Ch 3, turn.

Now work **pattern.**

Row 1 (right side): Dc in 6 [7, 8, 8] sc, (raised st around bar of next marked dc below) twice; skip sts behind raised sts, dc in 9 sc, pc st in next sc, dc in 5 sc, (raised st around bar of next marked dc below) twice; skip sts behind raised sts, dc in 9 [10, 11, 11] sc. Ch 1, turn.

Row 2: Sc in each st across. Ch 3, turn.

Row 3: Dc in 8 [9, 10, 10] sc, (raised st around bar of next raised st below) twice; skip sts behind raised sts, dc in 5 sts, pc st in next sc, dc in 9 sc, (raised st around bar of next raised st below) twice; skip sts behind raised sts, dc in 7 [8, 9, 9] sc. Ch 1, turn.

Row 4: Rep Row 2.

Row 5: Work as for Row 1, making each raised st around bar of corresponding raised st below. Ch 1, turn. Pattern is established.

Next Row: Make 2 sc in 1st st—inc made; work in pattern across, inc in top of ch-3. Ch 3, turn. Keeping inc sts in pattern, work 5 [5, 5, 3] rows even. Rep last 6 [6, 6, 4] rows until there are 49

[51, 55, 59] sts. Work even until total length is 17 [17, 18, 18] inches, end on right side.

Top Shaping. Rows 1–2: Rep Rows 1 and 2 of Armhole Shaping of Back. Ch 1, turn.

Row 3: Draw up a loop in each of 1st 2 sts, yarn over and draw through all loops on hook—sc-dec made; sc in each st to last st and ch-3, make sc-dec. Rep last 2 rows alternately until 19 [21, 23, 29] sts remain.

Next Row: Work even.

Following Row: Dec one st at each end, work across. Rep last 2 rows alternately 0 [1, 2, 5] more times. Work 1 row even. Fasten off.

Pin pieces to measurements excluding ribbing, dampen, and leave to dry. Sew side, shoulder, and sleeve seams; sew in sleeves, holding in to fit.

Neckband: With D hook, ch 7. Work ribbing as for Back over 6 sc until band slightly stretched will fit neck opening. Fasten off. Sew in place.

With pins mark position of 4 button-holes evenly spaced on right back opening, having first pin ½ inch from base of opening and last pin at center of neckband. With right side facing, attach yarn at upper corner of right back opening, ch 1, (sc along edge to next pin, ch 3, skip ⅜ inch along edge) 4 times; sc to base opening, sc along edge to left corner of neckband. Fasten off. Sew buttons in place.

SUNNY TOP

This design offers the perfect topping for a bathing suit. Roomy and airy, it is both attractive and practical.

Information to Check Before You Start

Sizing: Directions are written for Small Size (8–10). Changes for Medium Size (12–14) and Large Size (16–18) are in parentheses.
Materials: The top is made of Bernat Linette using 50 gram pull pouches. You need 10 (11, 13) pouches.
Tools: Afghan Hook (Bernat U.S.)— Size I (5.5 mm)
Crochet Hook (Bernat U.S.)— Size G (4.5 mm)
Gauge: 4 sts in pattern st = 1 inch
2 rows = 1 inch

Directions to Follow

Pattern Stitch: Row 1: Yo, draw up a loop in 3rd ch from hook, * yo, skip 1 st of ch, draw up a loop in next st of ch, repeat from * across row; take off loops as follows: yo, draw through 1 loop, * yo, draw through 2 loops, repeat from * across row. The loop remaining on hook counts as 1st loop of next row.

Row 2: Skip 1st upright bar, * yo, draw up a loop in next upright bar, repeat from * across row; take off loops in same manner as Row 1. Repeat Row 2 for pattern stitch.

Back: Using afghan hook, ch 67 (71, 75) sts. Work even in pattern st until piece measures 13 inches. Change to crochet hook and work as follows:

Row 1: Ch 1, 1 sc in each st—67 (71, 75) sts.

Row 2: Ch 1, turn, 1 sc in each st. Repeat Row 2 until 2 inches have been worked in sc, ending with a wrong side row. Fasten off.

Yoke and Sleeves: Using afghan hook, ch 59 sts. Working in pattern st, pick up loops in these 59 sts in same manner as before; working across 67 (71, 75) sts of back, skip 1st sc, * yo, draw up a loop in next sc, repeat from * across sts of back, yo, break off yarn; still using afghan hook, ch 59 sts, working in pattern st, pick up loops in these 59 sts in same manner as before; continuing to work in pattern st, take off loops on all 185 (189, 193) sts. Now work even in pattern st for 6 inches. Change to crochet hook and work in sc in same manner as before for 8 rows. Fasten off.

Front: Work to correspond to back.

Finishing: Leaving 12 inches open for neck, sew shoulder seams. Sew underarm and sleeve seams.

Lower Edging. Round 1: With wrong side facing you and using crochet hook, join yarn in underarm seam at lower edge and work 1 sc in each st, join.

Rounds 2 and 3: Ch 1, turn, 1 sc in each st, join. Fasten off.

Cuffs. Round 1: With right side facing you, join yarn in sleeve seam and work 1 sc in each st, join.

Rounds 2 through 8: Ch 1, turn, 1 sc in each st, join. Fasten off.

BELTED TUNIC

A pleasing combination of colors gives importance to this garment made of single crochet stitches. The unusual construction details provide added interest.

Information to Check Before You Start

Sizing: Directions are written for a Small Size. Changes for Medium and Large sizes are in brackets.
Working Measurements:
—Width across back or front at underarm— 18½ [20, 21] inches
—Length from shoulder to lower edge— 21¾ [23¼, 24¾] inches
—Length of sleeve seam—
17 [17, 17½] inches
—Width across sleeve at upper arm—
14½ [15½, 16½] inches
Materials: The tunic is made of Coats & Clark Red Heart® Sport Yarn, Art. E. 281, in 2-ply skeins. You need for each size:
—11 [12, 14] ounces of No. 111 Eggshell
—6 [6, 7] ounces of No. 802 Baby Blue
—2 ounces of No. 920 Cranberry
Tool: Crochet Hook—Size G
Gauge: Long sc pattern 4 sts = 1 inch
11 rows = 2 inches

Directions to Follow

Center Panel of Back: Starting at lower edge, with Eggshell ch 47 [51, 55], having 4 ch sts to the inch.
Foundation Row (right side): Sc in 2nd ch from hook and in each remaining ch across—46 [50, 54] sc. Ch 1, turn.
  Row 1: * Sc in next sc; insert hook in same place where next sc was made on row below, yarn over and draw up a long loop, yarn over and draw through 2 loops—long sc made; skip the sc covered by long sc. Rep from * across—46 [50, 54] sts. Ch 1, turn. Repeating Row 1 for long sc pattern, work even until length is 18¼ [19½, 21] inches. Fasten off.
  Center Panel of Front: Work as for Center Panel of Back until length is 14¼ [15, 16] inches. Ch 1, turn.

  Neck Shaping. Row 1: Work in pattern across 1st 10 [10, 12] sts; do not work over remaining sts. Ch 1, turn. Work even in pattern over these sts until total length from lower edge is 18¼ [19½, 21] inches. Fasten off. Skip next 26 [30, 30] sts on last long row worked before neck shaping, attach yarn to next st, and work in pattern across the remaining 10 [10, 12] sts. Then complete as for other side.
  Sew shoulder seams.
  Neckband: With right side of tunic facing, attach yarn to a shoulder seam at neck edge.
  Rnd 1: Ch 1, being careful to keep neck edge flat, sc evenly around entire neck edge. Join with sl st to 1st sc. Ch 1, turn.
  Rnd 2: Sc in each sc around, dec 2 sc at each corner at shoulder and 2 sc at each corner at lower edge of front neck; to dec 1 sc, draw up a loop in each of next 2 sts, yarn over and draw through all loops on hook. Join to 1st sc. Ch 1, turn.
  Rnd 3: Sc in each sc around. Join. Ch 1, turn.
  Rnd 4: Rep Rnd 2. Fasten off.

Outer Border of Back and Front. Rnd 1: With wrong side of tunic facing, attach Eggshell to any shoulder seam; ch 1, (* working along side edge of tunic and in sps formed by the pattern, sc in each of next 5 sps, make 2 sc in next sp. Rep from * to last sp before lower corner; make 2 sc in next sp, sc in corner; working along lower edge, make 2 sc in next st, sc in each st to st before next corner; 2 sc in next st, sc in corner, 2 sc in next sp of next side edge) twice. Then work as before along remaining side edge. Join to 1st sc. Fasten off.
  Rnd 2: With right side of tunic facing, attach Cranberry to joining; ch 1, sc in each sc around, inc 1 sc before and after each corner. Join. Fasten off.
  Rnd 3: With wrong side of tunic facing, attach Eggshell to joining, ch 1, sc in each sc around, making 2 sc in corner

sc at each of the 4 corners. Join. Fasten off. Turn.

Rnd 4: With Blue work as for Rnd 2, but do not fasten off at end of rnd. Ch 1, turn.

Rnd 5: With Blue, work as for Rnd 3.

Rnd 6: Rep Rnd 2.

Rnd 7: With Blue work as for Rnd 3, but do not fasten off at end of rnd. Ch 1, turn. Working with Blue only and alternating the incs as established on Rnds 2 and 3, work 10 [12, 12] more rnds. At end of each rnd ch 1, turn. At end of last rnd, fasten off.

Sleeves: Starting at lower edge, with Blue ch 59 [63, 67], having 4 ch sts to 1 inch.

Foundation Row (right side): Sc in 2nd ch from hook and in each remaining ch across—58 [62, 66] sc. Ch 1, turn.

Row 1: Sc in each sc across. Ch 1, turn. Repeating last row work even for 2¾ [2¾, 3¼] inches, end with a row on wrong side. Continuing to work even, work in stripes as follows: 1 row Cranberry, 1 row Blue, 2 rows Eggshell, 1 row Cranberry, 1 row Eggshell. Do not break off Eggshell at end of last row. Ch 1, turn. With Eggshell work in long sc pattern same as on Center Panel of Back for 11¼ inches, end with a row on wrong side. Fasten off Eggshell, attach Cranberry, ch 1, turn.

Next Row: Sc in each st across. Ch 1, turn. Rep last row until total length of sleeve is 17 [17, 17½] inches. Fasten off. With Back and Front together and leaving 7¼ [7¾, 8¼] inches free from shoulder, sew side seams for 8½ [9½, 10½] inches, leaving remainder of side edge open for slit.

Sew sleeve seams, matching stripes. Sew in sleeves.

Cord: Cut 3 strands of Cranberry each 8 yards long. Fold in half and knot ends together. Place folded and over a doorknob. Place a pencil through other end and twist yarn in one direction. Remove pencil and holding yarn taut at all times, fold in half. Release folded end a little at a time and it will twist into a cord. Knot each end and trim.

COPYRIGHT © 1979 COATS & CLARK, INC.

HOODED JACKET

Adding a hood to this pretty sweater produces a practical feature. The knitted band offers another pleasing touch.

Information to Check Before You Start

Sizing: Instructions are for Size 0–3 months. Changes for Sizes 3–6, 6, 9, 12, 18 months are in parentheses. Chest Measurement: 16½ (18, 19½, 20½, 21½, 23) inches, (42 [46, 50, 52, 54, 58] cm).

Materials: The jacket is made of Menortes, a Phildar yarn. You need 4 (4, 5, 6, 6, 7) balls.
—3 buttons

Tools: Crochet Hook—Size E (3½ mm)
—Knitting Needles—Size I (2½ mm)
　　　　　　　　—Size 3 (3 mm)
—Stitch Holder

Gauge: 19 sts = 4 inches (10 cm) using Size E Crochet Hook and measuring over crochet pattern
14 rows = 4 inches (10 cm)
—The gauge for the knitted band is 24 sts = 4 inches (10 cm) using Size 3 Knitting Needles

Special Abbreviations

cl = cluster. (Yrh, insert hook from right to left around stem of next tr in row below and draw loop through) twice, yrh, draw loop through 1st 4 loops on hook, yrh, draw loop through last 2 loops on hook.

dec 1 = decrease 1. Yrh, insert hook in next st and draw loop through, yrh and draw loop through first 2 loops on hook, yrh and insert hook in foll st, draw loop through, yrh, draw loop through 1st 2 loops on hook, yrh, draw loop through all 3 loops on hook.

NOTE: All figures on diagrams are in centimeters.

Directions to Follow

Main part—worked in 1 piece: Start at lower edge and make 82 (90, 98, 102, 106, 114) ch.

Foundation row (right side): 1 dc in 2nd ch from hook, 1 dc in each rem ch—81 (89, 97, 101, 105, 113) sts.

Row 1: 3 ch, miss 1st st, 1 tr in each st to end.

Row 2: 3 ch, miss 1st st, 1 tr in each of next 3 (3, 3, 1, 3, 3) sts, * cl, miss 1 st, 1 tr in each of next 3 sts; rep from * ending last rep 1 tr in each of next 3 (3, 3, 1, 3, 3) sts, 1 tr in next ch.

Row 3: As 1st row.

Row 4: 3 ch, miss 1st st, 1 tr in each of next 1 (1, 1, 3, 1, 1) sts, * cl, miss 1st st, 1 tr in each of next 3 sts; rep from * ending last rep 1 tr in each of next 1 (1, 1, 3, 1, 1) sts, 1 tr in next ch.

These 4 rows form patt.

Continue in patt until work measures approx. 4½ (4¾, 5, 5½, 6, 6¼) inches (11 [12, 13, 14, 15, 16]cm), ending with a 1st or 3rd patt row.

Divide for Armholes: Work each piece separately.

Next Row: Patt 15 (17, 19, 20, 21, 23) sts, turn.

Cont in patt on these sts for Right Front until armhole measures approx. 2½ (3, 3¼, 3¼, 3¼, 3½) inches (6½ [7, 7½, 7½, 7½, 8½] cm), ending with a 2nd or 4th patt row.

Shape Neck. Next Row: Patt to last 3 sts, turn.

Next Row: Ss over 1st 2 sts patt to end.

Next Row: Patt to last 2 sts dec 1.

Next Row: Ss over 1st st, patt to end—8 (10, 12, 13, 14, 16) sts.

5th and 6th Sizes

Next Row: Patt to last 2 sts dec 1—(13, 15) sts.

All Sizes: When work measures 8½ (9, 10, 10½, 11, 12) inches (22 [23½, 25, 26, 27½, 29½] cm), fasten off.

With right side facing, miss 9 sts, re-join yarn, 3 ch, miss 1 st, patt 32 (36, 40, 42, 44, 48), turn—33 (37, 41, 43, 45, 49) sts. Keeping patt correct, cont until 1 row less than on Right Front has been worked. Fasten off.

With right side facing, miss 9 sts, re-join yarn, 3 ch, miss 1 st, patt to end for Left Front—15 (17, 19, 20, 21, 23) sts. Finish to correspond with Right Front, rev shapings.

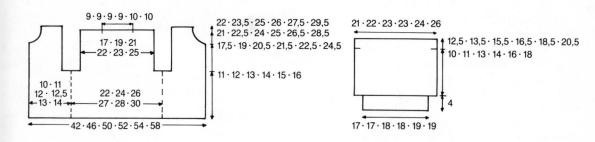

```
        9 · 9 · 9 · 9 · 10 · 10                22 · 23,5 · 25 · 26 · 27,5 · 29,5      21 · 22 · 23 · 23 · 24 · 26
                                             ↕ 21 · 22,5 · 24 · 25 · 26,5 · 28,5
            17 · 19 · 21                      ↕ 17,5 · 19 · 20,5 · 21,5 · 22,5 · 24,5                      12,5 · 13,5 · 15,5 · 16,5 · 18,5 · 20,5
            22 · 23 · 25                                                                                  10 · 11 · 13 · 14 · 16 · 18
                                             ↕ 11 · 12 · 13 · 14 · 15 · 16
  10 · 11
  12 · 12,5        22 · 24 · 26
  13 · 14          27 · 28 · 30                                                                                              ↕ 4
  ←     42 · 46 · 50 · 52 · 54 · 58     →              17 · 17 · 18 · 18 · 19 · 19
```

Sleeves: Start at lower edge and make 40 (42, 44, 46, 48, 50) ch.

Foundation Row (right side): 1 dc in 2nd ch from hook, 1 dc in each rem ch—39 (41, 43, 45, 47, 49) sts.

Row 1: 3 ch, miss 1st st, 1 tr in each st to end.

Row 2: 3 ch, miss 1st st, 1 tr in each of next 2 (3, 0, 1, 2, 3) sts, * cl, miss 1 st, 1 tr in each of next 3 sts, rep from * ending last rep 1 tr in each of next 2 (3, 0, 1, 2, 3) sts, 1 tr in next ch.

Row 3: As 1st row.

Row 4: 3 ch, miss 1st st, 1 tr in each of next 0 (1, 2, 3, 0, 1) sts, * cl, miss 1 st, 1 tr in each of next 3 sts, rep from *, ending last rep 1 tr in each of next 0 (1, 2, 3, 0, 1) sts, 1 tr in next ch.

These 4 rows form patt.

Work in patt until Sleeve measures approx. 5 (5½, 6, 6½, 7½, 8) inches (12½ [13½, 15½, 16½, 18½, 20½] cm). Fasten off.

Place a marker at side edges 1 inch (2½ cm) in below top of Sleeve.

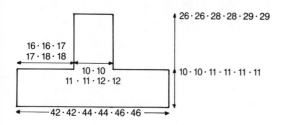

Hood: Start at front edge and make 82 (82, 86, 86, 90, 90) ch.

Foundation Row (right side): 1 dc in 2nd ch from hook, 1 dc in each rem ch—81 (81, 85, 85, 89, 89) sts.

Work in patt as for 1st size of main part until hood measures 4 (4, 4½, 4½, 4½, 4½) inches (10 [10, 11, 11, 11, 11] cm). Break yarn. Turn work, miss 1st 31 (31, 32, 32, 33, 33) sts, rejoin yarn, 3 ch, patt 18 (18, 20, 20, 22, 22) turn—19, (19, 21, 21, 23, 23) sts. Keeping patt correct, cont on these sts until hood measures 10 (10, 11, 11, 12, 12) inches (26 [26, 28, 28, 29, 29] cm). Fasten off.

To Make Up: Do not press.

Cuffs: With right side facing and 2½ mm needles knit up 40 (42, 44, 46, 48, 50) sts along Foundation Row of each sleeve.

Work in Knit 1 Purl 1 rib for 1½ inches (4 cm).

Cast off loosely in rib.

Join shoulder seams. Join sleeve seams to markers. Insert sleeves, joining free edges of sleeve seam to sts left at underarm. Join back seams of hood and sew in position around neck edge of main part.

Lower Border and Front Bands: With 1 mm needles, cast on 112 (120, 130, 134, 140, 150) sts and work in g st (every row sl 1 k, K to end) for 3 cms (1¼) ins *noting* that 1st row is wrong side, and ending with a right-side row.

Next Row: Slip 1 stitch, knit 5, inc 1, knit 1, turn, and leave rem sts on a spare needle.

Cont in g st on these 8 sts for Left Front Band until strip, when slightly stretched, fits up to Left Front to start of neck shaping, ending with a right-side row. Break yarn. Leave sts on a safety pin.

With *wrong* side facing and using contrasting yarn, Purl 98 (106, 116, 120, 126, 136) from spare needle. Break contrast yarn; leave sts on a stitch holder.

With *wrong* side facing, rejoin yarn to rem 7 sts and work as follows: K1, M1, K6.

Work Right Front Band on these 8 sts as for Left Front Band with the addition of 3 buttonholes, 1st to come 4 (4½, 4¾, 5, 5, 5½) inches (10 [11½, 12, 12½, 12½, 14] cm) from lower edge, 3rd to come level with start of neck shaping, and 2nd spaced evenly between.

To Make a Buttonhole (right side): Slip 1, knit 2, cast off 2 sts, knit 3, and back, casting on 2 sts over those cast off. Cont in g st until strip when slightly stretched fits right around edge of hood, ending with a *wrong* side row. Break yarn. Graft Front Bands together.

Alternatively, Front Bands may be cast off and seamed together on wrong side. Join Front Bands to main part and around hood. Join lower Border to Foundation Row of main part by undoing contrast yarn and work in back st through each st on right side.

Sew on buttons.

FILET JACKET

The Chanel-type styling of the cardigan
and the filet design produce an interesting fashion effect. The cardigan makes
an excellent jacket to wear when a
dressy touch is needed.

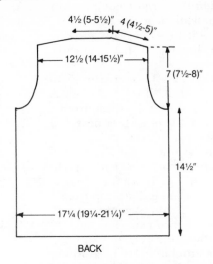

BACK

Information to Check Before You Start

Sizing: The directions are for Small
Size (8–10). Changes for Medium Size
(12–14) and Large Size (16–18) are in
parentheses.
Material: The jacket is made of Bernat
Zephyr yarn in 50 gram balls or Ber-
ella Sportspun yarn in 2 oz. balls. You
need 7 (7, 8) balls.
Tool: Crochet Hook (Bernat U.S.)—
Size F (4 mm)
Gauge: 2 spaces = 1 inch
2 rows = 1 inch

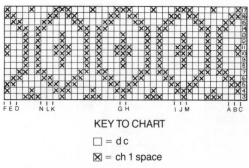

KEY TO CHART

□ = dc
☒ = ch 1 space

Directions to Follow

To Dec 1 Space: At beg of row, ch 3,
skip 1st space, 1 dc in next dc (counts as
1 dc), work in pattern st across row. At
end of row, work to last 2 spaces, ch 1,
yo, pull up a loop in next dc, yo, pull up
a loop in 3rd st of turning ch, (yo and
pull through 2 loops on hook) twice, yo,
pull through all 3 loops on hook.

To Inc 1 Space: At beg of row, ch 4,
1 dc in 1st dc, work in pattern st across
row. At end of row, (ch 1, 1 dc in 3rd st
of turning ch) twice.

To Make Spaces: 1 dc in dc, ch 1,
skip 1 st, 1 dc in next dc (1 space), ch 1,
skip 1 st, 1 dc in next dc for each additional space.

To Make Blocks (bl): 1 dc in each of
3 sts (1 block [bl]); 1 dc in each of next
2 sts for each additional block.

Back: Ch 74 (78, 82) sts. **Row 1:** 1 dc in
6th ch from hook (1 space), * ch 1, skip
next st, 1 dc in next st, repeat from *
across row—35 (37, 39) spaces.

Row 2: Ch 4, turn, skip 1st dc, * 1 dc
in next dc, ch 1, repeat from * across
row, ending skip next st of turning ch, 1
dc in next st of ch.

Starting with Row 3 of chart and con-

tinuing to work in dc pattern, work design as shown on chart until piece measures 14½ inches or desired length to
underarm.

Shape Armholes: Keeping pattern as
established, sl st over 2 spaces or bls,
work in pattern st to last 2 spaces or bls.
On the next row dec 1 space each end
of row—29 (31, 33) spaces and bls.
Work even until armholes measure 7
(7½, 8) inches.

Shape Shoulders: Sl st over 5 (6, 7)
spaces and bls, work 4 spaces. Fasten
off. Skip center 11 spaces and bls, join
yarn in next dc, ch 4, 1 dc in next dc,
(ch 1, 1 dc in next dc) 3 times. Fasten
off.

Left Front: Ch 40 (42, 44) sts. Work in
same manner as back for 2 rows—18
(19, 20) spaces. Now starting with Row 3
of chart and continuing to work in dc

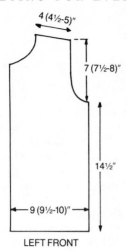

4 (4½-5)″

7 (7½-8)″

14½″

9 (9½-10)″

LEFT FRONT

pattern, work design as shown on chart until piece measures 14½ inches or desired length to underarm, ending at arm edge.

Shape Armhole: Keeping pattern as established, sl st over 2 spaces or bls, work to end of row. Dec 1 space or bl at arm edge of next row—15 (16, 17) spaces and bls. Work even in pattern st until armhole measures 4 (4½, 5) inches.

Shape Neck: Working in pattern st, sl st over 4 spaces or bls at neck edge. Dec 1 space or bl at same edge *every row* twice—9 (10, 11) spaces and bls. Work even until armhole measures 7 (7½, 8) inches.

Shape Shoulder: At arm edge sl st over 5 (6, 7) spaces or bls, work to end of row. Fasten off.

Right Front: Ch 40 (42, 44) sts. Work 2 rows in pattern st as for left front. Now starting with Row 3 of chart and continuing to work in dc pattern, work to correspond to left front, reversing all shaping and placing of design.

Sleeves: Ch 50 (54, 58) sts. Work in same manner as back for 2 rows—23 (25, 27) spaces. Now starting with Row 3 of chart and continuing to work in dc pattern, work design as shown on chart until piece measures 15½ (16, 16½) inches.

Shape Cap: Keeping pattern as established, sl st over 2 spaces or bls each end of row, then dec 1 space or bl each end of *every row* 7 (8, 9) times—5 spaces and bls. Fasten off.

Finishing: Sew shoulder seams. Set in sleeves. Sew underarm and sleeve seams.

Edging. Row 1: With right side facing you, join yarn in side seam of lower edge of right front and work 1 round sc, working 3 sc in corner sts, join. Fasten off.

Row 2: With wrong side facing you, join yarn in side seam of lower edge of left front and work 1 sc in each st of front and neck edges, working 3 sc in corner sts.

Row 3: Ch 1, turn, 1 sc in 1st sc, * ch 3, 1 sc in 3rd st of ch (picot), skip next sc, 1 sc in next sc, repeat from * along front and neck edges. Fasten off. Work same edging around lower edge of sleeves.

Directions on Use of Chart

NOTE—Work right-side rows from right to left; work wrong-side rows from left to right.

For back
For Small Size: Start at A, work to D.
For Medium Size: Start at B, work to E.
For Large Size: Start at C, work to F.

For left front
For Small Size: Start at A, work to G.
For Medium Size: Start at B, work to G.
For Large Size: Start at C, work to G.

For right front
For Small Size: Start at H, work to D.
For Medium Size: Start at H, work to E.
For Large Size: Start at H, work to F.

For sleeves
For Small Size: Start at I, work to K.
For Medium Size: Start at J, work to L.
For Large Size: Start at M, work to N.

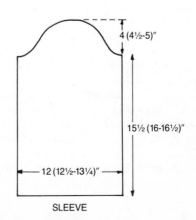

4 (4½-5)″

15½ (16-16½)″

12 (12½-13¼)″

SLEEVE

WOVEN JACKET AND SCARF

Weaving color through single crochet stitches adds a dashing touch to this easy-fitting topper. Adding a scarf provides a certain smartness.

Information to Check Before You Start

Sizing: Directions for the Jacket are written for a Small Size. Changes for a Medium and Large Size are in brackets.
Working Measurements:
—Width across back at underarm: 18¼ [19¾, 21¾] inches
—Width across each front at underarm, excluding border: 9½ [9¾, 10¾] inches
—Length of side seam, excluding border: 18½ [19½, 20½] inches
—Width across sleeve: 16 [17, 18] inches
—Length of sleeve seam: 16½ [17, 17½] inches

Materials: The jacket and scarf are made of Coats & Clark Red Heart® Fabulend™ Wool Blend Worsted Yarn, Art. E. 235, in 4-ply skeins. You need:
—30 [32, 34] oz. of No. 407 Lt. Natural
—11 [11, 12] oz. of No. 12 Black
—2 oz. of No. 1 White for each size
—2 oz. of No. 909 Scarlet for each size
—3 Toggle Buttons, 1½ inches long

Tools: Crochet Hook—Size J
—Tapestry Needle, No. 13, for weaving (J. & P. Coats)

Gauge: 4 sts = 1 inch
4 rows = 1 inch

Directions to Follow

JACKET

Back: Starting at lower edge, with Natural ch 74 [80, 88], having 4 ch sts to the inch.

Row 1: Sc in 2nd ch from hook, * sc in next ch, ch 1, skip next ch. Rep from * across to last 2 ch; sc in each of last 2 ch—73 [79, 87] sts, counting each ch-1 as a st. Mark this row for right side. Ch 1, turn.

Row 2: Sc in 1st sc, * ch 1, skip next sc, sc in next ch-1 sp. Rep from * to last 2 sc; ch 1, skip next sc, sc in last sc. Ch 1, turn.

Row 3: Sc in 1st sc, * sc in ch-1 sp, ch 1, skip next sc. Rep from * to last ch-1 sp; sc in last ch-1 sp, sc in last sc. Ch 1, turn. Repeating Rows 2 and 3 for pattern work until total length is 18½ [19½, 20½] inches, end on wrong side. Turn.

Armhole Shaping. Row 1: Sl st in 1st 5 [5, 7] sts, ch 1, sc in last st used, sc in next ch-1 sp; work in pattern to last 5 [5, 7] sts; sc in next sc, do not work over remaining 4 [4, 6] sts. Ch 1, turn. Work in pattern over 65 [71, 75] sts until length from 1st row of Armhole Shaping is 8 [8½, 9] inches, end on wrong side. Ch 1, turn.

Shoulder Shaping: Work in pattern across 1st 20 [22, 24] sts, sc in next sc. Fasten off. Then skip next 23 [25, 25] sts for back of neck; attach yarn to next sc, ch 1, sc in same sc, sc in next ch-1 sp, work in pattern across. Fasten off.

Left Front: Starting at lower edge, with Natural ch 38 [40, 44], having 4 ch sts to 1 inch. Work in pattern same as for Back over 37 [39, 43] sts to Armhole Shaping, end on wrong side. Turn.

Armhole Shaping. Row 1: Sl st in 1st 5 [5, 7] sts, ch 1, sc in last st used, sc in next ch-1 sp, complete row in pattern. Ch 1, turn. Work in pattern over 33 [35, 37] sts until length from 1st row of Armhole Shaping is 3½ [4, 4] inches, end at Armhole edge. Ch 1, turn.

Neck Shaping. Row 1: Work in pattern to last 5 sts; sc in next sc, do not work over remaining 4 sts—29 [31, 33] sts. Ch 1, turn.

Row 2: Work even in pattern. Ch 1, turn.

Row 3: Work in pattern to last 3 sts; sc in next sc, do not work over remaining 2 sts. Ch 1, turn. Rep last 2 rows until 21 [23, 25] sts remain. Work even in pattern until length from 1st row of Armhole Shaping is same as on Back. Fasten off.

Right Front: Work as for Left Front to Armhole Shaping, end on wrong side. Ch 1, turn.

Armhole Shaping. Row 1: Work in pattern across to last 5 [5, 7] sts; sc in next sc, do not work over remaining 4 [4, 6] sts. Ch 1, turn. Work even over the 33 [35, 37] sts in pattern until length from 1st row of Armhole Shaping is 3½ [4, 4] inches, end at neck edge. Turn.

Neck Shaping. Row 1: Sl st in 1st 5 sts, ch 1, sc in last st used, sc in next ch-1 sp; complete row in pattern—29 [31, 33] sts. Ch 1, turn.

Row 2: Work even in pattern. Turn.

Row 3: Sl st in 1st 3 sts, ch 1, sc in last st used, sc in next ch-1 sp; complete row. Ch 1, turn. Rep last 2 rows until 21 [23, 25] sts remain. Complete as for Left Front.

Sleeves: Starting at lower edge, with Natural ch 66 [70, 74], having 4 ch sts to 1 inch. Work in pattern same as for Back over 65 [69, 73] sts until length is 16½ [17, 17½] inches. Fasten off. Mark last row for armhole edge.

Pocket (make 2): Starting at lower edge, with Natural ch 28 [30, 30], having 4 ch sts to 1 inch. Work in pattern same as for Back over 27 [29, 29] sts for 7 [7, 7½] inches, end on right side. Mark last row for upper edge.

Pin pieces to measurements, dampen, and leave to dry.

Sew side and shoulder seams.

Weaving: NOTE—Each sc consists of 2 vertical stems. Weaving is done under the 1st vertical stem of each sc across the designated rows indicated on Chart.

Weaving on Sleeves: To weave a row, place a sleeve with right side up and armhole edge toward you on a flat surface. Cut 3 strands of Black each 10 inches longer than width of sleeve. Thread strands into tapestry needle and weave through next row up from armhole edge as follows: Insert needle under the 1st vertical stem of each sc across this row and draw yarn through, leaving a 4-inch end at beg of row and the excess at end of row. Ends will be secured later.

Cut 3 strands of White and weave

these strands through scs on next row as before. Starting at A on Chart continue to work weaving as before following the Chart to C. Secure ends.

Weaving on Pockets: With right side up and upper edge toward you, work weaving on pockets same as for sleeves, starting on the next row up from upper edge and following Chart from B to C. Secure ends.

Pocket Border. Row 1: With right side of a pocket facing, attach Black to sc at right upper corner, ch 1, sc in same st, make 2 sc in each ch-1 sp across upper edge, end with 1 sc in last sc. Ch 1, turn.

Row 2: Sc in 1st sc, * ch 1, skip next sc, sc in next sc. Rep from * to last sc; sc in last sc. Ch 1, turn.

Row 3: Sc in 1st sc, * ch 1, sc in next ch-1 sp. Rep from * to last sc; sc in last sc. Fasten off.

Having side edge of a pocket at side seam of jacket and lower edge meeting lower edge of front, pin a pocket to each front. Sew side edges only of each pocket in place.

Matching weaving lines, sew sleeve

WEAVING CHART

Black	—C
White	
White	
No Weaving	
No Weaving	
Scarlet	
Scarlet	
Scarlet	
Scarlet	
No Weaving	
Black	
Black	
No Weaving	
White	
White	—B
White	
No Weaving	
Black	
Black	
No Weaving	
Scarlet	
Scarlet	
Scarlet	
Scarlet	
No Weaving	
No Weaving	
White	—A
White	
Black	
No Weaving	

Each space on Chart represents a pattern row; use indicated color for weaving strand.

▲
Armhole Edge

seams to within 1 inch from top edge. Sew in sleeves.

Outer Border. Rnd 1: With right side facing, attach Natural to a side seam, ch 1, sc where yarn was attached.

NOTE—Work through both thicknesses of edges where pockets and fronts are together. (* Ch 1, skip ¼ inch along edge, sc in edge. Rep from * to next corner, ch 1; in corner make sc, ch 1, and sc) 4 times; ** ch 1, skip ¼ inch along edge, sc in edge. Rep from ** to beg of rnd. Join with sl st to 1st sc. Fasten off, attach Black to joining.

Rnd 2: Ch 1, making sc, ch 1 and sc in corner ch-1 sp of each of the 4 corners, make 2 sc in each ch-1 sp around. Join to 1st sc.

Rnds 3–4: Ch 1, making sc, ch 1, and sc in corner ch-1 sp at each of the 4 corners, work in pattern as for Back around. Join. At end of last rnd, fasten off.

Sleeve Border: With right side facing attach Natural to seam, then omitting corners work as for the 4 rnds of Outer Border.

Toggle Loop (make 3): With Black, ch 34. Join with sl st to form ring; then ch 1 and sl st in each ch around. Join. Fasten off. Form ring into a figure 8 and tack at center, then bring center of one of the 2 loops to previous tack and secure.

With large loop toward edge of right front, sew loops in place, having first loop 2 inches below neck edge and remaining loops 4 inches apart.

Toggle Covering (make 3): Ch 3, join to form ring. Ch 1, make 5 sc in ring. Then work sc in each sc around until cover is 1½ inches long. Fasten off, leaving a 6-inch end. Insert a toggle in cover and sew end.

Sew covered toggles in place on Left Front.

SCARF

Starting at narrow edge, with Black ch 30, having 4 ch sts to 1 inch. Work in pattern same as on Back of jacket over the 29 sts until total length is 80 inches. Fasten off.

Fringe: Cut 3 strands of Black, each 16 inches long. Double these strands to form a loop. Insert hook from back to front in 1st ch-1 sp of one narrow edge and draw loop through. Draw loose ends through loop and pull up tightly to form a knot. Knot 3 strands as before in every ch-1 sp across. Work fringe along other narrow edge in same way. Trim evenly.
COPYRIGHT © 1979 COATS & CLARK, INC.

GARDEN TRELLIS AFGHAN

The floral design makes this a bright and cheerful throw. The embroidery on a plain background changes the appearance completely.

Information to Check Before You Start

Sizing: Approximate measurement is 56 × 70 inches, not including fringe.
Materials: The afghan is made of Brunswick Windrush® yarn. Germantown Knitting Worsted can be substituted using the correct number of grams. You need for the Afghan:
—12 4 oz. skeins of 90100 Ecru
—2 skeins of 9094 Medium Lime
For the Embroidery: 1 skein each of
9092—Lt. Lime
9045—Lt. Desert Flower
90453—Dark Desert Flower
90381—Goldenrod
90383—Dk. Goldenrod
9033—Wood Brown
Tools: Afghan Crochet Hook—Size No. 8 or H (5.5 mm)
Tapestry Needle
Gauge: 4½ sts = 1 inch

Directions to Follow

Afghan Stitch Row 1: Keeping all lps on hook, pull up a lp in 2nd ch from hook and in each ch across.

To Work Lps Off: Yo hook, pull through 1st lp, * yo hook, pull through next 2 lps, repeat from * across until 1 lp remains. Lp that remains on hook always counts as 1st st of next row.

Row 2: Keeping all lps on hook, skip 1st vertical bar (lp on hook is 1st st), pull up a lp under next vertical bar and under each vertical bar across to last st, insert hook under last vertical bar and in lp at back of bar, pull up a lp. Work lps off as before. Repeat Row 2 for afghan stitch.

CHART FOR GARDEN TRELLIS AFGHAN

☐ Ecru	⊙	Goldenrod
◖ Med. Lime	◉	Dk. Goldenrod
◼ Lt. Lime	⊠	Lt. Desert Flower
⊡ Brown	◳	Dk. Desert Flower

Main Panel: Make 3. With Ecru, loosely chain 56 sts. Work in afghan stitch for 270 rows. Fasten off. Embroider each panel in cross-stitch following color key. Working from bottom of chart repeat the 108 rows from A to C twice, then work the 54 rows from A to B once. Weave in loose ends neatly.

Narrow Panels: Make 4. With Medium Lime, loosely chain 6 sts. Work in afghan stitch for 270 rows. Fasten off.

Crochet Borders: Work as follows on each long side of Ecru panels and Lime strips: With Ecru, attach yarn at end of long side of one panel. Ch 1, sc in each st down side of panel, working 1 st in each st. Ch 3, turn, * skip 1 st, dc in next st, then dc in st just skipped; rep from * across, ending dc in last st. Fasten off.

Finishing: Alternating lime strips with embroidered panels, place 2 panels with right sides together. Sew together by catching only the outside loop of each st on each side.

With Ecru, attach yarn on right side and work as follows across top and bottom of afghan: Ch 3, * skip 1 st, dc in next st, then dc in st just skipped; rep from * across, ending dc in last st. Fasten off.

Fringe: Knot 3 12-inch strands of Ecru into every other st across top and bottom of afghan. COPYRIGHT © MCMLXXIX BRUNSWICK WORSTED MILLS, INC.

GRANNY AFGHAN

One of the most popular afghans is formed of granny squares. Working in small pieces makes the afghan easy to handle.

Information to Check Before You Start

Sizing: Approximately 54 × 80 inches
Materials: The afghan is made of Bernat Berella "4" in 4 oz. balls. You need:
—7 balls Black (MC)
—2 balls Paiute Red (Color A)
—4 balls Natural (Color B)
—6 balls Topaz Gold (Color C)
Tool: Crochet Hook (Bernat-Aero)—Size F (4 mm)
Gauge: Each motif should measure 4½ inches on each side.

Directions to Follow

Motif: Make 216. Using Color A, ch 4, join with a sl st to form a ring.

Round 1: Ch 3, working in center of ring, 2 dc, * ch 1, 3 dc, repeat from * twice more, ch 1, join with a sl st to top of ch-3. Fasten off Color A.

Round 2: Join Color B in any ch-1 space, ch 3, 2 dc, ch 1, 3 dc in same space, * 3 dc, ch 1, 3 dc in next ch-1 space, repeat from * twice more, join with a sl st to top of ch-3. Fasten off Color B.

Round 3: Join Color C in any ch-1 space, ch 3, 2 dc, ch 1, 3 dc in same space, * 3 dc in next space, 3 dc, ch 1, 3 dc in next ch-1 space, repeat from * twice more, ending 3 dc in next space, join with a sl st to top of ch-3. Fasten off Color C.

Round 4: Join MC in any ch-1 space and work in same manner as Round 3, having 1 more group of 3 dc between ch-1 corner spaces. Fasten off. This completes one motif.

Finishing: To join, using MC and working through *back loops only*, sew motifs tog—12 motifs in width and 18 motifs in length. COPYRIGHT © 1978 BERNAT YARN & CRAFT CORPORATION

BEDSPREAD OR AFGHAN

This lovely colonial coverlet can be constructed in three sizes. The size is controlled by the number of squares you use. Working with small pieces makes the coverlet easier to handle as you crochet.

Information to Check Before You Start

Sizing: Each square measures 10½ × 10½ inches.
—The *Afghan* is approximately 65 × 75 inches and is made of 42 squares
—The *Twin-size Bedspread* is approximately 65 × 96 inches and is made of 54 squares
—The *Double Bedspread* is approximately 75 × 96 inches and is made of 63 squares
Materials: The cover is made of Brunswick Pomfret® Sport Yarn in 50 gram (1.75 oz.) balls, using No. 5000 Ecru. Fore 'N Aft Sport Yarn can be substituted if you wish, using the correct number of ounces. You need:
34 balls for the afghan
45 balls for the twin bedspread
52 balls for the double bedspread
Small amount of batting to stuff baubles
Tool: Aluminum Crochet Hook— Size 6 or G (4.5 mm)
Gauge: 4½ dc = 1 inch
2 rows = 1 inch

Directions to Follow

Popcorn Stitch: Dc 4 times in 1 st, remove hook and insert in 1st dc of group, catch loop of last dc and draw through 1st dc, tighten stitch.

Each square will measure 10½ × 10½ inches. Make 42 squares for afghan; 54 for twin size; 63 for double size.

Square: Chain 4, sl st to join.
Round 1: Ch 1, work 8 sc in loop, sl st to join.
Round 2: Ch 3, * (dc 2, ch 2, dc 2) in next st, dc 1; rep from * twice more, (dc 2, ch 2, dc 2) in next st, sl st to join.

Round 3: Ch 3, dc in next 2 sts, * (dc 2, ch 2, dc 2) in corner ch-2 loop, dc in next 5 sts; rep from * twice more, (dc 2, ch 2, dc 2) in corner, dc in next 2 sts, sl st to join.
Round 4: Ch 3, dc in next 4 sts, * (dc 2, ch 2, dc 2) in corner, dc in next 9 sts; rep from * twice more, (dc 2, ch 2, dc 2) in corner, dc in next 4 sts, sl st to join.
Round 5: Ch 3, dc in next 6 sts, * (dc 2, ch 2, dc 2) in corner, dc in next 13 sts; rep from * twice more, (dc 2, ch 2, dc 2) in corner, dc in next 6 sts, sl st to join.
Round 6: Ch 3, (popcorn in next st, dc in next st) 4 times, * (dc 2, ch 2, dc 2) in corner, dc in next st, (popcorn in next st, dc in next st) 8 times; rep from * twice more, ending (dc 2, ch 2, dc 2) in corner, (dc in next st, popcorn in next st) 4 times, sl st to join.
Round 7: Ch 4, skip 1 st, dc in next st, (ch 1 skipping 1 st, dc in next st) 3 times, popcorn in next st, dc 1, * (dc 2, ch 2, dc 2) in corner, dc 1, popcorn in next st, (dc 1, ch 1 skipping 1 st) 8 times, dc 1, popcorn, dc 1; rep from * twice more, ending (dc 2, ch 2, dc 2) in corner, dc 1, popcorn, (dc 1, ch 1 skipping 1 st) 4 times, sl st into 3rd ch of beginning ch to join.
Round 8: Ch 4, skip 1 st, dc in next st, (ch 1 skipping 1 st, dc in next st) 4 times, popcorn, dc 1, * (dc 2, ch 2, dc 2) in corner, dc 1, popcorn, (dc 1, ch 1 skipping 1 st) 10 times, dc 1, popcorn, dc 1; rep from * twice more, ending (dc 2, ch 2, dc 2) in corner, dc 1, popcorn, (dc 1, ch 1 skipping 1 st) 5 times, sl st in 3rd ch of beg ch to join.
Round 9: Ch 4, skip 1 st, dc in next st, (ch 1 skipping 1 st, dc in next st) 3 times, popcorn, dc in next 5 sts, * (dc 2, ch 2, dc 2) in corner, dc in next 5 sts, popcorn, (dc 1, ch 1 skipping 1 st) 8 times, dc 1, popcorn, dc in next 5 sts; rep from * twice more, ending (dc 2, ch 2, dc 2) in corner, dc in next 5 sts, popcorn, (dc 1, ch 1 skipping 1 st) 4 times, sl st in 3rd ch of beg ch to join.
Round 10: Ch 3, (popcorn in next st,

dc in next st) 4 times, dc in next 8 sts, *
(dc 2, ch 2, dc 2) in corner, dc in next 9
sts, (popcorn, dc 1) 8 times, dc in next 8
sts; rep from * twice more, ending (dc 2,
ch 2, dc 2) in corner, dc in next 8 sts,
(dc 1, popcorn) 4 times, sl st to join.

Rounds 11 and 12: Ch 3, dc in each
st around, working (dc 2, ch 2, dc 2) in
each corner, sl st to join. Fasten off after
round 12.

Baubles: Make 30 for afghan; make 40
for twin; make 48 for double.

Round 1: Ch 4, sl st to join, ch 1, sc 8
in loop, sl st to join.

Round 2: Ch 1, * sc twice in 1 st, sc
1, rep from *, ending sc twice in last st,
sl st to join.

Round 3: Ch 1, * sc twice in 1 st, sc
1; rep from * around, sl st to join.

Round 4: Ch 1, * sc 1, dec on next 2
sts, rep from * around, sl st to join.

Round 5: Ch 1, * sc in next 2 sts, dec
in next 2 sts; rep from * around, ending

sc 1, dec on last 2 sts, sl st to join. Stuff
bauble firmly with batting.

Round 6: Ch 1, * dec on next 2 sts;
rep from * around. Fasten off and draw
tog rem sts with needle and yarn.

Finishing: Arrange squares and sew together with matching yarn. (Afghan is 6
squares wide and 7 squares long; twin
bedspread is 6 by 9; double bedspread is
7 by 9). Sew baubles at intersections of
4 squares (where 4 squares meet).

Border. Round 1: Attach yarn in st
just before 1 corner, ch 3, ** dc 5 in
corner, * popcorn, dc 1, ch 1 skipping 1
st, dc 1; rep from * across side of afghan ending with popcorn in last st before next corner; rep from ** 3 times
more, sl st to join.

Round 2: Ch 3, working 5 dc in each
corner, dc in each st around, sl st to
join. Fasten off. COPYRIGHT © MCMLXXIX
BRUNSWICK WORSTED MILLS, INC.

Bibliography

When one is preparing a book, browsing through the work that has already been written is stimulating and interesting. In my research, I found the books and booklets listed here as well as the instruction leaflets of yarn manufacturers informative and thought-provoking. I believe you will also.

Aytes, Barbara. *Adventures in Crocheting.* Doubleday & Company, 1972.

Blackwell, Liz. *A Treasury of Crochet Patterns.* Charles Scribner's Sons, 1971.

Coats & Clark. *Learn to Crochet—No. 210 B.* Coats & Clark, 1974.
———. *Hairpin Lace—No. 235.* Coats & Clark, 1974.

Coats Sewing Group. *Crochet Stitches & Edgings.* Charles Scribner's Sons, 1976.

Dawson, Mary M. *Crochet Stitches.* Crown Publishers, 1972.

Dittrick, Mark. *Hard Crochet.* Hawthorn Books, 1978.

Hurlburt, Regina. *Left-handed Crochet.* Van Nostrand, Reinhold Company, 1979.

Mackenzie, Clinton D. *New Design in Crochet.* Van Nostrand, Reinhold Company, 1972.

Editors of McCall's Needlework and Crafts Magazine. *McCall's Crochet/Knit for the Home.* The McCall Pattern Co., 1978.

Mon Tricot. *Dictionary, Stitches, Patterns.* Crown Publishers.

Read, Susannah, General Editor. *The Needleworker's Constant Companion.* The Viking Press, 1979.

Reader's Digest Complete Guide to Needlework. The Reader's Digest Association, Inc., 1979.

Editors of Sunset Books and Sunset Magazine. *Crochet Techniques & Projects.* Lane Publishing Co., 1979.

Taylor, Gertrude. *America's Crochet Book.* Charles Scribner's Sons, 1974.

Index